Table of Contents

M000159941

About the Authors

Mark Price - CEO and Co-Author

After crashing and burning on every app business he ever made, Mark decided to stop making apps and instead teach people how to make them - but now he's making an app to do that… He also has 5 kids, likes fast cars, shooting things, and making movies.

Evan Leong - VP of Product and Co-Author

Evan is obsessed with brilliant designs and aims to create meaningful experiences through products. Aside from Devslopes, he loves coffee, making music & playing poker.

Caleb Stultz - iOS Developer and Co-Author

Caleb is captivated by learning new technologies and seeks to live as a life-long learner. As a developer, he loves making magic with code and crafting excellent user experiences. Besides working with Devslopes, he loves traveling, caffeine, Netflix binging, & learning new things.

Jack Davis - Backend Developer and Co-Author

Jack is really in his element building backend servers and services to support public facing applications as well as automating a lot of that work. Jack is a maker at heart and outside of work loves experimenting and building electronic circuits and gadgets backed up with code. He also enjoys the outdoors as well as spending time in his shop making furniture and leather items.

Jacob Luetzow - iOS Developer and Co-Author

Jacob will always make sure everything is done to perfection. He has a knack for surpassing expectations. Coding for Devslopes, sailing, rock climbing and hiking are how he prefers spending his days.

Jonny Burgoyne - Android/macOS Developer and Co-Author

Jonny loves creating cool stuff. Whether it's programming, 3D printing, or building a drone, he can't get enough of it. When he's not creating cool stuff, Jonny like to watch movies, chill with family, and travel.

Jess Rascal - Web Developer and Co-Author

Jess is "the British one" that enjoys assembling things with Angular, trying out things with Typescript, having a go at HTML, and creating chaos with CSS. Outside of his coding bubble he likes to tire himself out with boxing training, listening to glorious music, and having the odd tipple when the opportunity arises.

Jason Brewer - Digital Content Manager and

Editor

Jason handles all of Devslopes digital content and media. Apart from slaying it at Devslopes, he's a passionate skateboarder, pianist and machete swinging adventurist.

Check Us Out

At Devslopes, our mission is to make learning to code fun & affordable for you. We offer excellent and effective video courses on a myriad of programming topics: iOS, Android, Unity, Web Development, Angular 2, and much more. We also have a large library of free content for your perusal.

These courses are available through our iOS, Android, macOS, and tvOS platforms. Check us out in the App Store or Google Play store today!

Check us out at www.devslopes.com!

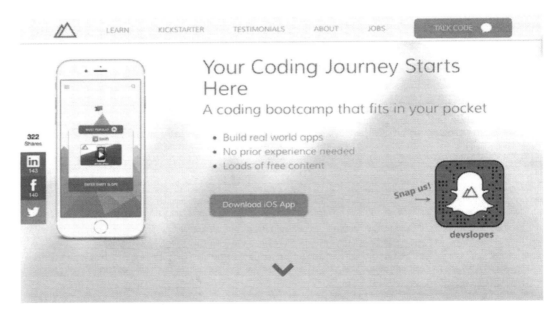

Preface

Welcome to the world of programming and iOS development. Learning to code can be tough. I taught myself how to write code in 2007 completely on my own. It was one of the most difficult experiences of my life. Resources were few, and support was non-existent.

Today is a lot different. Learning to code is now a *"thing"* and resources are everywhere. You have been set on a path for success. That doesn't mean that learning how to code is going to be easy. It probably won't be. You are going to get discouraged. You are going to tell yourself, *"I don't have the brain for this"* and you're going to want to give up. You are going to run into cyber-coder bullies who will belittle your coding skills and tell you that unless you have a degree in computer science, you aren't a *real* programmer.

I want to give you some advice to keep you on the straight and narrow when discouragement sets in:

1. Don't EVER compare yourself to other programmers. Compete against yourself. Someone will always be more skilled than you.

2. You DO belong here in the world of programming. No matter what anyone says. You have unique talents as a programmer that other programmers do not.

3. If the learning is painful and your brain is broken, then you are doing it right. Pain brings growth.

Programmers can live rewarding lives. I have spent over half of my programming career working from home. That meant more time with my family and also meant I could go to the movie theater whenever the frik I wanted.

Become a good programmer and you will have the chance to live whatever lifestyle you want. Whether that be a lifestyle with more personal time and freedom or whether that means receiving a big fat paycheck working for top companies - or perhaps both!

The last and most important thing I could ever tell you as you are learning how to code is this - Learn **EVERY** single day and do some hands-on coding **EVERY** single day.

Ready. Set. Go.

Mark Price

SECTION 1 - Learn to Code

Chapter 1: Installing Xcode

Canvas is to the artist as Xcode is to the iOS Developer. It serves as our workspace, creative outlet, source of frustration and more.

What you will learn

- How to install Xcode

- Opening Xcode

Key Terms

- **Xcode:** a software development suite created by Apple to allow for the creation of iOS apps.

Xcode is an amazing application. It is a fully-loaded suite of tools and applications that enable developers to create the future through apps. As you will see, it is simple to install and get started with minimal fuss.

Going to the macOS App Store

To begin, open the macOS App Store and in the search bar in the top right, type **Xcode** and press Enter to search for it.

Once the results load, Xcode will be the first result (Figure 1.1.1). Next, click GET and enter your Apple ID information to begin downloading it. Bear in mind that it is a massive application (4.5 GB) and after installation takes up nearly 12 GB.

Figure 1.1.1

Opening Xcode

To open Xcode, all you need to do is go into your Applications folder and click Xcode. It's that simple, really.

Once Xcode opens up, you will be presented with the 'Welcome to Xcode' screen which gives you several options to select (Figure 1.1.2).

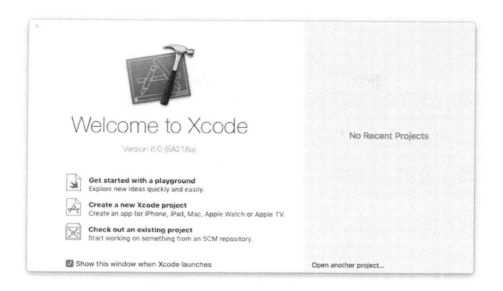

This will be our launchpad for all projects in this book. You will open Xcode and create projects from here. Once you understand the Xcode interface, you will see just how powerful and helpful it is in the app development process.

Wrapping up

This chapter was ridiculously short and for good reason – Apple has made our job so easy by making such a streamlined experience. The barriers to beginning iOS development are so few nowadays, we can get started with just a few clicks.

Chapter 2: Intro to Swift

Apple has always been on the cusp of new technologies. When they released Swift, (some of) the world cheered.

What you will learn

- What is Swift?

- What makes Swift different

- The future of Swift

- Variables

- Constants

- Types

- Collection Types

- Control Flow

- Conditionals

- Functions

Key Terms

- **Syntax:** the specific structure and order of a programming language.

- **Safe:** a characteristic of Swift which means that it is less prone to syntax errors or other compile-time errors.

- **Fast:** a characteristic of Swift which means that it is performed quickly and is efficient in nature.

- **Expressive:** a characteristic of Swift which means that its syntax is easily readable.

Swift is Apple's baby. According to Swift.org:

Swift is a general-purpose programming language built using a modern approach to safety, performance, and software design patterns.

If you don't come from a computer science or programming background you may be thinking, "That's neat. BUT WHAT DOES IT MEAN?   " Trust us when we say that it means that your learning-to-code life will be much easier than it could be.

Swift is an excellent first programming language to learn as it's syntax is generally easy to follow. There are also a ton of resources online (i.e. tutorials, YouTube videos, blogs, forums, etc.) to help you learn Swift.

This chapter serves as a precursor for the chapters to follow. It is mostly for your information and reference. We will dive in in detail later on. Let's get started!

Swift Foundations

Variables

Every programming language uses variables. They are like container which allow you to store data of many different types.

To declare a variable you must use the keyword `var`:

```
var message: String = "Hello, World!"
```

What we've just written tells our computer that we want to create a container (variable) with the name `message` of type `String` which contains the text "Hello, World!"

Something amazing about Swift is that it includes a feature called Type Inference. This means that Swift can analyze the data inside a variable (text, number, true/false, etc.) and infer it's type.

To test this, simply remove `String` after declaring the variable `message`:

```
var message = "Hello, World!" //Type-Inferred String
```

As you can see above, we never explicitly told our computer that we wanted `message` to be a `String` but because of the quotes around `Hello, World!`, Swift can infer it's type.

Variables are called variables because, well, they are variable – their value can be changed.

For example, if we wanted to change the value of our `message` variable we would need to write the name of our variable and change it's value like so:

```
var message = "Hello, World!"
message = "Hello, Swift!"
```

Now `message` is equal to "Hello, Swift!".

Constants

Sometimes, there are values you don't want to ever change. A date like your birthday, the version number of your application, or the name of your hometown for instance.

In Swift, we call these values constants.

To declare a constant, you must use the keyword `let`.

If we were to change the keyword `var` to the keyword `let` in our example above we would be presented with an error because we cannot modify a constant.

```
let greeting = "Hello, World!"
greeting = "Hello, Swift!" // Error
```

Types

String

So far, in the code above we've only referred to values of type `String`. A `String` can be used to hold textual data.

Strings are also powerful in how they can be modified, converted, and even hold values of many different types.

For example we can use String Concatenation to combine several `String` values together using the + operator.

```
let album = "Nevermind"
```

```
let artist = "Nirvana"
let review = " is amazing!    "
let description = "The album " + album + " by " + artist + review

//description = "The album Nevermind by Nirvana is amazing!    "
```

Another neat thing we can do is use String Interpolation to encapsulate other variables and pass them into a String value when we want.

```
let birthday = "May 15, 1992"

let bio = "My birthday is \(birthday)."

// bio = "My birthday is May 15, 1992."
```

You can even pass in values that are not of type String and Swift can convert them.

Int

The keyword Int is short for Integer. In math, an integer is most basically defined as a whole number.

We can use an Int value in a variable or a constant:

```
var age: Int = 24 // Explicitly declared Int
var salary = 70000 // Type-inferred Int
let birthYear = 1992
let daysInAYear = 365
```

Bool

The keyword Bool is short for Boolean. Booleans are simply true and false values. Just like all the above types, you can explicitly declare a variable of type Bool or let Swift infer it's type by setting the value of a variable to be either true or false.

```
var isFinishedLoading = true // Type-inferred
var dataLoaded: Bool = false // Explicit
```

Double / Float

A Double is a number value similar to the type beneath it - Float. The difference between the two is how precise you can be.

A `Double` is a 64-bit floating point number value which can be as precise as 15 decimal digits.

A `Float` is a 32-bit floating point number value which can be precise to 6 decimal places.

As you can see, a `Double` is more precise than a `Float`.

```
var intersectVersion = 2.0  // Type-inferred Double
```

Something to note: Swift defaults to type-infer decimal values as a `Double`, not `Float`. To declare a variable of type `Float`, be explicit:

```
var intersectVersion: Float = 2.0
```

Most of the time, you will be using `Double` values in Swift (and in this book).

Collection Types

In Swift, there are three different ways to store collections of values – `Set`, `Array`, and `Dictionary`. For the purposes of this book, we will only be using and learning about the `Array` and `Dictionary` in Swift.

Array

An array is a collection of values which are organized by index. The index is the count of how many objects there are inside of the array.
In Swift, zero-indexing is used meaning that the first item in the array actually has an index of 0. From then on, the number increases by one.

Defining an Array

Arrays are always written inside of brackets. Each value is separated by a comma.

```
var unoCards: [String] = ["Skip", "Wild", "Wild + Draw Four"] // Explicitly-
declared Array of Strings
```

```
var unoCards = ["Skip", "Wild", "Wild + Draw Four"] // Type-inferred as [String]
```

Arrays can contain values of a single type like the one above, but you also can include multiple types in an array.

To get the value for a single item from our array, we need to do the following:

```
...
print(unoCards[0]) // Prints
```

Using `print`, we can print the value of the first item (at index 0) in our `unoCards` array – "Skip".

Modifying an Array

I am going to create an array with a grocery list.

```
var groceryList = ["Milk", "Eggs", "Cheese"]
```

To add an item to our list, we simple use the `.append()` function in Swift:

```
var groceryList = ["Milk", "Eggs", "Cheese"]

groceryList.append("Marshmallows")

//groceryList = ["Milk", "Eggs", "Cheese", "Marshmallows"]
```

This will add the value "Marshmallows" to the end our `groceryList` array.

To add multiple items to our array, we can use the `.append(contentsOf:)` function in Swift:

```
var groceryList = ["Milk", "Eggs", "Cheese"]

groceryList.append("Marshmallows")

groceryList.append(contentsOf: ["Oreos", "Quinoa"])

//groceryList = ["Milk", "Eggs", "Cheese", "Marshmallows", "Oreos", "Quinoa"]
```

To insert an item at a certain point in an array, use the `.insert(_:at:)` function in Swift:

```
var groceryList = ["Milk", "Eggs", "Cheese"]

groceryList.append("Marshmallows")

groceryList.append(contentsOf: ["Oreos", "Quinoa"])

groceryList.insert("Potatoes", at: 2)

//groceryList = ["Milk", "Eggs", "Potatoes", "Cheese", "Marshmallows", "Oreos",
```

```
"Quinoa"]
```

The value "Potatoes" gets added and has an index of 2. Remember, that Swift uses zero-indexing.

To change a single item in an array, subscript the item you want to change and give it a shiny new value.

...

```
groceryList[0] = "Bread"

//groceryList = ["Bread", "Eggs", "Potatoes", "Cheese", "Marshmallows", "Oreos", "Quinoa"]
```

Dictionary

A `Dictionary` allows you to store data in pairs containing a key and a value. Just like a dictionary in a spoken/written language, each word has a definition. Comparing the two, in a Swift `Dictionary`, the key = word and the value = definition.

Look at the dictionary I have declared below:

```
var screenSizeInInches = ["iPhone 7" : 4.7, "iPhone 7 Plus" : 5.5, "iPad Pro" : 12.9]
```

To access the value of an item in a `Dictionary`, you could do the following:

```
print(screenSizeInInches["iPhone 7"]) // Prints 4.7
```

Notice how I called the `Dictionary`, then inside of the brackets subscript, I included the `String` value for the key? After putting that inside the `print` function, it prints the value.

Modifying a Dictionary

Now, I want to add an iPad Air 2 to my array of screen sizes. To do this, we need to type the name of our array, add brackets as a subscript, and add a value inside the brackets to add the key. To add the value, we add an equals sign (=) and set the value we want.

```
screenSizeInInches["iPad Air 2"] = 9.7

//screenSizeInInches = ["iPhone 7" : 4.7, "iPhone 7 Plus" : 5.5, "iPad Pro" : 12.9, "iPad Air 2" : 9.7]
```

20

Control Flow

Loops

There may be times where you'll want to loop through a collection of data and perform a certain task or do something while a certain condition is met.

There are 3 main loop types in Swift: `while`, `repeat-while`, and `for-in`.

The `while` loop

This, in my opinion, is the easiest loop to understand. It essentially states that while something is true, that it executes a block of code until it is false. Then it stops looping.

Here is an example:

```
var finished = false

while !finished {
    print("Loading...")
}
```

The code above, although it is a bad loop (meaning that it will run forever and crash Xcode), it means that while the variable `finished` is false, our code should print "Loading..." to the console. Note that the exclamation mark (!) before `finished` means the logical *not* and read as "not complete".

The `repeat-while` loop

The `repeat-while` loop operates very similarly to a regular `while` loop, with one key difference.

In a `repeat-while` loop, the code to be repeated is executed first, then the condition is checked to see whether or not the loop continues.

A `while` loop, the condition is checked first and that determines whether or not the code runs.

Here is an example:

```
var size = 10

repeat {
    size = size + 1
} while size < 15
```

This loop will continue increasing the size by adding the value of `size` plus one until it reaches 15. The thing to remember here is that the condition is checked after the code loops.

There are opportunities where you need to run code before checking if a condition is met. The `repeat-while` loop is the way to make it happen.

The `for-in` loop

Another type of loop is `for-in`. It is used to iterate through a collection of data and perform an action to each item in that collection.

For example:

```
var unoCards = ["Skip", "Wild", "Wild + Draw Four"]

for unoCard in unoCards {
    print(unoCard)
}
```

The code above would iterate through each item in the `unoCards` array and print the name of each item until it reaches the end. Then, our loop terminates.

You also can loop through a range of values. In Swift, a range is denoted by two or three dots.

1...5 is an inclusive range of the numbers from 1 until 5. The three dots means that values will be 1, 2, 3, 4, and 5.

1..< 5 is a non-inclusive range of numbers from 1 until 4. The two dots and less-than sign indicates that the values considered will be 1, 2, 3, and 4.

Conditionals

If Statements

Sometimes you might want to create conditional code that only will execute under certain conditions. That is where the `if` statement becomes very useful.

Basically, they work like this: if **x** is true, then perform **y**.

For example:

```swift
let carModel = "Delorean"

if carModel == "Delorean" {
    print("Great Scott!")
} else if carModel == "Geo Metro" {
    print("It drives, right?")
} else {
    print("If it's got wheels and drives, it's a car!")
}
```

In the above statement, we've said that if the `carModel` is equal to "Delorean", that it should print a message to the console.
If it is equal to "Geo Metro", it should print a message specific to that model. Finally, if it is neither a Delorean or a Geo Metro (thank goodness), then we should print a generic message.

The `if` statement combined with `else if` or `else` is frequently used.

If you have more than a few conditions to be met, then the next section will shed some light on what to do.

Switch Statements

The `switch` statement in Swift 3 is really useful for scenarios with multiple cases. Usually most decisions in code can be run through an "if/else" block, but for those that can't we can use a `switch` statement.

For example:

```swift
var unoCardValue = "Skip"

switch unoCardValue {
case "Skip":
    print("Skip") // "Skip" will be printed
case "Draw-Four":
    print("Draw-Four")
case "Reverse":
```

```
    print("Reverse")
case "Wild":
    print("Wild")
default:
    print("No card selected!")
}
```

In the above example, we have set the value of `unoCardValue` to "Skip". We have created a switch statement and named it the same name as our variable.

Now when our value changes, it will be passed in to our switch statement and if it meets one of our 5 conditions, it will run the code written for that case.

When creating a `switch` statement, you must be exhaustive and write a case for every possible scenario. If you don't need or want to do that, you can declare a `default` case at the bottom of the `switch` statement to handle any case that is not one of the cases you have written. Since the only value we're checking is a `String` which could be *anything*, we need to declare a `default` case since there are endless possibilities outside of our defined cases.

Functions

In Swift 3, we can write functions which are like a set of directions or code that can be written once and used in multiple places.

Basic Function

To create the most basic function we need to use the keyword `func` and give it a descriptive name to describe *what* it does.

For example:

```
func printName() {
    print("Devslopes")
}
```

Function With Parameter

The function above is great and all, but what if we want to print a name other than Devslopes?

We can pass in a parameter so that it can say any name by naming a parameter and giving it a type within the parentheses of our function.

Like so:

```swift
func printName(name: String) {
    print(name)
}
```

Now when we call our function, we can pass in a `String` value with the parameter `name` containing any name we want!

Function With Parameter and Return Value

Sometimes, you want to perform a function and return a value to a variable of some kind. To do this, you simply add the return type you want to return and ask the function to return the relevant value.

Here's an example:

```swift
var fullName = buildName(firstName: "Caleb", lastName: "Stultz")

func buildName(firstName: String, lastName: String) -> String {
    return "\(firstName) \(lastName)"
    // Returns "Caleb Stultz" to our variable above.
}
```

The function above requires two parameters – `firstName` and `lastName`. When we pass in those values, we return a `String` to the variable `fullName` returning the full name.

Wrapping up

This chapter has been a flyover of the Swift 3 programming language. I hope you can see how great it is, just by looking at it briefly. If you're completely new to programming, don't worry. If this is confusing or overwhelming, you're not alone. **But**, the most important thing at this moment is that you push through, remember that truly anyone can learn to code, and that you need to compete against yourself at this point to get better.

Chapter 3: Programming & Variables

In this exciting chapter, we are going to talk about variables, operators, and a little bit about how computers work. This is not a theoretical book, but I do want you to understand some of the basic principles that are happening underneath the hood so that you can have a foundation to build upon.

What you will learn

- Creating your first variable

- Unary, Binary, and Ternary Operators

- Another variable example

Key Terms

- **Variable:** A container used in programming to store a value of some type.

- **String:** A stored value consisting of characters or words.

- **Boolean:** A stored value consisting of a true or false property.

Variables are used in programming to store information which can be referenced and manipulated in a computer program. They also provide a way of labeling data with a descriptive name so that our programs can be understood more clearly by other programmers and ourselves.

If it's helpful, think of a **variable** as a container that holds information, their sole purpose is to label and store data in memory which can later be used in your program.

This is a basic flyover of what a **variable** is and how it works, but now you will create some **variables** in Xcode to help you understand how they work in the context of software development.

Creating your first variable

First, open Xcode if you haven't already and click `Create New Playground`. Give it a name like *Variables*, and click `Next`. Choose somewhere to save this .playground file and click `Create` to save it. You should see a screen like the one in Figure 1.3.1.

Figure 1.3.1

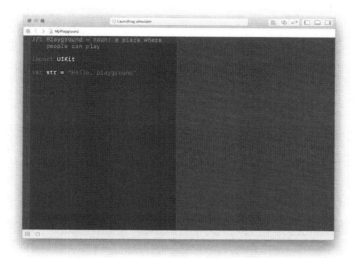

Playgrounds in Xcode are an amazing way to test code snippets to see if and how your code works. It's also a great way for me as an instructor to teach you basic coding principles in Swift.

By default, the Playground we just created already contains a **variable**. Figure 1.3.1 shows the code below.

```
var str = "Hello, playground"
```

Wherever you see `var`, that's short for **variable**. You're telling your computer that you want to create a **variable** (a container that you want to put data into). We can name it whatever we want for the most part, but some names are not allowed. For instance, we can't put numbers in front of a **variable** name (i.e. "2WeeksPay"), but you can use words first and then numbers (i.e. "day1").

```
var
```

In this case, let's use *message* as our **variable**'s name. **Variables** should always be descriptive and should tell you what's being stored in them.

```
var message
```

To give our **variable** a value, we need to use an equals sign just like in any math equation to show that our **variable** is equal to *something*.

```
var message =
```

We are storing some words in our **variable**, and the name for this is a **String**. To declare a **String**, you must use double quotes like so:

```
var message = "Insert String information here..."
```

The key term for what we have written in code here is **String Literal** because we have given our **String** an inherent value.
Later on, we will see how a **String** can be created with an empty value or no value at all.

Let's change the value of our **variable** `message` to be "Hello, playground" by deleting `Insert String information here...` from within the quotation marks and replacing it with `Hello, playground`.

This is your first **variable**. The data type is a **String**, made up of characters and words. That information will be stored in the **variable**.

Under the hood, this program is running on our mac, so it's actually being stored in the memory on the computer somewhere which is pretty cool! All of this is happening for us automatically.

So, in review we created a **variable** by specifying `var`, gave it a descriptive name, and then we gave it a **String** value of, "Hello, playground".

Variables can be changed as many times as you want. The data stored inside of them can change as our app needs it to. We will talk about this more later on when we compare it with a *Constant*.

Unary, Binary, and Ternary Operators

For a moment, let's talk about Operators. There are 3 types of Operators in Swift – unary, binary, and ternary. But what the heck do these words mean?

Unary operators only affect one target.

For example, you can create a **Boolean** (true/false value) which is called amICool:

```
var amICool = true
```

Based on the code above, I am definitely cool.

Then say a new fad or trend comes out that I haven't started yet... So now I'm "uncool". Well, now we can use a unary prefix operator to change that:

```
var amICool = true
amICool = !amICool
```

A unary operator basically inverts the value of `amICool`, our **variable**. Now `amICool` is false because it is the opposite of `amICool`.
Sadly, I'm no longer cool because I didn't follow the new fad or trend.

Unary operators affect one target, but binary operates on two targets.

Binary operators operate on two targets.

They are seen regularly throughout code as most **variables** and constants rely on another value to do their work. Here are some examples:

```
var accountBalance = 9.00
var isBatmanAmazing = true
var officialJobDescription = "Mad Scientist & Rare Cheese Connoisseur"
```

All of the above lines of code operate on two targets – the **variable** name (i.e. isBatmanAmazing) and the value following the equals sign (i.e. `true`).

Ternary operators affect three targets.

Now we are going to add another **variable** called *feelGoodAboutMyself* and set it's value to `true`.

```
var feelGoodAboutMyself = true
```

That's a **variable** and it's of type **Boolean**. We are storing the value `true` into this **variable**. Now let's use a ternary operator just for fun.

```
var feelGoodAboutMyself = true
feelGoodAboutMyself = amICool ? true : false
```

In a ternary operator, the question mark symbol (?) means "if" and the colon symbol (:) means "otherwise".

The code above means that if the value of `amICool` is `true`, then `feelGoodAboutMyself` should be set to `true`, otherwise it should be set to `false`.

It's a ternary operator because it works on 3 targets – `amICool`, `true`, and `false`.

Another variable example

In your Playground file, create a **variable** called *bankAccountBalance* and set it to equal 100.

```
var bankAccountBalance = 100
```

Next, create a **variable** named *cashRegisterMessage*. We want to have a message that will print out for someone who wants to buy something at a store.

```
var bankAccountBalance = 100
var cashRegisterMessage = "You are broke as a joke."
```

Now create a **variable** named *itemPrice* and set it's value to 60.

```
var bankAccountBalance = 100
var cashRegisterMessage = "You are broke as a joke."
var itemPrice = 60
```

We're also going to write a ternary operator to check if our bank account balance is greater than or equal to 50. If the operator returns `true`, then you are able to buy the item, otherwise, you can't buy the item because you are broke.

```
var bankAccountBalance = 100
var cashRegisterMessage = "You are broke as a joke."
var itemPrice = 60

bankAccountBalance >= itemPrice ? "Item purchased!" : cashRegisterMessage
```

Now, change the price of the item to 150 and add in the following conditional if/else statement (more on these in a following chapter).

```
var bankAccountBalance = 100
var cashRegisterMessage = "You are broke as a joke."
```

```
var itemPrice = 150

if bankAccountBalance >= itemPrice {
    cashRegisterMessage = "Item purchased!"
    print(cashRegisterMessage)
} else {
    print(cashRegisterMessage)
}
```

What do you notice changed in the console output on the right-hand side of your Playground window? "You are broke as a joke."

The if/else code above means that if the value of bankAccountBalance is greater than or equal to the itemPrice, then cashRegisterMessage should be set to "Item purchased!", otherwise it should be set to the default message we set.

There are other operators that we'll learn about later such as math operators for adding, subtracting, multiplying, and dividing. There is even a remainder operator for doing division and getting only the remainder of the result. We will talk more about those later.

Wrapping up

This chapter was a flyover of how **variables** work and what a **variable** is. We talked about unary operators, binary operators, and ternary operators. You learned that you can create a container called a **variable** by starting with the keyword var and giving the container a descriptive name like *bankAccountBalance*.

You learned that you can store a value into that container such as a **string** (text), **boolean** (true/false), or even a number (integers/decimals). You can assign the value using the assignment operator (equals sign).

Finally, I want to encourage you to dig more into this! Search online for the three types of operators and look up what a **variable** is. It's important to know these things because you want to become a great programmer!

Exercise

Create 4 variables to hold these types of data:
* Your name (String)

* Your age (Int)
* The temperature in your location (Double)
* Something that is true about yourself (Bool)

Chapter 4: Functions

Functions are a core component in programming. They are building blocks in building functional applications. Functions help our code to be more readable, compartmentalized, and ultimately more efficient. We can write a function to perform a specific task and then reuse it at will throughout our application.

What you will learn

- Creating your first function

- Another function example

- Constants

Key Terms

- **Function:** a container for a block of code that performs a specific singular task.

- **Parameter:** a value passed into a function. Can be of any type.

- **Constant:** a value in code that cannot be changed.

Every day, most humans live their lives under a set of routines. Things they do often times without even thinking about or realizing that they're doing them.

Think about what you do when you first wake up. I know for myself, I slither out of bed and stumble across the room to my noisy phone and silence the alarm. That event alone contains several different steps that I follow in the same order every day (unless I forget to set my alarm).

1. Wake up to alarm sound

2. Slide out of bed, trying not to accidentally wake my wife.

3. Stagger my way over to my alarm.

4. Silence my alarm.

The steps above are a **function**. A set of steps that I complete over and over again (every morning). In pseudo code, this could look like:

```
var awake = false
var inBed = true
var walking = false
var alarmSilenced = false

func getUp() {
    awake = true
    inBed = false
    walking = true
    alarmSilenced = true
}
```

Functions run the code inside them *asynchronously*, or, in a top-to-bottom manner. How's that for a five-dollar word?

In other words, `awake` gets set to `true`, `inBed` gets set to `false`, `walking` gets set to `true`, and `alarmSilenced` gets set to `true` – in that order.

My waking up metaphor is imperfect however, because it takes me probably 10-15 seconds to fully wake up, walk over, and silence my alarm. Modern devices can process the code inside **function**s so quickly that it is almost as if it's running instantly, even though it is running asynchronously.

Most simply put, **functions** are a way to perform an operation over and over. You will use them throughout many of the advanced projects you will complete later on in this book.

But enough *talking* about **functions**... Let's write some!

Creating your first function

If you've taken any advanced math courses, you probably have some background knowledge regarding **functions**. You probably know them by another name: Formulas. You can use `L x W` (length multiplied by width) to calculate the area of a rectangle or $a^2 + b^2 = c^2$ to determine the length of the hypotenuse of a right triangle.

We will create one of these formulas in Swift to illustrate how **functions** work.

First, open Xcode if you haven't already and click `Create New Playground`. Give it a name like *Functions* and click `Next`.

Choose somewhere to save this .playground file and click `Create` to save it. You should see a screen like the one in Figure 1.4.1.

Figure 1.4.1

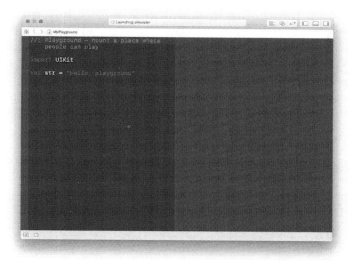

Delete all the boilerplate code on the left side but leave `import UIKit` as it is necessary.

To declare a **function**, we need to:

1. Begin with the keyword `func`.
2. Give it a descriptive name, similarly to how we name variables.
3. Include a set of parentheses and inside that any parameters we want to pass in.
4. Declare what value the **function** should return, if any.

In your Playground, type the following:

```
func calculateArea(length: Int, width: Int) -> Int {
//Code to calculate the area will go here.
}
```

As it currently exists, we have declared a **function** called `calculateArea(length:width:)`. There is no code inside our **function** and we are passing in a value for the length and width – both of type `Int`. We have also declared that we want to return a value of `Int` by typing `-> Int`. Let's add some code to calculate the area.

35

```
func calculateArea(length: Int, width: Int) -> Int {
    let area = length * width
    return area
}
```

Our **function** is now complete. We've created a **function** that calculates the area of a rectangle. We can pass in a value for the length and width (both are required) and the code inside the **function** multiplies them together to give us an area value.
We then `return` the value of `area` to our **function**. But in Playground, our **function** doesn't print to the console like it should.

That's because we haven't called it yet. We need to type the name of our **function** and pass in values for length and width so that Xcode knows to run the code inside.

At the bottom of your Playground window, call the **function** by typing it's name. Use Xcode's AutoComplete feature and press the `Enter` key when it pops up to make your life easier. Pass in a length of 10 and a width of 20.

```
func calculateArea(length: Int, width: Int) -> Int {
    let area = length * width
    return area
}

calculateArea(length: 10, width: 20)
```

To see the result of our **function**, look at the right-hand side of the Playground window (Figure 1.4.2) to see the value our **function** returns from our `area` variable.

Figure 1.4.2

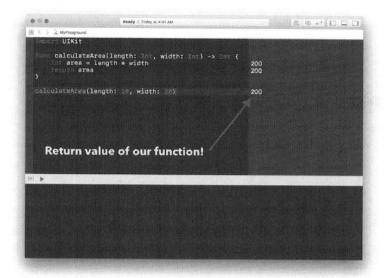

Return value of our function!

Let's try calling it again but pass in different values to calculate a different area (Figure 1.4.3).

```swift
func calculateArea(length: Int, width: Int) -> Int {
    let area = length * width
    return area
}

calculateArea(length: 10, width: 20)
calculateArea(length: 24, width: 15)
```

Figure 1.4.3

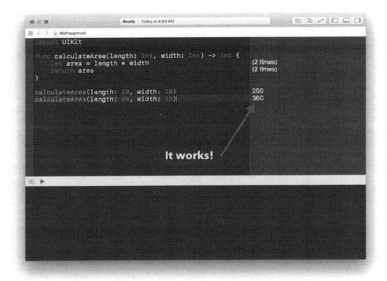

As you can see, the **function** works with a rectangle of any area with side lengths that are whole numbers.

Another function example

Functions can be used for anything! We used them above for a simple area calculation and now we will write one about our bank account.

At the bottom of your Playground file, type the following:

```
var bankAccountBalance = 500.00
var selfLacingNikes = 350.00
```

We created two variables – one to manage our bank account balance and one to declare the price of some cool self-lacing shoes. Great Scott!

We could just write out the conditional code to say that if we have enough money, then we can buy the shoes but a **function** is an even better way to do this. This way, we can reuse the **function** and apply it to other item prices.

```
var bankAccountBalance = 500.00
var selfLacingNikes = 350.00

func purchaseItem(currentBalance: Double, itemPrice: Double) -> Double {
```

```
    if itemPrice <= currentBalance {
        print("Purchased item for $\(itemPrice)")
        return currentBalance - itemPrice
    } else {
        print("You are broke. Balance still at $\(currentBalance)")
        return currentBalance
    }
}
```

What just happened?

Alright, woah.   That was a lot of code to write without any explanation. Let's talk about that now.

We declare a **function** named purchaseItem(currentBalance:itemPrice:).
We gave it two parameters to accept input values – currentBalance and itemPrice.
Next, we asked our **function** to return a value of type Double after it has finished running.

Inside our **function**, we wrote that if the itemPrice we pass in is less than or equal to our currentBalance value we passed in, then we should **1.)** print Purchased item for $\ (itemPrice) and **2.)** return currentBalance minus our item's price.

If that condition cannot be met, or in our code: else, our **function** will **1.)** print: *You are broke. Balance still at $(currentBalance)* and **2.)** return the value of our current balance unchanged.

At the bottom of our Playground, let's call our **function** now.

```
var bankAccountBalance = 500.00
var selfLacingNikes = 350.00

func purchaseItem(currentBalance: Double, itemPrice: Double) -> Double {
    if itemPrice <= currentBalance {
        print("Purchased item for $\(itemPrice)")
        return currentBalance - itemPrice
    } else {
        print("You are broke. Balance still at $\(currentBalance)")
        return currentBalance
    }
}

//Pass in the values for "bankAccountBalance" and "selfLacingNikes" below.
```

```
purchaseItem(currentBalance: bankAccountBalance, itemPrice: selfLacingNikes)
```

As you can see on the right-hand side, the **function** works! Our item's price is less than our account balance, so the operation 500.00 - 350.00 takes place for the price of the shoes to be subtracted by our account balance. This gives us a `bankAccountBalance` value of 150.00.

To actually do something with that value, we can override our `bankAccountBalance` to update it after our **function** runs.

```
...

bankAccountBalance = purchaseItem(currentBalance: bankAccountBalance, itemPrice:
selfLacingNikes)
```

Now `bankAccountBalance` is equal to 150.00 instead of 500.00 because our **function** has modified it *AND* we printed a message to the Debug menu (Figure 1.4.4).

Figure 1.4.4

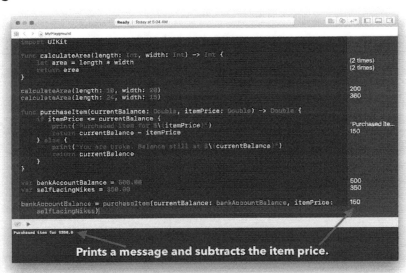

Prints a message and subtracts the item price.

We can create a new item to buy and pass it in through our **function**, too!

Create a variable beneath `selfLacingNikes` named *stainlessSteelAppleWatch* and give it a price of 599.00 like so:

```
var bankAccountBalance = 500.00
var selfLacingNikes = 350.00
```

```
var stainlessSteelAppleWatch = 599.00
```

Now pass it in to our `purchaseItem(currentBalance:itemPrice:)` **function**:

```
...
bankAccountBalance = purchaseItem(currentBalance: bankAccountBalance, itemPrice:
stainlessSteelAppleWatch)
```

As you can see in Figure 1.4.5, our **function** prevents the purchase from being made
and prints out an error message for us.

Figure 1.4.5

String Interpolation

As an aside, let's talk about why I used `\()` and placed `itemPrice` inside of it i.e. `\`
`(itemPrice)`.

In Swift, when you want to print a message or create a `String` value and include a value
of a different type, we can pass it in and convert it using String Interpolation. Like so:

```
var price = 250
var message = "The item's price is $\(price)."
```

The message that will print to the console is: "The item's price is $250."

The variable `price` is of type `Int` (inferred by Swift) and it's passed in and interpolated by using the syntax `\()`. Pretty cool!

Return Values Are The End of the Road

Whenever you call a return in a **function**, that is the end of that **function**. Code written after a return will never run. So make sure that any code written goes before the return statement.

Here's a bad example:

```
var pizzaSlices = 8
var amountOfPizzaEaten = 2

func eatPizza(slicesEaten: Int, pizzaSlices: Int) -> Int {
    if slicesEaten >= 1 {
        let updatedSlices = pizzaSlices - slicesEaten
        return updatedSlices
        print("\(updatedSlices) slices of pizza left!")
    } else {
        print("Meh, not hungry.")
        return pizzaSlices
    }
}

eatPizza(slicesEaten: amountOfPizzaEaten, pizzaSlices: pizzaSlices)
```

Do you smell something funky? In programming, we actually call this a "code smell" – when something just ain't right.

The print **function** called after `return` will never run because it was called too late. In fact, Xcode will even warn us that the code written afterward will not run. Our **function** *SHOULD* look like this:

```
var pizzaSlices = 8
var amountOfPizzaEaten = 2

func eatPizza(slicesEaten: Int, pizzaSlices: Int) -> Int {
    if slicesEaten >= 1 {
        let updatedSlices = pizzaSlices - slicesEaten
        print("\(updatedSlices) slices of pizza left!")
        return updatedSlices
    } else {
```

```
        print("Meh, not hungry.")
        return pizzaSlices
    }
}
```

```
eatPizza(slicesEaten: amountOfPizzaEaten, pizzaSlices: pizzaSlices)
```

Choosing To Not Return Anything

What if we don't want to deal with return values? Well, thanks to `inout` parameters, we don't have to.

An `inout` **parameter** allows for us to directly modify variables outside our **function** instead of having to return a value to them in order to update their value.

You can use an `inout` **parameter** by modifying the pizza **function** we wrote above:

```
var pizzaSlices = 8
var amountOfPizzaEaten = 2

func eatPizza(slicesEaten: Int, pizzaSlices: inout Int) {
    if slicesEaten >= 1 {
        pizzaSlices = pizzaSlices - slicesEaten
        print("\(pizzaSlices) slices of pizza left!")
    } else {
        print("Meh, not hungry.")
    }
}
```

```
eatPizza(slicesEaten: amountOfPizzaEaten, pizzaSlices: &pizzaSlices)
```

Inside the *if* block of our **function**, we are able to directly modify the variable `pizzaSlices` which is super cool.

When we call the **function** `eatPizza(slicesEaten:pizzaSlices:)` we add an ampersand to the front of the `pizzaSlices` variable we pass in. This is the syntax to tell Xcode that we want to use an inout **parameter**.

By writing a **function** this way, we aren't required to return a value but we can still modify the variables we want. You want to use this sparingly, and you don't **need** to know about this yet, but it's good to have in your tool-belt.

Constants

43

Throughout this chapter, you have seen the keyword `let` used in a similar way to how we create variables. That keyword is actually incredibly important. It is used to declare a **Constant** in Swift.

A **constant** is exactly like a variable except for the fact that it can never change once it is given a value.

Some examples of data that could be **constants** are: your birthday, a city name, car model, etc. Things that never change and remain **constant** (hence the name!). The keyword `let` is used in a "let that value stay the same" kind of manner.

Here are some pseudo-code examples:

```
let birthYear = 1992
let mothersMaidenName = "Squillagree"
let jennysPhoneNumber = 8675309
```

These values are all unchanging and we won't need to change them. If we try to change them, Xcode will yell at us, show the `let` we created as a `var` in gray, and give us an error asking us to change our `let` into a `var` so it can be modified as in Figure 1.4.6:

Figure 1.4.6

To be honest, that is the only information you will need to know about **constants** as they are identical to variables except that they cannot be changed once given a value.

Wrapping up

We've learned a lot in this chapter about **functions** – reusable bits of code that perform specific tasks. 99.9% of coding is writing and using **functions** so this is very important for you to know and understand well.

We talked about the anatomy of a **function** which contains the keyword `func`, a descriptive name of what the **function** does, a set of parentheses optionally including **parameters** to pass in, and a return type if needed.

In the following chapters, you will use **functions** frequently so if there are any parts of this chapter you don't fully understand read back through it again and make sure you really get it down.

Exercise

Write a function called `canDivideSlices` that takes in two values – `numberOfSlices` and `numberOfFriends` and returns a value of type `Bool`(true or false). This function will be used to determine whether or not a pizza can be divided evenly by your group of friends.

Chapter 5: Arrays

*An **array** is a collection type. It stores collections of data of multiple types and orders them numerically.*

What you will learn

- Creating your first Array

- Appending an item To an Array

- Removing an item From an Array

- Creating an empty Array

- Other neat things Arrays can do

Key Terms

- **Zero-indexing:** a term to describe the starting point (0) at which a Swift Array begins counting.

- **Array:** a collection type in Swift where values are collected and ordered numerically.

- **Append:** to add a value to an **array**.

- **Empty Array:** an **array** with no values stored inside – how sad.

The variables we learned about in chapter 3 are great for storing single values. In the real world, we need to keep track of multiple pieces of data that are all a part of the same category. For example – employee salaries, the value of each comic book in our collection, or the cost per item in a store inventory.

It is time and labor-intensive to create an individual variable for each of the above items and honestly it wouldn't be good code. This is where **arrays** come in *cue triumphant music!*

Arrays are a collection of values that allow us to store multiple values. In this chapter, we will see just how useful they can be.

Setting up a Playground

First, open Xcode if you haven't already and click `Create New Playground`. Give it a name like *Arrays* and click `Next`.

Choose somewhere to save this `.playground` file and click `Create` to save it. You should see a screen like the one in Figure 1.5.1.

Figure 1.5.1

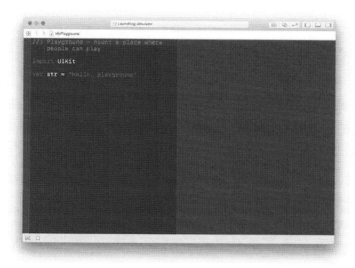

Delete all the boilerplate code on the left side but leave `import UIKit` as it is necessary.

Creating your first array

Let's use one of the above examples: the value of each comic book in our collection. Imagine that you have a collection, albeit a small one, that includes 5 comic books. They each have differing values. We *could* create a variable for each comic book and store the

47

value like so:

```
var comicBook1 = 10.0
var comicBook2 = 27.50
var comicBook3 = 1015.0
var comicBook4 = 55.0
var comicBook5 = 2.0
```

What if someone stole one of your comic books? What if you sold one? You would need to manually remove that line of code and then re-number the variables that follow it because each variable has a specific number and order.

Instead, create an **Array** called `comicBooks` and place the values inside of it like so:

```
var comicBooks = [10.0, 27.50, 1015.0, 55.0, 2.0]
```

Now we have a single line of code to replace the five lines we wrote above. We've written an **array** of type `Int` and have filled the braces ([]) with data.

Appending an item to an array

When we foolishly wrote the 5 variables above, it was difficult to manage and change. If we wanted to add a new comic book, we would have to add it at the end otherwise we would have messed up the number order of each variable. With an **array**, it is easy to manage and modify our data.

For instance, let's pretend that you scored and found an ultra-rare comic book at a garage sale. After researching, you learn that it's value is $500.

To add is to our **array**, simply type:

```
var comicBooks = [10.0, 27.50, 1015.0, 55.0, 2.0]

comicBooks.append(500.0)
```

On the right-hand side of the Playground window, you should see the **array** print out, this time with a new value at the end – 500.0!

Other things arrays can do

Arrays can do a couple cool things to help us manage a collection of data. For instance, we can calculate the total number of objects in our **array**. Just for explanation purposes, we are going to print the number of items in our **array** before we added our new $500 comic and after, too.

Try this:

```swift
var comicBooks = [10.0, 27.50, 1015.0, 55.0, 2.0]

print(comicBooks.count) // Prints 5 because of total above.

comicBooks.append(500.0)

print(comicBooks.count) // Prints 6 because we added a new value!
```

Pretty cool! What if you sold one of your comic books on eBay? How would we remove that item from the **array**?

Removing an item from an array

Arrays in Swift include a function called `.remove(at:)` which allow us to remove a certain item at a certain point in our **array**.

To remove the third value from our **array**, we need to add the following line of code:

```swift
var comicBooks = [10.0, 27.50, 1015.0, 55.0, 2.0]
print(comicBooks.count) // Prints 5 because of total above.

comicBooks.append(500.0)
print(comicBooks.count) // Prints 6 because we added a new value!

comicBooks.remove(at: 2)
```

Wait a minute... Didn't I just say to remove the third value from our **array**? Yes, and that is exactly what I did. You should see the third value (1015.0) printed out on the right-hand side of the Playground. So it worked, but if this is confusing it's okay because this is where I will talk about zero-indexing.

In most programming languages, **arrays** use what is called **zero-indexing** meaning that the first value in our **array** is given an identifier of 0 to indicate the first value. The second value has the identifier (or index) of 1, and so on. If you want the fourth value, you need to ask Swift for an index of 3. It may seem confusing, but that's just the way it is.

In the above code, we wanted to remove the third comic book from our **array**, so we asked to remove the item at index 2.

If we print `comicBooks.count` below `comicBooks.remove(at: 2)` you should see that the count is back down to 5.

```
...
comicBooks.remove(at: 2)

print(comicBooks.count) // Prints 5
```

Creating an empty array

Let's move on to another example – students in a classroom. Type the following beneath all the code you wrote above:

```
var students = [String]()
```

The above code is an empty **array**. We have declared a variable called `students` and have asked Xcode to make it an empty **array** containing String values. In regards to an **array**, "empty" means that it doesn't yet have any values – like an empty box or container would be with nothing inside.

To show that there is nothing inside, add the following:

```
var students = [String]()

print(students.count) // Prints 0 because our array is empty!
```

Now we can add students to our **Array**! Use the `.append()` function to do so:

```
var students = [String]()

print(students.count) // Prints 0 because our array is empty!

students.append("Jon")
students.append("Jacob")
students.append("Jose")
students.append("Jingle")
students.append("Heimer")
students.append("Schmidt")
```

In your Playground window, you should see the following (Figure 1.5.2):

Figure 1.5.2

```
//: Playground — noun: a place where
   people can play

import UIKit

var students = [String]()                    []

print(students.count) // Prints 0            "0\n"
   because our array is empty!

students.append("Jon")        ["Jon"]
students.append("Jacob")      ["Jon", "Jacob"]
students.append("Jose")       ["Jon", "Jacob", "Jose"]
students.append("Jingle")     ["Jon", "Jacob", "Jose", "Jingle"]
students.append("Heimer")     ["Jon", "Jacob", "Jose", "Jingle", "Heimer"]
students.append("Schmidt")    ["Jon", "Jacob", "Jose", "Jingle", "Heimer", "Schmidt"]
```

The pyramid-like print out of values on the right-hand side shows how each time we run
`.append()` to add a value, the **Array** becomes longer and includes more values.

Wrapping up

There are many more cool things that **arrays** can do, but you have learned the essentials
in this chapter. **Arrays** are collection type and as such, they are great for storing
collections of values. Whatever you have a list of – teachers, hot wheel cars, Minecraft
collectibles, you name it – **arrays** are a great way to store that data.

We are starting to get better at organizing and writing cleaner code and will continue to
do so throughout this book. Nicely done on getting this far! You deserve a cookie!

Exercise

Create an Array called `favoriteAlbums` and fill it with the titles of four albums that you
love. (Hint: They should all be values of type String). Add a new album title to your array
by using the `.append()` feature in Swift. Print the total count of the items in the array using
`.count`.

I'm going to make you be picky now... Use Swift's `remove(at:_)` feature to remove an
album from your array.

Chapter 6: Loops

Loops are repeating blocks of code that we can use to perform one action to multiple pieces of data in Swift.

What you will learn

- Writing your first `repeat-while` loop

- Writing your first `for-in` loop

- Writing your first `for-each` loop

Key Terms

- **Loop:** a section of code that repeats until a condition is met.

- **The DRY Principle:** a programming principle meaning "Don't Repeat Yourself", in an effort to remind programmers to use the most efficient coding practice.

The **DRY principle** states "Don't Repeat Yourself". It is a coding principle that has existed for a long time, but **loops** in Swift are blocks of repeating code.

How can using **loops** be a good practice? While a **loop** repeats the same code over and over, it does so within the confines of a single **loop**. We can pass in data from an array, for example, and the same operation can be performed on each item of that collection.

This is a very useful component of the Swift language. We will learn about the 3 popular types of Swift 3 **loops** in this chapter. Let's get loopy!

Setting up a Playground

First, open Xcode if you haven't already and click `Create New Playground`. Give it a name like *Loops* and click `Next`.

Choose somewhere to save this .playground file and click `Create` to save it. You should see a screen like the one in Figure 1.6.1.

Figure 1.6.1

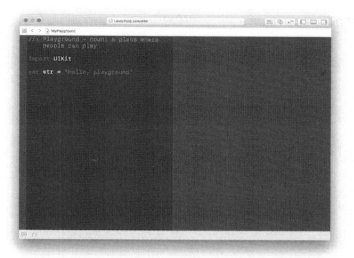

Delete all the boilerplate code on the left side but leave `import UIKit` as it is necessary.

Why you should use loops

Let's imagine that we have 4 employees working at our company. Each employee earns a different salary:

- **Employee 1:** $45,000

- **Employee 2:** $100,000

- **Employee 3:** $54,000

- **Employee 4:** $20,000 (Sorry, bro.)

Create 4 variables (one for each employee) and set the value of each variable to be the related salary above:

```
import UIKit
```

```
var employee1Salary = 45000.0
var employee2Salary = 100000.0
var employee3Salary = 54000.0
var employee4Salary = 20000.0
```

We just finished up Q4 of 2016 and we've had a very successful year. We want to give each employee a raise of 10%. In your Playground, type:

```
import UIKit

var employee1Salary = 45000.0
var employee2Salary = 100000.0
var employee3Salary = 54000.0
var employee4Salary = 20000.0

employee1Salary = employee1Salary + (employee1Salary * 0.10)
```

The above code performs the operation **45000.0 + (45000.0 * 0.10)** as it takes our variables value and adds it to 10% of itself.

On the right-hand side of the Playground, you should see a new value – 49500.

Let's perform this operation for each employee:

```
employee1Salary = employee1Salary + (employee1Salary * 0.10) // prints 49500
employee2Salary = employee2Salary + (employee2Salary * 0.10) // prints 110000
employee3Salary = employee3Salary + (employee1Salary * 0.10) // prints 59400
employee4Salary = employee4Salary + (employee1Salary * 0.10) // prints 22000
```

I don't know about you, but I smell some stanky code. If you were thinking, "WAIT. We're repeating ourself... What if we had 100 employees?" Doing this operation for 100 employees would be very exhausting and likely would result in errors.
We are also violating the **DRY principle** (Don't Repeat Yourself).

There is no need for us to have 4 separate variables for storing employee salaries. Let's instead consolidate them into a single array named `salaries`:

```
var salaries = [45000.0, 100000.0, 54000.0, 20000.0]
```

How can we cycle through these and add 10% to each person's salary? Well, we could type:

```
salaries[0] = salaries[0 + (salaries[0] * 0.10)
```

But that would result in the same issue. We still need to write a line of code for each employee and repeat ourself. Yuck! Delete that line of code leaving only the array called

```
salaries.
```

How do we solve this problem? This is where **loops** in Swift become very useful. For each employee, we've given them a salary and need to perform the same operation on each one – `salary + (salary * 10%)`. Let's write a **loop** to handle this.

Writing your first loop

The first **loop** we will write is called a `repeat-while` **loop**. There are a few different types of **loop**, but they all run code on repeat while or until a certain condition is met.

Writing a repeat-while loop

Below our salaries variable, type:

```
var salaries = [45000.0, 100000.0, 54000.0, 20000.0]

var x = 0
repeat {
    x += 1
} while (x < salaries.count)
```

You should see that on the right side of the Playground window our **loop** runs 4 times. But why?

We ask our **loop** to repeat taking the value of our variable x and adding one to it.
Then our **loop** checks against the condition we declared: `x < salaries.count`.
We ask it to see what the value of x is and then see if that is less than the total number of items in the array `salaries`.
The `.count` following an array will give you the value of how many items there are in that array. If we look, there are 4 salaries so, therefore, `salaries.count` = 4.

So under the hood, we are doing the following:

```
var salaries = [45000.0, 100000.0, 54000.0, 20000.0]

var x = 0
x + 1 // Now x = 1
// Check condition: 1 < 4 is true, continue to loop

x + 1 // Now x = 2
```

```
// Check condition: 2 < 4 is true, continue to loop

x + 1 // Now x = 3
// Check condition: 3 < 4 is true, continue to loop

x + 1 // Now x = 4
// Check condition: 4 < 4 is false, stop looping
```

Adding the 10% salary equation

Now all we need to do is add our salary equation but instead of using a number value to call a specific element of our array (i.e. `salaries[0]`), we will use our variable x (i.e. `salaries[x]`) because it's value iterates from 0 up until 3 when run through our **loop**. Remember, in arrays in Swift use zero-indexing, meaning that the first element is numbered 0.

Add the following to your repeat-while **loop**:

```
var salaries = [45000.0, 100000.0, 54000.0, 20000.0]

var x = 0
repeat {
    salaries[x] = salaries[x] + (salaries[x] * 0.10)
    x += 1
} while (x < salaries.count)
```

The variable x could be named anything, but x is simply a common choice used in **loops**. A variable that is more wordy but also more descriptive is `index`. Remember that in an array, the index is the number used to identify each element in the array.

To be more descriptive, change the variable x to be `index` instead. Like so:

```
var salaries = [45000.0, 100000.0, 54000.0, 20000.0]

var index = 0
repeat {
    salaries[index] = salaries[index] + (salaries[index] * 0.10)
    index += 1
} while (index < salaries.count)
```

So what is this doing? We begin with our `index` variable set to 0.
Then we declare a repeat-while **loop**. Inside the repeat block we add an equation which adds 10% of our salary to our current salary for the item at the index with the same value

as our variable `index` (at this point, it's equal to 0).

Then we add 1 to our `index` variable making it equal to 1.

Finally, we check using our `while` condition to see if index is still less than the total number of elements in our `salaries` array.

It probably seems that I am repeating myself, but it is really important that you understand this.

Writing a `for-in` loop

Another type of **loop** that you may want to write at times is called a `for-in` **loop**. It enables you to **loop** through a range of values and perform an operation for each value.

Here is an example of a `for-in` **loop**:

```
for x in 1...5 {
    print("Index: \(x)")
}
```

If you type the above code into your Playground, you will see the result "(5 times)" meaning that we have **looped** 5 times. In the console at the bottom of the playground window, you should see this message:

```
Index: 1
Index: 2
Index: 3
Index: 4
Index: 5
```

The value of x is being set to a value of 1, then we print the message `Index: 1` because x is equal to 1.

The **loop** then restarts but this time x is set to the next value in the range: 2.

The console prints `Index: 2` and the **loop** repeats. This continues until we hit a value of 5.

The use of `...` means "inclusive" and indicates that we should include every value from 1 until 5.

If we wanted to make it "exclusive" – so that our **loop** considers everything except the last value in the range – we would need to add a new "exclusive" **loop** as follows:

```
for x in 1...5 {
    print("Index: \(x)")
```

```
}

for x in 1..<5 {
    print("Exclusive Index: \(x)")
}
```

You should only see 4 lines print out for the second **loop**. This is because we have asked it to exclude the final value of 5 from being used.

The beginning of a `for-in` **loop** is indicated by the keyword `for`. Then we create a variable named x, but it could be named anything.
Next, we use the keyword `in` to indicate that we are about to declare a range of values.
At the end we state which values the **loop** should operate within.

To continue with out salaries example above, type the following `for-in` **loop** in your Playground window:

```
for i in 0..<salaries.count {
    salaries[i] = salaries[i] + (salaries[i] * 0.10)
    print(salaries[i])
}
```

This **loop** creates a variable named i and declares a range of 0 to "less-than" the value of `salaries.count`. Since `salaries.count` is equal to 4, our **loop** is exclusive and can only check values between 0 and 3 since 4 is not less than 4.
This is perfect, however, because the index of our salaries array begins at zero and ends at 3.

The flow of the above **loops** goes like this: the variable i gets set to 0 – the first value in our range.
Then i is passed in as the index for our `salaries` array.
Afterward, we do the math to add a 10% raise like before.
Finally, we print the raised salary to the console below.

Here is the key difference between a for-in **loop** and a repeat-while **loop**:
in a for-in **loop**, the value of our placeholder variable (in this case i) is modified by the range of values we set at the end.

In a repeat-while **loop**, we need to increment the variable `index` by writing `index += 1`.

Creating a `for-each` **loop**

The next **loop** is for when you may have a variable number of items to **loop** through. We've used predefined ranges or an array with static information inside of it.
What if all salary information was stored on a server which could change from day to day with new hires and fires? If we were to enter in everybody's salary information manually in a static array, it would be much harder to change or modify anyones salary. It also would be a troublesome task to locate a certain employee's salary if they were fired.

To write a `for-each` **loop**, type the following:

```
for salary in salaries {
    print("Salary: \(salary)")
}
```

As you can see in the console at the bottom of your Playgrounds window, every salary in our array is printed nicely.

The above code works by starting with the keyword `for` to indicate we are creating a **loop**.
Then, we create a variable called `salary` and ask it to **loop** through each item in the `salaries` array until we reach the end.
For each item **loop** through in the array we print it's value into a String like so: "Salary: 24200.0"

Personally, I find `for-each` **loops** the easiest for a beginner to understand as you can name the variable something specific related to the contents of your array.

Wrapping up

Loops are a foundational concept to understand when learning to code. If you feel confused about how they work, I encourage you to re-read this chapter. Try typing out the examples a few times.
It's also a great idea to do some research online. Find examples and real-life scenarios where people are using **loops** and learn from them.

We've learned about `repeat-while`, `for-in`, and `for-each` **loops** in Swift. Now you can **loop** through collections of data and write better, more efficient code. Whenever you need to perform the same operation over and over, instead of writing multiple lines of almost duplicate code use a **loop**!

Exercise

Create an Array that stores the names of all four members of the Beatles. Write a for-each loop that walks through the Array and prints the name of each Beatles member.

Create another Array that stores four countries populations. Write a for-in loop that walks through the array and prints a sentence with the population value passed into the sentence using String Interpolation. The population is 12378932, for example.

Chapter 7: Dictionaries

Similar to a Swift array, dictionaries are a convenient way of cataloging information. They are super useful if you need to store data with two related values (i.e. word and definition).

What you will learn

- Creating your first dictionary

- Adding an item to the dictionary

- Accessing the amount Of items in a dictionary

- Checking to see if a dictionary is empty

- Overriding a dictionary value to modify it

- Iterating through a dictionary

- Clearing out a dictionary of all data

Key Terms

- **dictionary**: a collection type in Swift 3 which allows for the storing of data in a key-value pair.

- **Key:** a unique identifier that is associated with a value.

- **Value:** a value which is identified and linked to a unique key.

When you were in school, you were probably asked at one point to look up the definition of a word to determine it's meaning. You knew that the words were sorted alphabetically, so you could efficiently track down the general location of the word, then fine-tune your search as you flipped through a couple pages as you got closer to your target word.

Once you had found your target word, you would read the definition and use that in whatever assignment you were working on.

In Swift, a dictionary (called hash tables or hash maps in other programming languages) is a collection type which associates a **key** with a value similarly to how a **dictionary** for a language associates words with their definition.

Swift **Dictionaries** operate just like a language **dictionary** does. You start with a **key** of some type (String, Int, Double, etc.) and a **value** of the same or a different type. While the **value** per **key** can vary, each **key** in a **dictionary** must be unique.

The thing that makes them unique is that they are much more efficient to search through than an Array and they are much easier to find particular items. An Array in Swift orders items numerically, which is great in some circumstances, but if you want to find a specific piece of information a **dictionary** is better. You can associate a **key** with a **value** so you can track down the item by it's **key** – just like you would in a language **dictionary**.

Let's dive into creating a **dictionary** in Swift now.

Setting up

First, open Xcode if you haven't already and click `Create New Playground`. Give it a name like *Dictionaries* and click `Next`.
Choose somewhere to save this .playground file and click `Create` to save it. You should see a screen like the one in Figure 1.7.1.

Figure 1.7.1

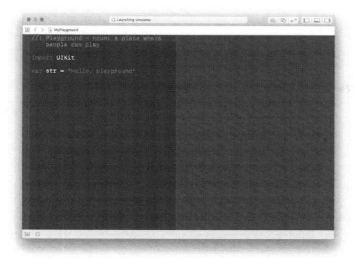

Delete all the boilerplate code on the left side but leave `import UIKit` as it is necessary.

Creating your first dictionary

To create your first Swift **dictionary**, create a variable called `namesOfIntegers` like so:

```
var namesOfIntegers = [Int: String]()
```

What we have done above is declared a variable and called it *namesOfIntegers*. We've set it to be equal to a **Dictionary** as indicated by the square brackets. Inside, we have declared that the key type should be `Int` and the value type should be `String`.

This means that any data we try to add to this **dictionary** has to adhere to that rule. We also declared this as an empty **dictionary** as indicated by the parentheses following the **dictionary** brackets.

You should see the following print out in the console indicating that we successfully created an empty **dictionary** (there are no values, but brackets and a colon in the middle):

```
[:]
```

Adding an item to the dictionary

A **dictionary** is no use if it is empty! Let's add some data so that it is a bit more useful to us.

Type the following on a new line beneath the variable *namesOfIntegers*:

```
var namesOfIntegers = [Int: String]()
```

```
namesOfIntegers[3] = "Three"
```

You might be thinking, "Hey! That's just like an Array!
3 must be the index and "Three" must be the data that's stored!
While that is a fair assumption at the moment, you will soon see how a **dictionary** is quite different.

The number 3 is actually the name of the **key** (of type Int) in our **dictionary** and the **value** associated with it is a String with a **value** of "Three".

We added a new **key** called 3 with a **value** of "Three".
These **key-value** pairs are what make **Dictionaries** in Swift so powerful.

Let's add another **key** and **value** pair to our **dictionary**.
Add the following at the bottom of your Playground file:

```
var namesOfIntegers = [Int: String]()
```

```
namesOfIntegers[3] = "Three"
namesOfIntegers[44] = "Forty Four"
```

The thing to note here is that it **does not matter** at what order you add these **values**. We access the items in a **dictionary** by their **key** not their number order.

Another dictionary example

Let's pretend for a moment that we're building an app that monitors and keeps track of important flight data for all the world's airports. Each airport should definitely have it's own unique code separating if from the others.

If Stockholm, Los Angeles, and Dubai all shared the same airport code, LAX, it would cause a massive amount of confusion and headache all the time.

Luckily, each airport has a unique airport code so that they are all differentiated from one another. A few airports could actually have the same name as long as their code was unique.

The thing about **Dictionaries** in Swift is that every **key** must be unique. This is so that all of the data you want to save into it can be differentiated and easily accessed just like each airport code needs to be easily accessible and quickly understood.

Continuing with this example, let's create a **dictionary** for a list of airport codes. Add the following **dictionary** at the bottom of your Playground:

```
...

var airports: [String: String] = ["YYZ": "Toronto Pearson", "LAX": "Los Angeles
International"]
```

OK, cool. So what is happening here? We created a variable called *airports* and explicitly declared it as a **dictionary** of type `[String: String]`.
We used the assignment operator (=) and added a pair of square brackets. Inside, we created two **key-value** pairs.

For each pair, we added a **key** of type `String` for each airport code followed by a colon (:).
We then added a **value** of type `String` containing the airports name. Since we created two **key-value** pairs, we used a comma to separate the **values** just like we would in an Array.

Accessing the amount of items in a dictionary

In order to access the amount of items in our **dictionary**, we can use the same function we do with Arrays. Let's print out a `String` and pass in the `airports.count` to show how many airports we've added to our **dictionary**. Like so:

```
var airports: [String: String] = ["YYZ": "Toronto Pearson", "LAX": "Los Angeles
International"]

print("The airports dictionary has: \(airports.count) items.")
```

In the console, you should see the following: "The airports dictionary has: 2 items." This should seem familiar from our chapter on Arrays like I said above. Arrays and **Dictionaries** both share this ability – to count their total number of objects.

Checking to see if a dictionary is empty

We can also look to see if we have any **values** at all. Use the built in function `isEmpty` to check this:

```
...

if airports.isEmpty {
    print("The airports dictionary is empty!")
}
```

Since we have two items in our **dictionary** nothing will print. If you were to remove everything from the **dictionary**, this `String` would print out in the console.

Overriding a dictionary value to modify it

Let's add a new **value** to our *airports* **dictionary**. At the bottom of your Playground, add the following:

```
airports["PDX"] = "Portland"
```

We have now added a new **key-value** pair, but what if you want to update the **value** to something different. To override the **value** we just set all we need to do is change it like so:

```
airports["PDX"] = "Portland"
airports["PDX"] = "Portland International"
```

Now, the old **value** `"Portland"` is gone and the current **value** for the **key** `"PDX"` is `"Portland International"`. Easy as that!

Removing an item from our dictionary

Let's add a new imaginary airport with a **key** of `"DEV"` and a **value** of `"Devslopes International""`

```
...

airports["DEV"] = "Devslopes International"
```

To remove this item completely from our **dictionary**, all we need to do is the following:

```
airports["DEV"] = "Devslopes International"
airports["DEV"] = nil
```

Now our **key-value** pair of "DEV": "Devslopes International" is gone forever from our **dictionary**.

Iterating through a dictionary

We can use a `for-in` loop to do something with the **keys** and **values** in our **dictionary**. Let's make one now! Add the following loop at the bottom of the Playground window:

```
...

for (airportCode, airportName) in airports {

}
```

Now, before we write any code inside of our loop let's talk about what we're doing here.

Since a **dictionary** works under the condition of **key** and **value** together, we need to loop through both **values** simultaneously. Thus, we have the tuple.

Here is how Apple's Swift 3 documentation defines a tuple: "Tuples group multiple values into a single compound value. The values within a tuple can be of any type and do not have to be of the same type as each other."

We are doing just what the definition describes when we loop through our **dictionary**. We combine the airport code and the airport name into a singular compound **value** and can modify it as we please.

Using both Key and Value

Let's put our tuple to use. Inside the `for-in` loop, add the following:

```
for (airportCode, airportName) in airports {
    print("\(airportCode): \(airportName)")
}
```

In the console below, you should see the following print out:

```
LAX: Los Angeles International
YYZ: Toronto Pearson
```

Using only Keys from a dictionary

If we only wanted to print the airport codes (the keys in our **dictionary**), all we need to do is create another `for-in` loop and access the `keys` property of our **dictionary** like so:

```
for key in airports.keys {
    print("Key: \(key)")
}
```

After writing that code, you will see the following print out in the console:

```
Key: LAX
Key: YYZ
Key: LHR
```

Any **dictionary's keys** can be accessed this way. Pretty cool! But so can the **values**. Check it out below!

Using only Values from a dictionary

We can do the same thing as above, but for the inverse – the **values** inside our **dictionary**.

Create another `for-in` loop to demonstrate this:

```
for value in airports.values {
    print("Value: \(value)")
}
```

The following will print out in the console:

```
Value: Los Angeles International
Value: Toronto Pearson
Value: London Heathrow
```

Clearing out a dictionary of all data

To clear out your **dictionary**, you can simply set it to be equal to an empty **dictionary**. Like so:

```
namesOfIntegers = [:]
```

This will reset and clear out all data from our **dictionary**.

Wrapping up

Dictionaries are super powerful and can be used in a ton of different ways. I personally think **dictionaries** are a super cool feature of Swift and programming in general.
It is a much more orderly and efficient way to organize data when you want to be able to access that data by a **key** and **value** pair.
Arrays are great and have their place, but Dictionaries are much more versatile in their everyday use.

You will especially use **Dictionaries** when you get into the later chapters that guide you to build apps that pull data from API servers online. The data is stored in a format called JSON (JavaScript Object Notation) which largely relies on Arrays and **Dictionaries** for storing and organizing information.

For example, the screenshot below (Figure 1.7.2) is from SWAPI.co (The Star Wars API – amazing, right?   ). If you look closely you'll notice data encapsulated inside of curly {} and square [] brackets (Figure 1.7.3).

The square brackets indicate Arrays and the square brackets indicate **Dictionaries**. Make sure that you understand both Arrays and **Dictionaries** well because it can be confusing navigating through JSON calls like the one below.
Sometimes, depending on the API, data will be downloaded in a simple Array or **dictionary**. But for some APIs, the data is more complex and can be stores in Arrays of **Dictionaries**.

Figure 1.7.2

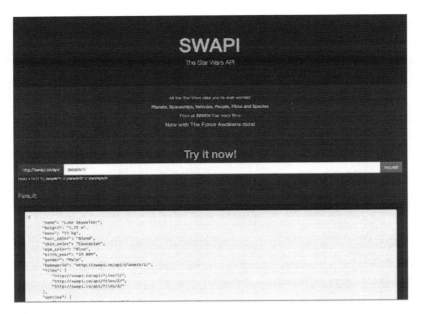

Figure 1.7.3

```
{
    "name": "Luke Skywalker",
    "height": "1.72 m",
    "mass": "77 Kg",
    "hair_color": "Blond",
    "skin_color": "Caucasian",
    "eye_color": "Blue",
    "birth_year": "19 BBY",
    "gender": "Male",
    "homeworld": "http://swapi.co/api/planets/1/",
    "films": [
        "http://swapi.co/api/films/1/",
        "http://swapi.co/api/films/2/",
        "http://swapi.co/api/films/3/"
    ],
    "species": [
        "http://swapi.co/api/species/1/"
    ],
```

Knowing the subtle differences between the two will make all the difference when building those later apps. If you still feel confused, it's always a good idea to read Apple's documentation on Swift 3. Learning to read documentation is an important part of becoming a developer. Don't overlook that!

Nicely done on completing this chapter! Let's move on.

Exercise

Create a Dictionary called `movieReleaseYears` that stores the title and year of release for three movies you love. The title of the movie is the `key` and the release year is the `value`. Write a `for-in` loop to pass in the movie titles and release years together and print them both, IMDb-style (i.e. "Toy Story (1995)")

Chapter 8: Boolean Logic & Conditional Statements

In this chapter, we will discuss Booleans, Conditionals, and Comparison Operators. Booleans are a foundational piece of programming that you will use throughout your code. They are used to compare things or perform an action based on a condition.

What you will learn

- Creating your first Boolean

- Type Inference

- Conditional Statement Basics

- Comparison Operators

Key Terms

- **Boolean:** a binary variable, having two values – "true" and "false."

- **Conditional Statement:** a block of code with one or two conditions that only runs when certain requirements are met.

- **Comparison Operator:** a function used to determine equality, inequality, or difference between two.

When you were a kid, there may have been a time where your parents said, "if you clean your room", then _____ would be the reward. You can fill in the blank. A trip to Disneyland   ? A Japanese-imported Robby the Robot toy   ? Perhaps a near-mint copy of Action Comics No.1 "Superman"   ?

But if you failed to clean your room, then the consequence would be not getting that reward.

If x is true, then y happens. Otherwise, z happens. This "cause and effect" relationship is the foundation that **Booleans** rest on.

Simply put, a **Boolean** is true or false.

Creating your first Boolean

First, open Xcode if you haven't already and click `Create New Playground`. Give it a name like *BooleansConditionalsComparisonOperators* and click `Next`. Choose somewhere to save this .playground file and click `Create` to save it. You should see a screen like the one in Figure 3.1.

Figure 1.8.1

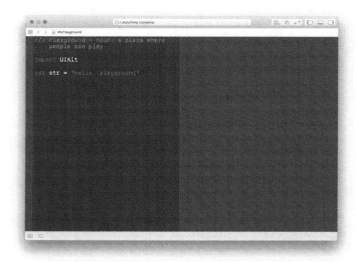

Delete all the boilerplate code on the left side but leave `import UIKit` as that is necessary.

Type the following code:

```
var isThisTheBestBookEver = true
```

You should see on the right-hand side, that the variable is equal to `true`.

Since we have declared our variable `isThisTheBestBookEver` as `true`, we have actually used one of Swift's most helpful features – Type Inference!

Swift Magic: Type Inference

Remember back to **Chapter 3** where we learned that variables can be of many types: Characters or words (`String`), numbers (`Int`, `Float`, `Double`), or even of type `Bool` (short for **Boolean**).

Thanks to Swift, we don't need to tell Xcode that we are declaring a **Boolean** when we type `true` or `false` because those are the only two values that a **Boolean** can be. In **Chapter 3**, when we wrote the following code, we used Type Inference as well:

```
var message = "Insert String information here..."
```

We used quotation marks (") to help Swift infer that the variable we wrote was of type String.

To explicitly declare a variable you can use the following syntax:

```
var message: String = "Insert String Information here..."

//or

var isThisTheBestBookEver: Bool = true
```

Thanks to Swift, we don't **need** to explicitly declare these types, although at times it is necessary which I will explain later on.

Back To Bools

Alright, now that we understand Type Inference, let's journey back over to our Swift Playground in Xcode.

We left the following code in our Playground:

```
var isThisTheBestBookEver = true
```

Beneath that code, we're going to change the value of our variable to now be `false`.

```
var isThisTheBestBookEver = true
isThisTheBestBookEver = false
```

By writing the name of our variable and setting it to be equal to `false` it is now false!

Conditional Statement Basics

Conditional statements help our code make decisions and run code depending on certain conditions. We can use conditionals to check against all kinds of values and conditions.

Write the following `if` statement and `if/else` statement at the bottom of your Playground:

```
var numberOfMinutes = 525600
var hasMedals = true

if numberOfMinutes == 525600 {
    print("Time to pay the rent.")
}

if hasMedals == true {
    print("You're amazing, Felix! Let's have a party!")
} else {
    print("Go away, Ralph!")
}
```

As you can see in the console, the first `if` statement prints out "Time to pay the rent." And the second `if/else` statement prints out "You're amazing, Felix! Let's have a party!".

If you want to add a third condition, you can also use `else if` like so:

```
let num = 9

if num < 0 {
    print("Number is negative.")
} else if num < 10 {
    print("Number is single-digit.")
} else {
    print("Number is multi-digit")
}
```

The above code will print "Number is single-digit." because `num` is less than 10.

In the rest of this chapter, we will use conditionals and **comparison operators** together in new and exciting ways.

Comparison Operators

Declaring something as `true` or `false` is great and all, but what can we actually do with it? We can use **Comparison Operators** to make our code compare things!

To begin, here are the six **Comparison Operators** in Swift:

```
Equal to: ==
Not equal to: !=
Greater than: >
Greater than or equal to: >=
Less than: <
Less than or equal to: <=
```

Let's see how these work with a commonly-used example – a bank account.

Example 1: Bank Account

At the bottom of your Playground, add the following variables *bankBalance* and *itemToBuy*:

```
...

var bankBalance = 400
var itemToBuy = 100
```

So we have a bank account holding $400 and want to buy an item with a price of $100.

Let's use a conditional and a **comparison operator** to determine whether or not we can purchase the item we want.

```
...

var bankBalance = 400
var itemToBuy = 100

if bankBalance >= itemToBuy {
    print("Purchased item!")
}
```

On the right-hand side of the Playground, you should see "Purchased item!" print out. The "" part is a console message in Xcode telling you that after our message is printed it should create a new line. It isn't actually a part of your String data.

I'm sure you see how powerful and useful **comparison operators** are. Here is yet another example of using **comparison operators**. We will write some code to check if a download has completed or not.

Example 2: Download completion checker

At the bottom of your Playground, type:

```
...

var downloadHasFinished = false

if downloadHasFinished == true {
    print("Download complete!")
} else {
    print("Loading data...")
}
```

Or we could simply use the "Not Equal To" **comparison operator**: !=

```
...

var downloadHasFinished = false

if !downloadHasFinished {
    print("Download complete!")
} else {
    print("Loading data...")
}
```

It's okay if the code above is confusing and seems flipped from the example above it. That's because it is! But let me explain.

1. First, we declare `downloadHasFinished` and set it's value to `false`.

2. Then, inside of an `if/else` statement we type `!downloadHasFinished` meaning whatever value `downloadHasFinished` currently has, in this case `false`, make it NOT equal to that (invert it to `true`).

3. Afterward, since the value of `downloadHasFinished` is now true, print "Download complete!"

The same principle can be applied to check or verify `String` values or any other values so long as they are of the same type.

Example 3: Book title verification

Imagine that you hired a new librarian who was always messing up the titles of books when entering them into the computer:

```
...

var officialBookTitle = "Harry Blotter and the Moppit of Meyer"

var attemptedEntryBookTitle = "Harry Plotter and the Muppet Mayor"

if officialBookTitle != attempedEntryBookTitle {
    print("Need to check spelling, try again.")
}
```

Closing thoughts

Booleans, **Conditional Statements**, and **Comparison Operators** are foundational components of programming in any language, but especially in Swift. You will use **Booleans** for all kinds of verification, completion handling, etc.

Wrapping up

We learned that a **Boolean** is a true or false value. We also learned that a **conditional statement** only runs code that meets a certain condition (hence the name!). Finally, we learned that the six **comparison operators** come in handy for comparing values of all kinds.

You rock!   Way to complete another chapter!

Exercise

Create a variable of type Bool named `syncComplete` and set it to false. Write a conditional statement to check whether or not syncing is complete. If syncComplete is true, print "Sync complete!". If syncComplete is false, print "Syncing...".

Create a variable and write a conditional statement that will check the balance of arcade tokens. If the balance is equal to or greater than 500, print out "Gamer Supreme!". If the balance is less than 500, print out "Child's Play...".

Chapter 9: Math Operators

Math, being an integral part of programming, can be used easily in Swift with a bit of know-how and a basic understanding of arithmetic.

What you will learn

- Basics of Math in Swift

- The Assignment Operator

- Arithmetic Operators

- The Modulo Operator

Key Terms

- **Assignment Operator:** the equals sign used in Swift to show assignment to a certain value or equality to another value.

- **Arithmetic Operators:** the four basic math operations – addition, subtraction, division, and multiplication.

- **Modulo Operator:** a math operator in Swift that allows for calculating the remainder of a division problem.

Math is a necessary part of programming. There's no getting around it. Those who are learning to program who don't come from a math/science background; those of you who don't have a degree in engineering (hint: I don't either), can still learn to code, though!
The math needed in programming doesn't often go far beyond what a majority of the population knows.

In Swift, there are several operators that we can use to perform mathematical equations. In this brief chapter, we will discuss each one.

Setting up

First, open Xcode if you haven't already and click `Create New Playground`.
Give it a name like *Math Operators* and click `Next`.
Choose somewhere to save this .playground file and click `Create` to save it. You should see a screen like the one in Figure 1.9.1.

Figure 1.09.1

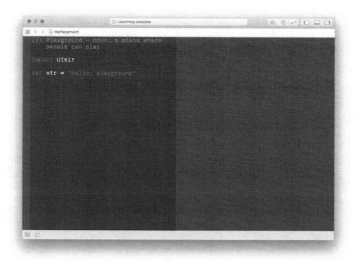

Delete all the boilerplate code on the left side but leave `import UIKit` as it is necessary.

The Assignment Operator

The **assignment operator** (=) is used just like the equals sign is used in math – to declare equality. Type out the example below in your Playground to see how this works:

```
var three = 3
```

When we create the above variable and name it *three*. We set it to literally equal three. The name of the variable is actually irrelevant. We could have named it anything and it still would serve as a way to use the value 3 throughout our code.

Arithmetic Operators

The four basic **arithmetic operators** (+, -, * , /) are used in Swift just as you would in a math class or in a graphing calculator. Here are some examples to show you how they can be used in Swift. Add the following to your Playground:

```swift
var product = 10 * 20 // Multiplication operator = *

var sum = 5 + 6 // Addition Operator = +

var difference = 10 - 3 // Subtraction Operator = -

var quotient = 30 / 3 // Division Operator = /
```

The Modulo Operator

There is an amazing operator in Swift (and other languages, too) called the Modulo (sometimes referred to the remainder operator).
It's purpose is to show the remainder left over when dividing two numbers. Here is an example of it in use for you to try in your Playground:

```swift
var remainder = 13 % 5 // Prints 3 because 10 / 5 is the nearest whole number
division that is possible. Three is left over as a remainder.
```

Here is another way you could look at the **modulo operator** to help it make sense:

```swift
var quotient = 13 / 5 // Prints 2 because Swift rounds up when it divides.

var remainder = 13 % 5 // Prints 3 because that is the remainder.

var result = "The result of 13 / 5 is \(quotient) with a remainder of \(remainder)"

// Prints "The result of 13 / 5 is 2 with a remainder of 3"
```

Wrapping up

That wasn't so bad was it? Using math in Swift is basic and easy. There's not much to it. Remember these operators and they will get you far as you go deeper into learning Swift.

Exercise

Create a variable that stores the result of 4 x 7. Create another variable that stores the result of 4 * (5 − 6) − 5. Use the modulo operator (%) to calculate the remainder of 123 / 7.

Chapter 10: Classes

Classes have been a part of society for as long as humans have been around. Each class has specific traits unique to itself. In Swift, this is no different. Classes are the cornerstone of Object-Oriented Programming.

What you will learn

- Creating your first Class

- Adding Variables and Functions

- Understanding OOP

- Reference Types

Key Terms

- **Class**

- **Object-Oriented Programming**

- **Reference Type**

If you are just starting your learn-to-code journey, you may have heard of **Object-Oriented Programming**.
It's a widely popular and highly revered model for programming that has stood the test of time. It is starting to get to a point where it may be replaced by other more modern models like *Protocol-Oriented Programming*, but it's still very important to understand.

Classes are a key component of OOP (**Object-Oriented Programming**) which allow us to create a blueprint of sorts and then copy it and modify it as needed.

An example could be a car in a car factory. Imagine an engineer created a blueprint for a car. In the factory, you can use that blueprint to create multiple copies of the same car by following the plans laid out in the blueprint.

Let's create our first **class** and use the car example from above.

Setting up

First, open Xcode if you haven't already and click `Create New Playground`.
Give it a name like *Classes* and click `Next`.
Choose somewhere to save this .playground file and click `Create` to save it.
You should see a screen like the one in Figure 1.10.1.

Figure 1.10.1

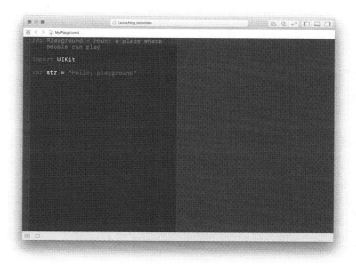

Delete all the boilerplate code on the left side but leave `import UIKit` as it is necessary.

Creating your first Class

Declaring a Class

In your Playground window, create a **class** by typing the following:

```
class Vehicle {
```

85

```
}
```

We used the keyword `class` followed by the name of our **class** `Vehicle`.

Adding Variables And Functions

Now, we need to add in variables for properties that we want all of our cars to have. Like so:

```
class Vehicle {
    var tires = 4
    var headlights = 2
    var horsepower = 468
    var model = ""

    func drive() {
        //Accelerate the vehicle
    }

    func brake() {
        //Stop the vehicle
    }
}
```

As you can see, a **class** can have properties (i.e. *tires*, *headlights*, *horsepower*, *model*) and functions (i.e. *drive()*, *brake()*) to describe it.

Understanding OOP

To understand **OOP**, you really need to try to visualize the world around you. This concept is usually pretty easy to understand for people who are more artistic and have a designer brain because you can easily visualize things as objects.
If your brain operates more on the numbers and logic side, this can be difficult to understand because you may want to turn it all into numbers or algorithms of some kind.

Here's another example, I hope this helps to explain **OOP** a little more.

Instagram has users who can like other photos, so you may have a `User` object which contains a user id, account, password, amongst other properties.
This user may also have functions like: `resetPassword()` or `deleteAccount`. Even the photos on Instagram could be objects.

If we have a `Photo` **class**, it may have properties for: `selectedFilter`, `numberOfLikes`, `numberOfComments`.

Some functions a `Photo` may have could be: `addLike()`, `removeLike()` – kind of actions to perform on that object.

Start trying to look at objects in the real world in regards to their properties and functions (what they're like and what they do).
Everything around you can be put into an object in code.

Creating an Instance of a Class

Let's create an instance of our `Vehicle` **class** by adding the following at the bottom of our Playground:

```
let delorean = Vehicle()
```

We created a constant called *delorean* and initialized it as an instance (or copy) of our `Vehicle` **class** by typing `Vehicle` and following it with parentheses.

The *model* property from above is initialized as an empty `String` above, so let's give our car a model name.

```
let delorean = Vehicle()
delorean.model = "DMC-12"
```

Create a few more instances of our **class** at the bottom of the Playground:

```
let delorean = Vehicle()
delorean.model = "DMC-12"

let bmw = Vehicle()
bmw.model = "328i"

let ford = Vehicle()
ford.model = "F150"
```

Can you see what's happening? We wrote the code for a Vehicle once, but we created multiple instances of that code and setting the properties of it.

We can also call the functions for `Vehicle` as well. Just so you're aware, once we create an instance of a **class**, we call it an object.
Just like when the car leaves the factory it's then considered an object.

Try this out by adding the following to your Playground:

```swift
let delorean = Vehicle()
delorean.model = "DMC-12"
delorean.drive()

let bmw = Vehicle()
bmw.model = "328i"

let ford = Vehicle()
ford.model = "F150"
ford.brake()
```

We called `drive()` on our `delorean` object and `brake()` on our `ford` object. We've told these objects to do something.

Again, think of a **class** like a blueprint – does it have any properties I should note? Are there any abilities it has or things it can do? In most cases, the answer will be yes.

Classes Are Reference Types

In Swift, there are **reference types** and value types. They are different, but we only need to know about reference types today.
I won't be going in depth into what it means, only what it means for you as the reader right now.

To demonstrate how **classes** are **reference types**, add the following function and print `ford.model` at the bottom of your Playground:

```swift
func passByReference(vehicle: Vehicle) {
    vehicle.model = "Cheese"
}

print(ford.model) // Prints "F150"
```

Next, call `passByReference(vehicle:)` and pass in the *ford* model:

```swift
func passByReference(vehicle: Vehicle) {
    vehicle.model = "Cheese"
}

print(ford.model) // Prints "F150"

passByReference(vehicle: ford) // Pass the ford class by reference
```

```
print(ford.model) // Prints "Cheese"
```

I thought when we declared `ford` we made it a constant by using `let`!
How is it that the model value can be changed? Well, to put it simply an object has a reference in memory.

You can't copy an object. Things like *Integers* and *Doubles* can be copied because they are value types, but not objects.

Here's another example to show how passing by reference works. Add the following variable and function to the bottom of your Playgroud:

```
var someonesAge = 20

func passByValue(age: Int) {
    age = 10
}
```

You probably notice that Xcode displays an error saying that `age` is a `let` constant. Because an *Integer* is a value type, we can't modify it in the same way we can a reference type. Let's try calling our function and passing in `someonesAge`:

```
var someonesAge = 20

func passByValue(age: Int) {
    age = 10
}

passByValue(age: someonesAge)
```

Xcode won't allow for this to work. **Reference types** can be modified and they are stored in a specific place in memory, but value types (i.e. Integer, Double, Float, etc.) cannot be modified, but can be copied.

Wrapping up

This chapter covers the basics of **Classes** in **Object-Oriented Programming**. A **class** can contain properties that describe it and actions (functions) that it can perform.

We can create a copy of a **class** by instantiating it as well. While this may still be confusing, you will continue to use it in context throughout this book which will help you rapidly gain understanding.

Continue to do your research and always stay curious about learning to code. Don't ever settle with doing enough or knowing enough. There are always ways for us to improve and become better programmers.

Exercise

Create another instance of the `Vehicle` class for a car of your choice. Be sure to set a value of type String for the `model` property. Create a separate class named `Smartphone` and include some properties and/or functions that all smartphones need. Create an instance of the `Smartphone` class called `iphone` and another called `android` and set the properties to be unique to those devices. Create another instance of the `Smartphone` class for another type of smartphone.

Chapter 11: Inheritance

In programming, inheritance isn't at all about randomly gaining a large sum of money from a long-lost relative but understanding what it means is worth much more... Possibly.

What you will learn

- What is Inheritance?

- Creating a Parent Class

- Creating a Child Class

- Overriding functions from a Parent Class

Key Terms

- **Inheritance:** a term to describe when a class is based on another class and inherits its default variables and function implementations.

- **Parent Class:** a code template with default values for variables and default implementations for functions.

- **Child Class:** a copy of a parent class with the ability to override or modify default parent class implementations and values.

In this chapter, you will read about inheritance. No, not the kind where a wealthy relative passes away leaving you with a huge lump of cash and you quit your job and run away to Bali for a permanent vacation. We're talking about **inheritance** as in inheriting features or traits as in genetics.

We will talk more about this in a moment, but let's dive into the code first.

Creating a Parent Class

First, open Xcode if you haven't already and click `Create New Playground`. Give it a name like *Inheritance* and click **Next**.

Choose somewhere to save this .playground file and click `Create` to save it.

You should see a screen like the one in Figure 1.11.1.

Figure 1.11.1

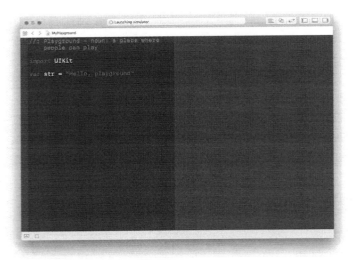

Delete all the boilerplate code on the left side but leave `import UIKit` as it is necessary.

What is Inheritance, really?

In iOS development, **inheritance** is a feature of Object-Oriented Programming which you learned about in the previous chapter on Classes. Classes can inherit traits from other classes which makes it very useful.

Think of this all in regards to a family. In every family, there are parents and children. The parents have certain traits which get passed down to the children.

For instance, my hair is brown and my dad's hair is brown. I received that trait from him. There are a number of other traits that are the same between the two of us, but I am different from my dad in a number of ways.

While much of me is similar, I have certain skills and traits that are not like my dad.

In Swift, we will create a class to act as a **parent class**. It will contain many general traits.

Then we will create a **child class** which will inherit traits from the **parent class**. The **child class** will have the same traits as it's parent but we can add in special traits unique to the **child class** alone. But let's start by building our **parent class**.

Building a Parent Class

While we could create a class about our actual parents and make this a sort of code-based genetics experiment, we are going to do something even cooler – think about super awesome cars!

Writing a Parent Class

In your Playground window, add the following `Vehicle` class and create a few variables for things that all vehicles have in common:

```
class Vehicle {
    var wheels = 4
    var make: String?
    var model: String?
    var currentSpeed: Double = 0
}
```

Every car has 4 wheels, which is why we created that variable. But why have we not given a value for the make or model of our car?

Well, every car has a make and model of some kind, so we actually don't need to specify these properties in our **parent class**.

Adding some functions

Inside of our `Vehicle` class, we can actually create some functions that all cars will do also:

```
class Vehicle {
    var wheels = 4
    var make: String?
    var model: String?
    var currentSpeed: Double = 0

    func drive(speedIncrease: Double) {
        currentSpeed += speedIncrease
```

```
    }

    func brake() {
        currentSpeed = 0
    }
}
```

The functions above may not be the best way to actually perform the driving and braking of a car, but you get the idea – you can add functions to a **parent class**.

Now let's see **inheritance** in action – with a **child class**.

Creating a Child Class

We will create a **child class** (or subclass) called *SportsCar* that inherits from `Vehicle`. This means that it will inherit all the properties and functions inside the `Vehicle` class unless we change them.

Writing A Child Class

Add the following code beneath the `Vehicle` class:

```
...
```

```
class SportsCar: Vehicle {

}
```

What we're doing above is declaring a class called `SportsCar` and using a colon : to identify that we want to inherit from another class (in this case – Vehicle).

If you're a visual learner, hopefully Figure 1.11.2 can help explain what's going on:

Figure 1.11.2

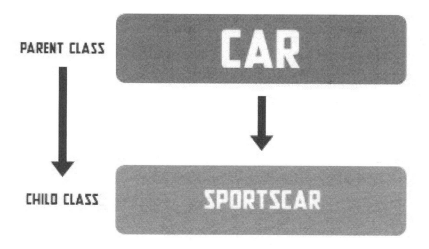

As our class currently stands, it is a clone of the class Vehicle. Everything will be implemented exactly the same way as Vehicle, unless we tell it to do otherwise. That is exactly what we will do now!

Before we can do anything with our SportsCar class we actually need to go back and add an initializer function to our Vehicle class.

Adding an Initializer function in the Vehicle Class

Inside of the Vehicle class, add the following init() function:

```
class Vehicle {
    var wheels = 4
    var make: String?
    var model: String?
    var currentSpeed: Double = 0

    init() {

    }

    func drive(speedIncrease: Double) {
        currentSpeed += speedIncrease * 2
    }
```

```
    func brake() {
        currentSpeed = 0
    }
}
```

This will give us access to the properties in `Vehicle` later on when we want to specify them in our `SportsCar` class.

We can actually do that now by overriding the `init()` function in the class `SportsCar`.

Overriding functions from `Vehicle`

Add the following code to `SportsCar`:

```
class SportsCar: Vehicle {
    override init() {
        super.init()
        make = "Lotus"
        model = "Elise"
    }
}
```

By overriding `init()` from the `Vehicle` class, we are able to change how we use it in our `SportsCar` class.
By using `super.init()` we actually are calling the function from within `Vehicle`.
Because of this we are able to initialize `make` and `model` giving them a combined value of "Lotus Elise".

Great, so our fancy-pants sports car has a name now, but we should also think about how it drives.
A sportscar drives differently than, say, a minivan, right? So we should override the `drive(speedIncrease:)` function, too. Try this out in the `SportsCar` class:

```
class SportsCar: Vehicle {
    override init() {
        super.init()
        make = "Lotus"
        model = "Elise"
    }

    override func drive(speedIncrease: Double) {
        currentSpeed += speedIncrease * 4
```

```
    }
}
```

We have overridden the function `drive(speedIncrease:)` so that the amount `currentSpeed` is increased by, is much faster since a sports car should drive faster than a regular car.

Creating a Sibling Class

If we continue with the example of classes being like a family, creating another class from the **parent class** results in another **child class** and we can actually call it a sibling class in relation to the other **child classes**.

Let's create a **child class** for another type of car – the minivan. I'm fairly certain that anyone without children reading this just shuddered at the sight of that word – minivan. Sorry about that.

Aside from being an icon of the classical American family, the minivan is very different from a sports car and therefore will need to have different information inside it's class. Let's make it.

Writing another Child Class

In your Playground, add a `Minivan` class, inheriting from `Vehicle` beneath the `SportsCar` class:

```
...

class Minivan: Vehicle {

}
```

Here's what we just did for all the visual learners reading this (Figure 1.11.3):

Figure 1.11.3

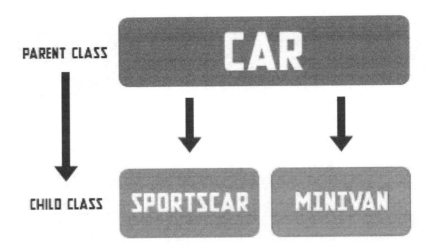

PARENT CLASS → CHILD CLASS

CAR → SPORTSCAR MINIVAN

Overriding functions from the Parent Class

If we want to add in a custom make and model value, we need to override the init()
function from Vehicle just like before. Add the following code to Minivan:

```
class Minivan: Vehicle {
    override init() {
        super.init()
        make = "Chevrolet"
        model = "Astro"
    }
}
```

We've now initialized the variables make and model and given them the values for a
Chevrolet Astro (ah, childhood).

What we should do now is override the drive(speedIncrease:) function to change how
our minivan drives. Anyone who's ever driven in or driven behind a minivan knows that
they aren't the quickest vehicles in the world – especially if loaded up with all the kids.

Inside of the Minivan class, override drive(speedIncrease:) like so:

```
class Minivan: Vehicle {
    override init() {
        super.init()
```

```
        make = "Chevrolet"
        model = "Astro"
    }


    override func drive(speedIncrease: Double) {
        currentSpeed += speedIncrease
    }
}
```

Wrapping up

Why does this matter? It allows us to compartmentalize our code and adapt it to meet specific needs.

In closing, here's a real-life example from Instagram.
For creating their filters, Instagram may have used a **parent class** including a generic filter. But each individual filter (i.e. Valencia, Inkwell, Nashville, etc.) could have been made into a **child class** containing a unique algorithm for filtering a photo a certain way.

Rather than putting all filters in one gigantic class, **child classes** could have been used to make a much more readable and compact code base.

Inheritance is a foundational principle of Object-Oriented Programming and is super important to understand if you want to be a professional programmer.
Remember that this chapter is not exhaustive. There are endless resources online to help in understanding this. Never stop learning and seeking understanding.

Exercise

Create a class for a Pickup Truck that inherits from `Vehicle`. Override the initializer and set the `make` and `model` properties to fit the truck. Override the `drive(speedIncrease:_)` function so that the car can drive half as fast as the SportsCar.

In the `Vehicle` class, add a property of type `Bool` called `hasStorageSpace` but don't initialize it yet. Initialize that property in the classes which do or don't have storage space using `true` or `false`.

Chapter 12: Polymorphism

If you're expecting this chapter to be about a band of teenagers with "attitude" that transform into superhuman heroes, you're bound to be gravely dissapointed, but don't worry. Polymorphism is just as cool as any 90's TV show.

What you will learn

- What is Polymorphism?

- Creating a base Class with requirements

- Creating a Subclass

- Implementing base Class requirements in a Subclass

Key Terms

- **Polymorphism:** being able to assign a different usage to something (like a class) in different contexts - specifically, to allow something like a variable, a function, or an object to have more than one form.

In this chapter, you will end your voyage into the basics of Object-Oriented Programming by reading about Polymorphism.
Other than being a really cool word, polymorphism is a very important concept to understand when becoming a programmer.

It is common in a developer job interview to be asked, "Can you please define 'polymorphism'?" Instead of looking like a deer in the headlights, we are going to break down what polymorphism is, what it means, and how it actually plays out in code.

What is Polymorphism?

A long-winded programming definition for polymorphism is: "Polymorphism allows the expression of some sort of contract, with potentially many types implementing that contract in different ways, each according to their own purpose."

That may be a bit of a textbook definition, but the basic concept here is that our code can occur in many different forms and its functions can be implemented in different ways.

This may still be confusing and that is okay. Let's build a code example as it is much easier to understand polymorphism this way.

Creating a new project

First, open Xcode if you haven't already and click `Create New Playground`.
Give it a name like *Polymorphism* and click `Next`.
Choose somewhere to save this .playground file and click `Create` to save it.
You should see a screen like the one in Figure 1.12.1.

Figure 1.12.1

Delete all the boilerplate code on the left side but leave `import UIKit` as it is necessary.

Creating a base Class with default functions

101

To begin, we will create a class called *Shape* with an area property and a function to calculate the area of our shape. Add the following to your Playground:

```
class Shape {
    var area: Double?

    func calculateArea(valueA: Double, valueTwo: Double) {

    }
}
```

Our base class `Shape` contains everything we need – a variable to store the area and a function to calculate an area with two input values.

Let's create a child class to inherit from our `Shape` class. What we need to do to demonstrate polymorphism is to obey the "contract" set in `Shape`, which is to have a `calculateArea` function.

Creating a Triangle Subclass

Add the following class and override the function `calculateArea(valueA:valueB:)` at the bottom of your Playground:

```
class Shape {
    var area: Double?

    func calculateArea(valueA: Double, valueB: Double) {

    }
}

class Triangle: Shape {
    override func calculateArea(valueA: Double, valueB: Double) {
        area = (valueA * valueB) / 2
    }
}
```

We now have created a subclass called `Triangle` and have overridden the function to calculate the area.
We're calling the same function, but the code inside is relevant to a triangle only.

This is **polymorphism** in action. The class `Shape` has a contract that all subclasses must follow which is to use the function `calculateArea(valueA:valueB:)`.

We used it and wrote custom code inside to calculate a triangle's area.

Let's now create a Rectangle subclass and override `calculateArea(valueA:valueB:)`.

Creating a Rectangle Subclass

Add the following code beneath the `Triangle` class:

```
...

class Rectangle: Shape {
    override func calculateArea(valueA: Double, valueB: Double) {
        area = valueA * valueB
    }
}
```

Now we have two separate classes implementing the same exact function, but the logic inside is different – this is **polymorphism**.
One object (`Shape`) taking different forms (`Triangle` & `Rectangle`).
We are obeying the contract set by `Shape` by implementing
`calculateArea(valueA:valueB:)` but in different ways.

Wrapping up

If you're in a job interview and are asked to define polymorphism, you can instead give them an example to explain that you understand the concept.

For instance:

Imagine that you have a Shape class and you need to calculate the area of a shape, but you don't know which shape will be passed in at runtime.

So, we create a calulateArea function and we also create two more classes for Triangle and Rectangle that inherit from Shape and at runtime they can each perform their own area calculation independent of each other and assign it into the area value.

It doesn't need to know beforehand what type of shape to pick because we have a different implementation set for each shape.

Polymorphism is a simple concept with a really technical definition but I hope you can see how easy it is to implement in code.

In summary, we created a base class called `Shape` which had a variable called `area` and a function called `calculateArea(valueA:valueB:)`.

Then, we created two subclasses called `Triangle` and `Rectangle`. They each inherited from `Shape`.
We obeyed the requirements from `Shape` and implemented and overrode the function `calculateArea(valueA:valueB:)`.

Inside each individual subclass, we added custom logic to calculate the areas for those particular shapes.

Polymorphism is what makes this possible.

Exercise

Create an subclass of `Shape` for a parallelogram. Override the area function so that it can calculate it's area. The formula for the area of a parallelogram is `A = b x h`. You're welcome.

Chapter 13: About Version Control

When working alone or with a team, Version Control allows you to backup your code for later retrieval.

What you will learn

- About Git

- Using Git with a team

- How Version Control works

Key Terms

- **Commit:** to backup changes in code to a local Git repository.

- **Push:** to send local code repository to a remote server for yourself/others to access.

- **Pull:** to download a remote repository and merge it in to your local repository.

Imagine that you are working on a personal app project. You just downed three Red Bulls and are feeling hyper-productive (literally).
You write line after line of code and it's beginning to look as though the new feature you've been building is nearly finished.

Little to your knowledge and due to a foolish lack of testing, somewhere around line 3,498 you created a serious bug that will cause major issues in your app.

You've written 5,000 lines of code since then! Surely, you'll be up all night trying to find the source of the bug. At least you drank those Red Bulls...

Never fear! This is where Version Control swoops in and saves the day.

Now let's return to the start of our story: Imagine you are working on a personal app

project **and** have set up Version Control for your project.
Every significant change made you **push** to a remote server.
You write another significant portion of code and **push** that to the remote server, too.
This continues until you have **pushed** code several more times.

Suddenly, you identify a serious bug in your code. Instead of having to parse through our entire code base, we can revert back to a previous state that our code was in.

Nice.

About Git

The most prevalent and popular system for managing Version Control is called Git. You should be using Git throughout this book to **push** all your projects online.

This way, you are being a smart coder and saving online backups **and** you're building a portfolio to someday show a potential employer.

Git is relatively easy to learn and use – even for a beginner and it can streamline the process of working with multiple developers on the same application.
With Git, it is easy to **push** your changes, **pull** down the changes of others onto your local machine, and fix merge issues when trying to bring them together.

Using Git with a team

Let's imagine another scenario. First, we have just hired two new developers – Sam and Pete.

Sam is working on building a killer new feature and makes a couple changes to the code base on his local machine.

Pete is working on a different feature, but in the same app. Pete makes some changes to the code base on his local device.

Do you see the problem here? At this point, Sam and Pete both have differences in the code that they are working on (Figure 1.13.1).
How can the two become one so that both features can be included?

Figure 1.13.1

Before Version Control, Sam would have had to send his updated code files to Pete somehow.

Then Pete would have had to identify and copy and paste in Sam's changes into his project and save it.

Then, Pete would have to send the updated project including his changes back to Sam so that they both can have the current project (Figure 1.13.2).

Figure 1.13.2

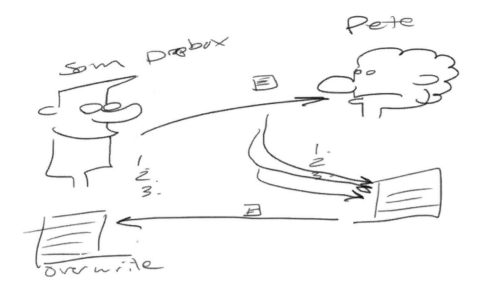

This situation is only between two developers. Imagine how the complexity of this issue increases with a larger team of developers!

How Version Control works

As previously stated, Version Control is an amazing way to handle backing up your code base and being able to revert back to previous changes if needed.
It also makes working with others **way** easier!

Imagine a development team with three developers named Jim, Sam, and Harry.

They are all working on an app and implementing various features.

Jim begins by writing some code and saves it into his version of the project.
Sam does the same and Harry does too.
Now all three of them have different versions of the same app (Figure 1.13.3).

Figure 1.13.3

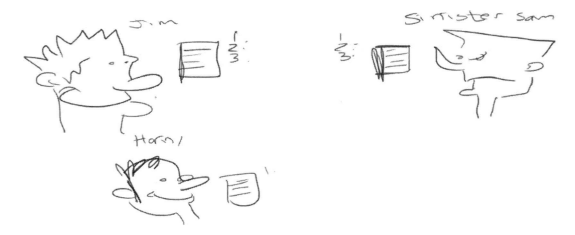

Now, Jim can now **commit** (**push**) his changes to a remote server (Figure 1.13.4).

Figure 1.13.4

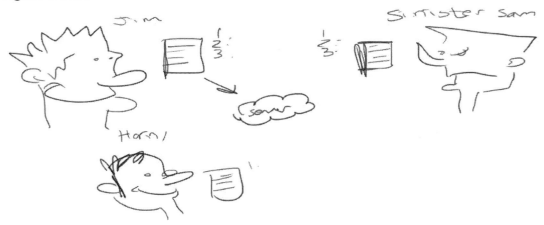

Once that is finished, Sam can access the remote server and **pulls** down Jim's changes. Version Control automatically merges in Jim's changes to Sam's project (Figure 1.13.5).

Figure 1.13.5

The two projects are now merged. Sam can now **push** his unique changes (including Jim's changes) back to the remote server so that another developer can access the updated project (Figure 1.13.6).

Figure 1.13.6

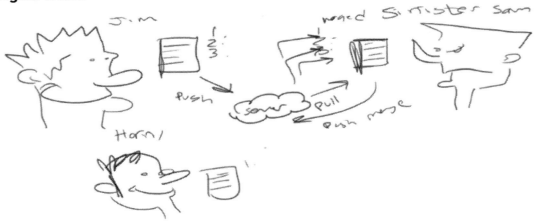

Harry the Junior Developer can now **pull** the project down to his local machine, make changes and add his features, then **push** his code to the remote server to merge them in and update the project (Figure 1.13.7).

Figure 1.13.7

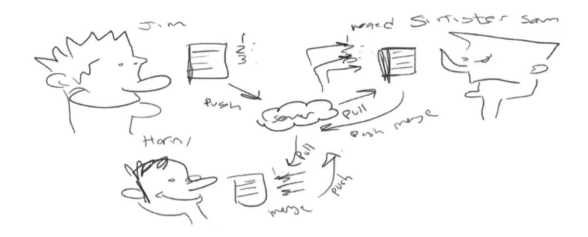

Wrapping up

Version Control is obviously extremely helpful when working alone and when working with a team. It is efficient, effective, and makes for a better development process overall.

The days of manually sending, merging, and re-sending code are gone. Git is an extremely helpful tool to learn. In the next chapter we will learn the basics of Git.

Chapter 14: Git Basics

There is nothing worse than getting a ton of work done only to realize later that there are major mistakes. Git is a powerful version control tool used to save backups of code so we can avoid this problem.

What you will learn

- Opening **Terminal** & setting up Git

- Initializing a Git Repository

- Committing files in Git

- Reverting back to a previous Commit

- Saving specific files to a Git Branch

Key Terms

- **Terminal:** a command-line application on macOS.

- **Commit:** to record changes made to a Git repository.

- **Branch:** an independent container to hold specific development changes.

Key Commands

- `cd [nameOfDirectory]` : a command to change directories.

- `ls` : a command to list all files within a certain directory.

- `git init` : a command to initialize a new Git repository

- `git add [fileName]` : a command to add a specific file to be tracked.

- `git add -A` : a command to track all changed/new files to be tracked.

- `git commit -m "message"` : a command to **commit** changes to our Git repository.

- `git log` : a command to view a list of all commits made.

- `git checkout [branchName]` : a command to switch **branches**.

- `git checkout -b [branchName]` : a command to create a new **branch**.

In this chapter, we will cover the basics of using Git for version control. While Git has lots of facets we could explore, we will be focusing on the basics in this chapter so that you can get up and running with it as soon as possible.

Opening Terminal & setting up Git

To begin, press ⌘ + Space to open Spotlight. Search for *Terminal* and press Enter to open the **Terminal** app (Figure 1.14.1).

Figure 1.14.1

Inside the **Terminal** window, we can write commands. If you've never written commands in **Terminal** before, this can seem scary or intimidating at first, but don't worry – we only have a few commands to learn.

Note: After typing a command in **Terminal**, you must press Enter to execute that command.

Creating a new directory

In **Terminal** type the following to change directories (cd) then press Enter:

```
$ cd Desktop/
```

The active directory in **Terminal** is now our Desktop.

Next, type the following to create a folder on our Desktop named *git-fun*:

```
$ mkdir git-fun
```

On the Desktop, there should now be a folder called *git-fun*.

If there isn't, ensure that the active directory is actually set to the Desktop (Figure 1.14.2).

Figure 1.14.2

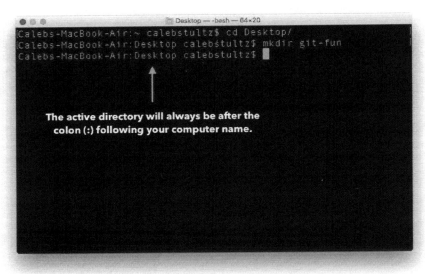

In **Terminal**, type the following to change directories to `git-fun`:

```
$ cd git-fun/
```

Creating a file for Git to manage

Git is already installed on your Mac (thanks, Apple!   ) so we can use it right out of the box.

But first, we need to create a file for Git to manage. Type the following to create a README.md file:

```
$ touch README.md
```

To verify that our file was created, we can use the command `ls` to list all files within our active directory, which happens to be `git-fun`.

114

```
$ ls
README.md
```

You should see that README.md appears beneath where we typed the `ls` command.

Now we have a file Git can manage and back up.

Opening & Editing README.md with Vim

We want to open our file to add something to it's contents so that we have something to revert back to later.

Vim is a terminal-based text editor which can edit documents directly within **Terminal** – no need for an external editor. Like Git, it is also installed on your Mac by default.

To edit README.md with Vim, type:

```
$ vim README.md
```

You should see a screen like the following (Figure 1.14.3):

Figure 1.14.3

Now, to insert data into README.md, we need to press i to begin 'Insert Mode'. You should see "-- INSERT --" at the bottom.

Type in a title like in Figure 1.14.4:

Figure 1.14.4

To close and save our file in Vim:
1. Press `Escape`.
2. Type `Shift + :`.
3. Type a lowercase x.
4. Press `Enter` to save README.md.

Initializing a Git repository

To begin using Git, we need to initialize a repository which will manage and store all of the files we tell it to. To see if we already have one (hint: we don't.), type the following:

`$ git status`

You should see an error message similar to the following:

`fatal: Not a git repository (or any of the parent directories): .git`

Ensure that your active directory is still `git-fun` and initialize a new Git repository (repo for short):

`$ git init`

Terminal should return with:

`Initialized empty Git repository in /Users/your-name/Desktop/git-fun/.git/`

Check the status of Git once more by typing:

`$ git status`

Now, we see a different message than we did before. When we run `git status` now, we see that we are `On branch master`, a list of untracked files that Git isn't sure what to do with, and that we have not yet added any files to a **commit** (Figure 1.14.5).

Figure 1.14.5

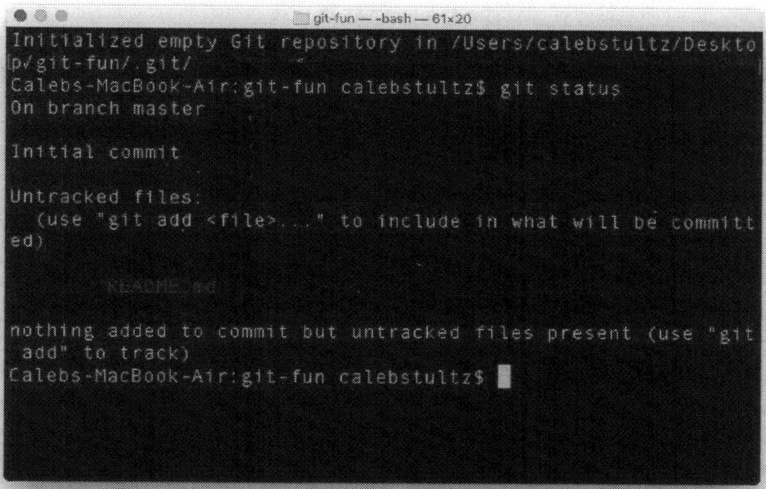

Great! This means that we are ready to start tracking and committing files!

Adding files to a Git repository

Git just told us that we aren't tracking README.md yet, so if we want to back it up we need to add it. In **Terminal**, type the following then press `Enter`:

`$ git add README.md`

Now if we type `git status` we see that our files which were once red show up in green now and that our changes are ready to be **committed** (Figure 1.14.6).

Figure 1.14.6

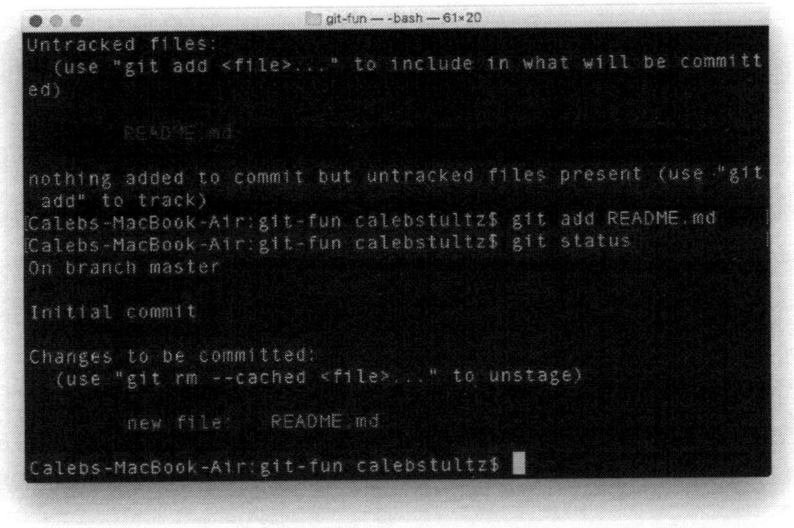

We are now ready to make our first **commit**. That simply means whatever files we have added to our Git repository will be timestamped and backed up as they currently are. After **committing** our changes, we can revert back to this exact point later on if we want.

Commitment is scary, but not in Git

Let's take a leap of faith and make our first **commit** to back up our README.md file.

Type the following then press Enter:

```
$ git commit -m "First commit ever."
```

To **commit** files it is required that you write a message in regards to the changes or additions you've made.

After typing, git commit, we used the command -m indicating that we want to write a message and then ended with a message in quotations.

Note: It is good to be specific about what changes have occurred.

After pressing Enter you should see the following message print out below (Figure 1.14.7):

Figure 1.14.7

```
Calebs-MacBook-Air:git-fun calebstultz$ git commit -m "First commit ever."
[master (root-commit) 345c39f] First commit ever.
 1 file changed, 1 insertion(+)
 create mode 100644 README.md
```

Now type git status to ensure that our **commit** was performed properly (Figure 1.14.8):

Figure 1.14.8

```
Calebs-MacBook-Air:git-fun calebstultz$ git status
On branch master
nothing to commit, working directory clean
```

This means that we have successfully **committed** our changes and backed up our code! Pat yourself on the back. Nicely done.

We are now going to make changes to README.md so we can practice this process one more time.

Making changes to README.md

Press ⌘ + K to clear the **Terminal** window. Ensuring that you are still in the active directory git-fun, type:

```
$ vim README.md
```

Now our file is open in Vim and we can modify it after pressing i to activate Insert Mode. Add a couple lines of writing so that we can make a change for Git to track (Figure 1.14.9).

Figure 1.14.9

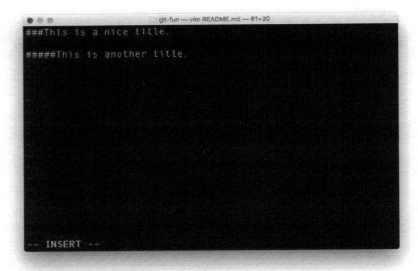

To save and exit Vim:
1. Press Escape.
2. Type Shift + :.
3. Type a lowercase x.
4. Press Enter to save README.md.

Type git status into **Terminal** and press Enter.
You should see the following message printed in the **Terminal**:

Figure 1.14.10

Now we are told that we have a file being tracked **and** a file that was modified and has changes in need of being **committed**.

We will **commit** those in a moment, but for now let's create a new file. This will show how to manage the scenario when you've created, tracked, and **committed** a file but add or modify a different or new file.

In **Terminal**, create a new JavaScript file like so:

```
$ touch code.js
```

Run git status to see what happened (Figure 1.14.11):

Figure 1.14.11

```
[Calebs-MacBook-Air:git-fun calebstultz$ git status
On branch master
Changes not staged for commit:
  (use "git add <file>..." to update what will be committed)
  (use "git checkout -- <file>..." to discard changes in working directory)

        modified:   README.md

Untracked files:
  (use "git add <file>..." to include in what will be committed)

        code.js

no changes added to commit (use "git add" and/or "git commit -a")
```

As you can see above, we have both files with changes and new files that have not yet been added.

While we can add and **commit** each file individually, it is much more efficient to perform two actions in one.

The add command in Git works on changed files and brand new files, too.

In **Terminal** run the following command then press Enter:

```
$ git add -A
```

Next run git status to check what happened (Figure 1.14.12):

Figure 1.14.12

```
[Calebs-MacBook-Air:git-fun calebstultz$ git status
On branch master
Changes to be committed:
  (use "git reset HEAD <file>..." to unstage)

        modified:   README.md
        new file:   code.js
```

The next step is to **commit** our changes. This will make a new backup including our changes to READMD.md and the new file code.js too. Type the following, just as before:

```
$ git commit -m "Modified README.md and added code file"
```

Press Enter and **Terminal** will tell you that you have modified and added a file similarly to before.

Next, enter git status and press Enter. You should see the same message from when we **committed** changes earlier on (Figure 1.14.13).

Figure 1.14.13

```
Calebs-MacBook-Air:git-fun calebstultz$ git status
On branch master
nothing to commit, working directory clean
```

Reverting back to a previous commit

What if we **committed** those changes, but then realized that we had introduced a massive bug into our code base? How would we fix this problem?

Reflecting on this chapter's example you may be thinking, "No big deal! We only have two files that we changed."
That's true, but when working on an app, especially with a team, there can be hundreds – even thousands – of lines of code that you're **committing** at a time.

If we want to revert back to a previous **commit** when things were happy and sunny and made sense, all we need to type into **Terminal** is:

```
$ git log
```

Press Enter and look at the message that get's printed out (Figure 1.14.14):

Figure 1.14.14

```
commit 845fd5837f0b8d87c2ab0ed75303b0fd1de22b6c
Author: Caleb Stultz <calebstultz@Calebs-MacBook-Air.local>
Date:   Tue Oct 18 04:42:42 2016 +0700

    Modified README.md and added code file

commit 69f008263f0306abb33fb2d5796a9a7b4287cd86
Author: Caleb Stultz <calebstultz@Calebs-MacBook-Air.local>
Date:   Mon Oct 17 18:02:36 2016 +0700

    First commit ever
```

We can see a list of all the **commits** we've made so far.
Each **commit** has a unique ID, author, date, and message. To exit the log, press Shift + Q.

I hope you can see how important writing a descriptive message is. It is really helpful in thinking back to what you were doing at the time of that **commit** so that you can pinpoint what may have gone wrong.

To go back in time (a la Huey Lewis and the News), you need to type `git checkout` followed by the first 7 digits of the unique ID for the **commit** you want to revert back to. For instance:

```
$ git checkout 69f0082
```

Terminal will return this message to us (Figure 1.14.15):

Figure 1.14.15

```
Note: checking out '69f0082'.

You are in 'detached HEAD' state. You can look around, make experimental
changes and commit them, and you can discard any commits you make in this
state without impacting any branches by performing another checkout.

If you want to create a new branch to retain commits you create, you may
do so (now or later) by using -b with the checkout command again. Example:

  git checkout -b <new-branch-name>

HEAD is now at 69f0082... First commit ever
```

To check to see the state of our `git-fun` folder, type `ls` into **Terminal** and press Enter.

You should only see README.md now. But where is code.js?

Since we reverted back to our first **commit**, code.js no longer exists because we created it after the fact. Amazing work, Git!

Let's check to see if the contents of README.md have changed back also. Type `vim` `README.md` and press Enter to open it in Vim. You should see the following (Figure 1.14.16):

Figure 1.14.16

Voilà! README.md has been sent back to the state of it's first **commit**.

To exit Vim:

1. Press Escape.
2. Type Shift + :.
3. Type a lowercase x.
4. Press Enter to save README.md.

Saving specific files to a branch

A **branch** in Git is a grouping of code. Usually, when working on a project you will be implementing one new feature at a time.

Developers usually make one **branch** per feature. But before I explain more what **branches** are in Git, first type git branch into **Terminal** and press Enter.

You should see something similar to the following (Figure 1.14.17):

Figure 1.14.16

```
[Calebs-MacBook-Air:git-fun calebstultz$ git branch
* (HEAD detached at 345c39f)
   master
```

124

As you can see, there are two **branches**: `master` and another that says (`HEAD detached at 345c39f`).

The asterisk (*) indicates what **branch** we are currently on.

The problem with the branch we are currently on is that it doesn't have a descriptive name... Let's give it one!

In **Terminal** type the following, then press `Enter`:

```
$ git checkout -b readme-one-line
```

Terminal will respond with something like:

```
Switched to a new branch 'readme-one-line'
```

The command we typed above, "checked out" a new **branch**, as indicated by -b and then at the end we gave our **branch** the name `readme-one-line`.

Now type `git branch` to see what **branches** are available to us (Figure 1.14.17):

Figure 1.14.17

```
[Calebs-MacBook-Air:git-fun calebstultz$ git branch
  master
* readme-one-line
```

As you can see, `readme-one-line` is now an official **branch**.

Switching branches

If we wanted to switch **branches**, we use the keywords `git checkout` followed by the name of the **branch** we want to switch to. For example:

```
git checkout master
```

After pressing `Enter`, **Terminal** should print:

```
Switched to branch 'master'
```

If you type `ls` and press `Enter` in **Terminal**, you will see both README.md and code.js now because master has always contained our most up-to-date code.

If you open README.md in Vim, you will see that both lines wrote are there.

When we went back in time earlier, Git actually created a temporary **branch** with our old files leaving our newest ones untouched on the **branch** `master`. When we created the

branch `readme—one—line` we saved those old files to `readme—one—line`.

Wrapping up

After going through this chapter, you are now ready to start using Git right away. You should be using Git with **EVERY** project.

If you want to be a professional developer, you will definitely be using version control (likely using Git), and even as an independent developer, it's a very efficient way to manage and safe-proof your code.

Exercise

For some good practice, create a new file in Terminal called `title.txt` using the `touch` command. Follow the steps necessary to add and commit the new file. Run `git status` to check that everything worked properly. If you get the message `On branch master nothing to commit, working directory clean`, revert back to a previous commit to remove the file `title.txt`.

Chapter 15: Setting up Github

Github is a powerful, advanced remote Git management tool. You should use this for personal projects as well as team projects.

What you will learn

- Creating a Github Account

- Generating an SSH Key

- Adding an SSH Key to SSH-Agent

- Adding SSH Key to Github account

Key Terms

- **Repository:** a central location where data is stored and can be managed.

- **Github:** an online Git management platform where code can be stored and managed.

- **SSH Key:** a means of identifying yourself to an SSH server for the secure transferral of data.

In this chapter, we are going to learn how to set up **Github** – an amazing online Git management tool. It allows for individuals or teams to push, pull, merge, and manage their entire code base.
You can create public or private **repositories** (great for companies working on new apps).

In the developer world, a **Github** profile can be equated with a portfolio of work. Therefore, it is paramount to build out a nice, beefy **Github** profile with all the projects you build throughout this book; Devslopes courses, or any other personal projects you want to post publicly.

Creating a Github account

First, open Safari or your browser of choice. Navigate to `www.github.com` and create an account by clicking the `Sign Up` button at the top of the page.
Create an account and follow the steps necessary to activate your account.

Next up, we need to create an **SSH key** to identify your computer as a trusted device so that **Github** knows that all code is coming from a secure device.
It works just like a key into a lock, but for your **Github** account.

Generating an SSH Key

On your Mac, go to `Applications` > `Utilities` and click on `Terminal`.
Alternatively, you can press ⌘ + `Space` and type *terminal* into Spotlight Search to find it.
Upon opening, a new Terminal window should pop up.

We need to generate an **SSH key** for **Github** to use.

First, type the following but add in your **Github** email in place of the example email:

```
$ ssh-keygen -t rsa -b 4096 -C "your_email@example.com"
```

Terminal will respond with the following:

```
Generating public/private rsa key pair.
```

Then Terminal will display:

```
Enter a file in which to save the key (/Users/you/.ssh/id_rsa): [Press enter]
```

Press `Enter` to save it to the default locations it chooses.

The next prompt will ask you to create/verify a password to secure the **SSH key**. This is entirely optional and up to you if you'd like to do so.

Adding an SSH Key to SSH-Agent

Now that we have an **SSH key**, we need to check if ssh-agent is working and then add it to the SSH agent:

In Terminal, type the following:

```
$ eval "$(ssh-agent -s)"
```

Press Enter and a message should print below similar to this one:

Agent pid 59566

Then type the following command:

```
$ ssh-add ~/.ssh/id_rsa
```

Adding SSH Key To Github Account

Now that we have created a secure **SSH key** and have added it to our SSH agent, we need to connect it with our **Github** account so that our Mac and **Github** can communicate.

In Terminal, type:

```
$ pbcopy < ~/.ssh/id_rsa.pub
```

This will copy our **SSH key** to our clipboard.

Return back to your web browser and click on your profile in the top right corner. In the following drop down menu, click Settings (Figure 1.15.1).

Figure 1.15.1

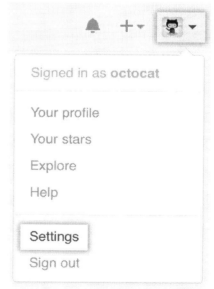

On the side of the page, click SSH and GPG keys (Figure 1.15.2).

Figure 1.15.2

Click New SSH key or Add SSH key to add our key that we have copied (Figure 1.15.3).

Figure 1.15.3

Type a descriptive title in the "Title" field (i.e. "Jerry's MacBook Air") and paste in your key to the "Key" field below (Figure 1.15.4).

Figure 1.15.4

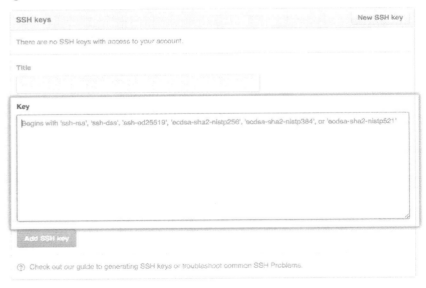

At the bottom of the page, click the `Add SSH key` button (Figure 1.15.5).

Figure 1.15.5

You may be required to enter your **Github** password to confirm making these changes.

Wrapping up

After following the steps in this chapter, you are now ready to learn how to use **Github**. In the next chapter, we will talk about local and remote code **repositories** and how to push our local code to **Github** for storage and management.

Chapter 16: Local vs. Remote Repositories

In previous chapters, we've set up and used local repositories on our computer, but now we are ready to begin backing up our files online. This is the first step in building an awesome portfolio to show a future employer!

What you will learn

- Creating a Remote GitHub Repository

- Adding a Remote Repository to Git in Terminal

- Committing, Pulling, and Pushing flow for GitHub

Key Terms

- **Remote Repository:** an online collection of code that can be managed and modified from a local device.

- **Pulling:** a term to describe when you download changes from your remote repository into your local repository.

- **Pushing:** a term to describe when you upload changes from your local machine to your remote repository.

At this point in the book, we've used Git to back up our code on our local machine, but as the world has progressively moved online it only makes sense for us to store our code online as well. Not just because the cool kids are doing it, but because it's a great way to build a portfolio of apps and coding projects to show off in a future job interview.

We're going to set up a remote Github repository which will allow us to push code from our repository and onto an online server and pull code from online into our local project.

Setting up a remote Github Repository

First, begin by going to **www.github.com** and log in to your account. If you haven't yet created an account flip back to **Chapter 15** of this section to set up your account.

Once there, click the green button that says `New Repository` (Figure 1.16.1). Alternatively, you can click on the + button in the upper right near your profile picture and select `New repository` there.

Figure 1.16.1

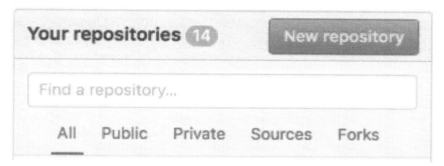

On the screen that follows, we will need to enter some information (Figure 1.16.2).

Let's begin by naming our repository something like *destroytheworld*.
Below the `Repository name` field, enter a description if you'd like. This is optional but helpful in explaining what is inside your repository.
Beneath the description field is the option to make this repository public or private.

Github offers unlimited free public repositories, but if you want to store your code on a private repository it costs money.
There are other Git repository websites like *BitBucket* which offers unlimited private repositories, but Github is certainly an authority in this realm and is the best known.

Beneath the public/private repository selection, you can tick a box to initialize your repository with a README.md file. I recommend this because any project you find on Github that is well-established and taken seriously has a thorough and nicely-formatted README.md file explaining their project in detail.

Helpful Hint:
If you want to see an amazing example of this, search Google for *Alamofire* and click on

the first result.

Scroll down the page that loads and you will see the README.md file for Alamofire which is very well written and looks amazing.

The left-most option at the bottom allows you to add `.gitignore`. This allows you to declare which files you want GitHub to ignore when you push your local changes up to your remote repository.

We won't be using this, but it is useful if you're building an app that includes any type of information you wouldn't want everyone to know – like secret API keys or account information.

The right-most option at the bottom lets you add a license to your project. We won't be doing this either, but it's nice to know that you can.

Figure 1.16.2

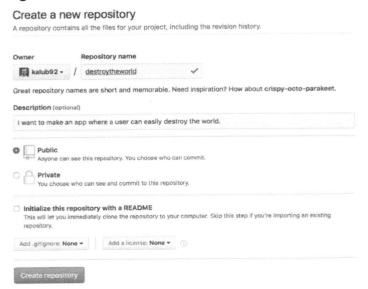

After filling out the `Repository name` field, giving it a description, ticking the `Initialize with README.md` box, and ensuring that we're making a public repository, click `Create repository`.

Preparing to connect a Local Repository to a Remote GitHub Repository

We are now at a good place to connect our remote repository on GitHub to our local machine so that any files we create or changes we make can be pushed up and saved online.

Since we've already set up SSH keys to connect our computer to our GitHub account, we can use SSH as a method to transfer files.

Click the green `Clone or download` button then click `Use SSH` (Figure 1.16.3).

Figure 1.16.3

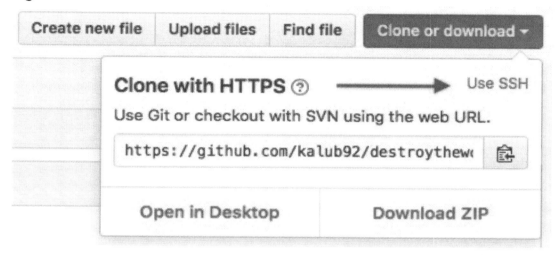

Copy the link that is provided and save it for later (Figure 1.16.4). We will use this to connect our remote repository to our local machine.

Figure 1.16.4

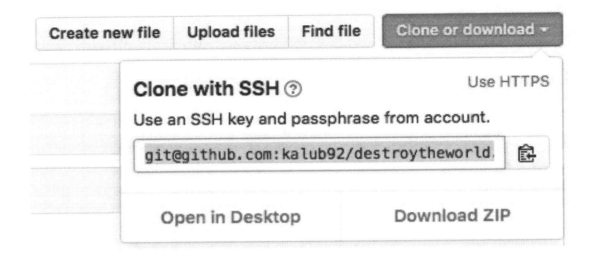

Setting up our project and Terminal

Next, open Terminal and Xcode as we will be using both of them.

In Xcode, click `Create A New Xcode Project`, then `Single-View Application`, name it *destroy-the-world*, tick `Create Git repository on My Mac`, and then save it to the Desktop.

By ticking the "Create Git repository..." box, we essentially run the command `git init` and initialize an empty local Git repository.

Switch over to Terminal and type `cd Desktop/` then `cd destroy-the-world` to enter our project folder.
Type `ls` and press `Enter` to see the contents of our project folder (Figure 1.16.5).

Figure 1.16.5

```
[Calebs-MacBook-Air:~ calebstultz$ cd Desktop/
[Calebs-MacBook-Air:Desktop calebstultz$ cd destroy-the-world/
[Calebs-MacBook-Air:destroy-the-world calebstultz$ ls
destroy-the-world               destroy-the-world.xcodeproj
Calebs-MacBook-Air:destroy-the-world calebstultz$
```

As you can see, there is a folder and an `.xcodeproj` file with the name *destroy-the-world*.

Making changes to commit

Click on the folder *destroy-the-world* on the Desktop and double-click on `destroy-the-world.xcodeproj`. We're going to make some changes to our project.

Click `ViewController.swift` and inside of the `viewDidLoad()` function, add the following:

```
override func viewDidLoad() {
    super.viewDidLoad()
    // Do any additional setup after loading the view, typically from a nib.
    print("Hello, World!")
}
```

Now we've made a change we can commit.
Switch over to Terminal, type `git status`, and press `Enter`.
You should see some red text saying that you've made changes to `ViewController.swift`.

If we were to commit these changes right now, it would only commit them to our local machine as we have not yet set up our remote repository on GitHub. Let's do that now!

Connecting a Local Repository to a Remote Repository

In Terminal, we need to add a **remote repository**. Earlier, you copied a link from GitHub for later use. Now is the time!

Type the following command and then paste the link you copied from GitHub into the Terminal. It should be similar to mine below:

```
$ git remote add origin git@github.com:kalub92/destroytheworld.git
```

Press `Enter` and just like that we've added a remote repository named `origin` and linked it to the link from our GitHub account.
We can now commit and push our code up to GitHub!

Committing files, Pulling in changes, and Pushing to GitHub

Committing Local changes to Git

To push our files to GitHub, we need to go through our standard Git procedure.

Enter the commands below followed by Enter in Terminal:

1. `git add —A`
2. `git commit —m "First commit to push to GitHub."`

Pulling Remote Changes Into Our Project

Let's pause for a moment and think about what we have going on.
We have a local repository containing an Xcode project and we have a remote repository containing a README.md file. We need to pull down the README.md file and merge it into our project.

To do this, type the following:

`$ git pull origin master`

This command downloads files from our remote repository called `origin` and pulls it into our `master` branch (Figure 1.16.6).

Figure 1.16.6

```
Calebs-MacBook-Air:destroy-the-world calebstultz$ git pull origin master
remote: Counting objects: 3, done.
remote: Compressing objects: 100% (2/2), done.
remote: Total 3 (delta 0), reused 0 (delta 0), pack-reused 0
Unpacking objects: 100% (3/3), done.
From github.com:kalub92/destroytheworld
 * branch            master      -> FETCH_HEAD
 * [new branch]      master      -> origin/master
```

Run `ls` in Terminal again to check if Git was able to pull down that README.md file (Figure 1.16.7). Looks like it did!

Figure 1.16.7

```
Calebs-MacBook-Air:destroy-the-world calebstultz$ ls
README.md                          destroy-the-world.xcodeproj
destroy-the-world
```

Pushing Local changes to GitHub

All we need to do to push our local changes up to GitHub is enter the following command:

`$ git push origin master`

The message that prints out in Terminal explains everything that Git is doing to push our files online, but all you need to know is that the current commit is being pushed. The result should look similarly to this (Figure 1.16.8):

Figure 1.16.8

```
Calebs-MacBook-Air:destroy-the-world calebstultz$ git push origin master
Counting objects: 21, done.
Delta compression using up to 4 threads.
Compressing objects: 100% (18/18), done.
Writing objects: 100% (21/21), 7.37 KiB | 0 bytes/s, done.
Total 21 (delta 1), reused 0 (delta 0)
remote: Resolving deltas: 100% (1/1), done.
To git@github.com:kalub92/destroytheworld.git
   fb97d86..061a223  master -> master
```

Verifying that we pushed it real good

Let's go to back to our web browser and find our project. It should be hosted at: github.com/your-username/destroytheworld in case you closed the tab.

Before we pushed changes we simply had a single README.md file. Now refresh the page and see what's changed (Figure 1.16.9):

Figure 1.16.9

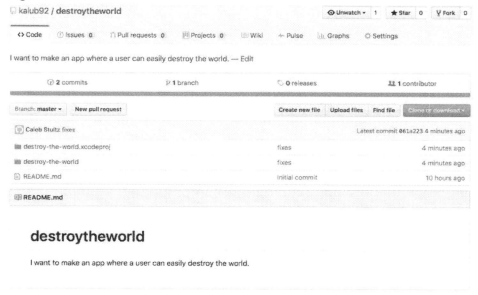

139

Wrapping up

Yay! We have now updated our remote repository and have saved a backup of our code online. We also covered the basic steps of managing both a local and remote repository in Git with GitHub.

The steps we followed were:
1. Set up remote repository on GitHub and initialized a README.md file
2. Created a new Xcode project and initialized a local Git repository
3. Made local changes to our project
4. Added our remote repository in Terminal by using `git remote add origin` `git@github.com:your-username/destroytheworld.git`
5.) Added and committed our local changes by using `git add -A` and `git commit -m` `"message"`
6.) Pulled in changes from our remote repository (i.e. README.md) and merged them into our project by using `git pull origin master`
7.) Pushed up our changes to GitHub by using `git push origin master`

Exercise

Create a new folder on your Desktop and copy in the .playground file from the Polymorphism chapter. Open Terminal, 'cd' into the Desktop then the folder you created, and initialize a git repository.

Go to github.com and create a new repository. Connect your remote repository to the one you initialized locally on your Mac by copying and pasting the SSH command found under the `Clone or download` menu after clicking on `Use SSH`.

Add the remote repository by using the command `git remote add` `git@github.com/username/your-repository.git`.

Add and commit the files in Terminal, then pull in any remote changes from the remote repository. Then push your local changes to the remote repository.

Refresh the Github page to verify you pushed all changes successfully.

Section 1 Project

Woohoo! You made it through section 1 and now have a good understanding of the fundamentals of Swift! That wasn't so bad, right? Now let's put your skills to the test.

Requirements:

Task 1

1. Create a new Swift Playground.

2. Declares a few variables to your Playground of the following types and assign them any valid values:

- `String`

- `Int`

- `Double`

- `Float`

- `Bool`

3. Write a function which calculates the volume of a cube. It should accept one parameter (side length) and return a value of type `Double` for the volume. The formula to determine the area of a cube is: $V = a^3$

4. Create an array containing the names of your 4 favorite Pokémon. The values should be of type `String`.

5. Write a `for-in` loop that loops through the Pokémon array and prints `"[Pokémon name goes here], I choose you!"`

6. Create a Dictionary that contains the make and model of 4 different cars you

like. If you don't like cars, you can use something else.

7. Create a Boolean variable called `downloadFinished` and write a conditional statement (`if/else`) which checks to see if it is true or not and then prints a relevant message.

8. Create a class called `Shoe` and give it properties for `hasLaces` of type Bool, `color` of type String, and `releaseDate` of type Int.
   9.) Create subclasses of `Shoe` for three different models of shoes that you like and initialize the variables with the relevant data for each shoe model.

Task 2

1. Create a folder and put your .playground file in it.

2. Create a Github account if you haven't already.

3. Create a new repository on Github.

4. Follow the guide in **Chapter 15** (Setting Up Github) to get your computer's SSH key on Github.

5. On your computer, from the Terminal app, initialize the folder containing your Playground as a local Git repository.

6. Add all files and then make a commit with a message.

7. Add your SSH Github repository URL (click the clipboard button on Github) as a remote repository (remember: `git remote add`).

8. Pull from Github (which will merge any files you already have in that repo).

9. Push to Github.

The End Result

If you refresh your repository on github.com you should see the Playground file loaded up on your Github page.

SECTION 2 - Beginning iOS

Chapter 17: Your First iOS App

Get pumped because in this chapter, you're going to build your very first app! That's right, you will build an app. Not just any, "Hello, World" app though – we're doing this the Devslopes way!

What you will learn

- Xcode Project Creation

- Navigating through Xcode

- Adding Objects to Interface Builder

- Connecting UI Objects and Code

Key Terms

- View Controller

- Utilities

- Attributes Inspector

- Assistant Editor

- UIButton

- UIImageView

- @IBOutlet

- @IBAction

- Aspect Fill

- Aspect Fit

Resources

Download here: https://github.com/devslopes/book-assets/wiki

Welcome to Section 2 – Beginning iOS! In this section, you be guided through the building of several amazing iOS apps. This book is project-based to give you real-world and in-context learning opportunities. The app we build in this chapter will teach you the basics of working with Xcode and more. If you've ever done any programming before, this project is our version of "Hello, World!" But don't worry... Ours is going to be awesome! Let's dive in.

Creating A New Xcode Project

First, open Xcode if you haven't already and click `Create a new Xcode project`.
Click `Single View Application`.
Click `Next`.
Give your project a name like *HelloooooWorld*. Below the name field, there are a few drop down menus, but for the sake of this chapter, you won't need to change any of them. Click `Next`. Choose somewhere to save this project file and click `Create` to save it. You should see a screen like the one in Figure 2.1.1.

Figure 2.1.1

Choose options for your new project:

Product Name: HelloooooWorld

Team: Devslopes, LLC

Organization Name: Devslopes

Organization Identifier: com.devslopes

Bundle Identifier: com.devslopes.HelloooooWorld

Language: Swift

Devices: Universal

☐ Use Core Data
☐ Include Unit Tests
☐ Include UI Tests

Cancel   Previous   Next

After clicking Create, the following window will appear (Figure 2.1.2):

Figure 2.1.2

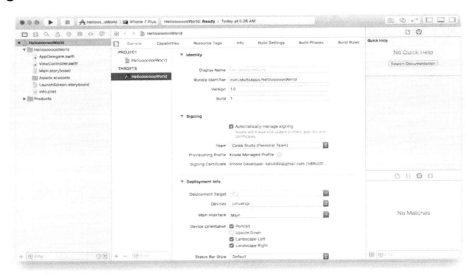

Navigator

On the left, you can see a list of all the files and folders in your project:

- AppDelegate.swift

- ViewController.swift

- Main.storyboard

- Assets.xcassets

- LaunchScreen.storyboard

- Info.plist

These are the files generated by Xcode when creating a new Single-View Application.

The column that they are in is called the `Navigator` and if you hover over each item in the row of buttons at the top (Figure 2.1.3), you will see that you can select between several "Navigator"s:

- Project Navigator

- Symbol Navigator

- Find Navigator

- Issue Navigator

- Test Navigator

- Debug Navigator

- Breakpoint Navigator

- Report Navigator

Figure 2.1.3

The center pane in Xcode is basically an editor. When you click on a file in your project, it will be opened into the center pane for you to modify. To check this out, click `ViewController.swift` and that file will be opened (Figure 2.1.4):

Figure 2.1.4

Helpful Hint:
My Xcode code editor is a different color than is given by default. To change your color scheme, go to the Menu Bar at the top and click on Xcode > Preferences > Colors & Fonts and choose a theme!

We will write the code for our app in this file. Before diving into that, though, let's check out where you will build the user interface (the part the user will see and interact with).

Click on `Main.storyboard` from the Project Navigator. You should see a rectangle with the title `View Controller` in the center panel of Xcode (Figure 2.1.5). This **View Controller** does exactly what it sounds like it does: control the view. The view, as you will soon learn, is the part of the app a user sees. This **View Controller** will handle the displaying, changing, and interactivity of certain elements in the view.

Figure 2.1.5

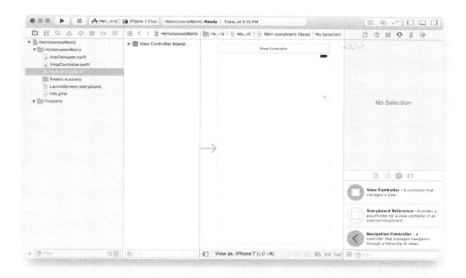

Utilities/Inspectors

Before we go any further, there is another section of the Xcode window you need to know about. The panel on the right-hand side of the window is called Utilities and you should be able to see an assortment of buttons across it's top (Figure 2.1.6). The section you will use the most is called the **Attributes Inspector** and it's icon looks like this:

Figure 2.1.6

In addition to the **Attributes Inspector**, there are also several other "Inspectors" including:

- File Inspector

- Quick Help Inspector

- Identity Inspector

- Size Inspector

- Connections Inspector

The inspectors you'll use the most are the **Attributes Inspector** (as I stated above, the Identity Inspector, and Size Inspector.

At the bottom of the **Utilities** panel, there is a Libraries section (Figure 2.1.7). The one you will use the most is the Object Library and this is where you will find labels, images, buttons, etc. to drop into your **View Controller**.

Figure 2.1.7

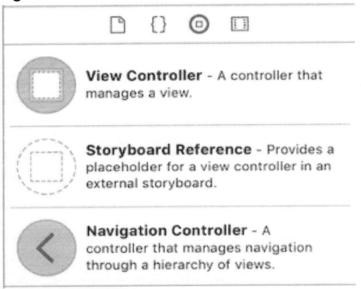

View Controller - A controller that manages a view.

Storyboard Reference - Provides a placeholder for a view controller in an external storyboard.

Navigation Controller - A controller that manages navigation through a hierarchy of views.

Document Outline

After clicking on `Main.storyboard`, or any Storyboard file for that matter, you've entered the Interface Builder.

On the left-hand side, but to the right of the Project Navigator panel, you can see the Document Outline. Here you can see a hierarchical list of all the components you have in your **View Controller** (Figure 2.1.8). We don't have anything yet, so our list of items is a bit bare, but soon we will change that.

Figure 2.1.8

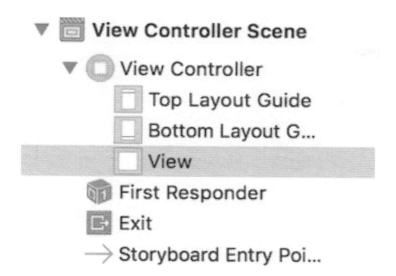

Adding Objects to the View Controller

In the Object Library at the bottom right-hand side of the Xcode window click the `Filter` search bar at the bottom and search for `UIImageView`. The only result will be an Image View (Figure 2.1.9):

Figure 2.1.9

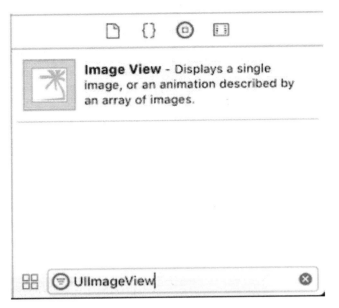

Image View - Displays a single image, or an animation described by an array of images.

⊖ UIImageView

Click and hold on the Image View then drag it to the View Controller. Let go once it is inside the View Controller (Figure 2.1.10):

Figure 2.1.10

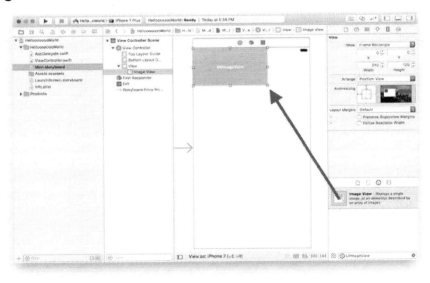

Drag the bottom-right corner of the **UIImageView** so that it fits to the entire bounds of the View Controller (Figure 2.1.11):

Figure 2.1.11

Great! Now we have an Image View in place! A `UIImageView` basically acts like a picture frame for an image. We need to fill our frame, so let's add in an image!

The download link above contains an `Assets` folder which we are going to need now. Open it and there should be two images inside: `bg.png` and `helloLogo.png`. All we need to do in order to copy these into Xcode is click on the `Assets.xcassets` in the Project Navigator and drag in the two images to the Document Outline like so (Figure 2.1.12):

Figure 2.1.12

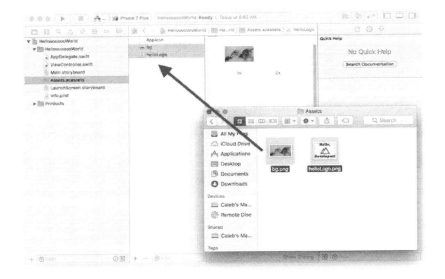

Click once again on `Main.storyboard` to enter the Interface Builder.

Click on the `UIImageView` then click on the `Attributes Inspector` ( ).

You should see a list of `UIImageView`-specific properties appear (Figure 2.1.13):

Figure 2.1.13

154

In order to set the **UIImageView** to use our bg image, we need to click the downtick button to the right of the Image property in the **Attributes Inspector**. Then click on bg to set it in the **UIImageView** (Figure 2.1.14):

Figure 2.1.14

Your View Controller should now look a little more amazing (Figure 2.1.15)!

Figure 2.1.15

The current image is quite squished and we want to create the best possible user interface and experience. So let's fix it. Click on the UIImageView if it has somehow become deselected. Ensure that the **Attributes Inspector** is selected and then change the Content Mode property from Scale to Fill to Aspect Fill. Now the image is maintaining it's aspect ratio while also filling the entire UIImageView (Figure 2.1.16):

Figure 2.1.16

Ahh, much better. Now repeat what we just did to add a UIImageView to add another UIImageView (except set to Aspect Fit) containing the logo image like in Figure 2.1.17:

Figure 2.1.17

So now that the we have our images in place, we can add a button which will control these images.

156

Adding UIButton

From the Object Library, search for UIButton and drag it onto the View Controller in the center and near the bottom of the screen.

You should see a rectangle box with the word Button inside (Figure 2.1.18). This is the default way a **UIButton** looks. We can customize it to our heart's content, but for the purposes of this app we will only change it to say, Welcome!.

Figure 2.1.18

To do this, click on the **UIButton** if it isn't already selected and in the **Attributes Inspector** on the right delete the text Button from the field immediately beneath the Title dropdown then change it to read Welcome! (Figure 2.1.19):

Figure 2.1.19

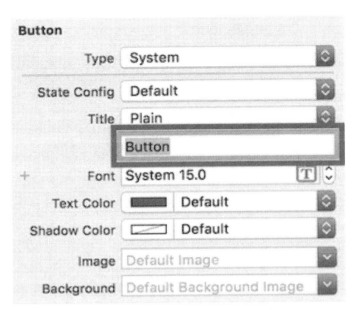

Press Enter to lock in that text. Now our button is too small and the text is being squished! Drag the corner or edge to resize it and then re-center it using Interface Builder's handy snap guides (Figure 2.1.20).

Figure 2.1.20

Testing Our Current App As-Is

It's a good idea to check to see how you are progressing when building an app, so building and running your program often is a good practice for ensuring that you know what's working and what isn't as often as possible. There is nothing worse than working for a few hours, running into problems, wasting time in confusion trying to find the issue, and later realizing something you did long ago is the source of the issue.

At the top-left corner of the Xcode window, you should see the following buttons and drop-down menus (Figure 2.1.21):

Figure 2.1.21

To build and run this application as is, we will need to click on the triangular, play-style button. It's standard behavior is to build and run our application. When you click it, it will compile all of your code files and other assets into an application and send it over to a macOS app called Simulator which comes bundled with Xcode. Simulator is basically a virtual iPhone/iPad/Apple Watch that allows you to test your applications without even needing the physical device present. It's always a good idea to test on a physical device as well. There can be serious performance differences and other issues that can arise.

Change the device from `iPhone 7 Plus` to `iPhone 7`. Now click the `Build & Run` button and wait while your app is compiled and loaded over to Simulator!

Once it loads you should see something like Figure 2.1.22:

Figure 2.1.22

Great! Our app looks great and is running but if you try to click on the button at the bottom it doesn't do anything! That's because we haven't written any code to tell it how it should behave!

Click the square, stop-style button to stop our app from running in Simulator. No need to waste our processing power on an app we're not using at the moment.

We are about to dive into writing some code to hide the images when the app launches and only show the `Welcome!` button, then when we press the button, the images appear!

Creating @IBOutlets/@IBActions

In Xcode, an @IBOutlet is a way for us to connect a UI elements like a button or image to a code file so that we can program it. It's a way to change properties and control it.

An **@IBAction** is a function which let's us perform actions when a certain UI element is interacted with. For this app, our **@IBAction** will be connected to our button. When we press it, it will cause the images to unhide.

We are now going to open up what is called the `Assistant Editor`. It allows us to see Interface Builder and associated code files on the same screen. Click the interlocking circles icon in the top-right corner of the Xcode window (Figure 2.1.23):

Figure 2.1.23

Your screen will change to look something like this: Interface Builder on the left, ViewController.swift on the right (Figure 2.1.24):

Figure 2.1.24

We need to create two **@IBOutlets**, one for each image and one **@IBAction** for the **UIButton**. Let's begin with **@IBOutlets**.

Adding Some @IBOutlets

To create an **@IBOutlet**, all you need to do is right-click and drag from the element you want to gain an **@IBOutlet** and move the mouse over to ViewController.swift. Do this from the bg image view. When you are over the code file, a blue line will pop up saying Insert Outlet or Outlet Collection. Position your mouse so that it is directly above the function viewDidLoad() like so (Figure 2.1.25):

Figure 2.1.25

Let go of the mouse and a pop-up will appear asking you how you'd like to configure your **@IBOutlet**. We will simply fill in the Name field with `bgImageView` and click `Connect` (Figure 2.1.26).

Figure 2.1.26

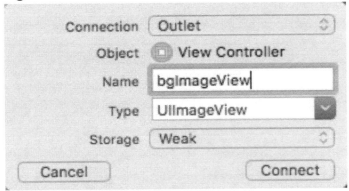

Now, your code fill will include this line of code:

```
@IBOutlet weak var bgImageView: UIImageView!
```

Follow the same steps above to create an **@IBOutlet** called `logoImageView` for the `helloLogo` image right below the previous **@IBOutlet**.

Afterward, your code file should look like this:

162

```
import UIKit

class ViewController: UIViewController {

    @IBOutlet weak var bgImageView: UIImageView!
    @IBOutlet weak var logoImageView: UIImageView!


    override func viewDidLoad() {
        super.viewDidLoad()
        // Do any additional setup after loading the view, typically from a nib.
    }

    override func didReceiveMemoryWarning() {
        super.didReceiveMemoryWarning()
        // Dispose of any resources that can be recreated.
    }
}
```

So now, believe it or not, we can interact with both of our **UIImageViews**! Let's try it out.

Inside of the `viewDidLoad()` function (which runs code as soon as the app has launched, add the following code:

```
override func viewDidLoad() {
    super.viewDidLoad()
    bgImageView.isHidden = true
    logoImageView.isHidden = true
}
```

Now click the triangular `Build & Run` button to check to see if we've properly hidden our Image Views (Figure 2.1.27):

Figure 2.1.27

163

Huzzah! It worked! Now let's write the **@IBAction** which will let us control our Image View to unhide themselves!

Adding An @IBAction

Adding an **@IBAction** is very similar to adding **@IBOutlets**. We need to `right-click` and drag from the element we want to act upon and drop the mouse in our code file. It's standard practice that **@IBActions** go at the bottom of a class.

`Right-click` and drag from the **UIButton** to ViewController.swift and let go beneath the function `didReceiveMemoryWarning()` like so (Figure 2.1.28):

Figure 2.1.28

When you release the mouse over the code file, the same pop-up will appear from when we made our **@IBOutlets**, but we need to change the `Connection` type to be `Action` instead of `Outlet`. Change that then type `welcomeBtnWasPressed` into the `Name` field (Figure 2.1.29).

Figure 2.1.29

An **@IBAction** should describe what action is taken on the connected UI element. Descriptive is best so that another developer looking over your code knows what that **@IBAction** does just by looking at it.

Now, you probably noticed that an **@IBAction** looks a lot like a function. That's because it is! It's a function that can be triggered by a specific user input.

When our button is pressed we want to set the UIImageViews** containing the background image and logo to become unhidden. So inside the brackets of the **@IBAction**, write the following lines of code:

```
@IBAction func welcomeBtnWasPressed(_ sender: Any) {
    bgImageView.isHidden = false
    logoImageView.isHidden = false
}
```

We're basically undoing what was done in `viewDidLoad()` when the app launched.

Ready to test this out? Me too! Click `Build & Run` and when Simulator opens, click the `Welcome!` button to see what happens!

Figure 2.1.30

Wrapping Up

`Hello, Devslopes!` It works! You just built your very first iOS app. Amazing work. This is the start of something very cool. You are on your way to creating much bigger and better things. This book will take you from here to building your very own real-time chat apps, games with SpriteKit and more. This is a journey and it won't always be easy, but it's a journey worth taking.

Exercise

Your challenge, should you choose to accept it, is to re-create this app from memory. If you need to, run through the chapter again but try to build this all from memory. Part of the learning curve here is learning how to use Xcode's many tools.

After you've re-created it, add another **UIButton**, connect it to an **@IBAction** and set it to re-hide the background and logo image views.

Chapter 18: UIStackView

Interface Builder and Storyboards make creating app interfaces extremely easy and straight-forward. UIStackView is a way we can quickly optimize and organize views in our interface, while offering the flexibility needed to make changes down the road.

What You Will Learn

- Use UIStackViews to align objects within the View Controller

Key Terms

- **UIStackView**

- **Content Mode**

- **Aspect Fit**

- **Distribution**

- **Axis**

- **Alignment**

Resources

Why Use UIStackViews?

So why use UIStackViews when Interface Builder already lets you create constraints for your storyboard assets? Here are the few main reasons:

- **Flexibility** - UIStackViews offer immense flexibility when rearranging assets within the storyboard. For example, with a row of icons you would need to create constraints individually in the context of the surrounding assets.

168

UIStackViews will allow you to add or remove assets within that row without a massive overhaul of reconfiguring constraints.

- **Less Math with Points & Pixels** - UIStackViews allows you to distribute items evenly, saving you the trouble of figuring out how spaced out certain elements should be.

- **Ease of Use** - On top of it all, UIStackViews are extremely easy to use once you get the hang of it, so let's dive right in!

Getting Started

Go ahead and open up a new XCode project and create a `Single View Application`. We'll name this project "UIStackViews," and save it to your computer. (Figure 2.2.1)

Figure 2.2.1

First, we'll need to import our assets. Click & drag all the assets from the resources folder into your `Assets.xcassets` folder in XCode. Be sure to include the 1x, 2x, and 3x versions! (Figure 2.2.2)

Figure 2.2.2

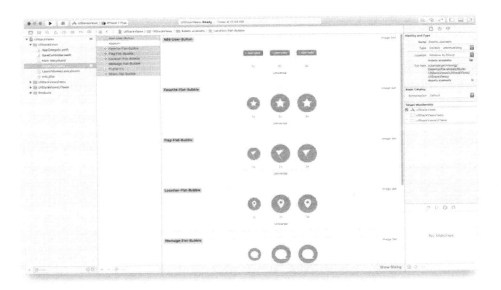

Now let's head over to our `Main.storyboard` and click on the `UIViewController` in our Interface Builder. Start by searching for a "UIView" in the Object Library, and dragging it onto our storyboard. Have it span the width of the View Controller, and give it a height of 64. Go ahead and also fill it in with the color of your choice. I'll be using **#148BAD**. (Figure 2.2.3)

Figure 2.2.3

Now let's add some constraints. With our UIView selected, click the constraints icon on the bottom right. Let's pin the view **0 from the top, 0 from the left, and 0 from the right**. Let's also give it a **fixed height of 64 points**. (Figure 2.2.4)

Figure 2.2.4

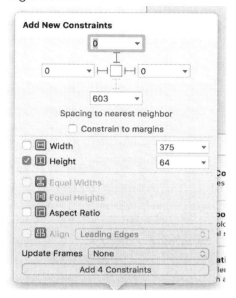

Now let's grab an `Image View` from the Object Library, and drag it on to the View Controller. Adjust the width and height to be 100pts by 100pts and place it slightly above the center of the View Controller. Now in the attributes inspector under **Image** find our `Profile-Pic`, and change the **Content Mode** to `Aspect fit`. (Figure 2.2.5)

Figure 2.2.5

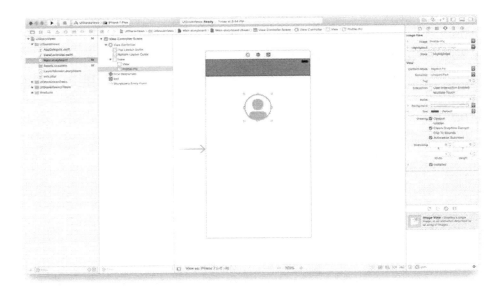

Let's drag another `Image View` on to the View Controller right below our `Profile-Pic` and give it a **width of 160pts, and a height of 50pts.** In the attributes inspector, change the **Image** to `Add-User-Button`, and make sure the **Content Mode** is `Aspect Fit` as well. (Figure 2.2.6)

Figure 2.2.6

Now let's drag a `UIView` under our "Add User" button. Since this will merely be a subtle line to separate the screen, let's **make the width 300pts, and the height 1pt.** We can fill it with our Navigation Bar color (In my project I'm using #148BAD). (Figure 2.2.7)

Figure 2.2.7

Great! Now we're going to place 5 `Image Views` beneath our line. These should all be 50pts by 50pts respectively. You can either drag each one individually, or configure 1, and then copy paste them next to each other 4 times. (Figure 2.2.8)

Figure 2.2.8

Now go ahead and place the remaining images into each Image View. Be sure to have their **Content Mode** Aspect Fit. Lastly, add a text Label from the Object Library with the text "View Bio." Just to make our UI look great, be sure to have the text color the same as your Navigation Bar & line. Feel free to choose whichever font you like best for this project! (Figure 2.2.9)

Figure 2.2.9

Implementing Stack Views

If you'll notice we haven't added any constraints just yet. Running this project as is would probably result in these assets being offset and not entirely where we want them. Have no fear! That's about to change.

First, let's go ahead and select our Profile-Pic and look for the stack view icon on the bottom right of the screen. (Figure 2.2.10)

Figure 2.2.10

Once you click it, you might notice the image may have slightly gotten bigger, or shifted. Don't worry! You just put the Profile-Pic into it's own stack view. Now go to the attributes inspector, and change the **Axis** to Horizontal. (Figure 2.2.11)

Figure 2.2.11

It may not seem like much because we only have 1 element in our stack view. Let's continue to do that for the Add User Button and the line separator. Remember to select them individually and change the **axis** to Horizontal.

Now you're going to click all 5 of the circular icons. Make sure they are all selected by holding down shift as you click. Once they are all selected, go ahead and click the stack view button. Make sure the **axis** is also Horizontal. (Figure 2.2.12)

Figure 2.2.12

Lastly, go ahead and put the View Bio label in its own horizontal stack view.

Now take all of your horizontal stack views you've just created (Profile-Pic, Add User Button, Line separator, Icons, and the View Bio label), and select them all in the left pane. With all of them selected, create another stack view but this time keep the **axis** Vertical. (Figure 2.2.13)

Figure 2.2.13

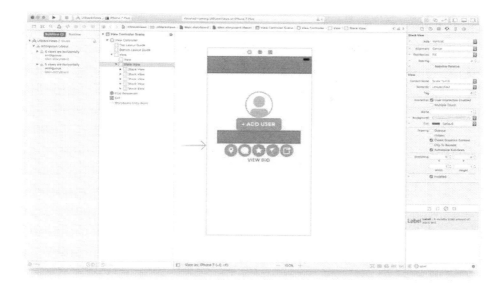

Whoa! What just happened? Let's break down exactly what we have done so far:

- We put all 5 elements into a horizontal stack view (Think 5 bars going across).

- We then put all those bars into a vertical stack view

Now all we need to do is configure them to iron out the UI!

With your vertical stack view selected, in the attributes inspector, change the **Distribution** to Equal Spacing, and the **Alignment** to Center. This evenly spaces our elements with our parent stack view.

Now go ahead and click the icon next to the stack view icon. Instead of pinning the edges of our stack view, let's center it Vertically and Horizontally in the container. This means no matter what we do, the stack view remains in the center of the view. (Figure 2.2.14)

Figure 2.2.14

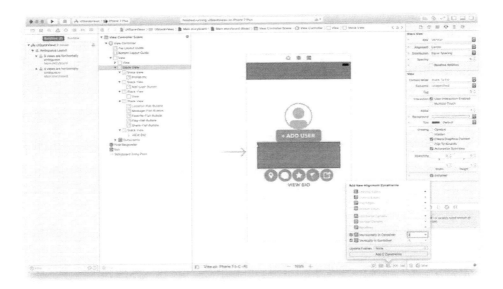

Note: *You can also update any frames or constraints that may be missing at this time to get rid of warnings.*

So what's even cooler about stack views, is that we can adjust the spacing of our elements within it on the fly. While our parent stack view is selected, find **Spacing** in the attributes inspector. From here we can increase or decrease the spacing in between elements. I'm going to make the **Spacing** 35. (Figure 2.2.15)

Figure 2.2.15

Now that we know we can equally space elements, lets do the same for our circle icons! Select the stack view with the circle icons, and make sure the **Distribution** is Fill Equally. Then increase the **Spacing** until they are a desired width apart. I'm going to keep mine at 6. (Figure 2.2.16)

Figure 2.2.16

Lastly, we're going to want to fix this enormous blue block that has been created from our thin line separator. Select the UIView within the stack view, and let's add an individual constraint. Let's give it a fixed height of 1pt. (Figure 2.2.17)

Figure 2.2.17

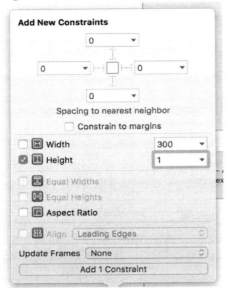

As you can see, since our line separators height becomes smaller, all the other elements within the stack view *automatically adjust*. If we were to delete any element within our parent stack view, all the elements would automatically fill the space equally, without us having to reset individual constraints!

Complete.png

Wrapping Up

Stack views are incredibly powerful for building flexible UI. Of course, not every interface calls for the implementation of a stack view, but when it does, it will make your life a whole lot easier!

Exercise

Find some new icons and elements off of the internet, and re-create a profile screen similar to this using stack views.

Chapter 19: Tipsy Tip Calculator App

How many times have you been out for dinner with friends, received your bill, then awkwardly fumbled around trying to mentally calculate an appropriate tip for your meal? I do this all the time. So if you're anything like me, you know how uncomfortable this is. In this chapter, we will build a tip calculator to help us out.

What You Will Learn

- Model-View-Controller

- How To Use UITextField & UISlider

- Creating a Data Model

- Using Data Encapsulation

Key Terms

- **Model**

- **View**

- **Controller**

Resources

Download here: https://github.com/devslopes/book-assets/wiki

This chapter is all about a programming design pattern called Model-View-Controller (MVC). It has been used in conjunction with Object-Oriented Programming for many years and is very widely used in development today.

Each component of Model-View-Controller has a unique function – let's break them down.

The **Model** layer is for holding data. We will create a class which holds some properties and functions related to that class. Remember the Classes chapter from Section 1? We will make a class of our own to store information like the bill amount, tip percentage, tip amount and total amount. We will also write a function containing the formulas that will calculate the tip amount for us.

The **View** layer is essentially a visual representation of our **Model** layer. It shows and presents what data we've stored. According to Apple's documentation, "A major purpose of view objects is to display data from the application's model objects and to enable the editing of that data."

The **Controller** layer is a go-between for the **View** and Model layers. It controls (hence the name **Controller**) the View to display **Model** data. Think of it like an interior designer telling the **View** layer where items should go on the screen and asking the **Model** layer to present data on the **View**. The **Controller** is also like a manager because it tells the **View** what and when it should change based on changes in the **Model** layer.

With that understanding under your belt, let's move on to creating our project.

Setting Up A New Xcode Project

First, open Xcode if you haven't already and click `Create a new Xcode project`. Click `Single View Application`.
Click `Next`. You should see a screen like the one in Figure 2.3.1. Give your project a name like *TipsyCalcApp*. Below the name field, there are a few drop down menus, but for the sake of this chapter, you won't need to change any of them. Click `Next`. Choose somewhere to save this project file and click `Create` to save it.

Figure 2.3.1

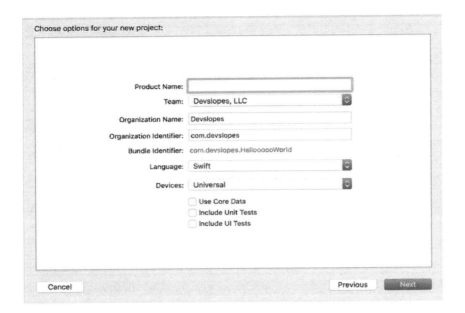

Choose options for your new project:

Product Name:

Team: Devslopes, LLC

Organization Name: Devslopes

Organization Identifier: com.devslopes

Bundle Identifier: com.devslopes.HelloooooWorld

Language: Swift

Devices: Universal

☐ Use Core Data
☐ Include Unit Tests
☐ Include UI Tests

Cancel   Previous   Next

Project Setup

Let's begin by setting up our project with some folders – one for each of the components of MVC.

On the left-hand side of the Xcode window, right click on the yellow `TipsyCalcApp` folder and click `New Group`. Name it `Model`. Repeat this for two more group folders but name them `View` and `Controller` respectively. At the end, your Project Navigator should look like Figure 2.3.2:

Figure 2.3.2

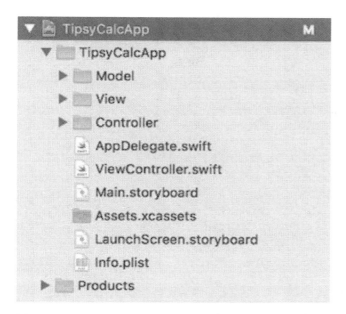

Move `ViewController.swift` into the `Controller` folder and click on `Main.storyboard`. It's now time to build the User Interface (UI) for our app.

Building the User Interface

You already have some experience with using Interface Builder and this chapter will be even more practice. Let's begin by seting a background color for our app. Click on the white background of the ViewController in Interface Builder and on the right-hand side, you should see the Attributes Inspector show up with loads of options for configuring the way the ViewController looks and behaves.

For the `Background` property, click the drop-down and select a light grey color. I'm using hex color #EBF0F1.

Your ViewController should look like Figure 2.3.4:

Figure 2.3.4

Next, we will be adding a banner bar to the top of our app to display the name Tipsy. In the bottom-right of the Xcode window you should be able to see the Object Library. If you can't, click the icon of a little circle with a square inside (⊙).

Search for UIView in the search bar at the bottom and the last result (simply labelled 'View') is the one we want. Click, drag, and drop the View from the Object Library to the ViewController. Position and resize the view then change the Background color property so that it matches Figure 2.3.5:

Figure 2.3.5

Now let's drag on a UILabel, which will let us display the "Tipsy" text. In the Object Library, search for UILabel and drag on the result called "Label" to the banner bar view in your ViewController. Use the handy snap guides to position it horizontally and vertically centered. To change the text in the label, click on it and in the Attributes Inspector (⬇) change where it says Label to say Tipsy. Press Enter so save that text.

To set a custom font and avoid using the yucky system font, click on the UILabel and on the right-hand side, click the 'T' box on the right side of the Font property (🔲) in the Attributes Inspector, then click System — System and change it to Custom.

At this point, you can choose whatever font you'd like and set the style and size. For this project, I'm using 'Avenir Next', 'Demi-Bold', size 30 like in Figure 2.3.6. After doing that, change the font color to white.

Figure 2.3.6

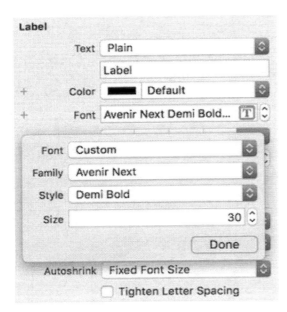

Looking back at our ViewController, our label is now showing some ellipses because our label is too small for the font size we just chose. So re-size the label to fit (Figure 2.3.7) and afterward change the text alignment to Center in the Attributes Inspector (Figure 2.3.8).

Figure 2.3.7

Figure 2.3.8

Now let's add constraints for these items. First, click on the blue view. Then at the bottom of the Xcode window, click the Pin button (). Add the following constraints to the blue UIView then click Add 4 Constraints (Figure 2.3.9):

Figure 2.3.9

Next, we need to add constraints to the label to keep it in the center of the blue UIView and also for it to maintain it's size. Click the label and click the Pin button. Set the following constraints and click Add 2 Constraints (Figure 2.3.10):

Figure 2.3.10

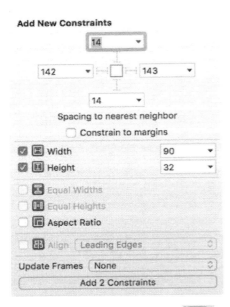

Then click the Align button () to the left of the Pin button. Add the following constraints and click Add 2 Constraints (Figure 2.3.11):

Figure 2.3.11

Now we need to start adding on the rest of our UI elements. We will make good use of UIStackView to make this process as simple as possible. No need to over-complicate

190

things!

To begin, search for UIStackView in the Object Library and drag a `Vertical Stack View` on to the ViewController. Position it like in Figure 2.3.12 and set constraints to pin the UIStackView to all four sides as seen in Figure 2.3.13:

Figure 2.3.12

Figure 2.3.13

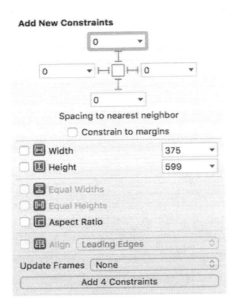

Add New Constraints

Now we need to start dropping in all the elements we will need. First, lets add a `UITextField` where the user will enter their bill amount. Search in the Object Library and drag on a `UITextField`. Drop it into the Vertical Stack View.

You probably notice that the TextField is massive and taking up the entire UIStackView. That will be fixed as we add more elements. Working with Stack Views can be tricky and takes persistent tweaking and modification but we will get it to look great

Click `Stack View` from the Document Outline to the left of Interface Builder. Then click on the Attributes Inspector if it isn't already.

Now we should add a slider for the user to modify with a label beside it to display the tip percentage. To do this we're actually going to drop a Stack View inside of our Stack View. Search for Horizontal Stack View in the Object Library and drag one into our original Stack View but at the bottom so that it is beneath the UITextField (Figure 2.3.14):

Figure 2.3.14

Now, drag on a UILabel and UISlider (find them in the Object Library and drop them into the Horizontal Stack View you just created (Figure 2.3.15) so that the label is on the left and the slider is on the right.

Figure 2.3.15

Obviously this doesn't look nice and it isn't the right size yet so click on the UILabel, click the `Pin` button, and add a `Width` constraint of 50. As you can see, the label is no longer being cut off by the slider (Figure 2.3.16):

Figure 2.3.16

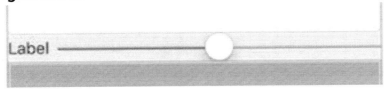

Now, let's keep on adding UI elements.

Next, beneath the slider we need to display the tip amount in dollars. To do this, we will add a nice little money icon, a label which simply says "Tip:", and another label which we will update when the slider slides showing a dollar amount. Just like before, we're going to use UIStackView!

Drag on another Horizontal Stack View beneath the previous Stack View containing the tip slider and place a UIImageView inside. To the left of that drag two UILabels side by side. Your results may vary, but my labels were hidden by the UIImageView. (Figure 2.3.17):

Figure 2.3.17

We want to make everything look nice and make sure that everything is visible so to do that, click the UIImageView, click the `Pin` button, and give it a `Width` constraint of `60`.

Do the same for the first label (which is now visible). While you're at it, click on the label, and in the Attributes Inspector change the text to `Tip:` (Figure 2.3.18).

Figure 2.3.18

We can leave the final label alone as it's width is fluid since we haven't changed anything about it. It is dependent on the other two elements which have their width locked thanks to constraints.

Beneath the lowest Stack View, we need another Stack View with duplicate contents so click on the Stack View in the Document Outline, press ⌘ + C then ⌘ + V and you should see a duplicate Stack View appear below (Figure 2.3.19):

Figure 2.3.19

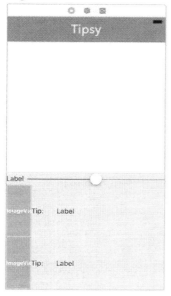

Alright, so now we have all the important UI elements we need for our app, but let's make them look better.

First of all, our main outer Stack View that is holding the UITextField and the other Stack Views is pinned to the outer edges of our screen and I think it would look better if we pulled it in a little from each side.

To do this, click the top-most Stack View in the Document Outline, click the Size Inspector () on the left-hand side of Xcode and in the `Constraints` section you can see the 4 constraints we created earlier.

Click the `Edit` button on the `Trailing Space` constraint and set the `Constant` value to `30`. Press `Enter` to lock it in place. Repeat this process for all three of the remaining constraints. The UI should look like Figure 2.3.20:

Figure 2.3.20

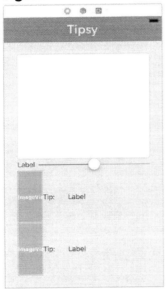

Now let's add some spacing between each vertical element of the outermost main Stack View. Select it using the Document Outline and in the Attributes Inspector, change the Spacing property from `0` to `20` (Figure 2.3.21):

Figure 2.3.21

Spacing ⬚⬚⬚⬚⬚⬚⬚⬚⬚⬚⬚⬚⬚⬚⬚⬚⬚⬚⬚⬚⬚ 20

Your ViewController should look like Figure 2.3.22:

Figure 2.3.22

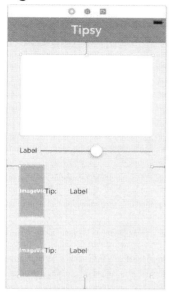

Alright, now let's set up the UITextField so it isn't so massively tall. Click on it and click the `Pin` button to add a `Height` constraint of `70`. Click `Add 1 Constraint` to add constraints. Now, in the Attributes Inspector set the `Alignment` to `Center` and set the font to Custom and use any font you'd like. In the `Placeholder` field, type `enter bill amount here` and press enter. A little further down, change the `Keyboard Type` from `Default` to `Decimal Pad`.

Now our UITextField is starting to look right (Figure 2.3.23)!

Figure 2.3.23

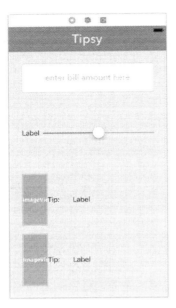

At the moment, we are pinning our main outer Stack View to the bottom which is why it's pulling down the other two Stack Views inside. To fix that, we simply need to experiment with changing the `Constant` of the bottom constraint until the spacing looks right. So to do this, click on the outermost Stack View from the Document Outline and click the Size Inspector (▯).

Click `Edit` to change the constant value for the `Bottom Space` constraint. Instead of 30 change it to something between 300-350. Whatever looks best to you.

Stack View can be inconsistent in how it displays in Interface Builder, so let's make sure that it will evenly space our two identical Stack Views inside (including the image view and two labels) by giving both of those Stack Views a height constraint of 30.

Your ViewController should look like Figure 2.3.24:

Figure 2.3.24

Now let's change the color and text of the label to the left of our slider. Click on it and in the Attributes Inspector change the color to the same blue color as the UIView above (#52ADFF). Then change the text to say `Tip:`. Press `Enter` to save it.

Change the color of the other two labels that say `Tip:` to match.

It also looks as though we should change the `Width` constraint of the `Tip:` label (in the Stack View) as well because of too much spacing between it and the the other label. Click on that label, open the Size Inspector, click `Edit`, and change the `Constant` value to 40 instead of 60 (Figure 2.3.25):

Figure 2.3.25

Now we need to add some spacing to our two identical embedded Stack Views. In the Document Outline, select one of the Stack Views (containing the Image View and two labels) and in the Attributes Inspector change the Spacing property from 0 to 10. Then select the other Stack View and repeat this process (Figure 2.3.26):

Figure 2.3.26

Change the label in the bottom-most Stack View to say `Total:` instead of `Tip:` (Figure 2.3.27):

Figure 2.3.27

Now select every label we've made (except the "Tipsy" label at the top) and in the Attributes Inspector change the font from the System font to whatever custom font you're using.

Finally, the very last (phew, finally!) thing we need to do is set our UIImageViews to the images we downloaded from the resources above. In Xcode, select `Assets.xcassets` and then open the `Tipsy Assets` folder from the downloaded resources. Drag in the image files from that folder (Figure 2.3.28):

Figure 2.3.28

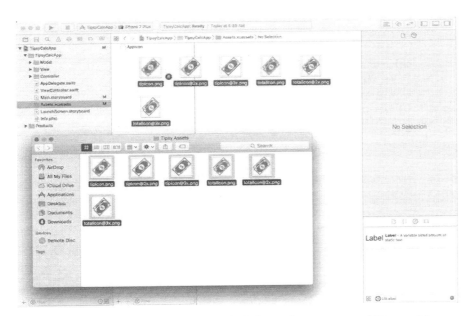

Now, return to `Main.storyboard` and click on the top-most UIImageView next to the `Tip:` label. In the Attributes Inspector, in the `Image` text field, type `tipIcon` and press `Enter` to lock it in place.

Next, click `Content Mode` and change it to `Aspect Fit`.

Do the same process for the UIImageView beneath this one, but set the image to `totalIcon`.

At the very end, your completed UI should look like Figure 2.3.29:

Figure 2.3.29

Pat yourself on the back and give yourself a blue ribbon because the user interface is now done! Let's move on to the fun stuff now – writing code!

Creating A Data Model

We're going to dive into the code by creating our data model. Remember, the model layer is all about data. It will be the "brains" of our calculator as it will help with storing and calculating the bill amount, tip percentage, tip amount, and total amount (after tip).

To get started, right-click on the yellow Model folder in the Project Navigator and click New File... (Figure 2.3.30):

Figure 2.3.30

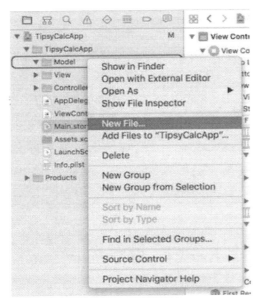

On the pop-up that follows, click iOS in the top left, then double-click on Swift File. Name it TipModel and click Create.

You now should be looking at a blank TipModel.swift file in the Xcode code editor (Figure 2.3.31):

Figure 2.3.31

```
//
//  TipModel.swift
//  TipsyCalcApp
//
//  Created by Caleb Stultz on 1/23/17.
//  Copyright © 2017 Caleb Stultz. All rights
    reserved.
//

import Foundation
```

Let's begin by declaring the class. Beneath `import Foundation` type:

```
import Foundation

class TipModel {

}
```

This is the body of our model class. Next, we need to add some properties for data that needs to be stored and managed by our app. We will need to consider the bill amount, tip percentage, tip amount, and the total amount.

Add the following properties like so:

```
import Foundation

class TipModel {
    private var _billAmount: Double = 0
    private var _tipPercent: Double = 0
    private var _tipAmount: Double = 0
    private var _totalAmount: Double = 0
}
```

The reason why you've used the keyword `private`, is to render the variables above as, well, private... This means that they are not accessible from outside this class. We call this **Data Encapsulation** and it means that the way we're using this code is kept hidden from the user and the user can only do a limited number of things to this code by calling functions unique to this class. If you're wondering why we used underscores before the names of our variable, I will explain it in a moment.

In order to access the variables above we need to use accessors which are affectionally called `getters and setters`. Essentially, we will create four new variables which will have the same name as the private variables from above just without the underscore. These variables will allow for you to read (get) the value of a variable and write (set) a new value to that variable. They also will be available to us outside of this class. They are sort of like an intermediary between us and the private variables.

To do that, add the following code beneath where you created the private variables:

```
class TipModel {
    private var _billAmount: Double = 0
    private var _tipPercent: Double = 0
    private var _tipAmount: Double = 0
    private var _totalAmount: Double = 0
```

```
    var billAmount: Double {
        get {
            return _billAmount
        } set {
            _billAmount = newValue
        }
    }

    var tipPercent: Double {
        get {
            return _tipPercent
        } set {
            _tipPercent = newValue
        }
    }

    var tipAmount: Double {
        return _tipAmount
    }

    var totalAmount: Double {
        return _totalAmount
    }
}
```

Whew, that was a lot of code! Let's unpack it now.

What we've done is create four new variables with the same names as the private variables above just without the underscore. For the first two, `billAmount` and `tipPercent`, we used `get` return the value of `_billAmount`. We used `set` to change the value of `_billAmount` and used `newValue`. `newValue` is built in to Xcode and basically, when using a setter it sets the value of the private variable to whatever value a particular variable is changed to. However it's modified, the `newValue` will be equal to that value.

Since we don't need to write a value for the `tipAmount` and `totalAmount` variables, we didn't explicitly use `get` or `set`. In returning values we are essentially "reading" the values of those variables like when we use `get`.

Now, when we use this data model later on, we will need to pass in values for `billAmount` and `tipPercent`. In order to make sure this happens, let's write an initializer function.

Writing A Custom Initializer

At the bottom of `TipModel`, beneath where you created the variables including getters and setters, write the following function:

```
...
init(billAmount: Double, tipPercent: Double) {
    self._billAmount = billAmount
    self._tipPercent = tipPercent
}
```

When we create an instance of TipModel in our ViewController later on (don't freak out, I will go over this in detail), we will use the `init(billAmount:tipPercent:)` function to give the instance some initial values to work with.

What we need to do to wrap up our data model is write a function to calculate the tip we need to pay. We can use the values passed in when TipModel is instantiated. Let's write that function now.

Writing A Function To Calculate the Tip Amount

So let's think about how we should calculate the tip amount. If we know the bill amount (i.e. $36.50) and the tip percentage (i.e. 15%), we can multiply the bill amount by the percentage to get the tip amount (i.e. $5.47).

So, using our variable names the formula would look like this: `tipAmount = billAmount * tipPercent`

Beneath the initializer function, write the skeleton of the following function and the formula needed to calculate the tip amount:

```
func calculateTip() {
    _tipAmount = billAmount * tipPercent
}
```

Great! So now our formula can calculate the tip amount. But that isn't completely helpful in and of itself. We want to know the total amount for the meal and the tip included. To calculate that, we should add the following line of code to add the bill amount to the tip amount:

```
func calculateTip() {
    _tipAmount = billAmount * tipPercent
    _totalAmount = billAmount + tipAmount
}
```

Now both values _tipAmount and _totalAmount will be set thanks to their setters!

At this point, go grab another cup of coffee and high five yourself cause our data model is done! BOOM! Now we're going to set up the ViewController (i.e. the **Controller** layer) to handle passing data to the **View** layer making our app interactive and fun!

Setting Up the ViewController

At the moment, there is nothing inside our **Controller** folder, but we should drag ViewController.swift into that folder. You know, for organization's sake and all. Once you've done that, click on ViewController.swift and you should see the following screen (Figure 2.3.32):

Figure 2.3.32

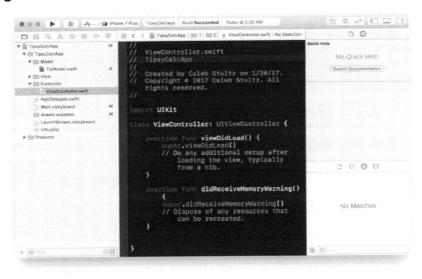

Delete the function didReceiveMemoryWarning() and everything inside. This is a boilerplate function we won't be using. Delete the commented-out line from within viewDidLoad() but leave the function in place like so:

```
import UIKit

class ViewController: UIViewController {

    override func viewDidLoad() {
```

```
        super.viewDidLoad()

    }
}
```

At the top, `import UIKit` tells Xcode to include the UIKit framework which contains everything you will need for interacting and manipulating UI elements and much more.

The function `viewDidLoad()` is called after the controller is loaded into memory. To put it simply, the code in `viewDidLoad()` basically run as the app loads past the launch screen.

As you will see in later chapters, there are ways to call code before and after the view loads/appears also.

Now, we need to create some @IBOutlets so we can talk to our UI elements like the slider, labels, and text field.

Creating @IBOutlets

Click on `Main.storyboard` and once it's opened, click on the `Assistant Editor` button in the top-right of Xcode (Figure 2.3.33):

Figure 2.3.33

The `ViewController.swift` file should automatically load beside Interface Builder but in case it doesn't, click on the `Automatic` button at the top of `ViewController.swift` (Figure 2.3.34), click `Manual` and navigate through the folders to find the ViewController file in the `Controller` group (Figure 2.3.35).

Figure 2.3.34

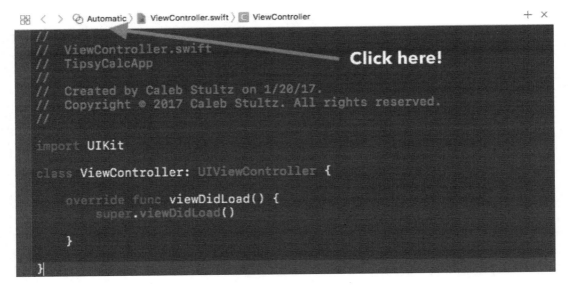

Figure 2.3.35

Now let's actually create some @IBActions. We will start with the text field.

`Right-click` and hold on the UITextField and drag until the cursor is above `viewDidLoad()` but beneath the class declaration of `ViewController` (Figure 2.3.36):

Figure 2.3.36

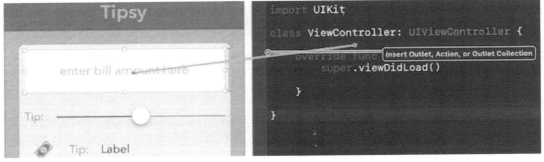

When you release the mouse, you will be presented with a pop-up just like in Figure 2.3.37 and an empty `Name` text field. Type `textField` and press `Connect`. Now we've properly connected our text field so that we can read values from it.

Figure 2.3.37

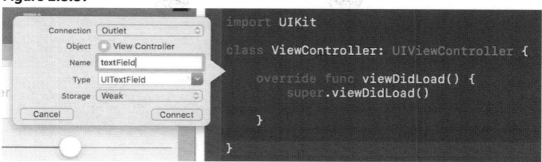

Following the same steps, you will need to create @IBActions for the UISlider as well as some of the labels with names from Figure 2.3.38:

Figure 2.3.38

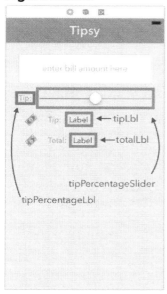

In all you should have the following @IBOutlets in your ViewController class (Figure 2.3.39):

Figure 2.3.39

```
import UIKit

class ViewController: UIViewController {

    @IBOutlet weak var textField: UITextField!
    @IBOutlet weak var tipPercentageSlider: UISlider!
    @IBOutlet weak var tipPercentageLbl: UILabel!
    @IBOutlet weak var tipLbl: UILabel!
    @IBOutlet weak var totalLbl: UILabel!

    override func viewDidLoad() {
        super.viewDidLoad()

    }

}
```

Setting Up UISlider

UISlider can be set up with a `value`, `minimum`, and `maximum` property.

The `value` property is what UISlider is first loaded with. It will display at this value. The `minimum` and `maximum` values are essentially the range that the UISlider can handle.

To modify these values, click on the UISlider and ensure that the Attributes Inspector is open. Set the `value` property to 0.15 for a default tip amount of 15% (standard in the U.S.), the `minimum` property to 0.1 and the `maximum` property to 0.25 (Figure 2.3.40):

Figure 2.3.40

Creating an Instance of our Data Model

Now, we're going to create an instance of our data model so that we can pass in values and calculate the tip as we'd like.

To do this, add the following variable beneath the @IBOutlets:

```
var tip = TipModel(billAmount: 0.0, tipPercent: 0.0)
```

We've created an instance of the class `TipModel`. Since classes are reference types, we have created a reference to the original class (sort of like a link on a website).

We passed in a static amount of $0.00 and a tip percentage of 0% but we will change that later on. So the variables `billAmount` and `tipPercent` are now set and are ready for use by the rest of the class.

If you glance back in this chapter to when we were creating TipModel, we wrote a function called `calculateTip()` which calculates our tip amount (believe it or not!) by multiplying the bill amount by the tip percentage which we now have. We will use this function momentarily, but first, we should set up some @IBActions to control the changing of the bill amount text field and tip percentage slider value.

Setting up @IBActions

To create an @IBAction, as you may remember from previous chapters, you simply need to right-click and drag from the element you want to give an @IBAction then drop it at the bottom of your class file. Do this for the UITextField.

When you reach `ViewController.swift`, let go and on the following pop-up click on the `Connection` drop down menu. Change it from `Outlet` to `Action`. Give it a descriptive name like `billAmountWasChanged`. Then, since we're dealing with a UITextField, change the `Event` property to `Editing Changed`. This is so that when we enter a value into the text field it can update as we type. After that's done, click `Connect` (Figure 2.3.41):

Figure 2.3.41

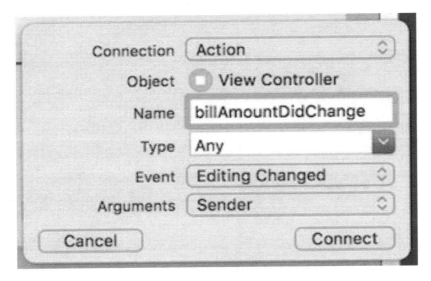

Helpful Hint:

It is not mandatory to put @IBActions at the bottom of your code files, but it is fairly common to separate @IBOutlets and @IBActions like this.

Now, we have an @IBAction for our UITextField and you probably noticed that it looks a lot like a function. That's because it is! Whenever the value is changed in the text field, we can call code to run! Let's just print a value for now. Inside of `billAmountWasChanged(_sender:)`, add the following line of code:

```
@IBAction func billAmountWasChanged(_ sender: Any) {
    print("My value changed!")
}
```

Now when we run our app and when we input a value and/or change it, the code inside the @IBAction will be called. Let's give it a shot!

Click the triangular `Build & Run` button to check if it works.

So far so good! As you enter and remove values, the console prints that the value was changed (Figure 2.3.42):

Figure 2.3.42

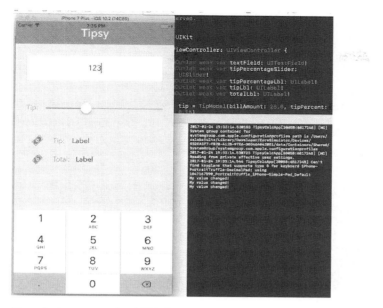

Now let's set up the UISlider's @IBAction and test it also. Switch back over to Xcode from the Simulator and in `Main.storyboard`, `right-click` and drag from the UISlider to beneath the @IBAction `billAmountDidChange`.

Set the `Connection` to @IBAction, the `Name` to `tipPercentageDidChange` and the `Event` to `Value Changed` (Figure 2.3.43):

Figure 2.3.43

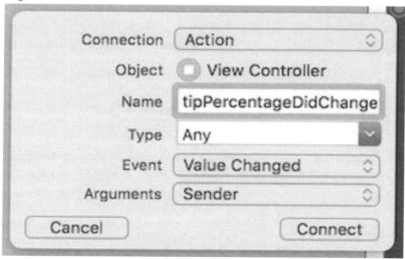

Click `Connect` and inside the brackets of `tipPercentageDidChange` add the following line to test if it's working:

```
@IBAction func tipPercentageDidChange(_ sender: Any) {
    print(tipPercentageSlider.value)
}
```

Click the Build & Run button again to check if our slider is working properly. Once it builds and opens in Simulator slide the slider around a bit and check out what happens (Figure 2.3.44):

Figure 2.3.44

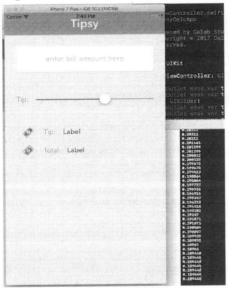

As you can see, the value prints out whenever we move the slider at all which is exactly what we're looking for.

Updating the Labels in the View Layer

Now that we know our @IBActions are working, we will write a few functions to set the tip calculation values as well as update the user interface.

Above the @IBActions but beneath viewDidLoad() add the following functions:

```
func setTipCalculationValues() {
    tip.tipPercent = Double(tipPercentageSlider.value)
    tip.billAmount = ((textField.text)! as NSString).doubleValue
```

```
        tip.calculateTip()
}

func updateUI() {
    tipLbl.text = String(format: "$%0.2f", tip.tipAmount)
    totalLbl.text = String(format: "$%0.2f", tip.totalAmount)
    tipPercentageLbl.text = "Tip: \(Int(tipPercentageSlider.value * 100))%"
}
```

Let me explain the first function, `setTipCalculationValues()`. First, we call `tip` which is the instance of our data model. Then, we set it's `tipPercent` property to be the same as whatever the value of the tipPercentageSlider is. We placed `tipPercentageSlider.value` inside of parentheses and wrote `Double` in front of it so that we are setting it as a double value instead of Float as provided by UISlider. Then, we set `tip.billAmount` to whatever value the UITextField has been set with. The interesting thing is that a UITextField deals with values of type String, so we wrap `textField.text` in parentheses and use a ! to tell Xcode that we definitely have a value. We force it to be "downcast" as type NSString which has a property `.doubleValue`. Essentially, we are converting a String (guaranteed to be a number) as a Double. At the end, we call `tip.calculateTip()` which sets the properties `tipAmount` and `totalAmount` in our data model. We use those values to modify the UILabels in our ViewController to show the tip and total values.

Next we call the function `updateUI()` which sets the `text` property of `tipLbl`, `totalLbl`, and `tipPercentageLbl`. We set the type of `tipLbl` and `totalLbl` to String but we use parentheses to include a custom feature which is displaying as U.S. currency ($). For the `format` property, we wrote **"$%0.2f"** which is a way of telling Xcode that any number value we pass in will be converted to look like a U.S. currency value (i.e. 5 becomes $5.00). For the `tipPercentageLbl` we set it to say "Tip: " and then we use String Interpolation to pass in the value of the `tipPercentageSlider` and multiply it to get the percentage as a whole number (i.e. 0.1 * 100 = 10%).

Calling the Functions from @IBActions

As you know, functions don't do anything unless they are called from somewhere else so let's do that. Our @IBActions are a perfect place to call them from.

When we enter in a value for the billAmount, we should call `setTipCalculationValues()` and `updateUI()` so that we can display a tip calculation every time we add or remove a value. We should call the same code when we change the value of the slider. Call both functions from each @IBActions like this:

```
@IBAction func billAmountDidChange(_ sender: Any) {
    setTipCalculationValues()
    updateUI()
}

@IBAction func tipPercentageDidChange(_ sender: UISlider) {
    setTipCalculationValues()
    updateUI()
}
```

There is one last place we need to call the `updateUI()` and `setTipCalculationValues()` function – in `viewDidLoad()`! This is so that when our view loads the labels display **$0.00** which is the amount we've entered when the app loads – nothing!

Add it like so:

```
override func viewDidLoad() {
    super.viewDidLoad()
    setTipCalculationValues()
    updateUI()
}
```

Testing

Click the triangular `Build & Run` button and let the app build and run in Simulator. Try it out! You should be able to add a value to the UITextField and the tip and total should display at the bottom. The tip amount should also be displaying.

Making UISlider Snappier

When sliding the UISlider from 12% to 13%, for example, you probably notice that the tip and total amounts keep changing. Our UISlider is fluidly sliding from 12%-12.1%-12.2% and so on. We want to set it to snap at whole number values. We can do this with a bit of math.

Add the following code to the `tipPercentageDidChange` @IBAction:

```
@IBAction func tipPercentageDidChange(_ sender: UISlider) {
    let steps: Float = 100
    let roundedValue = round(sender.value * steps) / steps
```

```
    sender.value = roundedValue

    setTipCalculationValues()
    updateUI()
}
```

Don't worry if you don't fully understand this bit of code, but essentially we are creating a Float type variable set to a value of 100 representing 100 "steps" a UISlider can take (percentages). Then, we round the value using a built-in Swift `round()` function. We take whatever value is being passed in and multiply it by `steps` (100). It is then rounded to the nearest whole number. Then after that, we divide it by 100 to get it back down to a number UISlider can understand.

Here's an example: We set UISlider to 0.12223182 which is a bit over 12%. We can use this value in the @IBAction by calling sender.value (assuming that the sender is of type UISlider. You can change it to be in the @IBAction if yours is set to `Any`.

Then, we create the constant `roundedValue` by passing in sender.value (0.12223182) multiplied by 100 (`steps`) which equals 12.223182. Since this is inside the `round()` function, it is rounded down to the whole number 12. We then divide it by 100 (`steps`) and it equals 0.12 again. We then set sender.value to be equal to `roundedValue` forcing it to snap into place at exactly 12%! Pretty cool.

Take a look at the app you've just made! I know it was difficult to understand and work through this chapter, but you did it! A major milestone on your path to becoming a developer!

Figure 2.3.45

Wrapping Up

You now have created an amazing app which can calculate the tip amount and total amount you need to know when paying your bill. This chapter taught the basics of Model-View-Controller and while we didn't dive in too deeply to the View layer, you will learn to rely on that much more heavily in the chapters to come. You will create custom view layers which can set a custom appearance for any of the UI elements. For the scope of this chapter, you learned what the View layer is and will soon put that practice into practice.

We created a data model that stored and performed calculations on several important variables. We used our ViewController to work with the View layer to display and show values from the data model.

Exercise

Are you ready for a challenge? Of course you are! Using what you've learned in this chapter, add functionality to split bills using a UISlider and dividing totalAmount to split the bill between a group of people. It could look like this, but you have free reign to customize and tweak this as you see fit:

Simulator Screen Shot Jan 26, 2017, 5.07.24 PM.png

Chapter 20: UIScrollView & Paging

Many apps feature content that must be scrolled through or paged through, but not many coding teachers will teach you how to use UIScrollView to do this. In this book, you will learn how so you're prepared.

What you will learn

- Creating a **UIScrollView**

- Allowing **UIScrollView** paging

- Adding UIImageView as a Subview

- Setting **UIScrollView**'s `contentSize` property

Key Terms

- **UIScrollView**

Resources

Download here: https://github.com/devslopes/book-assets/wiki

Apps like the Devslopes app use UIScrollView to allow a user to page between relevant content. In the case of the Devslopes app, you can scroll between pages including the different slopes you can learn from as in 2.6.0.

Figure 2.6.0

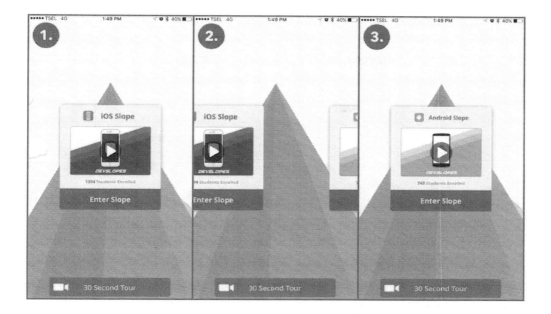

Setting up

Creating a new Xcode project

First, open Xcode if you haven't already and click `Create New Project`. Click `Single View Application`. Click `Next`. Give your project a name like *PageTheScroll*. Below the name field, there are a few drop down menus but for the sake of this chapter, you won't need to change any of them. Click `Next`. Choose somewhere to save this project file and click `Create` to save it. You should see a screen like the one in Figure 2.6.1.

Figure 2.6.1

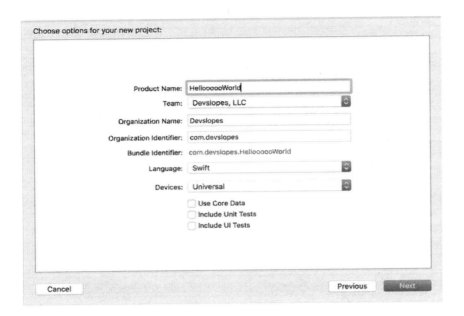

Building the User Interface

Click on `Main.storyboard` to open up Interface Builder. Next, download the assets for this project from the link above. Then, click on `Assets.xcassets` and drag all downloaded assets inside like in Figure 2.6.2:

Figure 2.6.2

224

Adding a UIImageView

Now we need to give our app a background image. In the bottom right of the Xcode window, search for UIImageView and drag one onto our ViewController. Position it so that it extends to the full size of the ViewController (Figure 2.6.3):

Figure 2.6.3

With the UIImageView selected, click the Pin button (⊡) at the bottom of the Xcode window and give it the following constraints pinning it a distance of 0 from all sides of the view (Figure 2.6.4):

Figure 2.6.4

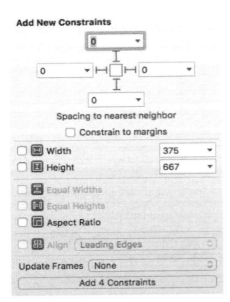

Add New Constraints

Spacing to nearest neighbor

Width 375

Height 667

Equal Widths

Equal Heights

Aspect Ratio

Align Leading Edges

Update Frames None

Add 4 Constraints

Next, click on the UIImageView and select the Attributes Inspector (⬇) if it isn't selected already. Set the `Image` property to be "Sky" and the `Content Mode` to be `Apsect Fill` (Figure 2.6.5). This is so that our image maintains it's aspect ratio, while filling to the edges of the UIImageView like a picture in a frame (Figure 2.6.6). It will look best on all screen sizes this way.

Figure 2.6.5

Image View

Image Sky

Highlighted Highlighted Image

State ☐ Highlighted

View

Content Mode Aspect Fill

Semantic Unspecified

Tag 0

Figure 2.6.6

Next, drag on another UIImageView and position it in the top right corner. In the Attributes Inspector for this UIImageView, set the `Image` property to "Sun" and the `Content Mode` to be `Aspect Fit` (Figure 2.6.7):

Figure 2.6.7

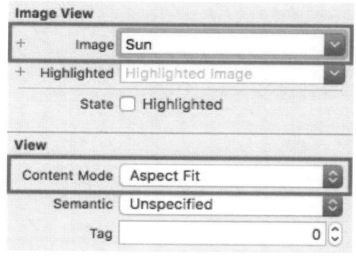

Drag the Sun UIImageView to the top right corner of the screen and position it like in Figure 2.6.8. Click the `Pin` button at the bottom and pin it to the right and top sides. Make sure you tick the `Height` and `Width` boxes to give it a fixed width and height so that it remains the size we want (Figure 2.6.9).

Figure 2.6.8

Figure 2.6.9

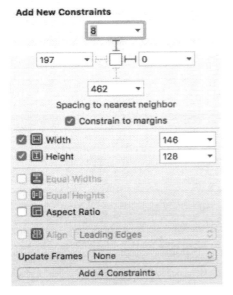

Drag on one last UIImageView and position it like so (Figure 2.6.10):

Figure 2.6.10

Click the Pin button and give it constraints which will pin it to the bottom, left side, and right side. Also, tick the Height box to give it a fixed height (Figure 2.6.11):

Figure 2.6.11

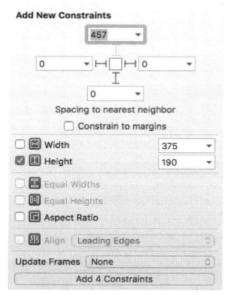

In the Attributes Inspector, set the Image property to "Mountains" and the Content Mode to Aspect Fill (Figure 2.6.12):

Figure 2.6.12

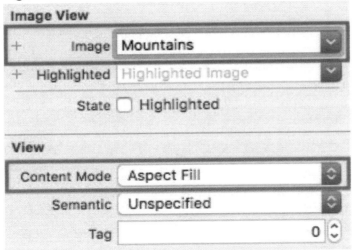

Your app's background should look like Figure 2.6.13:

Figure 2.6.13

Alright, so now we have a nice pretty background to be in the back of our app. We didn't have to spend time making this, but it's nice to always make things look nice in addition to running well.

Adding UIScrollView

Next, we are going to add in a **UIScrollView** which will perform all of the scrolling and paging we want for this app. Click on the search bar in the bottom-right corner of the Xcode window, search for "**UIScrollView**", and drag one into the Document Outline on the left-hand side of Interface Builder like so (Figure 2.6.14):

Figure 2.6.14

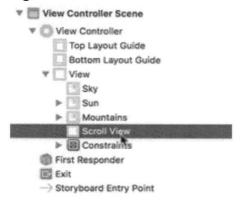

The reason we didn't drop the **UIScrollView** on top of the ViewController is because sometimes there are issues with **UIScrollView** in Interface Builder, so adding it to the Document Outline ensures that we position it in the right place – as the top-most item in front of everything else.

Next, drag and position the **UIScrollView** so that it takes up the entire frame of the ViewController – just like we did for the UIImageView with the background image (Figure 2.6.15):

Figure 2.6.15

UIScrollView is created transparent, but you can see the text '**UIScrollView**' in the center of Figure 2.6.15 above.

Next, with the **UIScrollView** selected **untick** the boxes for: Shows Horizontal Indicator, Shows Vertical Indicator and **tick** the box Paging Enabled (Figure 2.6.16).

Figure 2.6.16

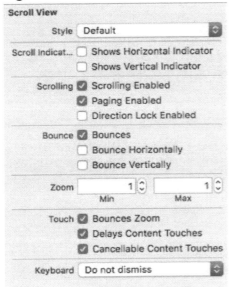

Adding content to UIScrollView

Great, now that we've added on a **UIScrollView** we need to give it some content so that it is useful! We've already included the assets you need in the source code you downloaded at the beginning of this chapter, so open `Assets.xcassets` in Xcode and you should see three images called `icon0`, `icon1`, and `icon2`. These are the iOS, Android, and Angular icons we'll use in our app.

Click on `ViewController.swift` in the Navigator on the left-hand side of the Xcode window and delete the boilerplate code leaving `viewDidLoad()` intact. Like so:

```swift
import UIKit

class ViewController: UIViewController {

    override func viewDidLoad() {
        super.viewDidLoad()
        // Do any additional setup after loading the view, typically from a nib.
    }
}
```

Next up, let's create an empty array of UIImageViews to contain all of our course icons we just added to our Assets folder. We also will create a for loop to create images to store inside each UIImageView. Add the following code above `viewDidLoad()`:

```swift
import UIKit

class ViewController: UIViewController {

    var images = [UIImageView]()

    override func viewDidLoad() {
        super.viewDidLoad()

        for x in 0...2 {
            let image = UIImage(named: "icon\(x).png")
            let imageView = UIImageView(image: image)
            images.append(imageView)
        }
    }
}
```

So you just wrote the code to create an array of UIImageView. Then you wrote a `for-in` loop which cycles from 0 up until 2. After, you created a constant called `image` which creates a UIImage and passes in the value for x into the filename for the picture (icon0.png, icon1.png, icon2.png). Then we create a constant of type UIImageView and pass in the UIImage. At the end of the loop, we append a UIImageView (containing a UIImage) to our array called `images`.

So after the loop runs, we have the following inside the `images` Array:
* UImageView -> UIImage -> icon0.png
* UIImageView -> UIImage -> icon1.png
* UIImageView -> UIImage -> icon2.png

If you build and run your app at this point, you will definitely see our nice mountain background image, but the icons are nowhere to be found. That is because we haven't yet placed them anywhere. We only created them.

Now let's get our images actually showing up in the **UIScrollView**.

Before we move forward though, I want you to think of **UIScrollView** like it's a magical window looking out into the world. When you drag your finger across the window, the world outside moves with your finger. Instead of you needing to move your head to see what is outside you can just swipe your finger over the glass.

UIScrollView has a property called `contentSize` which allows you to define how much content can be inside of a **UIScrollView**. As per the example above, the content size allows you to choose how big the world is through the window. Figure 2.6.17 shows how this will work in our app. We will set the `contentSize` momentarily.

Figure 2.6.17

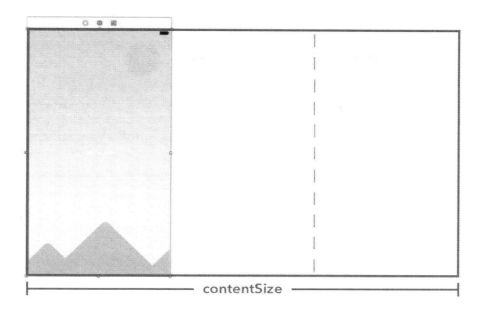

contentSize

Connecting UIScrollView to our ViewController.swift file

Let's create an @IBOutlet so that we can interact with our **UIScrollView** and add in those images.

Click on `Main.storyboard` and then click the `Assistant Editor` on the upper right-hand side of Xcode (⊗⊗) to bring up the associated `ViewController.swift` file.

Right-click and hold on "Scroll View" from the Document Outline and drag the cursor over to `ViewController.swift`. Release the cursor above `viewDidLoad()` like in Figure 2.6.18:

Figure 2.6.18

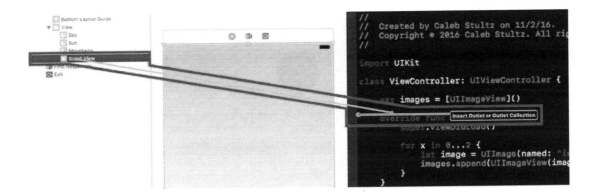

When you release the cursor give the @IBOutlet a name of scrollView and leave all other properties as they are like in Figure 2.6.19:

Figure 2.6.19

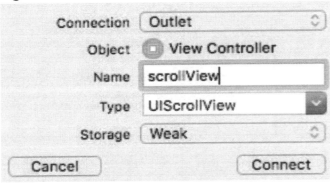

Now we can access the **UIScrollView** and make it do cool things!

Positioning UIImageView on UIScrollView

Now we need to set up some code which will be responsible for helping us to scroll our content and contain pages of content, too.

Inside the for-in loop you wrote earlier add these following lines of code:

```
...
for x in 0...2 {
    let image = UIImage(named: "icon\(x).png")
    let imageView = UIImageView(image: image)
    images.append(imageView)
```

```
    var newX: CGFloat = 0.0

    newX = view.frame.midX + view.frame.size.width * CGFloat(x)
}
```

What we have done is create a variable of type CGFloat called **newX**. We then set it's value, but it may be confusing to a new programmer to understand these values with no explanation.

Let me explain.

1.) `view.frame.midX` is a value that takes the current view (in this case, our screen) and looks for the size of it's `frame` (in this case, the same size as our screen). Then it calculates the midpoint on the X axis.

So, if your screen was 320 pixels wide, the `midX` point would be 160. Figure 2.6.19 shows how the grid actually works in iOS:

Figure 2.6.19

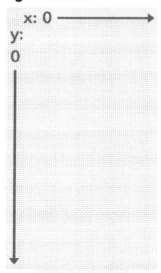

As you can see, the top left corner is x: `0`, y: `0` and as you move to the right or down towards the bottom the values increase.

2.) `view.frame.size.width` is a value that captures the width of our screen in this example. It looks inside of the view, then the frame, then captures it's size and stores the value for the width.

Since our imaginary screen is 320 pixels wide, it would return a value of 320.

3.) At the end we multiply `view.frame.midX + view.frame.size.width` by `CGFloat(x)`. Remember that we are in a `for-in` loop passing in values of 0, 1, and 2.

When the loop runs for the first time, we pass in the value `0` for x. Continuing with our example of a screen width of 320 pixels, `newX` calculation would go like this:

```
view.frame.midX = 160
view.frame.size.width = 320
CGFloat(0) = 0.0
```

So, for the first time through the for loop we are calculating `160 + 320 * 0` which gives us a grand total of 160 if we follow the order of operations.

The loop now will run again and our calculation changes. It now looks like this:

```
view.frame.midX = 160
view.frame.size.width = 320
CGFloat(1) = 1.0
```

We've just performed `160 + 320 * 1` which results in 480.

The loop runs one last time before stopping.

```
view.frame.midX = 160
view.frame.size.width = 320
CGFloat(2) = 2.0
```

We performed `160 + 320 * 2` resulting in 800.

So by the end we have changed `newX` to first be equal to 160, then 480, then 800.

Remember Figure 2.6.17 about `contentSize` from above? We need to offset each icon to have an entire screen width of space so that we can page between them properly. These `newX` values are what we will use to accomplish this.

We want our icons to show up in the middle of our screen which is why we are using `midX` as a property.

Adding each UIImageView as a Subview

Now that our loop creates a UIImageView and fills it with one of our icon images, we need to add it as a subview of **UIScrollView**. Think of this sort of similarly to how you would add a page in a Microsoft Word or Pages document.

At the bottom of the `for-in` loop, add the following:

```
...
for x in 0...2 {
    let image = UIImage(named: "icon\(x).png")
    let imageView = UIImageView(image: image)
    images.append(imageView)

    var newX: CGFloat = 0.0

    newX = view.frame.midX + view.frame.size.width * CGFloat(x)

    scrollView.addSubview(imageView)
}
```

We also need to give our images a frame size so that they are bound to a certain size. Set up the `frame` property of UIImageView like so:

```
...
for x in 0...2 {
    let image = UIImage(named: "icon\(x).png")
    let imageView = UIImageView(image: image)
    images.append(imageView)

    var newX: CGFloat = 0.0

    newX = view.frame.midX + view.frame.size.width * CGFloat(x)

    scrollView.addSubview(imageView)

    imageView.frame = CGRect(x: 0, y: view.frame.size.height / 2, width: 150,
height: 150)
}
```

Now every UIImageView we make in our loop will be bound to a frame size of 150 x 150.

We've positioned it at 0 on the x-axis and the middle of the screen (view.frame.size.height / 2) on the y-axis. We want it to be in the middle of the x and y-axis but as of now it's only centered on the y-axis.

We will modify the x-axis value using `newX` shortly.

Let's build and run our app at this moment to check and see how we did. As you can see in Figure 2.6.20, our image is now showing up, but sadly it is too low. That's because we set it's y-axis value to be `view.frame.size.height / 2` meaning that the top of our UIImageView is positioned in the middle of our screen on the y-axis. We want it to be centered, so let's do that now by subtracting half of the height of our Angular image.

Figure 2.6.20

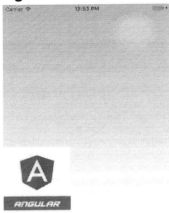

We know the height of our UIImageView is 150 because we set it to be so. We just need to subtract half of our UIImageView's height to bring it up to the center. Do that by surrounding `view.frame.size.height / 2` with parentheses and subtracting 75 like so:

```
...
imageView.frame = CGRect(x: 0, y: (view.frame.size.height / 2) - 75, width: 150,
height: 150)
```

Build and run the app again and check to see how the positioning has changed (Figure 2.6.21). Yay! It is nice and centered now!

Figure 2.6.21

Let's make the image centered on the x-axis now.

We already have the value in place to move our image to the center of the x-axis so change the x value in `imageView.frame` from 0 to use `newX` from earlier.

```
...
    imageView.frame = CGRect(x: newX, y: (view.frame.size.height / 2) - 75, width:
150, height: 150)
```

Changing the x-axis value here works identically to how we changed the y-axis above – meaning that the left side of the image (0 on the x-axis) will be positioned in the center. To make the image appear centered on our screen, we need to subtract 75 just like before.

```
...
    imageView.frame = CGRect(x: newX - 75, y: (view.frame.size.height / 2) - 75,
width: 150, height: 150)
```

Build and run to see if it worked. You should see something like Figure 2.6.22:

Figure 2.6.22

Woohoo! It's lookin' so good, but we still can't scroll. With everything centered and looking fancy, we only have a few more steps to go.

Let's make that **UIScrollView** scroll and page, too!

Making UIScrollView play nicely

Like I said before, **UIScrollView** has a property called `contentSize` which operates sort of like a magic window that allows us to move the world behind it as we move our finger around the glass. If we have content that is three times the width of our screen, we can set our **UIScrollView** to understand that.

Let's create a property to store the width of our content and change it's value based on the loop that we create so it expands as each UIImageView is created.

Add the following to ViewController.swift:

```swift
import UIKit

class ViewController: UIViewController {

    var images = [UIImageView]()
    var contentWidth: CGFloat = 0.0
```

```
    @IBOutlet weak var scrollView: UIScrollView**!

    override func viewDidLoad() {
        super.viewDidLoad()

        for x in 0...2 {
            let image = UIImage(named: "icon\(x).png")
            let imageView = UIImageView(image: image)
            images.append(imageView)

            var newX: CGFloat = 0.0

            newX = view.frame.midX + view.frame.size.width * CGFloat(x)

            contentWidth += newX

            scrollView.addSubview(imageView)

            imageView.frame = CGRect(x: newX - 75, y: (view.frame.size.height / 2)
- 75, width: 150, height: 150)
        }
    }
}
```

As you can see, we added a variable of type `CGFloat` called *contentWidth* and set it to equal `0.0`. Then, inside of the `for-in` loop we incremented it's value by `newX` each time the for loop runs. This creates enough space for a page for each image.

All we need to do now is to set the `contentSize` on our **UIScrollView** by adding a line of code beneath the `for-in` loop like so:

```
...
override func viewDidLoad() {
    super.viewDidLoad()

    for x in 0...2 {
        let image = UIImage(named: "icon\(x).png")
        let imageView = UIImageView(image: image)
        images.append(imageView)

        var newX: CGFloat = 0.0

        newX = view.frame.midX + view.frame.size.width * CGFloat(x)

        contentWidth += newX
```

```
    scrollView.addSubview(imageView)

        imageView.frame = CGRect(x: newX - 75, y: (view.frame.size.height / 2) -
75, width: 150, height: 150)
    }

    scrollView.contentSize = CGSize(width: contentWidth, height:
view.frame.size.height
}
```

Build and run the app to see how if our **UIScrollView** is now scrollable.

You should now be able to scroll from page to page seeing all three of our images snap nicely into place.

Wrapping up

At this point, you've learned all that you need to know about **UIScrollView** and I hope you can see how useful it can be to make accessing your content dynamic and fun in iOS apps.

Exercise

Currently, our app scrolls when we scroll on the UIScrollView. Extend this app by figuring out a way to make the entire screen page left and right instead of just being able to scroll on the UIImageView. *Hint:* Check out Chapter 23 for how to use UIGestureRecognizer in iOS.

Section 2 Project

Sweet! You made it through section 2 and now have a good understanding of the fundamentals of Swift! That wasn't so bad, right? Now let's put your skills to the test.

Requirements:

Task 1

1. Create a new Xcode project.

2. In the initial ViewController made in Main.storyboard, create a login screen similar to this:

   Hint: You will need to use `UIButton`, `UILabel`, `UIImageView`, and `UIStackView`.

3. Rename this initial ViewController to `LoginVC`.

4. In Interface Builder, drag on a UITabBarController which will act as our main app UI. Rename "Item 1" to say "Home" and "Item 2" to say "Settings".

5. Make the UITabBarController the "Initial ViewController" by dragging the arrow from LoginVC to be on top of the Tab Bar Controller until it turns blue like so:

6.) Create a new Cocoa Touch Class file by right-clicking on the project folder on the left-hand side of Xcode. It's class should be called "HomeVC" and it's subclass should be UIViewController. Be sure to delete the extra "ViewController" text it automatically adds in to the Class field. Click 'Next', click 'Create' and return to Main.storyboard. Click on the "Home" ViewController in the Tab Bar Controller and click the Identity Inspector. Set the identity of the "Class" to be "HomeVC" and press Enter.

7.) Drag a UITableView into HomeVC and drag a custom UITableViewCell inside. Create a custom cell like this Instagram-style post like so:

Sasha James
Sunny day in a wonderful place

This app will need to contain several photo posts. Our app will not be able to make posts, but will need to read from static data (for the purposes of this challenge). So, you will need to create a data model to store several posts. Create a data model to store:

* A Dictionary containing usernames (key) and posts (value).
* An Array of Photos (obtain nice free photos from pexels.com – no attribution required.)
* Use UIImage here
* The UIButtons don't need to actually do anything.

Helpful Hint:

Be a good programmer. Do your research, read back through the chapters in this section, and don't be afraid to reach out for help in the Devslopes chat or online. Struggling through this is the best way to learn and retain what you've learned. Good programmers are always seeking to learn and improve their practice.

Task 2

1. Open Terminal and `cd` into your Xcode project folder.

2. Create a new repository on Github.

3. If you haven't already, follow the guide in chapter 16 (Setting Up Github) to get your computer's SSH key on Github.

4. On your computer, from the Terminal app, initialize your project folder as a local Git repository.

5. Add all files and then make a commit with a message.

6. Add your SSH Github repository URL (click the clipboard button on Github) as a remote repository (remember: `git remote add`)

7. Pull from Github (which will merge any files you already have in that repo like README.md)

8. Push to Github

The End Result

If you refresh your repository on github.com you should see your project loaded up on your Github page.

SECTION 3 - Next Step iOS

Chapter 21: MyHood App

*A fun app to record images and details to be displayed in a table view. We will focus on saving and retrieving data using **UserDefaults**.*

What you will learn

- Use Table Views

- Store data and images with UserDefaults

- Style images

- Encode and decode data

Key Terms

- **UserDefaults**

- **TableView**

- **Table View Cell**

- **Protocol and Method**

- **Singleton**

- **Encode and Decode**

Resources

Download here: https://github.com/devslopes/book-assets/wiki

In this chapter, we are going to build an app called **MyHood**.
This is a fun little app that you can use to document your neighborhood (or with different

branding, anything really!) by taking pictures and adding descriptions. The images and descriptions will be saved to your apps **UserDefaults**, which is a way to permanently save data to your device, for as long as the app is installed. So lets get started!

Here is a sneak peek at the finished product!

Figure 3.1.0 (A & B)

Creating an Xcode project

Open Xcode and, from the File menu, select New and then New Project.
A new workspace window will appear, and a sheet will slide from its toolbar with several application templates to choose from. On the top, make sure to select iOS, and then look in the **Application** section.

From the choices that appear, select Single View Application and press the Next button (Figure 3.1.1).
(Note that Apple changes these templates and their names often. But it should be very similar to what is shown here.)

Figure 3.1.1

Then fill out the product name. I am calling mine **MyHood**.

You can select a Team and Organization Name. The organization identifier is usually in reverse DNS format. Make sure the language is Swift and select which devices you want your app to run on.

We'll keep it simple for this app and just do **iPhone**.

We do not need *Core Data*, *Unit* or *UI Tests* for this chapter, so you can leave those unchecked (Figure 3.1.2).

Figure 3.1.2

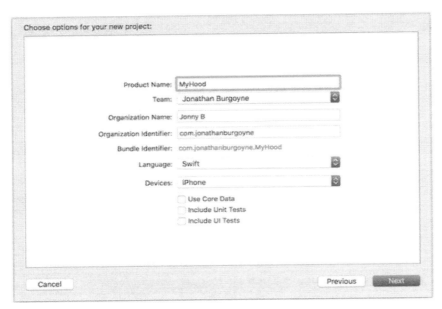

Finally choose a location for your app to be saved. I recommend checking the **Create Git repository** so that you can push your project to your Github (or Bitbucket) account and show off your awesome app to friends and potential employers!

Once the project loads, you will be looking at a brand new project that is just waiting to be turned into something great!

Getting started with the Data Model

We are going to start building our app now. And you can start with the data model or the user interface. Sometimes it makes more sense to do it one way or the other, but often its best to start with the data model. So that is what we are going to do here!

Now if you go back and reference the final product in Figure 3.1.0 (A & B) you see that we have a number of posts in a **TableView**, and each post has a Title, Description, and an Image.

Now, you would not normally save a bunch of images to your app using **UserDefaults**. **UserDefaults** is best used for a small amount of data, like setting your username and password. But because the purpose of this app is to learn about **UserDefaults**, we will be using it extensively to teach the principles involved with this class.

Also keep in mind, that what we are saving to **UserDefaults** for the image, is actually the `path` to the saved image on disc. So do keep in mind, that in the future when working with images and large amounts of data, you would want to use something like an online database or CoreData.

So, lets start on the data model. Right-click on your project and select 'New Group' and name that new group 'Model'. (Figure 3.1.4)

Figure 3.1.4

Then right-click on the **Model** folder and select `New File` This will open a new window as seen in Figure 3.1.5. Make sure `iOS` is selected at the top, and we want a `Swift File`. Select `Next`, then name the file `Post` and click `Create`. (Figure 3.1.6)

Figure 3.1.5

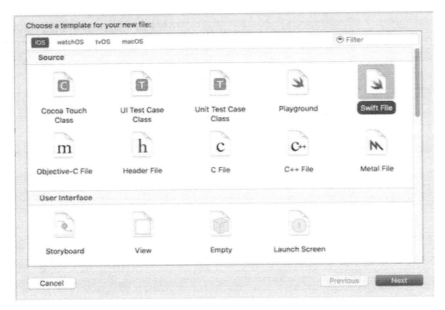

Figure 3.1.6

We just created the file that will become the custom class that will hold all the information displayed in each post in the table view.

Inside the `Post.swift` file, it should be empty save a lonely `import Foundation` line, so let's give it some company.

Remember, a custom class is like a blue print. So what do we want each post to be able to have? An image path, a description, and a title.

We will add those as private variables then create an initializer as follows.
We want every post to be required to have a title, description and an image, so we will include all three in the initializer.
Note that you should not use the reserved keyword **description** when naming properties, that is why we went with *postDesc*.

```swift
class Post {

    fileprivate var imagePath: String
    fileprivate var title: String
    fileprivate var postDesc: String

    init(imagePath: String, title: String, description: String) {
        self.imagePath = imagePath
        self.title = title
        self.postDesc = description
    }

}
```

Now when a new Post is initialized, the properties will be assigned the values that are passed into the initializer.

Now we can start on the UI, so hop on over to your `Main.storyboard` file.

User Interface

Referring back to Figure 3.1.0 A, we can see we will need a **TableView** to display the posts, and a View to contain the banner and navigation controls.
So go ahead and search for `uiview` in the **Object Library** and drag one to the top of your View Controller.
In the **Attributes Inspector** in the **Utilities** pane on the right, change the background color to any color you choose, but I will be using #2E87C3.
Then in the **Size Inspector** in the **Utilities** pane, change the height to **65**.

Figure 3.1.7

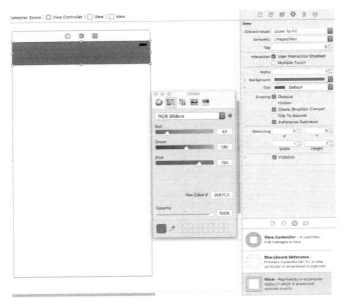

Now we will add constraints. With the **UIView** selected, click on the Pin button at the bottom right of the Storyboard.

Make sure Constrain to margins is not checked and set the left, top, and right constraints to 0.

Then set the height constraint to 65 by checking the Height box. Click Add Constraints.

Figure 3.1.8

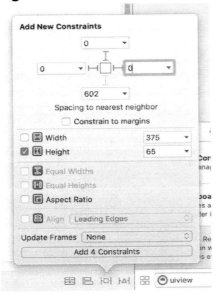

Now is as good a time as any to add our assets from the source code you downloaded earlier. Once you have the assets unzipped and in a folder, drag them into the Assets.xcassets folder.

Figure 3.1.9

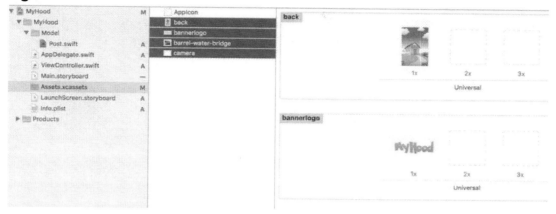

Now head back to the `Main.storyboard` file, and add an `Image View` to the blue View we added previously.

In the Attributes Inspector in the Utilities pan on the right, set the Image to `bannerlogo` and set the Content Mode to `Aspect Fit`.

Resize it to your liking. Then we will add our constraints.

Select the `Pin` button at the bottom right, and set the Width and Height constraints. Click `Add Constraints`.

Then select the `Align tool`, to the left of the `Pin` tool, and check `Horizontally in container` and `Vertically in container`.

This will align the banner image smack dab in the center of the View it is contained within. Figures 3.1.10 and 3.1.11

Figure 3.1.10

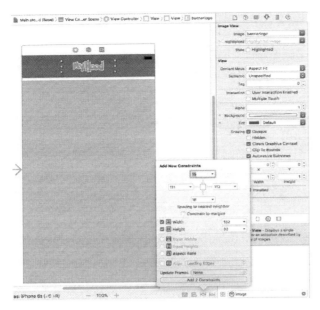

Figure 3.1.11

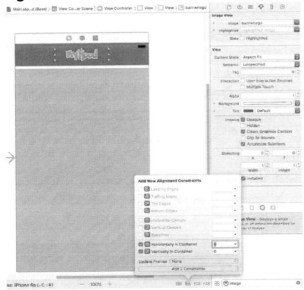

Next lets add the camera button. In the Object Library, search for *button*.
Then select and drag a button and place it in the top view on the right. In the Attributes
Inspector remove the default *Button* text, and change the Image to *camera*.
You will need to resize the button. I found 30 tall and 40 wide to be good.
Lastly lets add some constraints. Pin it 8 from the right, 8 from the bottom, and set the

258

width and height.

Figure 3.1.12

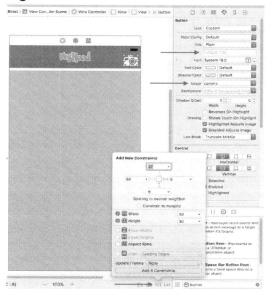

Next we need to add the **TableView**. In the object library search for **TableView**, and drag it into your view controller below your menu bar (which is what I will refer to the top blue view from now on).

Be sure not to grab a Table View Controller.
Add constraints and (with Constrain to Margins checked) pin it 0 from the left, 20 from the top, 0 from the right, and 20 from the bottom. Then press `Add Constraints`.

Figure 3.1.13

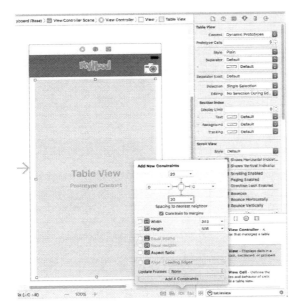

If, after you have added constraints, the element has orange dotted lines as seen below, this means that the constraints you added are different from what were previously displayed in the Storyboard.

So you need to update frames. This can be done by clicking the `Resolve Auto Layout Issues` button, and selecting `update frames`, or the keyboard shortcut `command + alt (option) + =`.

Figure 3.1.14

Now, we need to add a **Table View Cell**. In the Object Library, drag a **Table View Cell** into the table view. It will snap to the top of the **TableView** with the words 'Prototype Cells' above it.

Select the Content View under **TableView** in the View Controller Scene hierarchy and change the Background to blue.

This is just so that we can see the contents of the cell we are working with more easily, once we have all the elements inside it, we will change it back. At this point it should look like the contents of Figure 3.1.15.

Figure 3.1.15

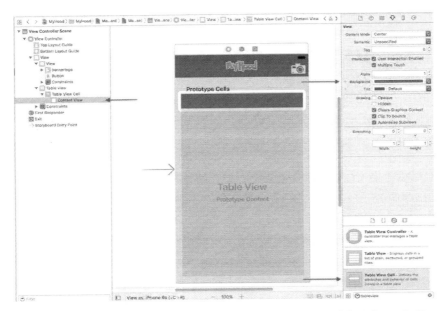

We need the cell to be a little bigger, so select the **Table View Cell** and in the size inspector make it 100.

Figure 3.1.16

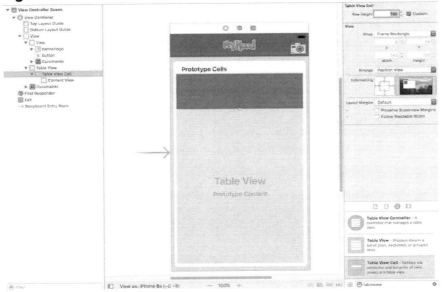

Now we can start adding our necessary elements. In each post, there is an image to the left and two labels to the right. So go ahead and add an Image View and two Labels as shown in Figure 3.1.17

Figure 3.1.17

Select the Image View, change the Image to one of the assets we added earlier which is 'barrel-water-bridge'.

This is just a place holder image for now. Set the Content Mode to `Aspect Fill` and check the box `Clip To Bounds`.

Then add constraints as follows, with `Constrain to margins` checked, pin it 0 from the top, left, and bottom and set the width to 83.

Figure 3.1.18

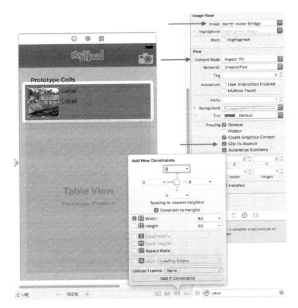

Now lets work with the labels. Select the top label and change the color to a Dark Gray Color, then select the `Font` and choose *Custom* and the Family of *Helvetica Neue* is good. Do the same thing with the second label, except make the style Light.

Design tip: Black text color is usually too black. It is better to go with a dark gray. And, when you have a header and text below it, you may think, "make the header bold and the text below regular". But it is actually better to make the header regular, and the text below light. That is why we made the second labels style = light.

Now add constraints. For the top one give the constraints of 8 from the left, 0 from the top, and 0 from the right, with `Constrain to margins` checked and set height = 20.

Figure 3.1.19

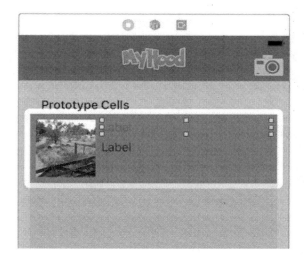

Figure 3.1.20

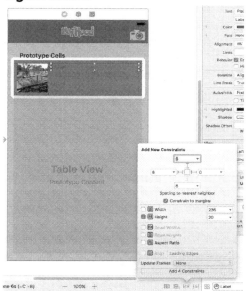

For the bottom label set the constraint with `Constrain to margins` checked 8 from the left, 8 from the top, 0 from the right, and 0 from the bottom.

Then set the number of "lines" to 3, and "Autoshrink" to *Minimum Font Size* set to 9.

This makes it so that if there is a long description, it wont truncate at first. It will shrink the font trying to fit the whole text until it gets down to font size 9, at which point it will finally truncate it.

Figure 3.1.21

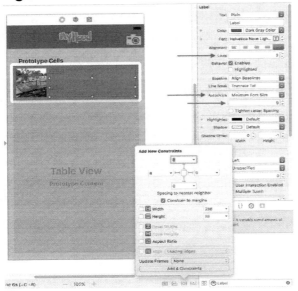

Lastly, remove the blue color from the Content View and change it back to Default.

Figure 3.1.22

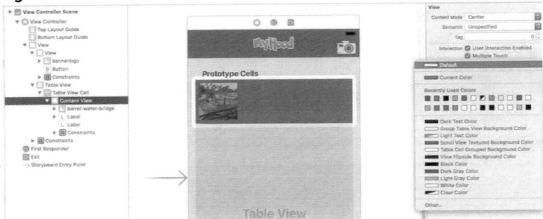

Working in the View Controller

Now what we need to do, is head into our `ViewController.swift` and start adding `IBOutlets` and `Delegates` so that we can work with the elements we just added to our

Storyboard.

First lets add the IBOutlet for the **TableView** by adding to the View Controller the following above viewDidLoad.

```
IBOutlet weak var tableView: UITableView!
```

You can also delete the didReceiveMemoryWarning function.

Then in your Storyboard, hook up the **TableView** to the IBOutlet by right-clicking View Controller and dragging from the **tableView** outlet to the **Table View** in the Storyboard. as shown in Figure 3.1.23

Figure 3.1.23

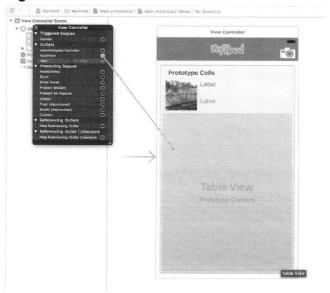

Now to work with the Table View in the View Controller, we need to add some **Protocols** and **Methods**.

A **Protocol** is used to declare a set of methods that a class adopts. It is a way of saying, "here is a set of behavior that is expected of an object in a given situation."

The **Methods** we implement then carries out the expected behavior.

So for a Table View we need to add two **Protocols** to the class of View Controller like this:

```
class ViewController: UIViewController, UITableViewDelegate, UITableViewDataSource
{
```

Once you have added those, you will have an error that says, "Type `ViewController` does not conform to protocol `UITableViewDataSource`".

So, we need to add some **methods** and other information. Go ahead and add to your viewDidLoad the following:

```swift
override func viewDidLoad() {
    super.viewDidLoad()
    tableView.delegate = self
    tableView.dataSource = self
}
```

Then we need to add the **methods**. Depending on the **protocol**, there are required and optional **methods**.

For **Table Views** we are required to provide information on how many rows there will be and a function to create the cells.

These methods look like the following:

```swift
func tableView(_ tableView: UITableView, cellForRowAt indexPath: IndexPath) ->
UITableViewCell {

    return UITableViewCell()
}

func tableView(_ tableView: UITableView, numberOfRowsInSection section: Int) ->
Int {

    return 10
}
```

So lets digest these two functions real quick. The first one you can get to autocomplete by typing "cellForRowAt" and the rest will pop up.

The second function you can get to autocomplete by typing "numberOfRowsInSection".

Now there are a number of optional **methods** that you can use besides these ones which implement further functionality.

For example - what happens when a cell is clicked on, or how many sections you want, or define cell size dynamically. But these two will be sufficient for us.

The first function is where we will initialize and display our custom Posts. For now I have a simple `return UITableViewCell()` to complete the function.

Later on we will be returning a custom cell that is initialized based on posts that are created and saved by the user.

268

The second function, manages how many rows there will be in the table view. I currently have it hard-coded at 10.

But what we really need is an array of type Post, and return the size of that array. So lets do that.

Below the `tableView IBOutlet`, declare a variable posts as follows:

```
var posts = [Post]()
```

and change the numberOfRowsInSection method to

```
    func tableView(_ tableView: UITableView, numberOfRowsInSection section: Int) ->
Int {
        return posts.count
    }
```

Now that you have the required **Methods** for the implemented **Protocols**, you will see that any errors have gone away.

Custom Cell

What we need to do now is create a custom class for the cell. If you look at the Storyboard, and the cell that we have our images and labels in, we need a way to communicate with those elements and have them update based on the data saved to our posts variable.

So to do that, we create a new group called *View*. (just like we did with Model in Figure 1.4). And then inside that group create a new file by right clicking on the group and select New `File`

Now this time, select `Cocoa Touch Class` and press `next`.

Then name it *PostCell* and make sure the subclass is `UITableViewCell`.

Then press `create`.

Figure 3.1.24

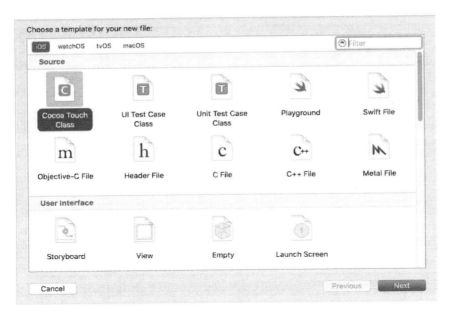

Figure 3.1.25

The PostCell file should open and look like this:

```swift
import UIKit

class PostCell: UITableViewCell {
```

```
    override func awakeFromNib() {
        super.awakeFromNib()
        // Initialization code
    }

    override func setSelected(_ selected: Bool, animated: Bool) {
        super.setSelected(selected, animated: animated)

        // Configure the view for the selected state
    }

}
```

You can go ahead and delete the `setSelected` function.

Now, this custom class is meant to communicate with the cell in Storyboard, so we need to add some `IBOutlets` as follows.

```
class PostCell: UITableViewCell {

    @IBOutlet weak var postImg: UIImageView!
    @IBOutlet weak var titleLbl: UILabel!
    @IBOutlet weak var descLbl: UILabel!

    override func awakeFromNib() {
        super.awakeFromNib()
        // Initialization code
    }
}
```

As you can see we have an outlet for the image, title, and description found in the Storyboard cell. Now lets go into Storyboard and hook those up the same way we did for the button.

But first we have to do something very important. And that is to change the Class of the **Table View Cell** to our newly created *PostCell*.
Do that by selecting the Cell in the hierarchy, then in the Identity Inspector click on the `Class` drop down and select our custom `PostCell` class.
Below that you will see Identifier, type in *PostCell* as seen in Figure 3.1.26.
This identifier will be used later to identify which cell to use when creating and displaying cells in the **Table View**.

Figure 3.1.26

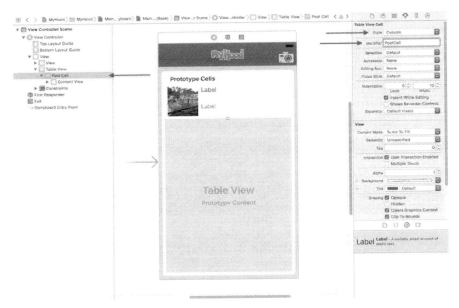

Right-click on PostCell and drag the outlet to its corresponding UI element as shown in Figure 3.1.27. Do this for each outlet we created in PostCell.

Figure 3.1.27

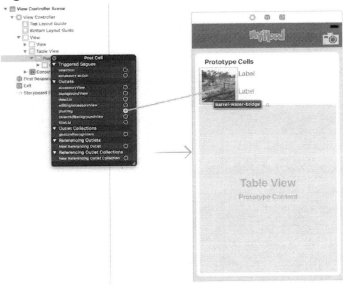

While we are in the Storyboard, lets go ahead and remove the **TableView** separators. Select the **TableView**, go to the Attributes Inspector, and go to Separator, select None.

Figure 3.1.28

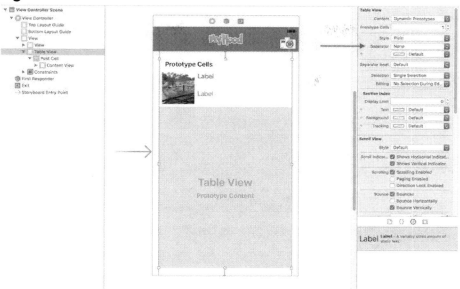

Now, we want to be able to configure a cell in the *PostCell* file.

To do that, we first need to modify the Post file. So head over to the Post file and make the following changes:

```
fileprivate var _imagePath: String!
fileprivate var _title: String!
fileprivate var _postDesc: String!

var imagePath: String {
    return _imagePath
}

var title: String {
    return _title
}

var postDesc: String {
    return _postDesc
}

init(imagePath: String, title: String, description: String) {
    self._imagePath = imagePath
    self._title = title
    self._postDesc = description
}
```

Lets talk about these changes real quick. The reason we made these changes is that when we first made this class, we made the properties private. Which is good practice because you don't want other files to be able to change these without special permissions.

However, we need to be able to have some way of accessing these properties, so we needed to create getters.

So we modified the declaration of the private variable by adding a _ to the front, then created getters for each. This practice is called "data encapsulation".

Now that we have our *getters*, or sometimes called *accessors*, we are able to go on to the next step.

Open your PostCell file, and add the following below the awakeFromNib function:

```
func configureCell(_ post: Post) {
    titleLbl.text = post.title
    descLbl.text = post.postDesc
}
```

This function takes in an object of type *Post* as a parameter. Then it sets the title and description labels that we set in the Storyboard, to the values of that specific post.

We aren't going to worry about the image for a while, it will just display our placeholder image we put in the Storyboard.

So where do we use this function? Lets go back to the ViewController file and update the cellForRowAt function to the following:

```
func tableView(_ tableView: UITableView, cellForRowAt indexPath: IndexPath) ->
UITableViewCell {

    let post = posts[indexPath.row]
    if let cell = tableView.dequeueReusableCell(withIdentifier: "PostCell") as?
PostCell {
        cell.configureCell(post)
        return cell
    }
    return PostCell()
}
```

Now lets run through this.

First we declare a constant post that is created from the posts array.

Next we grabbed the specific post that corresponds to the row that we are looking at in

274

the **TableView**. (That's what `IndexPath.row` refers too).

For example, if there are 10 entries in our posts array, there will be 10 rows in our table view, and each row corresponds exactly with its `IndexPath.row` property.

Then we are creating an *implicitly* unwrapped variable called `cell`, and setting it equal to `tableView.dequeueReusableCell(withIdentifier: "PostCell") as? PostCell`.

What is happening here, is with **TableViews**, they don't load all the data into cells. If you had thousands of posts in your posts array, that would crash the app.

So what it does is only load into memory as many as need to be shown on the screen at a time.

Then it will *dequeue* the cells as they go off the screen and push the new data into new cells as they come onto the screen.

We are also telling the **table view** which cell to use with the 'identifier' of `PostCell` that we added in Storyboard. And finally we cast it as a PostCell class.

We take that newly created cell, and we call the function we created in the PostCell `configureCell()` and pass in the post from the posts array that corresponds to that row. This will update the title, description, and eventually the image information that we created in the Storyboard.

Then we `return` the `cell`. Lastly, in the unlikely event that there is no *dequeued* cell available, we `return` an empty `PostCell()`.

Whew! I know that is a lot to take in and there are a lot of moving pieces here, so take some time and follow the bread crumbs to understand everything.

Now, we got everything set up, and we can run it, but we don't even have any data in our posts array, so lets just add some test data.

In `viewDidLoad`, add the following:

```
        let post = Post(imagePath: "", title: "Post 1", description: "Post 1
Description")
        let post2 = Post(imagePath: "", title: "Post 2", description: "I am the
second post. Yipeee!")
        let post3 = Post(imagePath: "", title: "Post 3", description: "I am the
most important post.")

        posts.append(post)
        posts.append(post2)
        posts.append(post3)
```

```
tableView.reloadData()
```

All we are doing here is creating three test entries of type Post, adding them to the posts array, and then reloading the Table View data.

You want to use `reloadData()` any time you make a change to your data, this notifies your table view that changes have been made so it will call your `cellForRow` and `numberOfRows` and any other **methods** related to table view and reload the Table View.

Run that now and make sure it is working. You should see the following:

Figure 3.1.29

Second View Controller

So we can see that it is working! Congratulations! You have done a lot so far, but now we need a way to add posts.

Lets create a second View Controller for that.

Create a new group in your project called *Controller*, by right clicking on the *MyHood* folder in the left pane and selecting New Group.

Then right click on the new group *Controller* and select New File select Cocoa Touch Class from iOS Source, then click Next.

Name it *AddPostVC* and set the subclass to UIViewController.

276

Figure 3.1.30

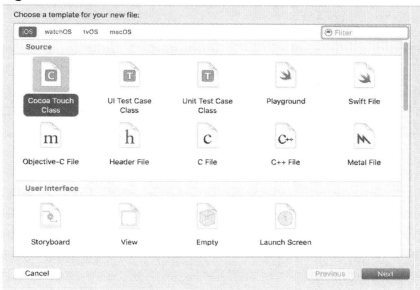

Figure 3.1.31

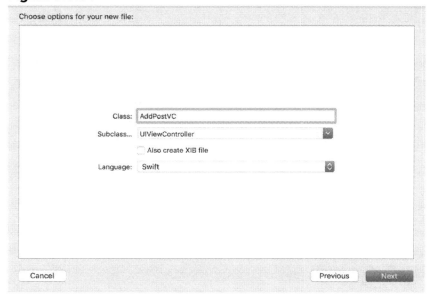

Delete the comments and `didReceiveMemoryWarning` function.

Before we begin building our second VC in Storyboard, lets revisit our finished product and remember what it looks like.

We have our menu bar at the top, an image, then two text fields, and a button.

Figure 3.1.0 B

Go to `Main.storyboard` and add a new View Controller by searching for **view controller** in the object library.

Drag it into the Storyboard next to our existing view controller.

Then set the Class to `AddPostVC` in the Identity Inspector.

Figure 3.1.32

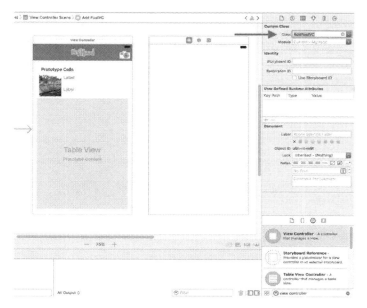

We can also add our segue from the first screen to the second screen by control dragging from our camera button to the new View Controller.

Select show then select the segue as it appears as an arrow connecting the two View Controllers, and name the segue *AddPostVC*.

Figure 3.1.33

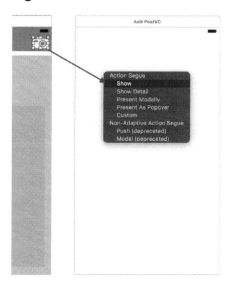

Figure 3.1.34

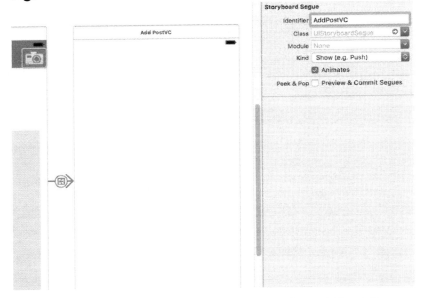

Now lets go ahead and add our menu bar to the *AddPostVC*.

This can be done by selecting the `MenuBar` view in the original VC, copying it with `cmd + c` , then selecting the new VC and pasting it with `cmd + v`.

Then drag it to the top, and pin it to the left, top, and right with the value of 0.

Figure 3.1.35

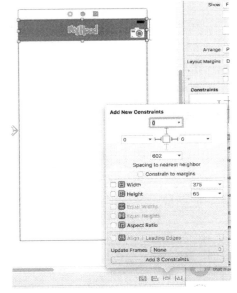

You can delete the Camera button and the banner image.
Add a label to the menu bar and set the text to "Make New Post".
Change the color to white, and change the font to *Helvetica Neue*.
Pin it 8 from the bottom, set the width and height, and center it.

Figure 3.1.36

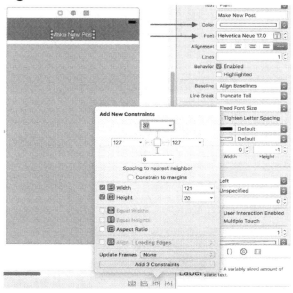

Figure 3.1.37

Next we need a button to cancel and go back to the original screen if we so choose. So drag a button to the left of the menu bar, and change the text to "Cancel", the color to white, and the font to *Helvetica Neue*.

Add constraints of 8 from the left, 8 from the bottom, and set width and height.

Figure 3.1.38

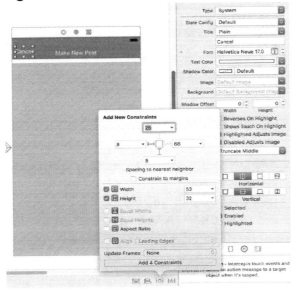

Next we need to add an image to the AddPostVC. Drag an Image View onto the screen and change the size to 240 x 240 in the size inspector.

Give it constraints of 35 from the top, set width and height, and center it horizontally in the container.

Figure 3.1.39

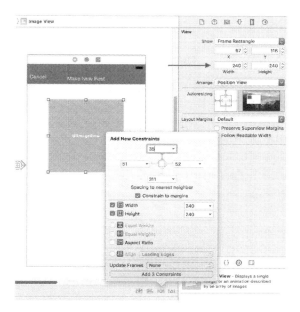

Figure 3.1.40

Go ahead and select the image, and set the image to our test image "barrel-water-bridge".

Set the Content Mode to Aspect Fill, and make sure the Clip To Bounds is checked in the Attributes Inspector.

This image is what we will click to add the images to be displayed in the Table View, so we need a way to click on it.

One way to do that is by taking a shortcut, and just add a button over the top of it that is the same size as the image.

Drag a new button onto the `AddPostVC` and make it the same size as the image, 240 x 240. Change the font to white, make the text say "+ Add Pic".

Next, select both the image and the button and in the `Pin toolbar`, select `Equal Widths` and `Equal Heights`.

Then in the Alignment tool bar select `Horizontal Center` and `Vertical Centers`.

Figure 3.1.41

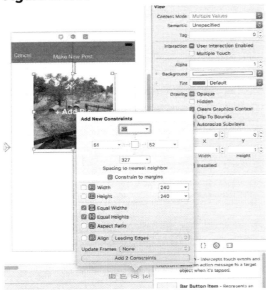

Figure 3.1.42

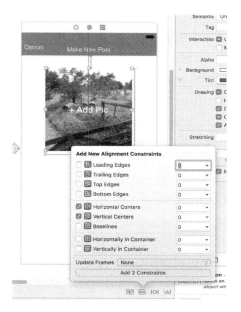

Now we need to add a couple text fields below the image so we can enter the Title and Description of our Post.

Add two text fields below the image as seen in the following figure.

Change the color to Dark Gray Color and change the font to *Helvetica Neue*.

Add a Placeholder text "Enter Title" for the top label and "Enter Description" for the bottom label.

Figure 3.1.43

For the top one, add constraints, pinning it 0 from the left, 20 from the top, and 0 from the right. Set height.

Figure 3.1.44

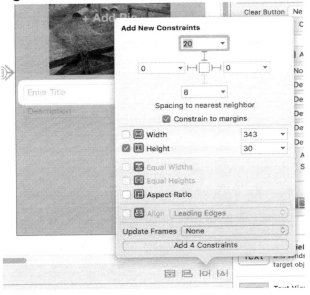

For the Description text field, add constraints, pinning it 0 from the left, 8 from the top, and 0 from the right. Set height.

Figure 3.1.45

Now we need a button that will make the post once the information is added. So drag in a new button below the text fields. Change the button text to 'Make Post', change the Text Color to White. Set the background to Blue. Add constraints as seen below, 8 from the top, set height, and width. Center horizontally.

Figure 3.1.46

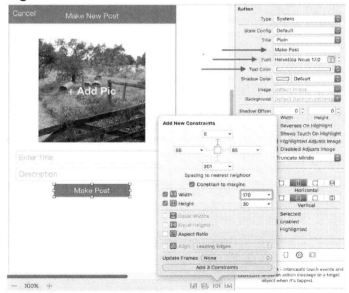

Figure 3.1.47

Now we are ready to get into some code and hook up these elements. Open the AddPostVC file and above the viewDidLoad() function add the following outlets.

```
@IBOutlet weak var titleField: UITextField!
@IBOutlet weak var postImg: UIImageView!
@IBOutlet weak var descField: UITextField!
```

then below the viewDidLoad() add the IBAction for the Make Post, AddPic, and Cancel buttons:

```
@IBAction func addPicBtnPressed(_ sender: UIButton) {

}

@IBAction func makePostBtnPressed(_ sender: UIButton) {

}

@IBAction func cancelBtnPressed(_ sender: UIButton) {

}
```

Now switch back to the Main.storyboard, right-click on the AddPostVC and drag from the outlets to the corresponding UI elements as seen in the below figures. When we hook up the IBActions for the Cancel, Make Post, and AddPic buttons, we also need to select the type of action, which is 'Touch Up Inside'.

Figure 3.1.48

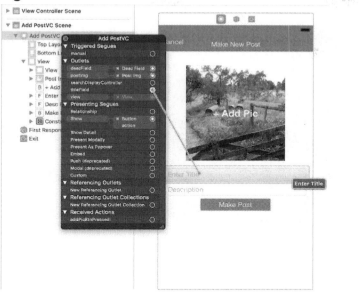

Figure 3.1.49

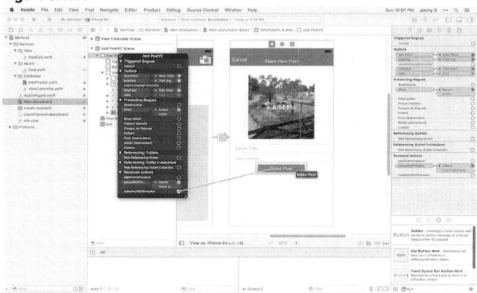

Figure 3.1.50

So at this point, you should have hooked up the Outlets for the postImg, titleField, and descField, and hooked up the IBActions for the addPic, Cancel, and Make Post buttons.

Now, real quick lets make it so that when we tap the + Add Pic button, it looks like the button goes away. We will do this by just removing the button text. So in the addPicBtnPressed function modify it to the following.

```
@IBAction func addPicBtnPressed(_ sender: UIButton) {
        sender.setTitle("", for: .normal)
    }
```

Next lets make it so when the cancel button is pressed, it takes us back to the initial screen. This is easy enough to do, simply modify that IBAction to the following:

```swift
@IBAction func cancelBtnPressed(_ sender: UIButton) {
        dismiss(animated: true, completion: nil)
    }
```

At this point, lets run it and make sure that we are able to click on the camera button in the first screen and segue to the second screen. Make sure when we click on the + Add Pic button in the second screen the button title disappears, and lastly make sure clicking on the Cancel button takes you back to the initial screen.

All right, hopefully that is working out just peachy for you!

Lets add a little styling to the main image on the second screen, and make it a circle. So in viewDidLoad() add the following:

```
postImg.layer.cornerRadius = 120
```

All we are doing here is setting the cornerRadius of the image to 120 which is one half the width of the image, effectively turning it into a circle.

At this point we can remove the test image from the Post Img Image View and instead set the Background to Light Gray Color.

Figure 3.1.51

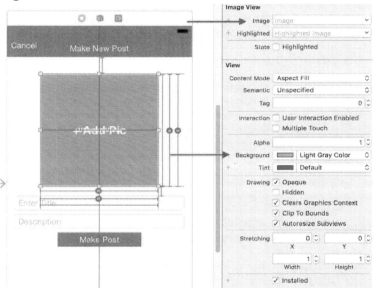

And when you run it, it should look like the following:

Figure 3.1.52

Now lets go ahead and add a little styling to the images in the table View. In the PostCell.swift file, in the awakeFromNib() function modify it to this. This gives the image in each post a nice rounded edge which looks nice.

```
override func awakeFromNib() {
        super.awakeFromNib()

        postImg.layer.cornerRadius = 15
    }
```

Adding UIImagePicker

Now we are going to write the code that will allow us to click on the AddPic button and select an image from our camera roll. This is done by means of a UIImagePickerController. Switch to AddPostVC.swift and under your IBOutlets, declare the following variable

```
    var imagePicker: UIImagePickerController!
```

Then in `viewDidLoad()` initialize it below everything else in that function:

```
        imagePicker = UIImagePickerController()
```

We also need to add a couple protocols that are required to work with the imagePicker, so modify your class as follows:

```
class AddPostVC: UIViewController, UIImagePickerControllerDelegate,
UINavigationControllerDelegate {
```

and just like we did with the Table View earlier, we need to add the delegate for the imagePicker in viewDidLoad() which should look like this at this point:

```
override func viewDidLoad() {
        super.viewDidLoad()

        postImg.layer.cornerRadius = 120
        imagePicker = UIImagePickerController()
        imagePicker.delegate = self

    }
```

Now we need to add a method as follows. You can add this to the bottom of the AddPostVC below the IBActions:

```
func imagePickerController(_ picker: UIImagePickerController,
didFinishPickingMediaWithInfo info: [String : Any]) {
        let selectedImage = info[UIImagePickerControllerOriginalImage] as! UIImage
        imagePicker.dismiss(animated: true, completion: nil)
        postImg.image = selectedImage

    }
```

What this function is doing is listening for when the imagePicker is presented, then when the user selects a picture, it takes that picture and assigns it to the constant `selectedImage` and casts it as a UIImage, then assigns that to the `postImg.image` so that it can be displayed and used later. Then it dismisses itself.

Then we need to present the imagePicker View Controller when the `addPicButton` is pressed:

```
@IBAction func addPicBtnPressed(_ sender: UIButton) {
        sender.setTitle("", for: .normal)
        present(imagePicker, animated: true, completion: nil)
    }
```

And lastly, before we can test this, we need to add a permissions to the `info.plist`. Open the `info.plist` from the left hand pane and in the last entry, when you hover over there should be a + sign that pops up.
Click on it and type **Privacy** and you should get some auto completed entries, and we

are looking for **Privacy - Photo Library Usage Description** then on the right there is space available to enter a message to the user why you would like to access their photos. Say something like "MyHood needs to access your photos."

Figure 3.1.53

Go ahead and run it, and verify that when you click the Add Pic button, you are asked to allow access to photos, then when you click a photo, it returns to the AddPostVC and the image you selected is now displayed as seen in following figure:

Figure 3.1.54

DataService

In our original View Controller file, we have our variable of `posts` array. But that is not globally accessible. So what we want to do is introduce a new data model called a **Singleton**, which is a single instance of data that is globally accessible.

So create a new group in your file tree, like we did with Model, View, and Controller, and inside that group, create a new `file` > select `Swift File` > and name it **DataService.swift**.

Once the file is opened modify it as follows:

```swift
import Foundation
import UIKit

class DataService {

    static let instance = DataService()

    private var _loadedPosts = [Post]()

    var loadedPosts: [Post] {
        return _loadedPosts
    }

    func savePosts() {

    }

    func loadPosts() {

    }

    func saveImageAndCreatePath(image: UIImage) {

    }

    func imageForPath(path: String) {

    }

    func addPost(post: Post) {

    }
```

```
}
```

And let's talk about what we got here. What we have done is laid the groundwork for the functions we will need to make this all work together. We have created and instantiated an instance of the `DataService`.

We have created a private array of posts, and created the getter for that array.
Then we have created empty functions for saving and loading posts, as well as saving images and creating the path for the image, a function to fetch that image given a path, and then finally a function to add posts that are created.

And as we move forward, each of these functions will get fleshed out. In fact we can start with the last `addPost` function.
Since we know that once we add a post, we will be adding it to the `_loadedPosts` array, then saving the posts, then reloading them, we can modify that function to be:

```
func addPost(post: Post) {
    _loadedPosts.append(post)
    savePosts()
    loadPosts()
}
```

Now those that may not do anything quite yet, but again we are laying the foundation.

Lets now work on the `savePosts()` function.
We are going to be using the **UserDefaults** class to save and load data, in conjunction with the `NSKeyedArchiver`.
So modify the `savePosts()` function as follows:

```
func savePosts() {
    let postsData = NSKeyedArchiver.archivedData(withRootObject: _loadedPosts)
    UserDefaults.standard.set(postsData, forKey: "posts")
    UserDefaults.standard.synchronize()
}
```

What we are doing here is taking the `_loadedPosts` array and using the `NSKeyedArchiver` class to transform that array into data.
Then we are using `UserDefaults` to save that data to a key we are calling "posts".
And finally, using `UserDefault` method called `synchronize()` to save the data to disc.

Next we can work on the `loadPosts()` function, so modify it as follows:

```
func loadPosts() {
    if let postsData = UserDefaults.standard.object(forKey: "posts") as? Data {
```

```
        if let postsArray = NSKeyedUnarchiver.unarchiveObject(with: postsData)
as? [Post] {
            _loadedPosts = postsArray
        }
    }
}
```

Here we are essentially reversing the process we took to save the posts.
First we are using **UserDefaults** to load the archived and saved data in the `savePosts()`
function, then un-archiving it and casting it to an array of type `Post`, then setting
`_loadedPosts` equal to that newly restored `postsArray`.

Now, we have a challenge to overcome. We can add a post, which will then save, and in
turn load the posts, however, there is currently no way of letting the Table View know
that there has been any change. So lets fix that.

First lets go into the AddPostVC.swift file and make it so we can actually make posts.
Modify the makePostBtnPressed action as follows:

```
    @IBAction func makePostBtnPressed(_ sender: UIButton) {
        if let title = titleField.text, let desc = descField.text, let img =
postImg.image {
            let post = Post(imagePath: "", title: title, description: desc)
            DataService.instance.addPost(post: post)
    dismiss(animated: true, completion: nil)
        }
    }
```

Lets break this down. First we have a string of `if let`'s to check that there is in fact
something inside each of the text fields and Image View.
Since we are requiring there to be an entry for each, the action will not continue if there
is not.
Then we create a post based on the input of the text fields (we are still not ready to test
images, so it is an empty string).
Then we call the `DataService.instance.addPost` function and pass into it the newly
created post. And remember that when the `addPost` function is called, that post is then
added to the `loadedPosts` array, and so are the `savePosts` and `loadPosts` functions.
Lastly we dismiss the view and return to the initial screen to see the **TableView**.

So now lets continue solving the problem of the Table View not knowing when a new
post has been added. We are going to solve this by using notifications.

Back in the `DataService.swift` file modify the `loadPosts()` function by adding:

```
func loadPosts() {
    if let postsData = UserDefaults.standard.object(forKey: "posts") as? Data {

        if let postsArray = NSKeyedUnarchiver.unarchiveObject(with: postsData)
as? [Post] {
            _loadedPosts = postsArray
        }
    }

    NotificationCenter.default.post(Notification(name:
Notification.Name(rawValue: "postsLoaded"), object: nil))
}
```

What we are doing here is using **Notification Center** to signal whenever this function is called. So it sends a signal out that posts have been loaded, and now we need to implement the listener in the `ViewController.swift` file that contains the Table View.

We can remove all the test data we used before as well as deleting var posts = [Post]() since we will be using the data from the singleton now. Modify the viewDidLoad() function as follows:

```
override func viewDidLoad() {
    super.viewDidLoad()
    tableView.delegate = self
    tableView.dataSource = self

    NotificationCenter.default.addObserver(self, selector:
#selector(ViewController.onPostsLoaded(_:)), name: NSNotification.Name(rawValue:
"postsLoaded"), object: nil)
}
```

We have deleted the test data, and added the **Notification Observer**.
This function is listening for the signal sent by the function we created just prior in the
`loadPosts()` function.
When it receives the signal, it will then call the function onPostsLoaded which we will create now. Below your other functions add:

```
func onPostsLoaded(_ notif: AnyObject) {
    tableView.reloadData()
}
```

This one is simple enough. Once the observer receives word that new posts have been loaded, it will call this function which will then reload the data.

We deleted the test data and the posts array we were using, so we need to change a couple functions as follows, swapping out `posts` for `DataService.instance.loadedPosts`:

```
func tableView(_ tableView: UITableView, cellForRowAt indexPath: IndexPath) ->
UITableViewCell {

    let post = DataService.instance.loadedPosts[indexPath.row]
    if let cell = tableView.dequeueReusableCell(withIdentifier: "PostCell") as?
PostCell {
        cell.configureCell(post)
        return cell
    }
    return PostCell()
}

func tableView(_ tableView: UITableView, numberOfRowsInSection section: Int) ->
Int {
    return DataService.instance.loadedPosts.count
}
```

The last thing we can do, before we test that our posts are being saved is prepare the **Post** class to be **encoded** and **decoded** by the Archiver and Un-archiver. Now, when using **UserDefaults**, you can save and retrieve simple objects very very easily. For example the following works right out of the box:

```
UserDefaults.standard.set("Jonny B", forKey: "userNameKey")

if let name = defaults.string(forKey: "userNameKey") {
        print(name)
}
```

No need to add any encoding or decoding. This works for Strings, integers, booleans, Double, Floats, and URLs.

```
let defaults = UserDefaults.standard
    defaults.set("Jonny B", forKey: "userNameKey")
    defaults.set(30, forKey: "age")
    defaults.set(true, forKey: "isAwesome")
    defaults.set("This is a string", forKey: "string")


    if let name = defaults.string(forKey: "userNameKey") {
        print(name)
    }
```

But when you want to save more complex data such as custom classes you have to be very explicit and tell **UserDefaults** how to **encode** and **decode** each property of the class. So that is what we are going to do next in the `Post.swift` file.

First off we have to modify the class to inherit from `NSObject` and `NScoding` as follows:

```
class Post: NSObject, NSCoding {
```

then after the initializer add the following:

```
override init() {

}

func encode(with aCoder: NSCoder) {
    aCoder.encode(self._imagePath, forKey: "imagePath")
    aCoder.encode(self._postDesc, forKey: "description")
    aCoder.encode(self._title, forKey: "title")
}

required convenience init?(coder aDecoder: NSCoder) {
    self.init()
    self._imagePath = aDecoder.decodeObject(forKey: "imagePath") as? String
    self._title = aDecoder.decodeObject(forKey: "title") as? String
    self._postDesc = aDecoder.decodeObject(forKey: "description") as? String
}
```

We are required to add that `override init`.
Then what we are doing is simply providing keys for each property to be encoded, then upon decoding explicitly stating what type of object they should be **decoded** to. It looks a little scary, but if you look at just one line at a time, its not too bad.

Now we are ready to test it out! Run it and make sure that you are able to add a picture, set title and description, then press **Make Post** and it should return to **TableView** and display the post you just made!

The image in the Table View isn't updated yet because we have not yet implemented that code, but we are getting there. And just to recap what is going on behind the scenes here, when we press **Make Post**, it is taking the information you input into the image, title, and description fields, creates a new post with that information, then calls the `DataService` function, `addPost()` which takes the new post, and adds it to the `loadedPosts` array in the `DataService`.

It then saves the entire `postsArray` which encodes the posts into data and saves it to a `UserDefault` key.

Then `loadPosts()` is called which retrieves the data that was just saved, un-archives it and turns it back into an array of usable posts, at which point we send a notification to the initial View Controller that the `loadedPosts` have been updated. So it should reload the **Table View** data.

Then we see the newly added posts! Whew! That is quite the rabbit hole eh?

Figure 3.1.55 and **Figure 3.1.56**

The last thing we have to do is get those images working!

Saving and retrieving images

I said earlier, that when I say we are saving an image to **UserDefaults**, what we are actually saving is a reference to the location of that image we save.

So we need a way to get the path to that image that we have saved. In the `DataService.swift` file, at the very bottom add this function:

```swift
func documentsPathForFileName(_ name: String) -> String {
    let paths = NSSearchPathForDirectoriesInDomains(.documentDirectory,
.userDomainMask, true)
    let fullPath = paths[0] as NSString
    return fullPath.appendingPathComponent(name)
}
```

You don't need to understand everything that is going on here, but basically we are passing in a file name and saying go into my file directory and return to me the path to that file.

Then we are appending that path string to the file name we passed in. So for example say I passed in `image001.png` into this function.

It goes and finds the path, then appends that path to my file name and returns `user/jonnyb/images/image001.png` (or whatever the path would look like).

Next we need to update the `saveImageAndCreatePath` function as follows:

```
func saveImageAndCreatePath(_ image: UIImage) -> String {
    let imgData = UIImagePNGRepresentation(image)
    let imgPath = "image\(Date.timeIntervalSinceReferenceDate).png"
    let fullPath = documentsPathForFileName(imgPath)
    try? imgData?.write(to: URL(fileURLWithPath: fullPath), options: [.atomic])
    return imgPath
}
```

Let's break it down. We pass into this function an actual image of type `UIImage`. We then turn that image into data. We create an image path and use the `Date.timeInterval` function to ensure that each time we save an image it will have a unique path name.

Then we pass that path into the `documentsPathForFileName` function we just created and use that path that is returned to write to disc the image data! Then we return the `imgPath`.

Now lets get ready to retrieve an image from storage by updating the `imageForPath` function as follows:

```
func imageForPath(_ path: String) -> UIImage? {
    let fullPath = documentsPathForFileName(path)
    let image = UIImage(named: fullPath)
    return image
}
```

In this function we are passing in a path and returning an actual `UIImage`. We get the `fullPath` by way of our `documentsPathForFileName` function and then create an image from the path, then return the image. Not too bad!

Now we are ready to modify our `makePostBtnPressed` action to work with images, so head on over to the `AddPostVC.swift` file and modify it as follows:

```
@IBAction func makePostBtnPressed(_ sender: UIButton) {
```

```
        if let title = titleField.text, let desc = descField.text, let img =
postImg.image {
            let imgPath = DataService.instance.saveImageAndCreatePath(img)
            let post = Post(imagePath: imgPath, title: title, description: desc)
            DataService.instance.addPost(post: post)
            dismiss(animated: true, completion: nil)
        }
    }
```

What we did here was create the variable `imgPath` and use the `saveImageAndCreatePath`
function in `DataService` which takes an image, turns that image into data, returns a String
that contains the path to that file.

Then we use that `imgPath` string in the initializer of our post to save the path.

Next we need to update the `configureCell()` function in the `PostCell` file so that when we
reload the data, the image in the cells load the saved image corresponding with each
cell. Modify the `configureCell` function as follows:

```
    func configureCell(_ post: Post) {
        titleLbl.text = post.title
        descLbl.text = post.postDesc
        postImg.image =          DataService.instance.imageForPath(post.imagePath)
    }
```

Here we are using the `imageForPath` function we created to take the `imagePath` we just
saved, and retrieving the data and turning it into a UIImage that will be displayed in the
Table View cell.

Finally, add one last thing to add to the `viewDidLoad()` function in `ViewController.swift`
file.
This is so that when we load the **TableView** we are loading the posts. Add this right
above the `NotificationCenter Observer`.

```
        DataService.instance.loadPosts()
    }
```

Wrapping up

And that's it! I know this was a bit of a journey, but look how much you have learned! You
know how to use **TableViews**, how to **encode** and **decode** data using **UserDefaults**,
how to use Notifications, and much more.

If things are still hazy I encourage you to go back over this and read through a few times to cement this knowledge. Way to go, give yourself a pat on the back and keep on learning.

Exercise

Now that you have learned about table views and segues, your exercise for this section is to make it so when you click on one of the table view entries, it takes you to a new view controller detail screen about that entry. Display the information and the picture in a larger format. Happy coding!

Chapter 22: Working with Maps - Park.ly Parking Spot Saver App

Apps using the iPhone's GPS capabilities help us get from place to place, give us to-the-minute traffic updates, and much more. In this chapter, we will build a useful tool which saves our parking spot on a map and gives us walking directions back to it.

What You Will Learn

- Using MKMapView

- Implementing MKMapViewDelegate Methods

- Creating the ParkingSpot Model Class

- Conforming to MKMapViewDelegate/CLLocationManagerDelegate with Extensions

- Using and adding MKAnnotation/MKAnnotationView/MKPinAnnotationView

- Creating a LocationService Singleton

Key Terms

- **MKMapViewDelegate**

- **CLLocationManagerDelegate**

- **Singleton**

Resources

Download here: https://github.com/devslopes/book-assets/wiki

If you're anything like me, the following scenario will sound familiar: You drive to the store, mall, or some other place. You go in and do whatever it is that you went there to do. When walking out to go home, you look around helplessly as you have forgotten where you parked. This can be a very frustrating event and I happen to forget where I've parked all the time.

We're going to build a nice little app in this chapter called *Park.ly* which will allow you to drop a pin on your location and tap on the pin to pull up GPS walking directions back to your car. The features of MapKit and MKMapView are many, and this chapter will cover the basics of using maps and location services in iOS.

Here is a screenshot showing you what this app will look like when we're done building it:

parkly-screenshots.png

Setting up

Creating a new Xcode project

First, open Xcode if you haven't already and click `Create New Project`. Click `Single View Application`. Click `Next`. Give your project a name like *Park.ly*. Below the name field, there

306

are a few drop down menus but for the sake of this chapter, you won't need to change any of them. Click `Next`. Choose somewhere to save this project file and click `Create` to save it. You should see a screen like the one in Figure 3.2.0.

Figure 3.2.0

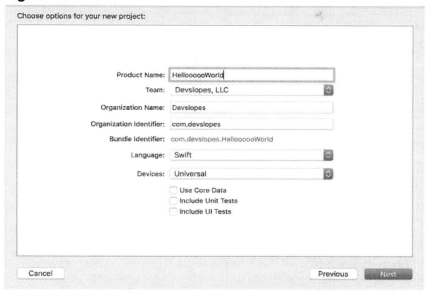

Building the User Interface

Click on `Main.storyboard` to open up Interface Builder. Next, download the assets for this project from the link above. Then, click on `Assets.xcassets` and drag all downloaded assets inside like in Figure 3.2.1:

Figure 3.2.1

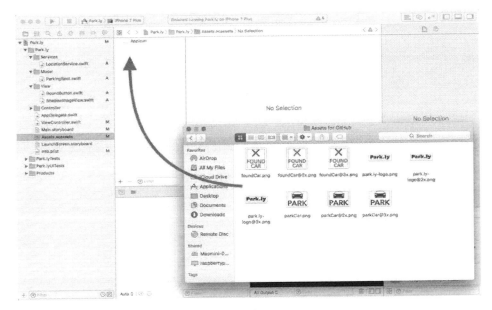

At this point, we're ready to dive in to the project.

Modifying Info.plist

What you are about to do doesn't have to be done first by any means, but it's a very small step that can easily be overlooked and will hinder your ability to use Maps in iOS, so I like to do this step from the beginning so that I don't forget down the road.

In the Project Navigator, you should see a list of your files. Click on Info.plist to open it and you should see a file like in Figure 3.2.2:

Figure 3.2.2

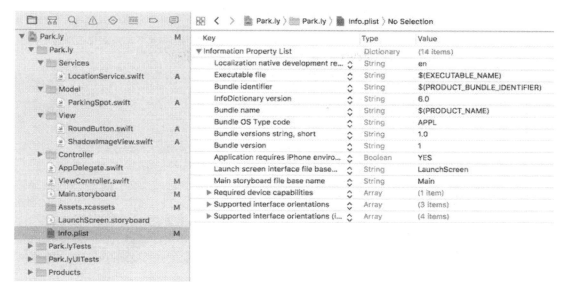

We need to add a row so right-click and then select Add Row from the drop-down menu (Figure 3.2.3):

Figure 3.2.3

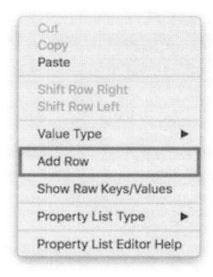

As soon as you've click Add Row, an editable field will appear as a new row in the column of other properties. We need to give permission for When In Use Maps usage. This means that our app will only be able to track our location when we're actively using the app. To do this, type `Privacy - Location When In Use Usage Description` and press `Enter`. What you will see is a new String property with no value. We need to give it a value now.

Helpful Hint:

MapKit, which we will be using in our app, has two usage capabilities: `When In Use` and `Always`. Think of an app like Google Maps as one that would use your location all the time since it monitors your location when you're using the app and when you request GPS directions. Even when you're phone is locked and you're not directly using Google Maps, it's still tracking your location to give you turn-by-turn directions.

Apple requires developers to give a reason for why they are requesting certain services such as access to the Photos library, Contacts, Touch ID, etc. We will type our reason as the value for the When In Use property we just added. Type a message similar to my example in Figure 3.2.4:

Figure 3.2.4

Application requires iPhone environment	↕	Boolean	YES
Launch screen interface file base name	↕	String	LaunchScreen
Main storyboard file base name	↕	String	Main
▶ Required device capabilities	↕	Array	(1 item)
▶ Supported interface orientations	↕	Array	(3 items)
▶ Supported interface orientations (iPad)	↕	Array	(4 items)
Privacy - Location When In Use Usage Description	↕ ⊖ ⊕	String	↕ We need your location to save parking pins. Thanks!

Press `Enter` to save that value. Now we've successfully added the required properties to Info.plist that our app needs to successfully use the MapKit framework. Let's move on to building our UI.

Building the Park.ly User Interface

Open up `Main.storyboard` from the Project Navigator and you will see a blank ViewController. Search for a UIButton from the Object Library in the bottom right (Figure 3.2.5):

Figure 3.2.5

Button - Intercepts touch events and
Button sends an action message to a target
object when it's tapped.

Drag a UIButton on to the ViewController from the Object Library and position it like so, giving it the following constraints (Figure 3.2.6/3.2.7):

Figure 3.2.6

Figure 3.2.7

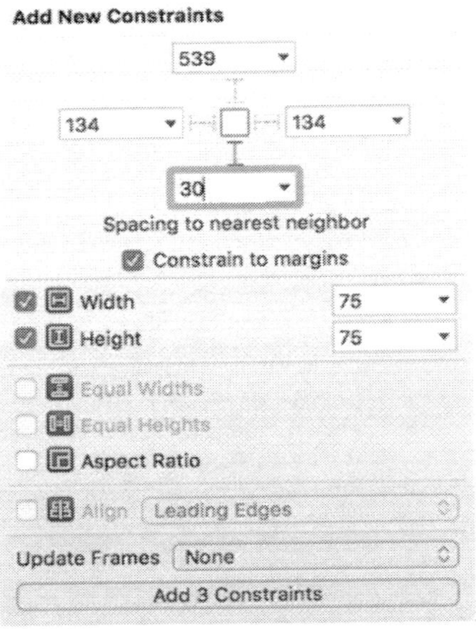

Add New Constraints

Next, with the UIButton still selected click the `Align` button ( ), select `Horizontally in Container`, and click `Add 1 Constraint`.

Open up the Attributes Inspector on the right-hand side of Xcode ( ) and click on the UIButton. We need to change our button to look like the design. First, delete the `Button` text from the text field beneath the `Title` property drop-down menu, then set the button `Image` property to `parkCar` and press `Enter`. Lastly, scroll down to the bottom of the Attributes Inspector panel and click `Background Color` and choose `White Color`. The background color is up to you, but white is what I thought looked best for constrasting the Map View.

Next up, we need to add a UIImageView to show the Park.ly logo. This is entirely optional, but I thought it looked nice. In the Object Library, search for UIImageView and drag one into our Storyboard just like we did with the UIButton.

Position it so that it looks the same as Figure 3.2.8. Use the handy snap guides in Interface Builder to position it equally from the left, right, and top.

Figure 3.2.8

Next, click on the UIImageView and ensure that the Attributes Inspector (⬦) is open on the left-hand side of the Xcode window. In the `Image` property box, type `park.ly-logo` and press `Enter` to confirm your selection. For the `Content Mode` property, change the mode to `Aspect Fit`.

Let's give the UIImageView some constraints. With the UIImageView selected, click the `Add New Constraints` button (▯) and give it the following constraints (Figure 3.2.9):

Figure 3.2.9

We are now at the last step of creating our UI – adding the Map View! In the Object Library, search for Map Kit View and you should see this result (Figure 3.2.11):

Figure 3.2.11

 Map Kit View - Displays maps and provides an embeddable interface to navigate map content.

Drag it onto the ViewController just like you would for a UIView or any other UI element however, we've run into an issue. If you try to drag the four corners of this Map View to the four corners of the ViewController, you will see that the Map View is currently covering up the logo and the button. We need to change that.

In the Document Outline, drag the Map View to be the top-most layer in the list of UI elements (Figure 3.2.12):

Figure 3.2.12

Now, click the Add New Constraints button () and pin the Map View to the top, bottom, left, and right like so (Figure 3.2.13):

Figure 3.2.13

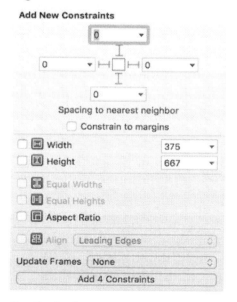

Finally, before we dive into the code we need to allow our Map View to show the User Location. Click the Map View and in the Attributes Inspector, tick the box labeled User

Location (Figure 3.2.14):

Figure 3.2.14

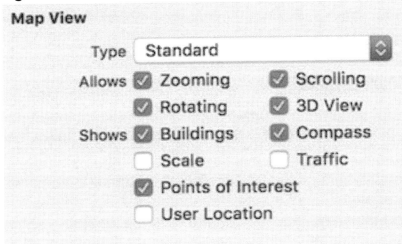

Excellent! Now we have a nice, simple User Interface for our app (Figure 3.2.15):

Figure 3.2.15

Custom UIButton/UIImageView Classes

Setting Up MVC Folders

In the completed app screenshot above, the Park Car button is circular and has a nice drop shadow. The Park.ly logo also has a drop shadow. We're going to make two quick, little subclasses to set up that view code.

First, we should set up our project with some folders. We will use standard Model-View-Controller setup by creating groups in Xcode for each of the three components by going into the Project Navigator on the left and then right-clicking on the yellow park.ly folder and selecting `New Group` (Figure 3.2.16):

Figure 3.2.16

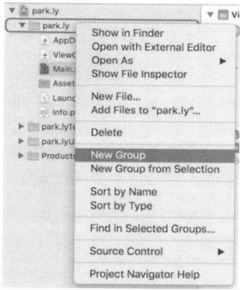

Edit the title to be `Controller` and press `Enter` to lock it in. Repeat that process for a `View` group and a `Model` group.

When finished your Project Navigator should look like Figure 3.2.17:

Figure 3.2.17

317

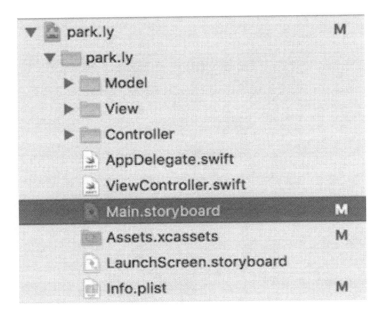

Creating Custom View Class Files

Right click on the View folder and click New File.... Click the iOS button at the top left of the window that came up and double-click Cocoa Touch Class. Name it RoundButton and in the Subclass of: field type UIButton. Ensure that Swift is selected for the language and click Next. The following pop-up window asks you where to save the file. Save it in the default location by clicking Create but make sure that the Park.ly box is ticked under Targets (Figure 3.2.18):

Figure 3.2.18

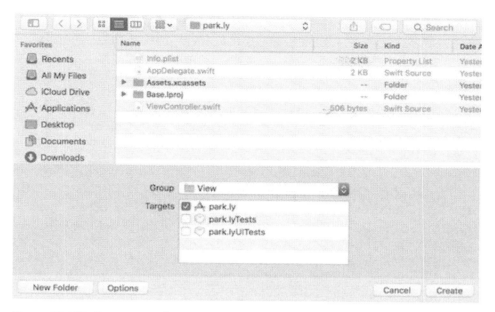

Open `RoundButton.swift` from within the `View` folder and delete the commented out code so that the `RoundButton` class is empty. To set up our custom round button, we only need to override one function and add a few lines of code.

Add the following code to override `awakeFromNib()`. Don't forget that you can use Xcode's speedy autocomplete feature to make this faster and easier.

```
class RoundButton: UIButton {
    override func awakeFromNib() {

    }
}
```

You may be wondering why we're overriding the default implementation of `awakeFromNib()`. According to Xcode's Quick Help: "*Typically, you implement awakeFromNib for objects that require additional set up that cannot be done at design time. For example, you might use this method to customize the default configuration of any controls to match user preferences or the values in other controls. You might also use it to restore individual controls to some previous state of your application.*"

Customizing the default controls is exactly what we want to do! So let's do it. Inside the `awakeFromNib()` function, we need to change a property called `cornerRadius`. We can use this to make rounded corners, but in our case we want a completely round button.

What we can do is we can set the corner radius to be half of the height of the button.

That means that the corners will be rounded perfectly to the middle. If our button was 50 pixels tall and we rounded each corner 25 pixels (half it's height), they would each meet in the middle making the button appear to be perfectly circular.

To set the cornerRadius property, add the following code to `awakeFromNib()`:

```
class RoundButton: UIButton {
    override func awakeFromNib() {
        self.layer.cornerRadius = self.frame.height / 2
    }
}
```

In that one line, we are setting the property `cornerRadius` to be the height of the button divided by 2. No matter what height we make our button in the future, now it will always be perfectly circular!

In order for our UIButton to use this code, we need to go set it to subclass `RoundButton`. To do this, click `Main.storyboard` and click on the UIButton at the bottom of the

ViewController. Click on the Identity Inspector (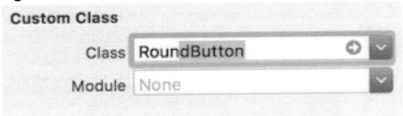) and in the `Class` field in the `Custom Class` section, type `RoundButton` and press `Enter` (Figure 3.2.19):

Figure 3.2.19

Testing and Fixing `ViewController.swift`

We should build and run the app to check if we were successful. Before we do that though, there's a tiny thing we need to do to keep our app from crashing. Since we're using a Map View from MapKit, we need to actually tell the ViewController how to handle that. So before we can run this app at all, we need to import `MapKit` in our ViewController.

Click `ViewController.swift` and add the following line of code:

```
import UIKit
import MapKit

class RoundButton: UIButton {
    override func awakeFromNib() {
        self.layer.cornerRadius = self.frame.height / 2
    }
}
```

And that's all we need at the moment to get our app running...for now. Click the triangular Build & Run button at the top left corner of Xcode (or press ⌘ + R) and wait for the app to open in Simulator.

You should see what I see in Figure 3.2.20 (your map may look different):

Figure 3.2.20

Great! So the our UIButton has been properly rounded. Now let's give it a nice pillowy drop shadow.

In RoundButton.swift add the following code to awakeFromNib():

```
override func awakeFromNib() {
    self.layer.cornerRadius = self.frame.height / 2
    self.layer.shadowRadius = 20
    self.layer.shadowOpacity = 0.5
    self.layer.shadowColor = UIColor.black.cgColor
```

}

After adding that code, `Build & Run` once more to check to see our beautiful view code in action (Figure 3.2.21):

Figure 3.2.21

Excellent. It's looking great so far. Believe it or not, the UI part of our app is complete.

> **For an extra challenge:** See if you can make a custom view class for UIImageView just like we did for UIButton and set the same code (be sure to delete the line of code changing the cornerRadius) inside of `awakeFromNib()`. Then go to
>
> `Main.storyboard` and set the custom class in the Identity Inspector ( ).

Setting Up A Data Model

For our app, we will be saving a location to a map, so we need to create a data model class which we will instantiate later on to create and save a location on our Map View. Let's dive in!

First, `right-click` the `Model` folder in the Project Outline. Click `New File...` and on the following window that pops up select `Cocoa Touch Class` from the iOS menu. Name it `ParkingSpot` and set it to subclass `NSObject`. Click `Finish` then `Create` to save it into your project. It will open automatically as you probably know by now.

You should see the following code inside ParkingSpot.swift:

```
import UIKit

class ParkingSpot: NSObject {

}
```

We haven't subclassed NSObject before and the reason we're doing that is because of MKAnnotation. According to Xcode's Quick Help, "The MKAnnotation protocol is used to provide annotation-related information to a map view." We will be using MKPinAnnotation later on to display the pin information on our map and the MKAnnotation to capture the location to help the pin know where it should drop and display itself on the map.

So, as you may have guessed, we need to inherit from MKAnnotation to use `ParkingSpot` on our Map View. We also need to import MapKit. Change the declaration of the ParkingSpot class to look like this:

```
import UIKit
import MapKit

class ParkingSpot: NSObject, MKAnnotation {

}
```

After doing this, you will immediately be shown an error. Xcode is warning you that you aren't conforming to the protocol `MKAnnotation` and you're not yet. Let's do that now. All we need to do is create three properties for the title, location name, and coordinate of the Map View annotation. Then we need to initialize them.

Add the following code to the ParkingSpot class:

```
class ParkingSpot: NSObject, MKAnnotation {
    let title: String?
    let locationName: String?
    let coordinate: CLLocationCoordinate2D

    init(title: String, locationName: String, coordinate: CLLocationCoordinate2D) {
        self.title = title
        self.locationName = locationName
        self.coordinate = coordinate
    }
```

}

As you can see in the code sample above, we create three constants. Two of these constants are optional and one is required. If you look deeper into MKAnnotation, you will see that it requires a coordinate value but it's title and subtitle are optional.

Then, we create an initializer function to initialize the values for `title`, `locationName`, and `coordinate` when an instance of ParkingSpot is created.

I just told you that MKAnnotation has an optional subtitle property, but how should we handle it? It's simple! We will just use a variable called `subtitle` and brackets to return `locationName` as it's value. This way we are actually setting the `subtitle` property of MKAnnotation and not creating a separate variable of the same name.

Do this like so:

```
...
class ParkingSpot: NSObject, MKAnnotation {
    let title: String?
    let locationName: String?
    let coordinate: CLLocationCoordinate2D

    init(title: String, locationName: String, coordinate: CLLocationCoordinate2D) {
        self.title = title
        self.locationName = locationName
        self.coordinate = coordinate
    }

    var subtitle: String? {
        return locationName
    }
}
```

The last thing we need to do before our data model is done is add a function that will pass in a coordinate (CLLocationCoordinate2D) and return an MKMapItem which encapsulates information about a specific point on a map. The function will set up that specific point for our function.

Write `import Contacts` beneath `import MapKit` at the top of `ParkingSpot.swift` and add the following code at the bottom, then I will break down what we wrote:

```
...
func mapItem(location: CLLocationCoordinate2D) -> MKMapItem {
    let addressDictionary = [String(CNPostalAddressStreetKey): subtitle]
    let placemark = MKPlacemark(coordinate: location, addressDictionary:
```

```
addressDictionary)

    let mapItem = MKMapItem(placemark: placemark)
    mapItem.name = title

    return mapItem
}
```

In this function, we pass in `location` as a CLLocationCoordinate2D. This is simply a GPS coordinate with a latitude and longitude property. Next, inside the function we declare a constant called `addressDictionary` which, as you probably guessed is a dictionary that holds addresses. Then we create `placemark` of type MKPlacemark. This takes in a coordinate (which we have) and an addressDictionary (which we also have) and creates specific point and connects it to a specific address. In our case, we won't be using an address but will be using a message describing the location name. Finally, we create `mapItem` which is of type MKMapItem and we pass in the `placemark` we created earlier. We set the `name` property of `mapItem` with the value of ParkingSpot's `title` property. Then, we return `mapItem`. Now when we instantiate ParkingSpot, we can call `mapItem(location:)` to create an MKMapItem for our Map View to understand. We will use it later so you can see how it's really used in context. We needed to import the Contacts framework so that we could access `CNPostalAddressStreetKey` which gives us a String value containing the street name.

And just like that, our data model is complete! We are now set to start in on programming our ViewController! Pat yourself on the back and give yourself (or your coding buddy) a high five!

Setting Up The ViewController

In the Project Navigator, click on ViewController.swift to open it in the code editor. We've already imported the MapKit framework, but there is one other key framework we need – `CoreLocation`. Update ViewController.swift to include CoreLocation and while you're at it, delete the boilerplate function `didReceiveMemoryWarning()`:

```
import UIKit
import MapKit
import CoreLocation

class ViewController: UIViewController {
```

```swift
    override func viewDidLoad() {
        super.viewDidLoad()
    }

}
```

Alright, so we can't interact with our ViewController without the proper @IBOutlets and @IBActions so let's switch over to `Main.storyboard` and set them up.

Once you've selected `Main.storyboard`, click the Assistant Editor (⊘⊘) button to open the code file associated with our ViewController. You should see a screen similar to mine in Figure 3.2.22:

Figure 3.2.22

Creating @IBOutlets/@IBActions

In order to interface with the elements in our UI, we need to create two @IBOutlets – one for UIButton and one for Map View.

You already know how to do this. Either `right-click` and drag from the UIButton to the code file and release above the `viewDidLoad()` function or manually type the @IBOutlet code and then drag from the little circle to the UIButton that is created to the left of your line of code like in Figure 3.2.23:

326

Figure 3.2.23

Now create an @IBOutlet for the MKMapView by doing the same thing you did for the UIButton. I named mine `mapView`.

Let's set up an @IBAction now for our UIButton so that we can drop pins on our map when we tap on it.

`Right-click` and drag from the UIButton to beneath `viewDidLoad()` and let go. Be sure to change @IBOutlet into @IBAction by clicking on the drop-down menu and changing the connection type. Name it something like `parkBtnWasPressed`. It's important to name your @IBActions descriptively relating to what is being done to trigger that action. We won't put any code inside of it yet, but soon enough we will.

Your code should look like this:

```swift
import UIKit
import MapKit
import CoreLocation

class ViewController: UIViewController {

    @IBOutlet weak var parkBtn: RoundButton!
    @IBOutlet weak var mapView: MKMapView!

    override func viewDidLoad() {
```

```
        super.viewDidLoad()

    }

    @IBAction func parkBtnWasPressed(_ sender: Any) {

    }
}
```

Excellent, so now you have @IBOutlets and an @IBAction! Let's carry on to the good stuff – getting our location!

Creating The LocationService Singleton

A **singleton** is one of my favorite things in programming. A **singleton** is actually a software design pattern that only allows a class to be instantiated with one object. This means that we can create one instance of a class and save information to it and use it throughout our class without needing to instantiate it.

We will use a **singleton** as a LocationService which will:

1.) Set up and configure a CLLocationManager to our liking.
2.) Manage our location and persistently update the coordinate property so our app can use our current GPS coordinate however and whenever we like.

We won't dive deep into detail about how **singletons** work or anything too complex, but you can certainly see how **singletons** work and imagine how useful they could be in your apps.

Let's begin by creating a new group and file in Xcode. `Right-click` on the yellow park.ly folder and click `New Group`. Name it `Services`. Then, `right-click` the Services folder and click `New File...`.

At this point, `double-click` on `Swift File` and name it `LocationService`. Click `Create` to save it.

Importing CoreLocation

Open `LocationService.swift` and directly beneath `import Foundation` add the line `import CoreLocation`. Now we can access all the fun location-related stuff we need!

Creating A Singleton Class

We will create the most simple of **singletons** first, then expand on it.

First, add the following class declaration to your Swift file:

```
class LocationService {
    static let instance = LocationService()
}
```

By declaring `instance` as `static` we are giving it the ability to "live" across the entire run of our app. Which is perfect if we want to be able to use the values in this class wherever and whenever we want. At the moment our **singleton** doesn't do anything, so let's give it some properties and methods.

First off, we need to have it inherit from NSObject and **CLLocationManagerDelegate**. Those are both needed when wanting to get a user's location because **CLLocationManagerDelegate** relies upon NSObject to work properly.

Add the following code:

```
class LocationService: NSObject, CLLocationManagerDelegate {
    static let instance = LocationService()
}
```

Next, we're going to add some variables – one which will manage our location and then other which we will save our current location to.

Add the following lines of code:

```
class LocationService: NSObject, CLLocationManagerDelegate {
    static let instance = LocationService()

    var locationManager = CLLocationManager()
    var currentLocation: CLLocationCoordinate2D?
}
```

The `locationManager` variable is instantiated and going to help us in managing our location. If you press press ⌘ and click on CLLocationManager, you can see all the fun location managing functions we can use! Our `currentLocation` variable is not yet instantiated, but it will be in a moment.

Overriding The Initializer

329

When we use this **singleton**, we want it to have certain properties saved like how our locationManager should work and set specific settings so that we don't have to write extra code in our ViewController. We can do this by overriding the initializer for the **singleton** class. We're going to set values for some properties of `locationManager` in addition to declaring the **singleton** as it's delegate.

Add this code to override the initializer:

```
class LocationService: NSObject, CLLocationManagerDelegate {
    static let instance = LocationService()

    var locationManager = CLLocationManager()
    var currentLocation: CLLocationCoordinate2D?

    override init () {
        super.init()
        self.locationManager.delegate = self
        self.locationManager.desiredAccuracy = kCLLocationAccuracyBest
        self.locationManager.distanceFilter = 50
        self.locationManager.startUpdatingLocation()
    }
}
```

So what did we just do? We told LocationService that when it is instantiated by `static let instance = LocationService()` to set the `locationManagers` delegate to be LocationService. Then we tell it what level of accuracy we'd like with `kCLLocationAccuracyBest`. We set a distance filter to tell CLLocationManager when it should update our location. We'll talk more about that one in a couple paragraphs. Finally, we tell our locationManager to start updating our location.

Now to finish this up, there is one delegate method we need to use to to update our location in our app and it is called `locationManager(manager:didUpdateLocations locations:)`.

Add it to the **singleton** class we just made:

```
class LocationService: NSObject, CLLocationManagerDelegate {
    static let instance = LocationService()

    var locationManager = CLLocationManager()
    var currentLocation: CLLocationCoordinate2D?

    override init () {
        super.init()
```

```
        self.locationManager.delegate = self
        self.locationManager.desiredAccuracy = kCLLocationAccuracyBest
        self.locationManager.distanceFilter = 50
        self.locationManager.startUpdatingLocation()
    }

    func locationManager(manager: CLLocationManager!, didUpdateLocations locations:
[AnyObject]!) {

    }
}
```

Awesome, now let's discuss what we will do with this. Earlier we set a property called `distanceFilter` to a value of 50. That means that every 50 meters CoreLocation will trigger a location update. We can use the delegate method we just added to run code every time our location is updated. Pretty cool!

All we need to do is save our current coordinates to our `currentLocation` variable and we're good to go.

To do that add in the following code:

```
...
func locationManager(manager: CLLocationManager!, didUpdateLocations locations:
[AnyObject]!) {
    self.currentLocation = locationManager.location?.coordinate
}
...
```

Beautiful. So now, whenever our location is updated and CLLocationManager notices, this function is called saving our GPS coordinates to our very own `currentLocation` variable. Once we've granted location services to our app (more on that later), we will be able to pull our GPS coordinates and use them whenever we want!

Let's move on to doing that. Click on `ViewController.swift` to open it up in the code editor.

Creating Our ParkingSpot

We will need to create a variable of type `ParkingSpot` so that whenever we tap our "Park" button, a pin annotation is made with our current location and dropped on the map appropriately. To do this write a single variable above `viewDidLoad()` like so:

```
var parkedCarAnnotation: ParkingSpot?
```

We will instantiate and it and set the `coordinate` property when the users location is updated, but that will be later on in this chapter.

Checking And Requesting Location Services

In order for us to actually get a user's location data to show up on the Map View, we need to request permission first. At the beggining of this chapter, we added a property to `Info.plist` with the message we will show when requesting location permissions, but now let's actually write the code to request it.

I wrote a function called `checkLocationAuthorizationStatus()` to put everything in to make my `viewDidLoad()` function look a little neater. Plus, I could reuse this elsewhere in this ViewController if I needed to.

Add the following function beneath the `@IBAction` called `parkBtnWasPressed`:

```
func checkLocationAuthorizationStatus() {
    if CLLocationManager.authorizationStatus() == .authorizedWhenInUse {
        mapView.showsUserLocation = true
        LocationService.instance.locationManager.delegate = self
        LocationService.instance.locationManager.desiredAccuracy =
kCLLocationAccuracyBest
        LocationService.instance.locationManager.startUpdatingLocation()
    } else {
        LocationService.instance.locationManager.requestWhenInUseAuthorization()
    }
}
```

This function will check to see if we are authorized for location services. If we are not, it will request "When In Use" authorization. If we are already authorized, it will show the users location on the Map View and tell our LocationService to start updating our location. In order for our app to work properly, we need to call this function from `viewDidLoad()` as well as set the delegate of our Map View.

In `viewDidLoad()` call the function you just wrote and set the delegate of `mapView` like so:

```
override func viewDidLoad() {
    super.viewDidLoad()
    mapView.delegate = self
    checkLocationAuthorizationStatus()
}
```

The delegate is `self` (referring to our ViewController) because, "a map view sends messages to its delegate regarding the loading of map data and changes in the portion of the map being displayed" according to Xcode's Quick Help. It makes sense that the delegate is set to be our ViewController because that is the thing that cares what is being displayed and how and when.

Creating A Function To Center MKMapView

When I was building this app for the first time, I thought it would be the best user experience if the users location was centered on the screen and it would be great on the code side to be able to center the map on the user's location at will.

To achieve this, you will write a little function which takes in a `location` property of type CLLocation (basically just a coordinate including longitude and latitude properties). Then you will create a coordinate region which tells the map what size it should zoom to. Then we set the region and it will animate automatically. MapKit gives us that for free.

First, we need to create a variable called `regionRadius`. This property will tell our function the length in meters (500) it should zoom in to on our map. You will see how it's used in a moment.

Add the following property beneath the @IBOutlets:

```
let regionRadius: CLLocationDistance = 500
```

Then, add the following function to the bottom of the ViewController class:

```
func centerMapOnLocation(location: CLLocation) {
    let coordinateRegion = MKCoordinateRegionMakeWithDistance(location.coordinate,
regionRadius * 2.0, regionRadius * 2.0)
    mapView.setRegion(coordinateRegion, animated: true)
}
```

As you can see the `coordinateRegion` property is created using the coordinates from the location we pass in (as a center coordinate), and two other values for longitudinal meters and latitudinal meters which are set using the `regionRadius` we created earlier with a value of 500 meters. Feel free to mess around with this value and tweak it to your liking.

Adding MKMapViewDelegate and

CLLocationManagerDelegate Extensions to ViewController

MKMapViewDelegate Extension

To get the functionality we want, we need to conform to **CLLocationManagerDelegate** and **MKMapViewDelegate**. We could add these to the end of our class declaration or for the purpose of writing clean code, we can create extensions of ViewController at the bottom of our code file which conform to the protocols we need.

Go to the bottom of ViewController.swift and beneath the closing brackets of the ViewController class add an extension of ViewController which conforms to **MKMapViewDelegate** like so:

```
...
extension ViewController: MKMapViewDelegate {


}
```

Now we can call some methods from **MKMapViewDelegate** that we need. First call mapView(mapView:viewFor annotation:) inside our extension like so:

```
extension ViewController: MKMapViewDelegate {
    func mapView(_ mapView: MKMapView, viewFor annotation: MKAnnotation) ->
MKAnnotationView? {
        if let annotation = annotation as? ParkingSpot {
            let identifier = "pin"
            var view: MKPinAnnotationView
            view = MKPinAnnotationView(annotation: annotation, reuseIdentifier:
identifier)
            view.canShowCallout = true
            view.animatesDrop = true
            view.pinTintColor = UIColor.orange
            view.calloutOffset = CGPoint(x: -8, y: -3)
            view.rightCalloutAccessoryView = UIButton.init(type: .detailDisclosure)
as UIView
            return view
        } else {
            return nil
        }
    }
}
```

We're doing a lot in the code above. First, we use an `if let` to create an annotation but only if it is of type `ParkingSpot`. We then set up an identifier ("pin"), create a `view` variable of type MKPinAnnotationView, and then proceed to set various settings and customizations. When we set `view.rightCalloutAccessoryView` we are telling our app that when we tap the pin, on the white pop-up that follows we want there to be a Detail Disclosure button on the right-hand side. You can see that in Figure 3.2.24 below. At the very end, we return `view` which is of type MKAnnotationView.

This function creates an MKAnnotationView which is the fancy codename for the view which holds the pin and the callout pop-up in the Apple Maps app. In the screenshot of our completed app above, this is what an MKAnnotationView looks like including the "callout" – the white view that pops up when tapping the pin.

Figure 3.2.24

Next, we need to handle what happens when we tap on the pin then tap on the Detail Disclosure button. We want it to copy the current location and send it to the Apple Maps app (bonus points if you can figure out how to send this to Google Maps instead).

To do this, we will add another delegate method of **MKMapViewDelegate** underneath the function we just wrote but still inside of the extension:

```
extension ViewController: MKMapViewDelegate {
    ...
    // Code redacted for space purposes
    ...
        func mapView(_ mapView: MKMapView, annotationView view: MKAnnotationView,
calloutAccessoryControlTapped control: UIControl) {
        let location = view.annotation as! ParkingSpot
        let launchOptions = [MKLaunchOptionsDirectionsModeKey:
MKLaunchOptionsDirectionsModeWalking]
        location.mapItem(location:
(parkedCarAnnotation?.coordinate)!).openInMaps(launchOptions: launchOptions)
    }
}
```

This function handles what happens when we tap on the Detail Disclosure button on the white pop-up view after tapping on the pin we drop.

We create a constant called `location` which we set with `view.annotation` and we downcast it with the type `ParkingSpot`. Then we create another constant called `launchOptions` which is a dictionary that MapKit uses to tell the Apple Maps app what type of directions we want to use. You can choose default, driving, walking, or transit. I used walking directions because most people will be walking to find their car. Finally, using the `mapItem()` function of `ParkingSpot`, we pass in our location from `parkedCarAnnotation` we created earlier and set it to open in Maps by calling the function `openInMaps(launchOptions:)` and passing in our dictionary of launch options. All this to send our location to the Maps app.

CLLocationManagerDelegate Extension

Now we will create an extension for **CLLocationManagerDelegate**. Beneath the closing brackets of the **MKMapViewDelegate** extension add the following extension:

```
extension ViewController: CLLocationManagerDelegate {

}
```

Inside, we are going to call one delegate method that is called when the user's location is updated. It is a perfect time to save our location to our LocationService **singleton** and also a perfect time to instantiate our `parkedCarAnnotation` and pass in our location so that we have an accurate pin drop every time.

Add the following code insite the **CLLocationManagerDelegate** extension:

```
func mapView(_ mapView: MKMapView, didUpdate userLocation: MKUserLocation) {
    centerMapOnLocation(location: CLLocation(latitude:
userLocation.coordinate.latitude, longitude: userLocation.coordinate.longitude))

    let locationServiceCoordinate =
LocationService.instance.locationManager.location!.coordinate

    parkedCarAnnotation = ParkingSpot(title: "My Parking Spot", locationName: "Tap
the 'i' for GPS", coordinate: CLLocationCoordinate2D(latitude:
locationServiceCoordinate.latitude , longitude:
locationServiceCoordinate.longitude))
}
```

In this function, we are first calling `centerMapOnLocation(location:)` and passing in the current user location (via `userLocation.coordinate.latitude/longitude`) provided to us by **CLLocationManagerDelegate**. Every time our location updates, the map will now center on our location.

Next, we create a constant called `locationServiceLocation` and set it to our LocationService **singleton** which is persistently managing our location and updating the `currentLocation` value with our current GPS coordinates. We use a variable like this so that we don't have to type `LocationService.instance.locationManager.location!.coordinate` twice as it's really lengthy.

Afterward, we set the value of `parkedCarAnnotation` to be of type ParkingSpot and we instantiated it with all the values it requires like a title, locationName, and latitude and longitude values which we take from `locationServiceCoordinate`.

For the `locationName` property I wrote "Tap the 'i' for GPS" which is what the Detail Disclosure button looks like. If the user taps on that it loads up the Maps app with GPS directions. We're using `locationName` as a subtitle for the MKAnnotation that shows up when tapping the pin.

Adding Code To Our @IBAction

Wait a minute! We haven't written any code to execute when our UIButton is pushed. Let's do that to ensure that our app actually does something.

Inside of the @IBAction named `parkBtnWasPressed` add the following code to check and see if there are any annotations in our `mapView`. If there are not, we will add an annotation to drop a pin on the map and change the UIButton's image to the red 'X' reading "FOUND CAR". If there are, we will remove it and set the UIButton's image back to the one with grey "PARK" text and the car icon. At the end, we center the map on the current user's location.

Add this code to the @IBAction `parkBtnWasPressed`:

```
@IBAction func parkBtnWasPressed(_ sender: Any) {
    if mapView.annotations.count == 1 {
        mapView.addAnnotation(parkedCarAnnotation!)
        parkBtn.setImage(UIImage(named: "foundCar.png"), for: .normal)
    } else {
        mapView.removeAnnotations(mapView.annotations)
```

```
        parkBtn.setImage(UIImage(named: "parkCar.png"), for: .normal)
    }
    centerMapOnLocation(location:
LocationService.instance.locationManager.location!)
}
```

If you're confused by why I checked to see if `mapView.annotations.count` was equal to 1, let me explain. When MKMapView is created, it stores a default annotation in an array of MKAnnotations. So when we start up the app, the array `mapView.annotations.count` is already equal to 1. Since that is the case, we call `addAnnotation` and pass in `parkedCarAnnotation`. Then we set the button image and center the Map View. At this point, `mapView.annotations.count` is equal to 2.

When we press the button again to delete the pin, we check the count of the `annotations` array and since it is not equal to 1, we enter the `else` block, remove any annotations in our mapView, and set the button image back to the default grey "PARK" image.

Building, Running, & Wrapping Up

At this point, you should be ready to build and run your app! Click the triangular `Build & Run` button or press ⌘ + R to see how we did.

The app should pop up, request location services, and then center in on your location. If you're not building to a physical device, ensure that you have a location set. To do this go up to the macOS Menu Bar when in Simulator, click `Debug` and scroll down to `Location`. Set one of the predefined locations like Apple or paste in an address of your own. You can also drop a pin and then set "City Bicycle Ride" or one of the other options to simulate the user's location moving on the screen.

MapKit is extremely useful and versatile. It can be used in a number of ways and we've just bnarely scratched the surface of what can be done. You also learned about and used **singletons** which wasn't neccessary but it definitely showed how they can be used and how useful they are!

Nicely done! This app introduced some new ideas and features of iOS you haven't used before. If you've made it thus far you should celebrate all the amazing learning you're doing. Keep it up!

Exercise

To extend this app, do your homework to enable this app to:

- Provide an option to open your parking spot pin in Google Maps and Apple Maps

- Utilize UserDefaults to save and retrieve the pin even if the app is quit or crashes

Chapter 23: AutoLayout Size Classes

AutoLayout is already an incredibly helpful tool in developing iOS apps, but the ability to use Size Classes will make it even more helpful for you as a developer.

What you will learn

- How to use AutoLayout size Classes

- Implementing device-specific features

Key Terms

- **Size Classes:** a way of configuring a user interface with device-specific features.

Resources

Download here: https://github.com/devslopes/book-assets/wiki

AutoLayout in Xcode is an amazing tool in regards to building apps that look beautiful on all screen sizes, but we can customize AutoLayout using **size classes** to make specific changes or UI decisions based on the screen size. Some things that look great on iPhone don't always look as great on an iPad (seriously, check out the Twitter app for iPad), but **size classes** allow us to fix this.

Creating a new Xcode project

To begin, open up Xcode and double-click `Single View Application` to create a new project. Name it something like `AutoLayoutSizeClasses` and save it anywhere.

Next, open up `Main.storyboard` and click on `View as: iPhone xx (wC hR)` (Figure 3.4.1) at the bottom of the window. `wC` means "Width: Compact" and `hR` means "Height: Regular".

Figure 3.4.1

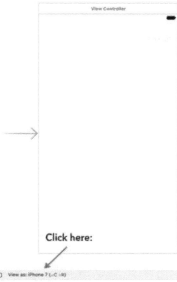

Click here:

View as: iPhone 7 (-C -R)

Note that the initial device loaded in Xcode is an iPhone 7 in Portrait mode which has a width skinner than it's height – therefore it's width is compact. It's height is considered "regular" because it is in Portrait orientation. If we rotated the device, it's height would then be compact.

What you will see pop up at the bottom of the window are the different screen sizes an iOS device can have (Figure 3.4.2):

Figure 3.4.2

We will talk about these in a moment, but for now let's place some things on our ViewController so we can later modify them for different screen sizes.

Adding items & constraints to ViewController

Review of AutoLayout

Drag a `UIView` onto your ViewController into the top left corner (Figure 3.4.3), set a custom background color, Click the Pin button (Screen Shot 2016-10-07 at 8.45.13 PM.png) and give it the following constraints (Figure 3.4.4):

Figure 3.4.3

Figure 3.4.4

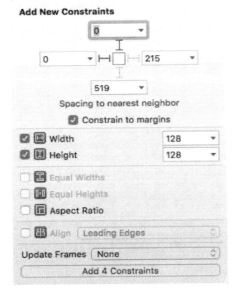

Now, if you click on one of the device options at the bottom, you can see what it looks like on different screen sizes. In Xcode 7, you used to have to go to the Assistant Editor and use the Preview feature to see differing screen sizes. In Xcode 8, you no longer need to do that. What you see in Interface Builder is what you get in the Simulator.

Click through the different screen sizes and see that our purple view maintains the same size and position.

Using AutoLayout is nothing new at this point in the book, but we needed to set up an example for using **size classes**. Let's do that now.

Using Size Classes in Interface Builder

Click the landscape orientation button at the bottom of the screen to rotate our device in Interface Builder (Figure 3.4.5):

Figure 3.4.5

If you look closely, you will see that now our iPhone has a compact width and compact height (Figure 3.4.6):

Figure 3.4.6

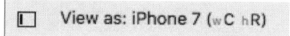

We will use **size classes** to change our UIView based on the width of the device. Click the Vary for Traits button and tick the Width box (Figure 3.4.7):

Figure 3.4.7

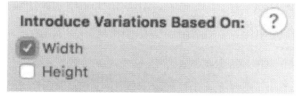

Now anything that we change will affect the devices and orientations shown in blue (Figure 3.4.8):

Figure 3.4.8

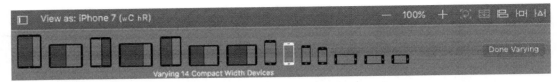
Click on the landscape-oriented iPhone 7 and select the UIView in the ViewController.

Make sure that the Size Inspector (⬚) is selected and double-click on the Width Equals: constraint to edit it.

You now should be able to see a list of properties all relating to our width constraint (Figure 3.4.9):

Figure 3.4.9

Width Constraint	
First Item	View.Width
Relation	Equal
Constant	128
Priority	1000
Identifier	Identifier
Placeholder	☐ Remove at build time
	☑ Installed

There is a little plus sign (+) next to the 'Constant' property. We want to change this value so that our UIView will be wider when the screen is wider. Click the plus sign and set both the width and height drop-downs to be 'Compact' (Figure 3.4.10). Leave 'Gamut' alone as we don't need to change that. Click Add Variation.

Figure 3.4.10

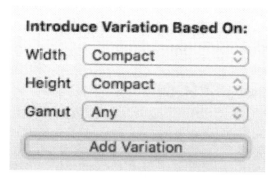

Introduce Variation Based On:

Width [Compact ◇]

Height [Compact ◇]

Gamut [Any ◇]

[Add Variation]

Now we have two 'Constant' properties that we can modify. One is named 'wC hC' and affects our UIView **only** when it's width and height are both compact. The other is just named 'Constant' and affects it in every other circumstance. Change the value of 'wC hC' from 128 to 300. See how it changes in Interface Builder (Figure 3.4.11)!

Figure 3.4.11

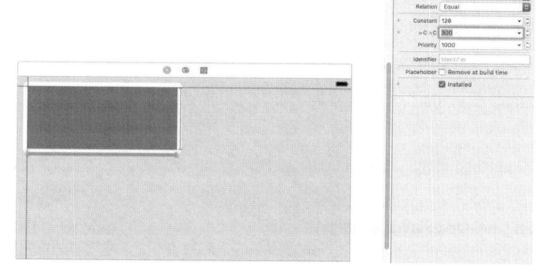

Here is where the magic happens...   Click on the Portrait-oriented iPhone at the bottom of the window. Notice that the UIView is back in it's original form of being a square. Why the change?

Well, the iPhone now has a compact width and regular height. We have it set to stretch to a width of 300 only when **both** the width and height are compact! So cool!

To finish up this example, click 'Done Varying' on the blue Size Class menu at the bottom of the window): Done Varying

A note about iPad and iPhone 7 Plus

If you were to switch devices to an iPad, you probably noticed that the height and width are both regular. The iPhone 7 Plus is different in landscape mode than any other iPhone because it has a bigger screen size.

Here is a helpful table to help you remember it all:

	Vertical Size Class	Horizontal Size Class
iPad Portrait	Regular	Regular
iPad Landscape	Regular	Regular
iPhone Portrait	Regular	Compact
iPhone Landscape	Compact	Compact
iPhone 7 Plus Landscape	Compact	Regular

These devices can sometimes cause headaches when trying to get your UI to look nice on both iPad and iPhone. Knowing what size classes to use is definitely a step in the right direction!

A more useful example

Now that we've used **size classes** to make changes depending on the screen width, let's make something a little more useful.

Setting up the UI

Select and delete the UIView that we've been modifying so that we have a blank ViewController once again. Drag on a UITableView and position it so that it fits in the

346

ViewController like so (Figure 3.4.12):

Figure 3.4.12

Click the Pin button (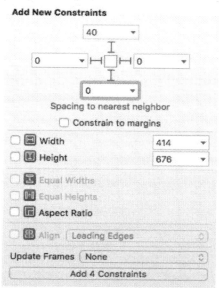) and give the UITableView the following constraints:

Drag in a UITableViewCell so that we aren't just looking at a grey box that says 'Table View' and afterward drag on a UIView to act as a banner bar at the top of our app. Give it a background color to set it apart from the UITableView. (Figure 3.4.13):

Figure 3.4.13

Click on the UIView you just made and click the Pin button (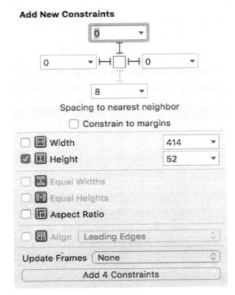) to give it the following constraints (Figure 3.4.14):

Figure 3.4.14

We pinned it to the top, left, and right sides of our screen and gave it a fixed height of 52.

Modifying the UI for iPad

Our banner's height is great for an iPhone-sized device, but on an iPad it looks a bit too skinny (you can check if you want by clicking on the iPad at the bottom of the screen). Let's make it so that when we're using an iPad, the banner is a bit taller.

Click on the UIView banner, then click `Vary for Traits` at the bottom of the Xcode window. We want to introduce variations based on height, so tick the 'Height' box (Figure 3.4.15):

Figure 3.4.15

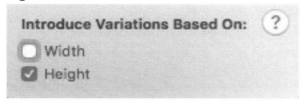

To change the height based on the device we're using, click on the Size Inspector (⬚) in the top right-hand side of the Xcode window and double-click on our `Height Equals:` constraint.

Just like before, we're going to click the plus sign button (+) next to the `Constant` property and on the following pop-up, select `Regular` for both height and width (Figure 3.4.16).
Again, leave `Gamut` alone. Click `Add Variation` and notice how there is a new field beneath `Constant` where we can customize the height of our UIView as the device we're using has a regular height and width (i.e. iPads of all shapes and sizes).

Figure 3.4.16

Introduce Variation Based On:

Width [Regular ⌄]

Height [Regular ⌄]

Gamut [Any ⌄]

[Add Variation]

Set the value of the wR hR field to be something taller than 52, like 100. Press Enter to set that value. Next, click on one of the iPads at the bottom of the screen and see if the height of our UIView changes.

Alas! It works! Your iPad view in Interface Builder should look similar to mine in Figure 3.4.17:

Figure 3.4.17

Click 'Done Varying' to end changing our variation and then click on the iPhone 7 to switch back to an iPhone screen size.

Adding a label to a UIView

350

Drag on a UILabel and position it at the top and in the center of our colorful banner UIView at the top of our screen (Figure 3.4.18). I gave mine a custom font and set the label to be centered:

Figure 3.4.18

Next, we need to add some constraints to keep the UILabel where we want it. Click on the UILabel then click the Pin button (⊡) to add the following constraints (Figure 3.4.19):

Figure 3.4.19

Add New Constraints

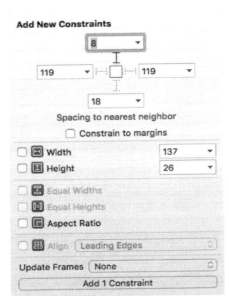

Spacing to nearest neighbor

☐ Constrain to margins

| ☐ ▣ Width | 137 ▾ |
| ☐ ▣ Height | 26 ▾ |

☐ ▦ Equal Widths
☐ ▦ Equal Heights
☐ ▣ Aspect Ratio

☐ ▦ Align [Leading Edges ⌄]

Update Frames [None ⌄]

[Add 1 Constraint]

Afterward, we need to make sure that our label stays centered. To do this, click the `Align`

button () and tick the 'Horizontally in Container' box. Click 'Add 1 Constraint'.

Now our label is staying put. But what if on iPad, we wanted the font size to be bigger. It looks pretty silly at the moment being so small. See what I mean in Figure 3.4.20:

Figure 3.4.20

Let's change the font so it is larger on a larger device. Click on the UILabel and ensure that the Attributes Inspector (⬇) is selected.

To change the font size on iPad, we don't even need to click the 'Vary for Traits' button but instead we can click the plus sign (+) to the left of the 'Font' property in Xcode (Figure 3.4.21):

Figure 3.4.21

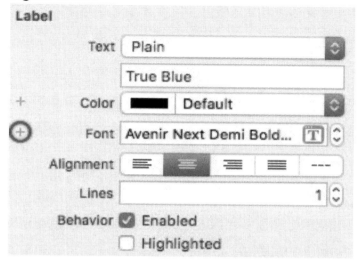

On the pop-up, choose 'Regular' for both width and height. Leave 'Gamut' alone again. Click 'Add Variation' to add our font variation.

Now, we see a duplicate font selector beneath the standard one named wR hR meaning "Width: Regular" and "Height: Regular". If we change the font size on wR hR, it will only affect iPad. Try it out and bump the font size up to 30 (Figure 3.4.22):

Figure 3.4.22

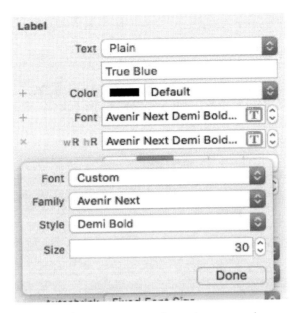

Now the font size is much easier to read on an iPad screen:

Before

True Blue

After

True Blue

Showing/Hiding elements on different devices

Another cool thing we can do is create a label for some subtitle text beneath our app name 'True Blue' and have it show up on iPad but leave it out of the iPhone interface.

To do this click on the iPad in the Device menu at the bottom of the window. Drag on a UILabel beneath the other label already on the screen. Position it like so (Figure 3.4.23):

Figure 3.4.23

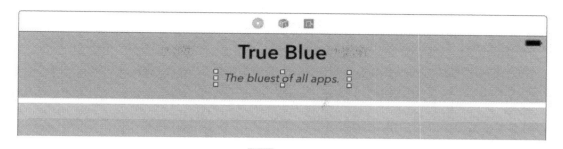

Click on the label, click the Pin button (⊡), and add the following constraints (Figure 3.4.24):

Figure 3.4.24

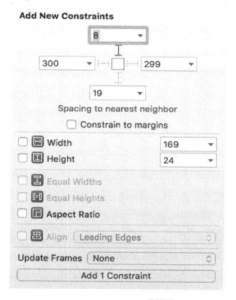

Click the Align button (⊟) and add the following constraints (Figure 3.4.25):

Figure 3.4.25

Add New Alignment Constraints

- ☐ ⊞ Leading Edges ▾
- ☐ ⊟ Trailing Edges ▾
- ☐ ⊡ Top Edges ▾
- ☐ ⊡ Bottom Edges ▾

- ☐ ⊞ Horizontal Centers ▾
- ☐ ⊞ Vertical Centers ▾
- ☐ ⊞ Baselines ▾

- ☑ ⊞ Horizontally in Container `0` ▾
- ☐ ⊞ Vertically in Container `0` ▾

Update Frames [None ⌄]

[Add 1 Constraint]

Now, this looks fine and dandy on an iPad, but what does it look like on an iPhone? Click on an iPhone model in the Device menu to check (Figure 3.4.26):

Figure 3.4.26

Yikes. That's not what we're looking for. We need to set our label to show on iPad only, so click on an iPad in the device menu again. Then click on the subtitle label if it isn't

356

selected anymore.

In the Attributes Inspector, scroll down to the very bottom. You should see a tick-box named 'Installed'. Click the plus sign (+) to add a variation for regular height and regular width just like before.

You should now see two tick-boxes – both labeled 'Installed' but one with an extra label saying wR hR. Leave that box ticked, but untick the default box (Figure 3.4.27). This is basically saying that we want this label only to show on iPads, but everywhere else it shouldn't even be loaded.

Figure 3.4.27

Let's go check to see if the subtitle label has been removed from our iPhone. Click on any iPhone from the Device menu at the bottom of the window. You should see the same result as Figure 3.4.28 which means that it worked!

Figure 3.4.28

Wrapping up

This chapter contained a few basic examples of how **size classes** work together with AutoLayout to make building user interfaces for multiple devices and screen sizes even easier. We learned how to make changes to our UI determined by screen height or width. We showed a subtitle label on iPads but not on iPhone screens. We made our banner talled on iPad screens as well.

Being able to make our UI this flexible is a very powerful advantage Apple has over other platforms of development. I'm sure you can see how useful this could be when designing full-fledged apps.

The best apps are made by developers who are attentive to detail and care about how the app is experienced on iPhone and iPad. If you're able to make an app that tailors to both devices, your app will be way ahead of many other apps out there now.

Exercise

Extend this app by adding a + button to the upper right-hand corner of our app as if we were to add a post or image to our imaginary app. Give it some constraints to keep it in place. Switch to an iPad in Interface Builder and add in some more buttons to the left of the + button. Set them so that they are only installed on an iPad device with a regular height and regular width.

Chapter 24: Working with Gestures - Tanstagram

Create an app with tangram shapes that can expand, shrink, pan around the screen, and rotate. You will also be able to save your shape configurations as an image to your camera roll.

What You Will Learn

- How to add multiple gesture recognizers to a `UIImageView`.
- How to save an image to your camera roll.

Key Terms

- **UIGestureRecognizer**
- **UIPinchGestureRecognizer**
- **UIPanGestureRecognizer**
- **UIRotateGestureRecognizer**
- **UITapGestureRecognizer**
- **UIGraphicsImageRenderer**
- **UIImageWriteToSavedPhotosAlbum**

Resources

Getting Started

Let's start by opening XCode and creating a new `Single View Application`. Go ahead and name it "Tanstagram," and save the project wherever you'd like. (Figure 3.5.1)

Figure 3.5.1

Now let's drag all of our image assets provided for us into the `Assets.xcassets` folder. You can drag and drop it in the left pane right under the App Icon folder. Once completed, make sure that each image it's 1x, 2x, and 3x versions as well. This will ensure the proper size and resolution for any apple device. (Figure 3.5.2)

Figure 3.5.2

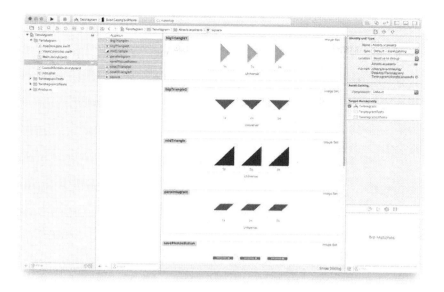

Let's head over to our Main.storyboard. Go to the Object Library on the bottom right and search for UIImageView, and drag it on to our storyboard. (Figure 3.5.3)

Figure 3.5.3

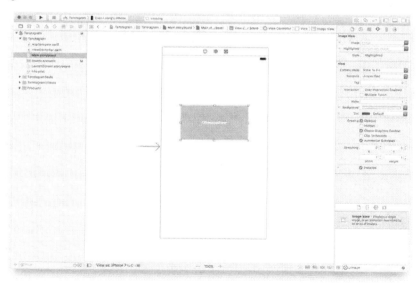

With the UIImageView selected, head on over to the attributes inspector in the right pane. Since we'll be pinching, zooming, and rotating, we'll want to check off User

`Interaction Enabled` and `Multiple Touch` under the **Interaction** section. Let's also change the **Content Mode** to `Aspect Fit`. (Figure 3.5.4)

Figure 3.5.4

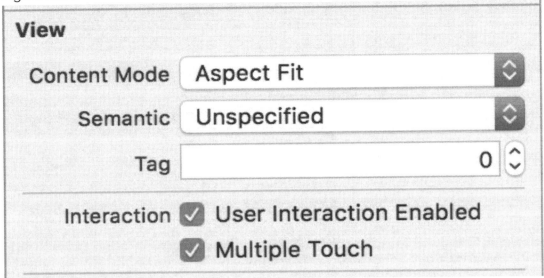

Now let's put an image in our UIImageView! Select a shape from the **Image** dropdown in the attributes inspector. Once the shape appears, you'll want to resize the UIImageView so it surrounds the shape, leaving as little whitespace as you can. (Figure 3.5.5)

Figure 3.5.5

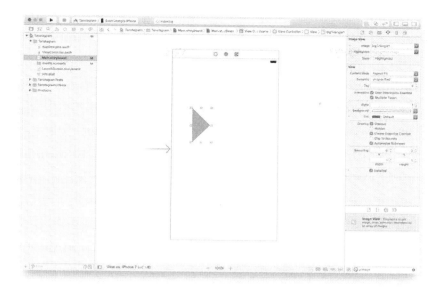

We'll need to make 6 more UIImageViews for the other shapes, so go ahead and copy and paste 6 more and fill them with their respective shapes. Don't forget to double check that they are all `Aspect Fit`, and `User Interaction Enabled` and `Multiple Touch` is checked off! Once done, you should have 7 shapes total. (Figure 3.5.6)

Note: These shapes do not need to be any exact size, just as long as you resize the UIImageView to fit around the shape as best as possible.

Figure 3.5.6

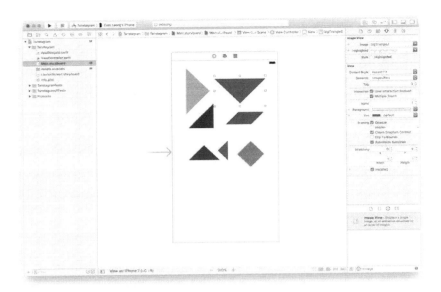

Now let's click the **Assistant Editor** to have our Main.storyboard and ViewController.swift side by side. We can delete the didRecieveMemoryWarning and comments in viewDidLoad. (Figure 3.5.7)

Figure 3.5.7

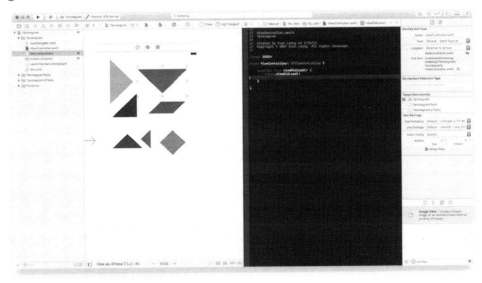

Go ahead and click on a shape in your storyboard. We'll want to control drag on to our

`ViewController.swift` right above `viewDidLoad`. Make sure to create an `@IBOutlet`
`Collection`, and name it **images**. (Figure 3.5.8)

Figure 3.5.8

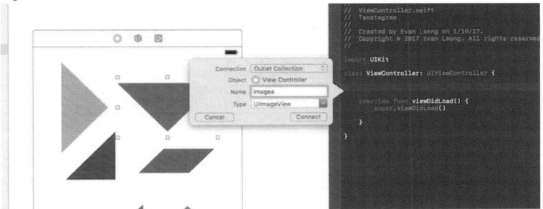

Once connected, you'll notice a small dot next to your `@IBOutlet`. Hovering over it will
turn it into a small plus symbol, and highlight the recently connected shape in the
storyboard. All we need to do now is click the plus, and drag it on to the rest of the
shapes to add it to the array of `@IBOutlet Collection`. Once you are done connecting all
the shapes, hovering over the small plus symbol will show all the shapes highlighted in
the storyboard. (Figure 3.5.9)

Figure 3.5.9

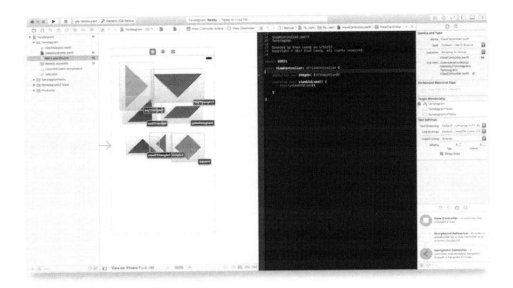

Now let's dive into some code! First, let's add the `UIGestureRecognizerDelegate` after `UIViewController`. This will allow us to access some of the built in functions for UIGestureRecognizer. These should be separated by a comma. (Figure 3.5.10)

Figure 3.5.10

```swift
import UIKit

class ViewController: UIViewController, UIGestureRecognizerDelegate {

    @IBOutlet var images: [UIImageView]!

    override func viewDidLoad() {
        super.viewDidLoad()

    }

}
```

Pinch Gesture

Create a function called `pinchGesture` with a parameter called `imageView` of type `UIImageView` that returns `UIPinchGestureRecognizer`. Since we told the function we were returning a `UIPinchGestureRecognizer`, we'll need to do so.

```swift
func pinchGesture(imageView: UIImageView) -> UIPinchGestureRecognizer {
    return UIPinchGestureRecognizer(target: self, action:
```

```
#selector(ViewController.handlePinch))
    }
```

You might notice we're getting an error. Don't worry! Before we fix it, let's break down what the return function is actually doing:

target: We're basically telling the function that it needs to look at `self` for the `UIPinchGestureRecognizer`.
action: This is what actually happens when we execute when the gesture.
#selector: the selector looks for the function that the action will execute. In this case, we are telling it to look for a function called `handlePinch`.

This is the reason we are getting an error. We haven't created the function `handlePinch` yet! Let's do that now.

Go ahead and write out the function `handlePinch` that takes a parameter called `sender` of type `UIPinchGestureRecognizer`.

```
func handlePinch(sender: UIPinchGestureRecognizer) {
        sender.view?.transform = (sender.view?.transform)!.scaledBy(x:
sender.scale, y: sender.scale)
        sender.scale = 1
    }
```

Since we've created the parameter (sender) of `UIPinchGestureRecognizer`, we can access some of it's properties and functions using dot notation. In this function we're basically looking to the `view` of the `sender` and accessing `transform`. Then we're telling it to scale both the x and y axis, specifically by 1, so when you put two fingers on the screen and expand or contract, the shape will react proportionally on a 1 to 1 ratio.

Now let's apply the `pinchGesture` function to our shapes! Create a function called `createGestures`. Inside it, we'll create a **for loop** with a constant that applies the gesture, and then adds it to the shape.

```
func createGestures() {
    for shape in images {
        let pinch = pinchGesture(imageView: shape)
        shape.addGestureRecognizer(pinch)
    }
}
```

The `pinch` constant that is looking for an `imageView` to apply to `pinchGesture`. Then we use dot notation again to add `pinch` to `shape`.

Now all we need to do is add `createGestures` to `viewDidLoad` so the function runs! (Figure 3.5.11)

Figure 3.5.11

```
override func viewDidLoad() {
    super.viewDidLoad()

    createGestures()

}
```

Run your project and you'll see you can pinch your shapes! Great work!

Looking at our code, you might notice it's broken up into 3 main parts - setting up the gestures, handling the gestures, and then applying them. Before we add our other two gestures, let's organize our code a little bit.

Add the following comments above their respective functions so we know what each block is responsible for.

```
// Set Gestures

func pinchGesture(imageView: UIImageView) -> UIPinchGestureRecognizer {
    return UIPinchGestureRecognizer(target: self, action:
#selector(ViewController.handlePinch))
}

// Handle Gestures

func handlePinch(sender: UIPinchGestureRecognizer) {
    sender.view?.transform = (sender.view?.transform)!.scaledBy(x:
sender.scale, y: sender.scale)
    sender.scale = 1
}

// Create Gestures

func createGestures() {
    for shape in images {
        let pinch = pinchGesture(imageView: shape)
        shape.addGestureRecognizer(pinch)
    }
}
```

Now all we need to do is add the rotation and pan gestures. These are in a very similar format as our pinch gestures. I encourage you to pause here and see if you can figure out how to add it on your own! Then you can cross reference your work with the code below:

```
// Set Gestures

func pinchGesture(imageView: UIImageView) -> UIPinchGestureRecognizer {
    return UIPinchGestureRecognizer(target: self, action:
#selector(ViewController.handlePinch))
}

func panGesture(imageView: UIImageView) -> UIPanGestureRecognizer {
    return UIPanGestureRecognizer(target: self, action:
#selector(ViewController.handlePan))
}

func rotationGesture(imageView: UIImageView) -> UIRotationGestureRecognizer {
    return UIRotationGestureRecognizer(target: self, action:
#selector(ViewController.handleRotation))
}

// Handle Gestures

func handlePinch(sender: UIPinchGestureRecognizer) {
    sender.view?.transform = (sender.view?.transform)!.scaledBy(x:
sender.scale, y: sender.scale)
    sender.scale = 1
}

func handlePan(sender: UIPanGestureRecognizer) {
    let translation = sender.translation(in: self.view)
    if let view = sender.view {
        view.center = CGPoint(x: view.center.x + translation.x, y:
view.center.y + translation.y)
    }

    sender.setTranslation(CGPoint.zero, in: self.view)
}

func handleRotation(sender: UIRotationGestureRecognizer) {
    sender.view?.transform = (sender.view?.transform)!.rotated(by:
sender.rotation)
    sender.rotation = 0
```

```
    }

    // Create Gestures

    func createGestures() {
        for shape in images {
            let pinch = pinchGesture(imageView: shape)
            let pan = panGesture(imageView: shape)
            let rotation = rotationGesture(imageView: shape)
            shape.addGestureRecognizer(pinch)
            shape.addGestureRecognizer(pan)
            shape.addGestureRecognizer(rotation)
        }
    }
```

If you'll notice, the `panGesture` and `rotationGesture` are essentially the same as our `pinchGesture`, except we are calling different functions in **action**. We are still setting the **target** as `self` to look for the gestures.

Similarly to our `pinchGesture`, we need to create the functions `handlePan` and `handleRotation`. The `handlePan` function basically moves the center point of the shape upon the UIPanGestureRecognizer, which is exactly what we want! The `handleRotation` function rotates our shape upon UIRotationGestureRecognizer.

Lastly, we'll need to create constants in our for loop, and add the gestures to our shape. Run your project and make sure you can pinch, rotate, and pan your shapes!

Rendering UIImageView to UIImage & Adding to Camera Roll

You should have an image in your `Assets.xcassets` folder called "savePhotosButton." If it's not there, go back to the resources folder and drag the 1x, 2x, and 3x versions into your `Assets.xcassets` folder.

Let's go into the `Main.storyboard` and drag a `UIImageView` from the Object Library. (Figure 3.5.12)

Figure 3.5.12

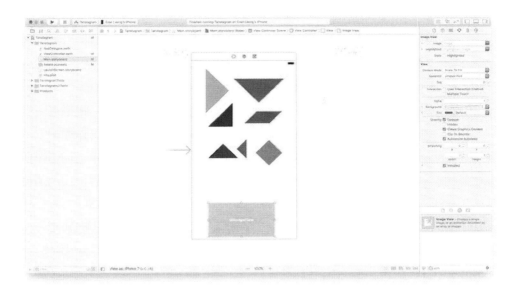

Go to the attributes inspector and make the image the "savePhotosButton." Also be sure that the **Content Mode** is set to Aspect Fit, then resize your UIImageView on your storyboard to eliminate the white space. (Figure 3.5.13)

Figure 3.5.13

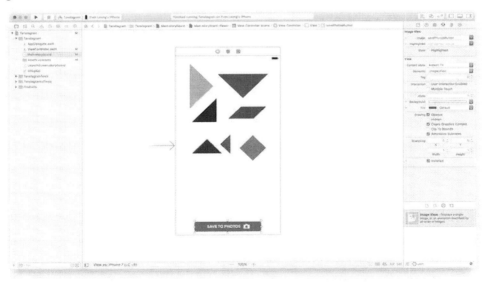

Now let's add some constraints. First, let's set it to a fixed width and height, and pin it 8

pts from the bottom. (Figure 3.5.14)

Figure 3.5.14

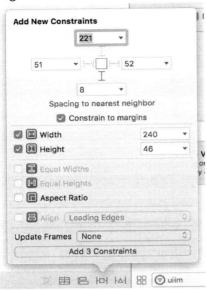

Next, let's make sure the button stays in the center for any device. Go ahead and constrain it horizontally in the container. (Figure 3.5.15)

Figure 3.5.15

Believe it or not, there is more than one way to add gestures! Instead of doing it programmatically, we're going to switch things up and add it from the storyboard.

Search for the `Tap Gesture Recognizer` in the Object Library, and drag it directly on to your `Save To Photos` image. (Figure 3.5.16)

You'll notice the Tap Gesture Recognizer is now added to the top of the View Controller with a small blue icon. (Figure 3.5.17)

Figure 3.5.16

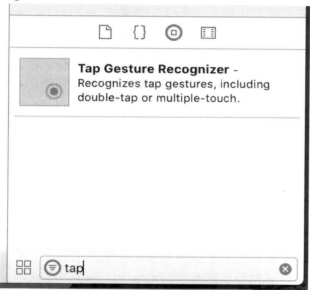

Figure 3.5.17

Now let's `control` drag from the Tap Gesture Recognizer to our `ViewController.swift`. You can place this right below `viewDidLoad()`. Be sure to change the **connection** to `Action`, and **type** to `UITapGestureRecognizer`. Let's also name it `saveToPhotosTapGesture`. (Figure 3.5.18)

Figure 3.5.18

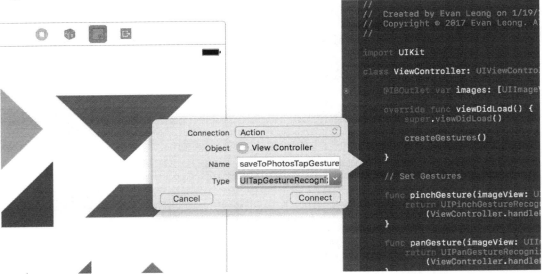

Next, we need to enable interactions in the **Attributes Inspector**. While the
SavePhotosButton image is selected, check off User Interaction Enabled and Multiple
Touch. (Figure 3.5.19)

Figure 3.5.19

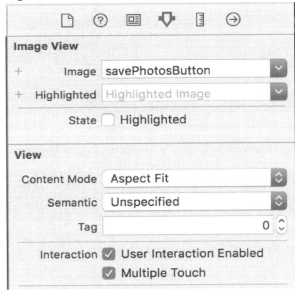

Let's test our button to make sure things are working. Go ahead and write a print statement in your `saveToPhotosTapGesture` and run your project! Tap the button and make sure your print statement is showing up. (Figure 3.5.20)

Figure 3.5.20

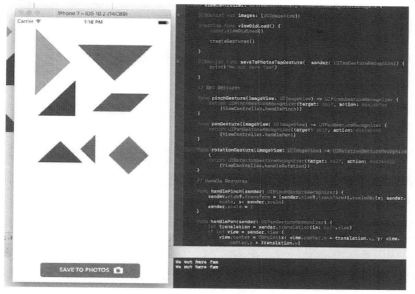

Rendering The Image View

First, let's create a function called `renderImage()` that holds two constants, `renderer` and `image`.

```
func renderImage() {
    let renderer = UIGraphicsImageRenderer(size: view.bounds.size)
    let image = renderer.image { (goTo) in
        view.drawHierarchy(in: view.bounds, afterScreenUpdates: true)

    }
    UIImageWriteToSavedPhotosAlbum(image, self,
#selector(ViewController.renderComplete), nil)
}
```

Our `renderer` constant is assigned to `UIGraphicsImageRenderer`, which will render at the specified size. In this case, we are specifying the size as the `view.bounds.size`.

Then we create our `image` constant, which will render the image in the correct `view.drawHierarchy`.

Lastly, our function is going to save the image with `UIImageWriteToSavedPhotosAlbum`. We are also telling our ViewController to look for and execute `renderComplete`. Let's go ahead and create that function now.

The purpose of this function is to let the user know that the image has either been saved successfully, or if an error has occurred.

```
func renderComplete(_image: UIImage, didFinishSavingWithError error: Error?,
contextInfo:UnsafeRawPointer) {

    if let error = error {

        // Error Occurred
        let alert = UIAlertController(title: "Something Went Wrong :(", message:
error.localizedDescription, preferredStyle: .alert)
            alert.addAction(UIAlertAction(title: "OK", style: .default))
        present(alert, animated: true)

    } else {

        let alert = UIAlertController(title: "Photo Saved!", message: "Your image
has been saved to your Camera Roll.", preferredStyle: .alert)
            alert.addAction(UIAlertAction(title: "OK", style: .default))
        present(alert, animated: true)
    }
}
```

Don't forget to call our `renderImage()` function in our `saveToPhotosTapGesture`! (Figure 3.5.21)

Figure 3.5.21

```
@IBAction func saveToPhotosTapGesture(_ sender: UITapGestureRecognizer) {
    renderImage()

}
```

Now let's run our project!

Uh Oh, we crashed! Let's read the error message in our console. (Figure 3.5.22)

Figure 3.5.22

```
2017-01-22 13:46:22.253427 Tanstagram[42998:6090486] [access] This app has crashed
because it attempted to access privacy-sensitive data without a usage description.
The app's Info.plist must contain an NSPhotoLibraryUsageDescription key with a
string value explaining to the user how the app uses this data.
(lldb)
```

All we need to do is add `NSPhotoLibraryUsageDescription` in our `info.plist`. We basically need to prompt permission for Tanstagram to access our users Photo Library.

Head over to your `info.plist` and add `NSPhotoLibraryUsageDescription` as a key. You'll notice when you hit enter, XCode will register the key as `Privacy - Photo Library Usage Description`. Under the "Value" column, let's write "Saving image to your camera roll!" This is just a description that will be in the Alert View when we prompt for permission. (Figure 3.5.23)

Figure 3.5.23

Launch screen interface file base...	◇	String	LaunchScreen
Main storyboard file base name	◇	String	Main
▶ Required device capabilities	◇	Array	(1 item)
▶ Supported interface orientations	◇	Array	(3 items)
▶ Supported interface orientations (i...	◇	Array	(4 items)
SPhotoLibraryUsageDescription	◇ ⊕ ⊖	String	◇

Privacy - Photo Library Usag...	◇ ⊕ ⊖	String	◇ Saving photos to your camera roll!

3.5.232.png

Now run your project and click the **Save To Photos** button! Success!

Success.png

Wrapping Up

As you can see, there is so much us developers can do with gestures. We learned how to pan, pinch, and rotate images, as well as rendering our images to be saved to our camera roll. With the endless possibilities with a touch screen, the concepts presented here can be applied in numerous creative ways. Code on!

SECTION 4 - App Design

Chapter 25: App Design Introduction

In this section, you'll learn a multitude of practices that will allow you to design professional and inspiring applications. Not only will we learn the basics of design and product creation, but we'll dive into real world examples of what to do after your product has been launched, and how to prioritize features in your upcoming versions that will ultimately lead you to successful product.

Often in startups & companies, you'll see an employee for each respective category:
* User Experience (UX)
* User Interface (UI)
* Developer
* Product Manager

By the end of this section, you will have the knowledge to conquer 3 of the 4 categories. And by the end of this book, you will have all 4 under your belt.

Who is this this for?

The Design portion of the book is written for solo developers, or small teams who are building mobile applications in the startup sphere. While all of the elements in this section can easily be applied in a mature company with any category, we're going to focus on turning you into a multidimensional product expert.

Chapter 26: User Experience / User Interface

Explore the difference between User Interface, User Experience, and the characteristics of each.

What you will learn

- The difference between User Experience (UX) and User Interface (UI)

- The role and use of UX/UI in your application.

What exactly is UX / UI?

Before we begin, we'll need to have a clear understanding of UX / UI, and the differences between each.

UX - User Experience

User experience, put frankly, is the *personality of your application*. Think about your best friend for a moment. What characteristics make them your best friend? Are they loyal? Easy to talk to? Fun? Inspiring? These types of adjectives are generally used to describe the user experience of an application.

Consider the following example (Figure 4.1.1):

Figure 4.1.1

These interactions are pretty standard for most applications, however they are poorly presented. Try to imagine every interaction in your application as a conversation. Imagine if this application was a person, and before you even knew anything about them, they were asking for your email and wanted to know where you are at all times. I'd bet they wouldn't make it to your top 10 friends on speed dial.

Now consider this interaction (Figure 4.1.2):

Figure 4.1.2

We can ask for user location and to enable push notifications later in the application. For now, your best friend is just really happy you stopped by in their world. This communication is something you might experience when talking to a real person. It's warm, inviting, and re-assuring your data won't be compromised.

UI - User Interface

So if User Experience is your personality, what is the User Interface? **User Interface is the way your application looks.** This should always match your application personality. For example - If you were building a professional business application, it might have more muted colors, and less whimsical fonts to portray a sense of authority.
Let's think about your best friend again. The way they dress & present themselves is most likely a reflection of their personality. The combination of the two (UI: how they look & UX: their personality) is what makes them unique.

Consider this application to help you locate the best coffee shops around you (Figure 4.1.3):

Figure 4.1.3

Although the functionality is there, it doesn't speak much for the applications personality. Let's say our application has a light, friendly, modern personality. Here's how we might spice up our UI to really let the User Experience shine through (Figure 4.1.4):

Figure 4.1.4

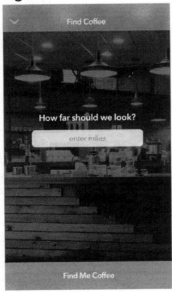

So is User Interface or User Experience more important?

User Experience. Why?

A great experience & functionality will always surpass the looks of an application. Remember, your applications personality will always express itself through design, but never in reverse.

Check out Craigslist.com for a moment. I bet there wasn't more than 5 minutes of thought put into the design, but it executes flawlessly, and is easy to use.

Key Takeaways:

- User Experience is your applications personality
- User Interface is the way your application looks
- Let your designs reflect your applications personality
- Interactions should mimic an actual human conversation

Chapter 27: Designing Your First application In Sketch - Part 1

Learn the basics of Sketch through designing an elegant application to find the best coffee or tea in your area.

What you will learn

- Basics of Sketch

- Implementing UX/UI principles

- Giving your Application personality

Designing Your First App

Before we dive right in to designing, we'll want to think about a few things first. Every time you are about to design a new product from scratch, think about the following questions:

1. What is the main goal of the application? (This should be no more than 2-3 sentences)

2. If your application was a person, describe them in 3 words.

3. Who is going to be using your application?

We'll be making an application that allows it's users to find the best coffee & tea in their area. So let's go ahead and answer the questions above.

1. What is the main goal of the application?
Our application allows you to find the best coffee or tea in your area.

2. If your application was a person, describe them in 3 words.
Our application is going to be modern, friendly, and warm.

3. Who is going to be using your application?

People who enjoy a really good cup of coffee or tea. They're more particular than your average drinker.

Great! We'll be using these answers throughout our design process to help keep consistency throughout our application.

Let's start designing! Go ahead and open Sketch and create a New project (Figure 4.2.1).

Figure 4.2.1

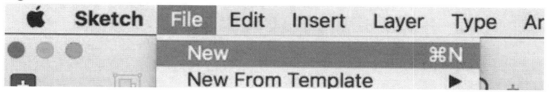

In the upper left corner click Insert +. From the drop down menu click Artboard (Figure 4.2.2).

Figure 4.2.2

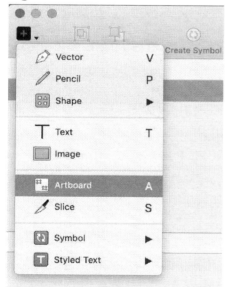

You will be using the Insert option for adding all your assets to the Artboard.

Selecting Insert you will find the following options:

* Vector

* Pencil

* Shape
* Text
* Image
* Artboard
* Slice
* Symbol
* Styled Text

Feel free to take a second and explore this menu. I encourage you to get really familiar with it.

On the right hand side you'll see a ton of great templates (Figure 4.2.3). We'll go ahead and click iPhone 7 for now, but feel free to peruse the others on your own time!

Figure 4.2.3

On the left hand side, you'll now see that Sketch has created an "iPhone 7" section under your current page. Now everything you put inside this Artboard will be organized accordingly.
Let's go ahead and rename *iPhone 7* to *Home*.

We're now going to create our first shape. Go to the upper left corner again, and this time we're going to Insert -> Shape -> Rectangle.
Start in the upper left corner, and drag across to the right until it snaps to the right

corner. We'll then drag it down to roughly half the screen. You'll notice that Sketch will automatically snap to the center.

Congratulations! You just inserted your first shape!

Your Artboard should now look like the following (Figure 4.2.4):

Figure 4.2.4

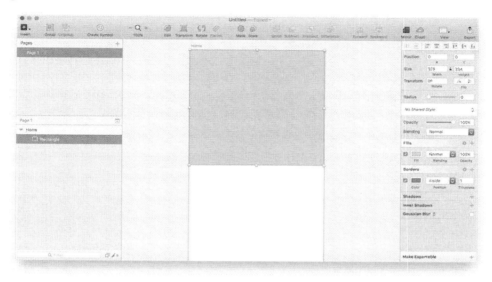

On the right hand side you'll notice an *Attributes Inspector* that correlates with the shape you just made. This will always show the attributes of an element you have currently selected.

From here we can alter properties like the opacity, shape fill, border, shadows, and even add blurs! We'll get into more of this later, but for now let's un-check the Borders box.

We're going to split our screen into two sections: one for finding coffee, and the other for finding tea. We've just created our coffee section, so let's create another rectangle for our tea. We could add another rectangle, but since the dimensions we want are already set in our first rectangle, let's just duplicate it.

While having our rectangle selected, **hold down** option, and left click.
Drag your mouse down and you'll see a new copy of the rectangle being created. Keep dragging down until the rectangle has snapped to the bottom of the Artboard. Your screen should now be entirely gray with two rectangles perfectly distributed on the screen (Figure 4.2.5).

Figure 4.2.5

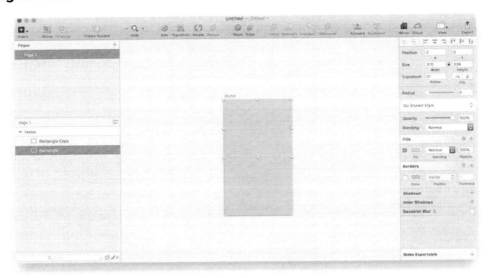

Now let's rename our rectangles. Under our renamed *Home* Artboard, let's click on our first rectangle (top one), and rename it *Coffee Box*, and the bottom one *Tea Box*.

Let's add some color to this now! Select your *Coffee Box* and click the Fill rectangle (color picker) on the right panel. Let's find a cool mocha color. Click or drag around in the "Hex Box" until you find something you like. You can also scroll through the color spectrum below on the multicolored bar. **If you're having trouble finding one you like, you can use the hex: #6F4E37.**

We'll now add an image to spice things up. Head on over to www.nounproject.com. They are a great resource for finding high quality icons (Figure 4.2.6).
In the search field type "coffee" and choose an icon you like. *This is a good time to reflect on one of the first questions we asked when we started this project.*
What is your applications personality like? Since our application's personality is modern, friendly, and warm, try to find one that fits that description.

Figure 4.2.6

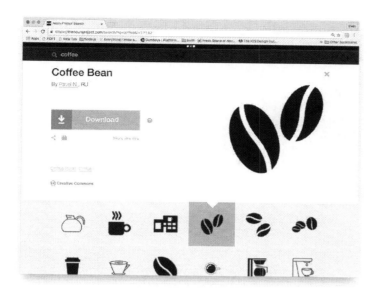

Once you have downloaded your image, you can just drag and drop it from your downloads folder (or any saved location) directly into Sketch. When you drop the image in, try to place your mouse directly over the Artboard. When you are done dragging, the image might be bigger than the Artboard. Don't worry! This happens all the time when dragging & dropping images.

You can zoom in and out of your canvas with command + and command –. You will want to make sure you have enough space to grab one of the corners of your image.
Grab a corner and while holding down shift, scale down your image by dragging it into the center.
Holding down shift will keep all the dimensions proportionate.

There will be some text on the bottom left that we wont want in our image. It's best practice to write all of these down to properly give credit to the artist in another section of the application, but for now we'll remove it.
Double click your image to go into edit mode. On the right hand side, make sure Selection is selected. Drag over the text and hit Delete.** This will remove the text and crop your image properly (Figure 4.2.7).

Figure 4.2.7

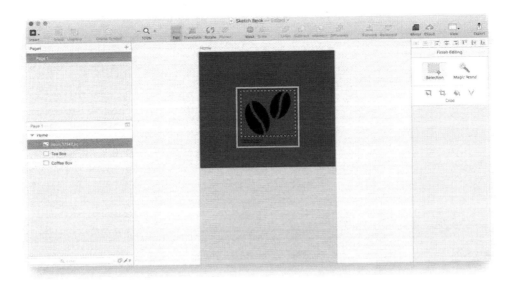

This is looking great! Let's rename our picture to *Coffee Beans*. The full black color of the coffee beans are a little too harsh. We want this image to blend with the background, so let's decrease the opacity. *While the Coffee Beans are selected, you can decrease the opacity with the slider on the right hand side, or type in a percentage. 20%-25% opacity looks great for this effect* (Figure 4.2.8)

Figure 4.2.8

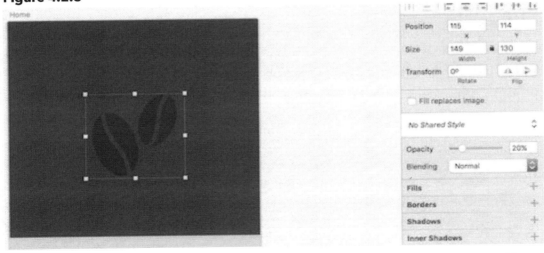

We're now going to add some text. Go to Insert -> Text and click right over the Coffee Beans. Type "Find the Best Coffee", center it and find a font you like. Keep in mind our applications personality when doing this!

If you're stuck on styling your text, I've used *Avenir Next - Demi Bold* in this example. Your Artboard should look something like this (Figure 4.2.9):

Figure 4.2.9

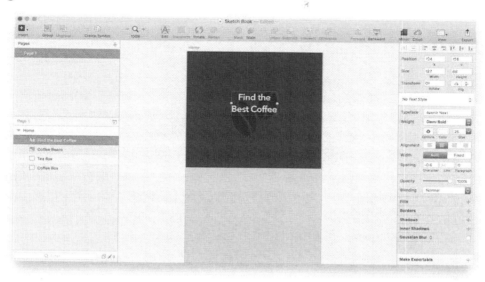

Now we want to make sure that the text is perfectly centered with our Coffee Beans, and luckily Sketch gives us a really easy way to do this! Select both the text and Coffee Beans by clicking *Coffee Beans* then holding down shift and clicking on the text. In the upper right of your panel you'll see some alignment icons (Figure 4.2.10).

Figure 4.2.10

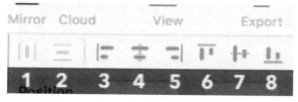

1. Distribute Horizontally - Create even spacing between horizontal elements

2. Distribute Vertically - Create even spacing between vertical elements

3. Align Left - Make your elements left aligned

393

4. `Align Horizontally` - Center your elements horizontally

5. `Align Right` - Make your elements right aligned

6. `Align Top` - Make your elements aligned to the top

7. `Align Vertically` - Center your elements vertically

8. `Align Bottom` - Make your elements align to the bottom

With both items selected, we are going to align them both vertically and horizontally Watch what happens!**

Our text is now perfectly in the center of our icon (Figure 4.2.11).

Figure 4.2.11

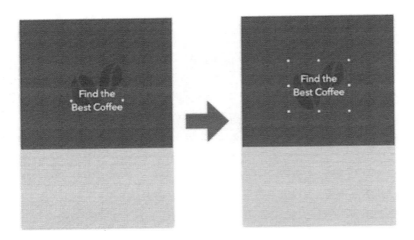

Now with those two elements still selected, let's `command + g` to put them in a group. This will create a folder with those two elements inside. Let's then rename the folder *Coffee Box Assets*.

- *Note: It is super important to keep your elements grouped in folders. It helps to keep your projects organized, and allows you to move elements all together. If you wanted to reposition your text and icon without them being grouped, you would have to select them individually. This may seem trivial now with only 2 elements, but as your designs become more complex, the easier it will make your life!*

Now try aligning your Coffee Box Assets folder vertically and horizontally to your Coffee Box in the same way we did the text and Coffee Beans.

Breakdown

Not only did you learn some basic Sketch elements, but you actually dove into the inner workings of UX. Let's break down what just happened.

We ask ourselves two questions with every screen:

1. What are we trying to accomplish / want the user to do?

2. What is the best way to present this, given our applications personality?

What are we trying to accomplish?

Upon launch, we are trying to let the user know that there are two things we do best. We find the best coffee & the best tea. We want the user to understand this, and quickly choose one. We then guide them on a path to discovering more about our app.

What is the best way to do this given our applications personality?

Our application is modern, friendly, and warm. We do not want to bombard our user with too many options, because more often than not, more options means more decisions the user needs to process. The best way for the user understand what we do and quickly choose an action, is to split the screen up into two sections. Right from the beginning the user can easily digest what's going on and make a decision.

Exercise: Complete the Tea section to match the Coffee section

1. Find a cool green tea color (use www.paletton.com or www.adobe.kuler.com).

2. Find a cool tea icon, and apply the same attributes to it as the Coffee Beans.

3. Add some text "Find the Best Tea" and group it with the tea icon.

4. Group your Tea Assets with your Tea Box

5. Make sure everything is aligned perfectly (horizontally & vertically)

6. Hi-five the closest person next to you

Chapter 28: Designing Your First App in Sketch - Part 2

Continue building your first app in Sketch while learning some UX principles and Sketch tools

What you will learn

- Playing off current user habits to your benefit

- Aligning elements

- Using more Sketch tools

Great! We've now designed a beautiful home screen, but what happens when a user selects either Coffee or Tea? We'll look into a few principles of building out a great product while creating this next screen.

Playing Off Current User Habits

You will want to keep in mind what other applications your customer base might be using, and what habits they may already be accustomed too. Many times it's playing off of the norm, but adding your own twist to it. Your users get what they were expecting, but also are delighted because you have added an element they're not used to. Let's start off by building a screen a user might already be expecting.

Building the Results Screen

Let's break down the elements we'll need for this screen:

1. A list of the results

2. A map

3. Metrics to rate the quality of results (i.e. stars)

Given these elements, it's best to set our screen up similar to an application like Google maps (Figure 4.3.1):

Figure 4.3.1

We'll start by adding a new page to our project. Click the + symbol on the Pages tab, and name the new page *Results*. We can also rename our first page to *Home* (Figure 4.3.2).

Figure 4.3.2

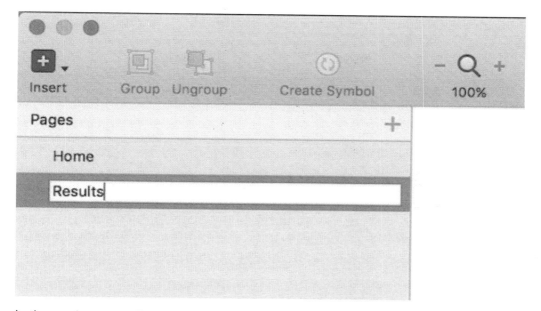

Let's now insert an `iPhone 7 Artboard`, and rename it *Coffee Results*. We'll then create the navigation bar by inserting a rectangle. *Be sure to have the sides snap to the edges of your Artboard, and bring the height down to 64pt.*

Since this is the Coffee Results screen, we'll want to fill the navigation bar with the same color as our Coffee Rectangle from our previous screen. Head on over to your "Home" page and click your `Coffee Rectangle`. Go to the Fill box to grab the HEX (color code).

Instead of constantly going back to previous assets to grab colors, Sketch makes it really easy for you to save HEX's as either **Global Colors** or **Document Colors**.

Global Colors save HEX's across the entire program. This means you will have access to these every time you open up Sketch. I recommend saving colors that you frequently use across many application designs.

Document Colors save HEX's only in the current document. You'll want to save these custom colors specific to your current project.

Let's go ahead and **Save** our Coffee color to our Document Colors (Figure 4.3.3). Now we can go back to our Navigation Bar in our *Coffee Results* and simply select our saved color to fill it in.

Figure 4.3.3

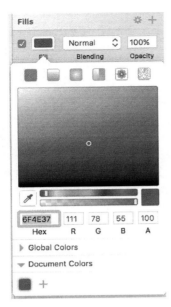

To finish up the navigation bar, go ahead and do the following:

1. Rename the rectangle to *Coffee Results Navigation*

2. Remove the border

3. Add a slight drop shadow

4. Add a Back button (You can either make this in Sketch, or find one online).

5. Add the title "The Best Coffee" and align it with your back button.

6. Group them all in a folder called *Navigation*

Note: Make sure your styling decisions match your applications personality! (i.e. font and icon style)
Have fun with this. This is where your creativity & personal touch comes in.

By the end of it, you're navigation bar should look like some variation of this (Figure 4.3.4):

Figure 4.3.4

Let's now insert a rectangle for our map. Make the edges snap to the corners and give it a height of 250.

Let's also remove the border and rename the rectangle *Map Image*. We can leave this for now, as it is just a placeholder for our map image.

For this next part, we'll simulate a table view to display some options.

Insert a rounded rectangle in the shape of a square by holding down `shift`. Go ahead and make it 90pt by 90pt and remove the border. This will serve as a placeholder for an image for the first result. We can also rename this *Result Image* (Figure 4.3.5).

Figure 4.3.5

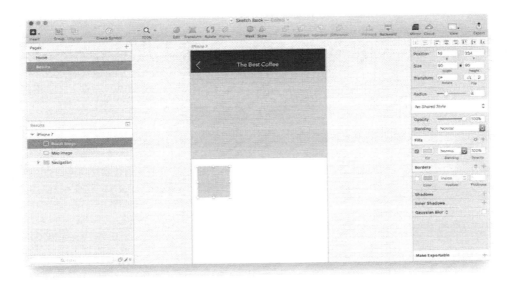

We've left some room on the right because we'll be placing a few things here:

1. Name

2. Ranking (Stars)

3. Short Description

4. Hours of Operation

Go ahead and Insert -> Text -> Type a name for your first coffee shop result. I'm also going to make my text semi-bold to have it stand out a bit more.

Tip: When selecting the text color, often times pure black text on a pure white background is too harsh. Having a dark gray colored text can help soften things up.

Now we're going to add some stars. Luckily Sketch has a preset star we can insert. Let's Insert -> Shape -> Star and make it 20pts by 20pts.
Remove the border on the shape, and don't forget to hold down shift to keep it proportional!

While the star is selected, hold down option and drag to the right. You'll notice that the star is being duplicated. Go ahead and do this 3 more times until we have 5 stars. Don't worry about positioning just yet (Figure 4.3.6).

Figure 4.3.6

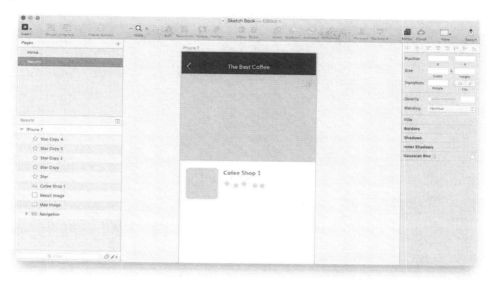

We're now going to align the stars using a few of Sketch's handy alignment tools. With all 5 stars selected, let's first `distribute horizontally`, which will ensure that the spaces between each star are equal. Then let's align them all vertically.

Wow! You have just turned a messy cluster of stars into a perfectly aligned constellation! While your stars are still selected, let's `control + g` to place them in a group named *Stars*. You're stars should now look like this (Figure 4.3.7):

Figure 4.3.7

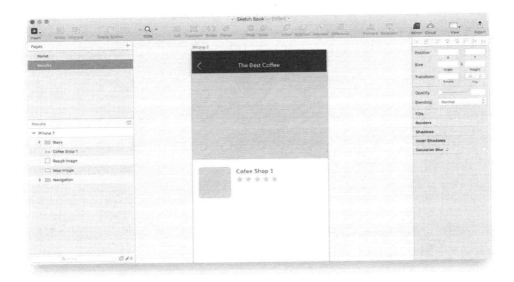

Feel free to color in your stars now. If you're showing 4/5 stars I'd recommend removing the fill in the empty star and give it a border, or removing the un-earned star all together.

Now let's add a small description and hours of operation. We can make the text 2pts smaller than the title, and choose a *light* or *regular* font type.

Let's select the 4 elements we created (title, stars, description, and hours), and left align them, as well as distribute vertically.
While they are all selected, let's put them in a group and name it *Cell Details*. Now we can select our Cell Details group, as well as the Result Image, and align vertically to make sure everything is pixel perfect.

Let's now add a thin line to simulate the table view separator. I'm going to Insert -> Shape -> Line and have it start where my Result Image begins, and drag it all the way to the (right) edge of the Artboard. Let's also make the thickness .5, and make sure it's 20pts below our Results Image (Figure 4.3.8).

Figure 4.3.8

Now all we need to do is put the **line, Cell Details, and the Result Image** in it's own group called *Cell Assets*. Now that we have one cell in its own group, we can hold down option and duplicate the cells to make the rest of our table view! You can also rename your copied Cell Assets to correspond with each cell.

Wrapping up

When designing your apps, be sure to take a look at similar products in the same space. Often it's best to use intuitive gestures and design principles your target market is already used to, but add your own spark into the mix that will make your product stand out.

Exercise

1. Go back and replace all our image placeholders with actual images! Feel free to do a Google search for some cool images that will put your application design in it's best light.

   When you have the placeholder shape selected, click Fill (Figure 4.3.9) and select Choose Image from the Pattern Fill section and select your image.

Figure 4.3.9

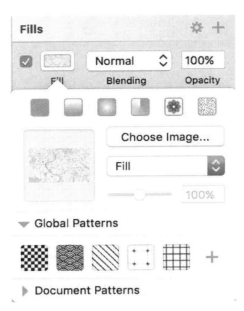

Global Patterns

Document Patterns

2. Edit each cells specific details to simulate a live application.

3. Recreate this screen for your Tea screen. *Remember, you can use copy paste to your advantage. There are only a few elements that are different from the Coffee screen ;)*

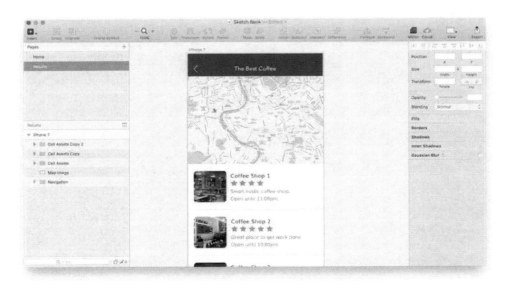

Final.png

Chapter 29: Magic Wand Theory

Learn how to reverse engineer your ideal user experience to better execute your product features.

What you will learn

- How to use the "Magic Wand Theory" to guide important product decisions

What do you want your users to do?

I want to take a moment and explain a concept that is often overlooked when brainstorming products and more specifically, product features. While this concept can be applied to all applications in some capacity, it becomes increasingly relevant in applications that require high engagement to succeed (i.e. a social network vs a utility application).

The Magic Wand Theory was coined by *BJ Fogg*, a behavioral scientist and innovator from Stanford University (I can't take all the credit for this!).
His wisdom on the relationship between user engagement and products are definitely worth checking out. I encourage anyone who is creating products in technology to check out his work. I will also reference tid-bits of his work throughout the rest of the chapters in this book.

The "Magic Wand Theory" basically asks, *"If you could wave a magic wand, and have your users do exactly what you want them to do, what would it be?"*

Sounds simple right? Almost too simple. Many people overestimate the power of approaching their products this way. If you have ever worked with a product team, or even brainstormed product ideas with a colleague, you've probably encountered a conversation like this in some shape or form:

Person 1: *"We need the users posts to be visible to all users."*
Person 2: *"But, what if that user only wants it to be seen amongst a certain group of*

people?"

Person 1: *"Well do you think it is fair to the other users that have signed up to access exclusive content?"*

Person 2: *"Well then we'll have specific features tailored to those individuals."*

Person 1: *"OK, then maybe we should have a tiered payment system for each level of membership."*

I hear these types of conversations far too often. They are largely abstract, and turn into debates of theory and "what if's." Without creating more context to the situation, you can gather the following:

1. Person 1 and 2 have a theoretical disagreement. It is basically a disagreement on privacy.

2. Person 2 is creating a scenario with an unknown frequency of occurrence.

3. Now both people are compromising by creating a solution to a problem they have created, and in turn creating a potentially useless features and payment system predicated on false assumptions.

4. It's difficult to justify any features because it is still unclear what the user should be doing.

Basically by going down this rabbit hole without addressing the *ideal* user experience, many product managers end up fabricating features based on false pretenses. This gets passed on to developers and designers who will spend months building the product, only to find that users are not using it as it was originally intended. Instead, you can open up the conversation by using the "Magic Wand Theory":

You: *"But wait! What should the user be doing the second they open the application? I think it should go straight to the post page, where the user would post a startup idea they had. Other users in the community will up-vote or down-vote their idea, and the user will comment and discuss pros and cons."*

Getting straight down to what the user *should* do, **turns abstract ideas into concrete, actionable features, and gives you a goal post to strive for.**
Now every feature, interaction, and discussion will hinge from what the user should be doing. This will make conversations more focused, less abstract, and actionable.

Now we can go back to the first conversation, and re-evaluate the ideas discussed:

Person 1: *We need the users posts to be visible to all users*

You: *Great, because our goal is to have people interact with that persons post, that seems to make the most sense. We can always make minor adjustments post launch.*

Done! Nothing further needs to be discussed. No added features or membership tiers etc, and now you and your team have a "true north" for every discussion thereafter :)

This is just one mock scenario of many *real ones*. I encourage you to think about this whenever discussing product features and ideas, and always ask yourself "What do I want the user to do?"

Wrapping up

Make sure to constantly ask yourself in each design decision, "Ideally, what would we have the user do?" This will help navigate the clutter of possible features and allow you to hone in on the most optimal experience for your users. It will also serve as a chopping block for many unnecessary conversations which can dilute the mission of your product or company.

Chapter 30: App - Savemate

Design a full fledged application that has room for rich micro-interactions

What you will learn

- Combining shapes

- Filling elements with color

- Various Sketch tools

We'll go ahead and design an app that will leave room for some creative micro-interactions which we'll cover in the next chapter.
Open up a new project in Sketch and name it *Savemate*. Savemate will be an app that allows users to keep track of an item they are saving money for.

Start by going to Insert -> Artboard -> and select iPhone 7 on the right hand side.
We'll then Insert -> Shape -> Rectangle for the navigation bar. Have it snap to the edges, and bring it down 64pts.
You can remove the border on the shape, and give it a dark gray color. If you can't decide on a dark gray, I'll be using the HEX #525252.

Let's Insert -> Text and type *savemate* at the top. I'm going to make "save" a thinner text style than "mate."
This is a great technique to style text when you want certain words to stand out.
Also, let's find a cool mint color to contrast with our gray navigation bar. Feel free to find a color that suits your personal taste. I'll be using the HEX #46C281. Our artboard should now look something like this (Figure 4.5.1):

Figure 4.5.1

Let's now `Insert` -> `Shape` -> `Rectangle` right below our navigation bar. This is going to be where we place the item details.

Be sure to have it snap to the left and right corners, and make it around 90pts high. Go ahead and choose a lighter gray for the fill, and remove the borders.

If you're having trouble with finding a light gray, I'll be using the HEX #E9E9E9.

- *Tip: Instead of using lines to separate elements in your designs, it's also great to use "off whites" & "grays" to signify different sections. It's easier on the eyes and gives a great minimalistic feel.*

Let's now `Insert` -> `Text` and type "Goal: New Guitar."

`Insert` another line of text and have it say "by January 7th, 2017." This will be our goal date and should be smaller than the goal text. Feel free to choose a dark gray HEX for the text color as well.

Using the align tools, let's select both of these text fields and align them horizontally. Let's also group them together with `command + g` and align it vertically and horizontally in the gray rectangle, and then group the rectangle and the text group together.

Feel free to name your groups appropriately as you create them (Figure 4.5.2).

Figure 4.5.2

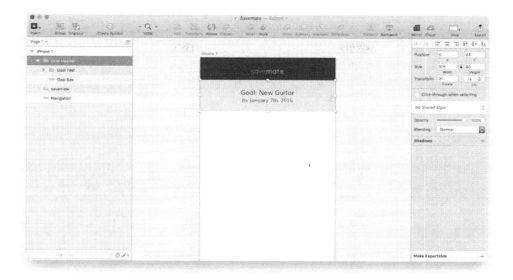

Now for some fun stuff! We'll be making a progress circle to reflect the goals progress. Sketch gives us some great tools to allow us to do this pretty easily.

First, let's Insert -> Shape -> Oval.
While holding Shift, left click and drag to make a perfect circle that is **180pts x 180pts**. Also remove the border and fill it with a color that is going to stand out.
(You'll see why we're doing this in a moment, don't worry about the specific color. We're just using it as a placeholder)

Now command + c, and command + v to copy and paste the circle. Let's make it a different color so we can see it, and scale it up to around **210pts x 210pts**.
Also be sure to place it behind the smaller circle, and with both of them selected, center them vertically and horizontally (Figure 4.5.3).

Figure 4.5.3

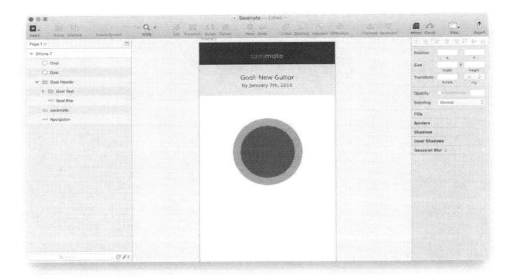

At the top you'll notice a few tools provided by Sketch (Figure 4.5.4).

Figure 4.5.4

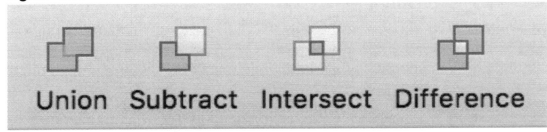

Union merges two shapes together

Subtract subtracts the top element from the one underneath it

Intersect intersects the top shape from the one underneath it

Difference subtracts the difference between two shapes

Well go ahead now and **select both circles** and click Subtract and BOOM! We now have the shape of our progress circle (Figure 4.5.5).

Figure 4.5.5

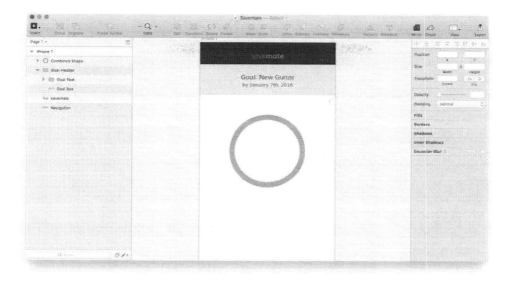

You'll notice now on the artboard panel, the two circles have been named as a *Combined Shape*. You can actually edit the elements in Combined Shapes, so if things didn't come out perfectly on the first try you can alter them later.

Now let's select our new Combined Shape, and click fill.
We want to give this a slight gradient with two colors. Select the Linear Gradient, which will give us two palettes to change colors, and span a gradient across our shape (Figure 4.0.6).

Figure 4.5.6

415

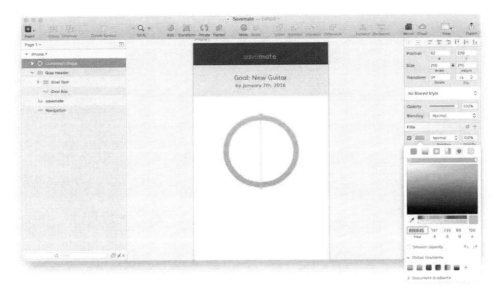

Let's start by making the bottom part of our circle the same color as our title in our navigation bar.

With Fill selected, click the right rectangle on the slider, or the bottom circle on the gradient line on our shape (Figure 4.5.7).

Figure 4.5.7

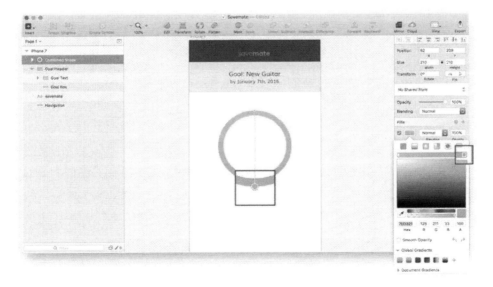

Sketch allows us to quickly find the HEX of any element on your screen.

Let's control + c and you'll notice you can hover the cursor over any element, and with the Fill selected, you can left click to insert that HEX. **Hover over our title and select the color to fill our bottom part of our circle.** (Figure 4.5.8)

Figure 4.5.8

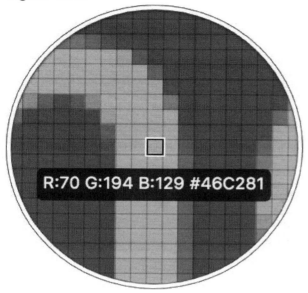

R:70 G:194 B:129 #46C281

For our other HEX in the gradient, we'll use #B5EB45.

Now, let's Insert -> Shape -> Triangle.

We'll make this **170pts x 100pts**. Go up to the top and click Rotate, and rotate our triangle -90 degrees (Figure 4.5.9).

Figure 4.5.9

If you guessed that we might subtract this triangle from our Combined Shape, you're right! With the triangle and Combined Shape (Circle) both selected, click Subtract. Now it's starting to look like a real progress circle! (Figure 4.5.10)

Figure 4.5.10

It looks a little funny with the dry cut edges doesn't it? Let's round them off a bit.

The difference between the two circles is roughly **30pts x 30pts**.

We'll divide that number by two and get a circle that's **15pts x 15pts**.

Click Insert -> Shape -> Oval, and give it the size of **15pts x 15pts**.

We'll use this to put at both ends of our progress circle. You may have to zoom in, as well as manually alter the x and y coordinates (using decimals help to align this perfectly). (Figure 4.5.11)

Figure 4.5.11

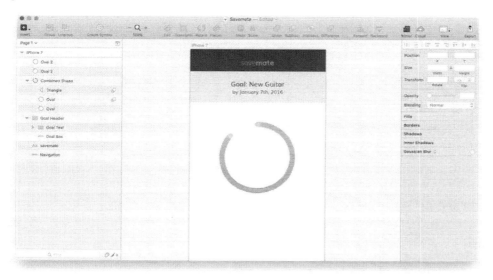

Now with both of the Ovals selected and the Combined Shape (our circle), click Union and have them join the shape. You'll also notice our ovals automatically inherited the colors so we don't have to fill them in!

Wrapping up

In this section we learned about some of the powerful Sketch tools that allow us to manipulate shapes to achieve a desired effect. It's also great to use whites and off-whites to differentiate different areas of your app without the use of harsh lines or colors.

Exercise

To complete this app, we'll add some elements that you already know how to implement, per the previous chapters!

- Add a money **amount saved** (i.e $1500) in the center of the circle

- Add the **full amount** (i.e. $2000) beneath the **amount saved**

- Add a button at the bottom of the screen that includes an icon

- The text of the button should say "Add $10"

By the end of it all, it should look like this! (Figure 4.5.12)

Figure 4.5.12

Goal: New Guitar
by January 7th, 2016

$1500

of $2000 Goal

ADD $10

Chapter 31: micro-interactions

Learn the fundamentals for creating rich micro-interactions.

What you will learn

- Learn how design and simulate micro-interactions through Invision

What is a micro-interaction?

A micro-interaction is any small task or form of communication between your app and the user. This could be actions from prompting settings, pop-ups, too singular call to actions. Users will be consciously or subconsciously drawn to this familiar form of communication.

For example, this could be a pop-up when you complete an action in an app such as double tapping a   , to like a photo on Instagram. (Example: Figure 4.6.1)

Figure 4.6.1

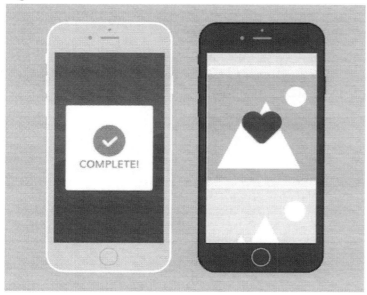

Why are micro-interactions Important?

The subtle but immediate responses given by micro-interactions are arguably the most important component when forming user habits. Not only is your app talking to your user, but its responding.
Your app is beginning to form a relationship with your user, and the way you craft this is extremely important.

Designing a micro-interactions

We'll use our Savemate app we just created to simulate a micro-interactions. In the design phase, you probably won't create actual animations just yet, but you can simulate the idea through some third party tools. This gives your team and developers an idea how the interaction should be executed.

First let's insert a new artboard. You can either do it in the Savemate project or create an entirely new one.
Go ahead and `Insert -> Artboard -> iPhone 7` to get started. This interaction is going to be a modal response to tapping the "ADD $10" button.

Let's now `Insert -> Shape -> Rounded Rectangle` and make it a perfect square in the middle of our artboard with the dimensions of 250pts x 250pts.
Remove the borders and give it the same HEX color as our button from the Savemate homepage. I'm using HEX: #12A792.

Now let's `Insert -> Text` and write *DEPOSIT COMPLETE!*. Leave it towards the bottom of the rectangle so we have room for a cool icon. (Figure 4.6.2)

Figure 4.6.2

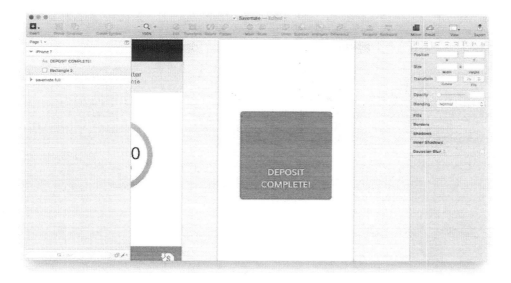

Next, find an icon that can make the user feel "accomplished".

Remember that this is going to display every time a user does what **you** (the product creator) wants them to do. This will eventually become validation they will subconsciously crave every time they deposit $10.

This may seem small, but goes a long way. (Figure 4.6.3)

Figure 4.6.3

Lets put those elements into it's own group and export them. With your group selected, click Make Exportable on the bottom right. (Figure 4.6.4)

Figure 4.6.4

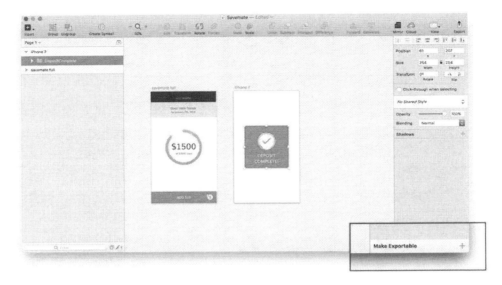

You'll notice an export pane pop up. For now, go ahead and change the size from **1x** to **2x**, and we can leave the suffix blank for now (Figure 4.6.5). Now click Export and save it to your computer.

Figure 4.6.5

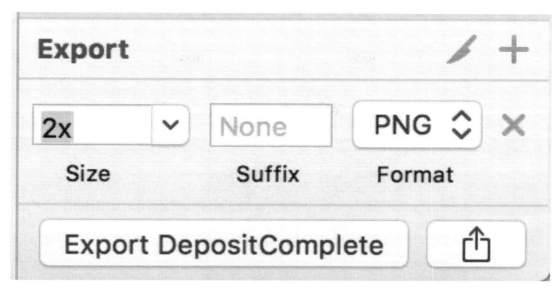

Lastly, let's select our home screen artboard and export that as well. Make sure to have the entire artboard selected and export it at 2x.

On the right hand side, you'll see a preview of the export. Be sure to check both `Background Color` and `Include in Export`. This will make our background white instead of transparent.

Creating the micro-interactions in Invision

Great! Now that we have both our home screen and our popover exported, let's create a simulated interaction using Invision. Invision is an awesome tool for creating interactive mock-ups and sending them to friends, teammates, or clients. It's also a great way to get a feel for a product idea before **any** code is written.

Head on over to www.invisionapp.com and sign up if you do not have an account. It's free to sign up, and well worth the money if you would like to upgrade to a paid account.

We'll start by adding a new project. Click the + symbol to add a new prototype. We can call this *Savemate*, and select `iPhone`. Make sure `Portrait` is selected and click `Create Prototype`.

Right off the bat you'll notice we're able to drag and drop our assets into Invision's interface.

Find your home screen and popover and drag them into Invision (Figure 4.6.6).
Now let's click our home screen to enter edit mode.

Figure 4.6.6

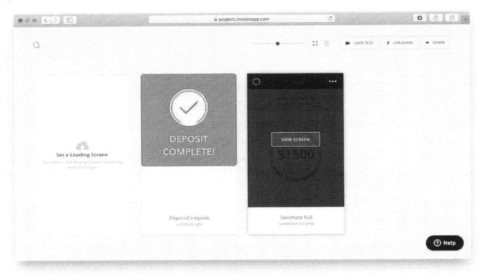

Figure 4.6.7

Here you'll find the interface you'll be working with the most.

1. These arrows allow you to move back and forth between your uploaded assets.

2. You can use these to navigate through sections of your entire project.

3. This contains Preview Mode, Build Mode, Comment Mode, and History Mode. This is what you will be interacting with the most. From here you can create your hot spots, comment on your prototype, and view your history.

4. This is where you would enter a phone number to send the prototype to. The recipient will be able to play with the prototype as if it were an actual app on their phone!

Let's jump into `Build Mode`, and click and drag over our button to create a hot spot. You'll notice another box appear. This allows us to choose a destination for the hot spot. Generally this could be another screen or interaction. For now, we'll select `Screen as Overlay`. We'll keep the Gesture to `Tap`, and let's select our micro-interactions popup. Keep the **Position** `Centered` and **Transition** `Fade In`.
Let's **increase the BG to around 40%** and leave everything else checked off (Figure 4.6.8).
Go ahead and hit save! Feel free to play around with all the options in the mean time. Invision does an amazing job at simulating app experiences. You can use swipe gestures, flips, popovers and much more.

Figure 4.6.8

Let's jump back into **Preview Mode** and click our button. Watch what happens! We've now simulated a micro-interactions that we can send to a developer or teammate without writing a line of code!

Wrapping up

We've merely skimmed the surface of possibilities for Invision. In this section we created a micro-interaction, but with Invision you can simulate entire app experiences before you or your developers dive into code. I'd highly encourage you to explore it in depth on your own time. I've personally used Invision for all of my personal projects as well as client mockups. It's an immensely powerful tool that can increase fluidity with your team and potential users.

Exercise

Use your imagination, and design another screen this app could have. Keep in mind the the target demographic and apps personality as you do this as well. Once your finished, go ahead and drop it into Invision and simulate the actual functionality.

Chapter 32: Night Owl App

We'll master some intermediate UX/UI principles and design an app that intelligently makes use of our screen real estate and target demographic.

What you will learn

- How to find great colors schemes for your app

- Screen Real Estate

- Exporting Assets

- More UX/UI principles

The app we're going to design in this chapter is called *Night Owl*. If you can remember back from Chapter 2 of this section, we need to answer a few questions first!

1. **What is the main goal of the application?**

   Night Owl allows users to chat with other people in their area that can't sleep. You will only be able to log on from 11:00PM - 5:00AM.

2. **If your application was a person, describe them in 3 words.**

   Sleek, Mysterious and Inviting.

3. **Who is going to be using your application?**

   People ages 18-35 who cannot sleep.

Great! Now that we have these answered. Let's go ahead and start designing.

Designing Night Owl

Open up Sketch and go to `File -> New From Template -> iOS UI Design`. You'll notice we have some symbols and templates we can work with. For now, let's click the + to add a new page, and title it *Login*.

Now let's `Insert` -> `Artboard` and select `iPhone 7`. We can rename our artboard *Login Screen*.

Go ahead and `Insert` -> `Shape` -> `Rectangle` and have it cover the whole artboard. Be sure to remove the borders. (Figure 4.7.1)

Figure 4.7.1

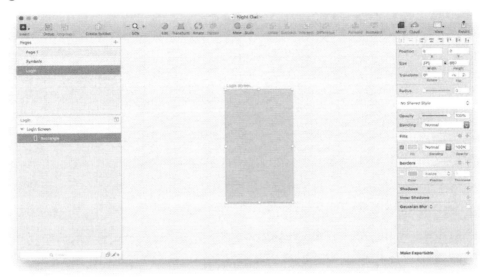

This will serve as the background for our login screen. Let's rename it to *Night BG*. Let's also find a cool mysterious dark blue color. We want to give the feeling of night time and mystery.

If you're having trouble finding a deep blue night HEX, I'll be using: #223543.

Once you have found your deep blue, click the `Linear Gradient` icon to give it a night sky feel (Figure 4.7.2).

It's almost as if the moon is giving off light to our night sky. Feel free to adjust the second color as necessary. (Figure 4.7.3)

Figure 4.7.2

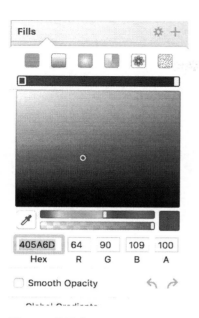

Figure 4.7.3

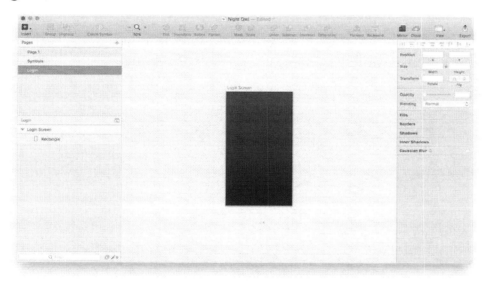

We're going to make the moon a part of our title logo. Go ahead and search the web for a crescent moon image.

Once you have your image, set the **Fill** to white, and let's also add a **shadow**. We want to give an illuminating effect for our moon, so let's change the black color of the shadow to white. Have the X and Y values both be 0. We don't want an offset for our illumination!

431

(Figure 4.7.4)

Figure 4.7.4

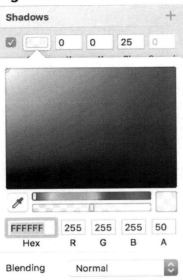

We can also crank up the blur of our shadow to roughly 25. This should give us a nice glowing effect for our moon. (Figure 4.7.5)

Figure 4.7.5

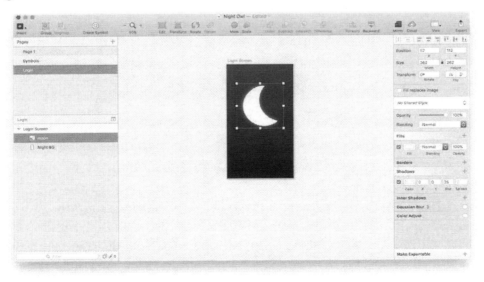

This is looking great!

Now let's Insert -> Text and type *NIGHT WL* in all caps. (Yes I left out the "O" intentionally :)).

Find a font you like that matches our apps personality, and leave a space for the "O." I'll be using *Avenir Next Ultra Light*. Let's make the size around 30, and center it horizontally. We'll also bring it up towards the top. (Figure 4.7.6)

Figure 4.7.6

We're going to use the moon as the "O" in "Night Owl" to give the title a little flair. Feel free to resize and alter the position and glow until you like the way it looks. (Figure 4.7.7)

Figure 4.7.7

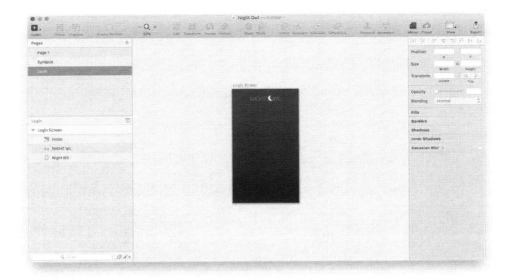

This is looking pretty sweet! Let's add some stars to top off our background.

Insert -> Shape -> Oval and make a small perfect circle. Remove the border and make the fill white.

Go ahead and apply the same "glowing" technique you did on your moon and adjust the opacity of the white glow to your liking.

Now that you have one completed star, you can copy & paste it to scatter them around the artboard to your taste.

Feel free to resize them to add some variety to your night sky. When you are done, let's group all the stars in a folder to keep things tidy. (Figure 4.7.8)

Figure 4.7.8

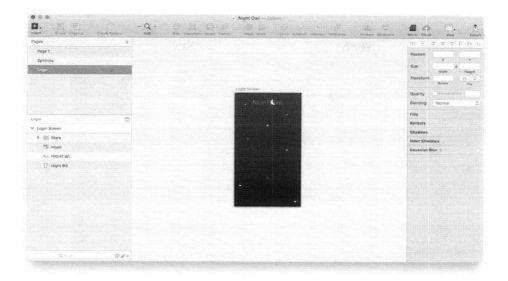

Now let's create our login button. Insert -> Shape -> Rounded Rectangle and place it right on bottom.

You can remove the borders, adjust the corners to your liking, and center it horizontally in the artboard.

Go ahead and make the fill pure white.

Let's then Insert -> Text and type *Login*. Then, use the same base color as our night background color. (Figure 4.7.9)

Figure 4.7.9

435

Lastly, find a picture of an cartoon owl, and place it right in the center of your screen to fill up the blank space a bit. Feel free to use the principles in this section to create an owl if you'd like as well.

The final login screen should look something like Figure 4.7.10.

Figure 4.7.10

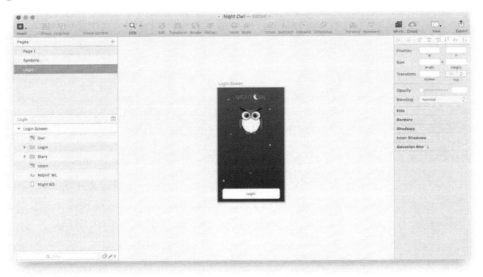

Creating the Home Page

Create another page and title it *Home*. This is where we'll design our home screen.

Go ahead and `Insert -> Artboard -> iPhone 7` and copy your Night BG from the Login screen. We can also bring over our "Night Owl" title (including the moon) and place it at the top.

We're going to want to make it a little smaller because it's more of a navigation title, rather than a login screen.

At the top, click `Scale`, and bring it down just a notch (maybe 95% of the 100%). (Figure 4.7.11)

Scaling works well when you want to keep all your elements proportionate. If you had grouped your text and moon together, and `Shift` + dragged the group inwards, the text would not scale appropriately to the moon. Don't forget to align it horizontally in the artboard when you're done!

Figure 4.7.11

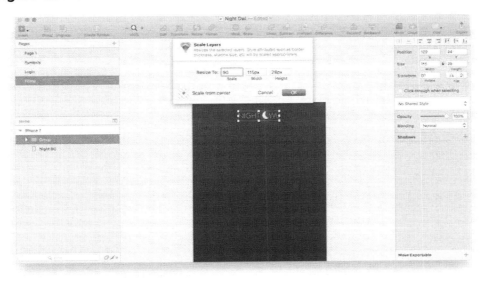

Great! Now we're going to create a little space for a user to write a status. Perhaps a reason why they can't sleep!

Let's `Insert -> Shape -> Rounded Rectangle` and place it right below our title. Make the fill white, and remove the borders. (Figure 4.7.12)

Figure 4.7.12

437

The white is probably a little harsh on the eye's (being that a user will use this app at night). Let's decrease the opacity to 25%. This is just enough for the user to know it's a text field without being obnoxious.

We can then `Insert` -> `Text` and type a placeholder text as a prompt to write a status. Be sure to decrease your placeholder text opacity to around 60% to denote it is in fact placeholder text. (Figure 4.7.13)

Tip: Placeholder text is a great way to prompt action without cluttering up the UI. If it weren't for the placeholder text, we'd have to put a call to action somewhere outside of the text field, which could get messy and confusing. Take advantage of placeholder text as a prompt for action anywhere you can. They are very useful on forms, status updates, and chat / messaging systems.

Figure 4.7.13

So what happens when a user posts a status? We can place the text right below the status bar.

To demonstrate this, let's Insert -> Text and say "No Recent Posts."

This will let people viewing our mockup know where their status would be posted. Let's also align it horizontally in the artboard. (Figure 4.7.14)

Figure 4.7.14

Lastly, we'll add a "Trending Topics" table view that users can browse through and chat

439

with other night owls.

Let's create a "Trending" header for our table view.

`Insert -> Shape -> Rectangle` and snap it to the left and right edges. We'll make this around 50 pts tall. Let's also remove the borders and make the fill a solid black color, and decrease the opacity to around 40%.

You'll see that our Night BG color will begin to bleed through giving it a nice complimentary shade to our theme.

Finally, let's `Insert -> Text` and type *Trending* inside of our header box. (Figure 4.7.15)

Figure 4.7.15

Now let's find a cool trending icon to put beside our text. Once you've found one, make the fill white and scale it down so it fits nicely right beside the "Trending" text.

Group these two items together and align it vertically and horizontally in the header box. You know the drill! ;)

(Figure 4.7.16)

Figure 4.7.16

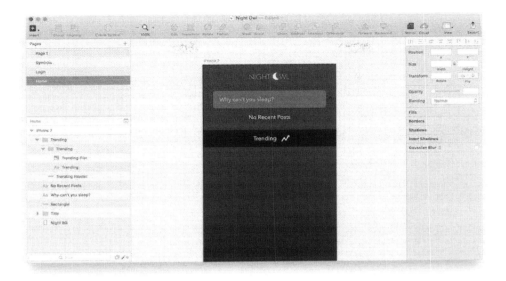

Let's create our table view cells. This will be topics a user can click on.

All we'll need to do is Insert -> Text and type any topic you'd like.

Go ahead and Insert -> Shape -> Line to act as a table view cell separator.

To match our theme, make the line white in color, and decrease the opacity to 50% to soften it.

We'll also decrease the thickness to .5 to further match a table view cell separator.

(Figure 4.7.17)

Figure 4.7.17

Now let's group these two items, and duplicate them down the artboard to simulate a table view. Then rename each item to simulate a variety of topics. By the end of it, you're Home screen should look something like (Figure 4.7.18)

Figure 4.7.18

Screen Real Estate

Before we move on, I want to emphasize a few things we accomplished here (aside from a beautiful home screen!).

First, we began to create a color scheme for our app without even realizing it! Notice how we didn't need to add any more colors other than the Night BG, and yet we have such a dynamic, great looking screen?
We accomplished this through lowering the opacity of white and black elements over our original color. This created depth from our original color, and allowed us to do two things:

1. **Speak to our users without words** - Instead of saying "This is a textfield!" we were able to convey that beautifully with a semi - transparent rounded rectangle. We *told* the user where to go with our color choice. This goes for the table view header as well.

2. **Separate elements with more than just lines** - Barring the table view separators, we were able to properly denote sections in our app through our color scheme.

Always look for ways to speak without directional text. Different colors and semi transparent black and white items do this wonderfully.

Second, we made great use of the screen real estate. As product designers, we must be very dialed into how elements will be displayed on various devices, and how much space we have to get our user to fully and properly digest our app.

Notice how the main elements take up *most, if not all of the screen real estate.*
We are only showcasing two actions: Posting a status and viewing trending topics to talk about. There are obviously a multitude of features we can throw on this screen, but the more that happens the harder it becomes to digest.

Also notice we still have room at the upper left and right corners for items like an "Inbox" and a "Hamburger Menu", etc. These secondary items can be placed at the top, bottom, and in the corners of our screen. And the main actions that will loop our users into our journey cycle should be front and center. Users these days need to be hooked, intrigued, and understand your app all within 1-2 seconds.

If more time is needed to understand where or how to start their journey through your app, you might lose a conversion. That's how quickly things can change. That's why the details matter.

Don't ever think you're over thinking it, because chances are you're doing the exact opposite.

Creating the Chat Screen

Lastly, we're going to design a chat screen between another user.
Let's go ahead and click + and create a new page called *Chat*. We'll also `Insert ->` `Artboard -> iPhone 7`, and title it *Chat Screen*. Then, copy & paste our Night BG from any of the previous screens and paste it on our Chat Screen.

Then, `Insert -> Symbol -> Keyboard -> Dark -> Lower` (Figure 4.7.19).
Go ahead and place the keyboard symbol at the bottom of the Chat Screen.

Figure 4.7.19

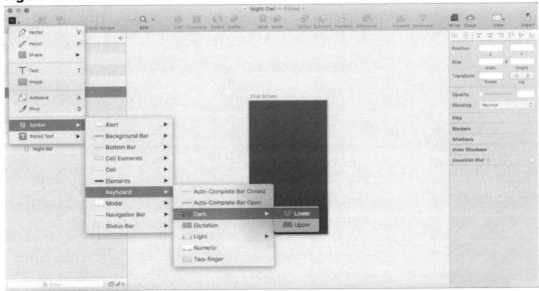

Symbols are elements you can create to reuse throughout your project. The beauty of symbols is that once you change the root symbol, all instances of that symbol change, so you don't have to go back and alter each one.
Similar to coding, we don't want to repeat ourselves, and any chance to optimize work

flow is encouraged. Can you guess any of our elements we've repeated so far? If you guessed our **Night BG** you're correct!

Feel free to click our Night BG and click `Create Symbol` in the upper left (Figure 4.7.20). Now every time we change our Night BG, all of our screens will change!

Figure 4.7.20

Let's create our navigation bar items. We won't have a separate rectangle, but go ahead and `Insert` -> `Text` and type a topic of choice. Align it horizontally on our screen, and find/add a "back" button. Make sure you make the fill white! (Figure 4.7.21)

Figure 4.7.21

Now, create the field where the user would type.

Insert -> Shape -> Rectangle and place it right above the keyboard symbol at 50 pts high. Remove the border and make the fill white. If you guessed that we should probably decrease the opacity, you're correct!

I would bring the opacity down to around 40%, and create a placeholder text in the same way we did for the status on our Home Screen. Don't forget to align it vertically in the rectangle. (Figure 4.7.22)

Figure 4.7.22

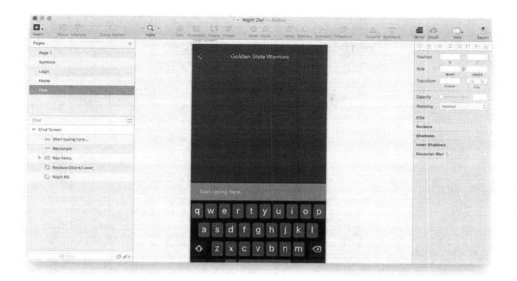

Next, find a "send" (i.e. airplane) button that is enclosed in either a circle or square to simulate a button. If you'd like, you can also find a send icon, and group it with a circle in Sketch. We'll use this as our "send" button for our chat. We'll keep the icon inside white, and fill the surrounding color.

Head over to www.paletton.com or www.color.adobe.com. These are **extremely** helpful tools when creating color palettes. We can input a HEX, and the tool will show complimentary colors in different schemes. It's a great starting place to explore colors that compliment your theme. I often start with a HEX provided, and adjust accordingly.

Let's take our base Night BG HEX (#223543) and add it into Paletton. We'll then go to the upper left corner and click Adjacent Colors (Figure 4.7.23)

Figure 4.7.23

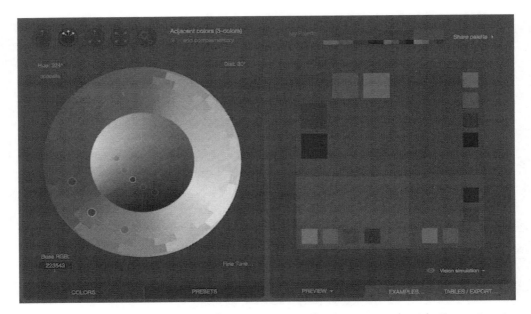

You'll notice right off the bat we have a variety of colors to work with. I'm going to grab one of the green HEXs by clicking the box. Find a green color you like and copy it to your clipboard. (Figure 4.7.24)

Figure 4.7.24

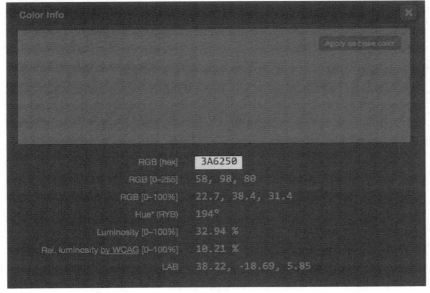

Now paste it into the Fill of your "send" button. It turns out this green works really well right out the gate! If yours doesn't look quite right, feel free to use this HEX as a starting point, or go back to Paletton and choose a different color all together. These tools work great for unleashing your creativity and giving you some options to work with. Once you have your "send" button, be sure to align it vertically in your text box and group them together to keep things tidy. (Figure 4.7.25)

Figure 4.7.25

Lastly, we're going to want to create a mock conversation. Let's Insert -> Shape -> Oval and create a perfect circle around 33pts x 33pts. We can remove the border as well. This will act as a user picture within the chat.

Next Insert -> Text for the name, date, and the message individually. We'll make the text for the date a little smaller, the message text a standard size, and the name a little bigger as well as **bolded** or semi ***bolded***. We want to emphasize the different elements within the cell, and this is a perfect way to do so.

We'll now add a thin separator line and style it similar to our home screen table view separators. Once you have all these elements configured, let's group them together! (Figure 4.7.26)

Tip: When creating table view cell separators, it often helps to have the left side align to the furthest left element, and scale to the end of the screen on the right. For example, our line separator is essentially left aligned with our image circle.

Figure 4.7.26

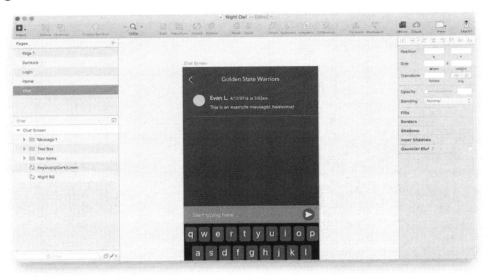

Now you can copy & paste this cell, and change it's elements accordingly to simulate real interactions! Feel free to fill in our placeholder/user images with actual faces!

Final Screens.png

Wrapping up

Be sure to keep your apps main functionality on the forefront of the screen. You have 1-2 seconds to grab the users attention and convey exactly what they're supposed to do. It's also great to use semi-transparent black and white shapes to break up elements of your screen, as well as placeholder text to suggest direction and instruction.

Exercise

The top of the Home screen has room for more functionality (ie. an Inbox or a Menu). Use your creativity and design more features that enhances the goal of the app, while keeping in mind the target demographic and use case scenarios.

Chapter 33: Exporting Assets

We'll take a brief look at the history of iPhones, screen sizes and resolutions. We'll then learn how to properly export assets to make them pixel perfect.

What you will learn

- How to properly export assets in Sketch for iOS

We've lightly touched on exporting assets in previous chapters, but we'll go ahead and export some of the icons in our Night Owl app as if we're ready to put them into our XCode project.

Understanding the iPhone resolution

First, we need to understand how the iPhone screen resolution works.
If you have worked with iPhone assets before, you've probably noticed you need to export them at 1x, 2x, and 3x.
So why exactly do we need to do this?

As the iPhone began to evolve, Apple began putting **retina** screens in their phones to enhance their displays.
The 2x suffix represents double the density of pixels. So instead of 1px by 1px, there are 2px by 2px's occupying the same space.

The same concept is applied to 3x, meaning there are actually 3px by 3px (9 pixels) occupying the same space, making the display **much** richer. Apple denotes this "space" as points, which is exactly what Sketch uses.

This is great for us, because all we have to do is select our images in Sketch, and export them at 1x, 2x, and 3x, and Sketch will automatically give us the correct pixels to be displayed for each respective resolution. From there we can drop them into XCode for pixel perfect images.

XCode also uses the point system, which works out *amazingly* because now we can design down to the pixel.

For example, if we have a UIImage in XCode at 30pts by 30pts, we can create a 30pt by 30pt asset in Sketch, export them at 1x, 2x, and 3x and our assets will come out perfectly. On the contrary, we can design in Sketch and know the *exact* dimensions we need to design for in XCode.

Exporting the Night Owl Assets

Go to your Night Owl Home page and find your "Trending" icon. On the bottom right you'll notice Make Exportable. (Figure 4.8.1)

Figure 4.8.1

Once clicked, you'll notice a few options (Figure 4.8.2):

Figure 4.8.2

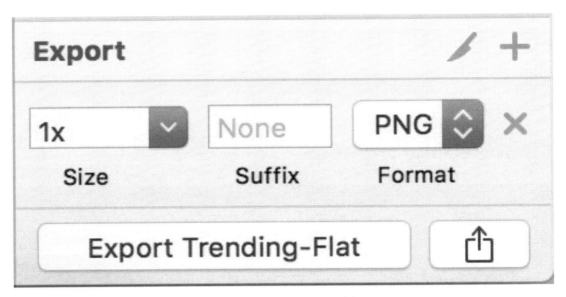

By clicking + Sketch will add 2x, and clicking + again adds 3x.

From here we can click Export and save our assets to a destination. (Figure 4.8.3)

Notice Sketch has added the suffix's automatically, making it readable in XCode right out of the gate.

Figure 4.8.3

You will also notice a little knife icon next to the +. Clicking this will create a **slice** instead of an exportable item. The only difference between slices and exportable items is that slices will pick up all the existing layers, whereas the exportable item will just be the layer selected.

Wrapping up

Create your designs in Sketch *exactly* how you would want them to look, and they can be easily exported at the correct sizes. This will make your icons and assets pixel perfect, and save you the headache of trying to scale sizes manually outside of Sketch and Xcode.

Exercise

Go ahead and export the rest of the assets in our Night Owl app using the same method above. Feel free to experiment with the other sizing options and formats to get a feel for their full capabilities!

Chapter 34: Designing Apps to Boost Retention & Increase Virality

In this chapter we'll explore a fundamental formula for retention and virality.

What you will learn

- Key components for optimizing a users initial experience with your app, which increases the likelihood of virality

- The Viral Coefficient

- How to trigger behaviors within your app

Three step process

There are three main elements that a user will go through when they experience your app, and it's your job to maximize each one of them. If your product can achieve this, not only will your users have a great experience, but retention will likely increase. This will also increase the likelihood of organic growth. (Figure 4.9.1)

Figure 4.9.1

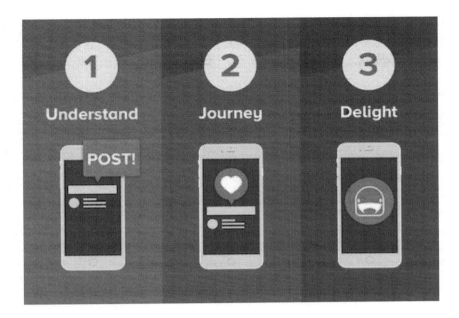

Understanding

Users need to understand why they are there, and what they need to do. At the very least, the user will have some context of what your app is, or what it does. Whether it is by keyword search in the App Store, or word of mouth from a friend, we need to assume their context with your app is as minimal as possible.

Therefore it's essential that the second your user opens your app, they understand exactly what they need to do to start using it. If you want the user to post something, this should be clear and not be buried and bogged down with secondary features.

Journey

The next component is the Journey. The journey begins the second your user interacts with your app, and ends when they have gone through the actions you've set forth. For example, the journey through experiencing Instagram for the first time would be tapping the post icon, choosing your favorite filter, writing a description, and finally posting it to your feed.

The journey should be taken **very** seriously. It is as if you are meeting someone for the first time. A first impression is generally an accumulation of how they present themselves (both physically and emotionally), how they speak, what they speak about, the common ground you establish, and a variety of other factors. This can be directly translated to the first journey your user goes through with your app.

I encourage you to be very deliberate through this process. Focus on a few key actions you want your user to engage in, and cut out all the unnecessary fat.

The user is in discovery mode, and excited to try out a new experience. Having too many options forces the user to think instead of enjoying the ride.

Imagine if you went on a roller coaster, but at every turn it comes to a jolting stop, and asks if you want to go left or right? Sure it might be fun to "customize" the ride, but it becomes less of an experience, and more of a duty.

Your users owe you nothing. Give them a great roller coaster ride.

I cannot stress enough the importance of remembering your target audience through this process. Because this is a first impression, you want to make sure your app personality shines strong here.

If your building a business or enterprise application, you might want to cut straight to the point and make it easy for a wide range of ages to use. Whereas an app focused on music for millennial's might call for a greater finessed experience, filled with more bells and whistles. This will vary immensely for every single app, and should be carefully crafted and tested throughout the entire lifetime of your app.

Delight

This is your moment. Your user has found your app, downloaded it, experienced a magnificent journey through their first interaction, and now it's time for you to close them. This can be tied into creating user habits with micro-interactions, elevating the experience to a new level after completing an action.

Let's go back to our Instagram example. Once a user goes through the journey of posting their first picture, the highlight of it all is when users like your picture! Displaying users liking your content is a micro-interaction that loops you back into the journey process.

Another example is finding a freelancer on a platform like Upwork. The journey could have been setting up your profile and posting your first job listing, and when a freelancer reaches out to fill the position, the loop has been closed. That's the crucial moment when Upwork will let you know you've succeeded in your post, and as a user.

458

Gratifying your users in this aspect can also have some great compounding effects. This is the moment where the value proposition of your app is being fully defined, and when the user has experienced the value firsthand. They might tell their friends about it!

This is arguably the most powerful form of marketing, it's what makes products go viral. All products strive for this, and dialing in on gratifying your users after they have gone through the first two steps is crucial for success.

Virality Coefficient

The virality coefficient is a way to quantify virality. Frankly put, it's the **average invites each existing user sends out, multiplied by the conversion rate of those invites.** Invites can come in many ways. They can be emails, share systems, and even word of mouth. For the sake of illustrating this concept, invites are - *how many people your current users talk about your awesome app to others.*

So if we were to rephrase the definition in our context, it would basically be **how many people your current user base talked about your awesome app, multiplied by the percentage of people who actually downloaded it.** (Figure 4.9.2)

Figure 4.9.2

Great, so now let's see this in action! Imagine we just finished building our awesome app that already has 100 committed users. Let's say that on average, each user tells 5 of their friends about it, and 25% of those people actually download it and do the same. Look at how this affects our users over time. (Figure 4.9.3)

Figure 4.9.3

Users	Friends Shared to	Users Converted
100	500	125
225	625	156
381	781	195
577	977	244
821	1,221	305
1,126	1,526	381
1,507	1,907	477
1,984	2,384	596
2,580	2,980	745
3,325	3,725	931
4,257	4,657	1,164
5,421	5,821	1,455
6,876	7,276	1,819
8,695	9,095	2,274
10,969	11,369	2,842
13,811	14,211	3,553

i (Average # of users friends that were shared to)	5
Conversion %	25%
k (Viral Coefficient)	1.25

As you can see, we have a healthy growth curve. At the end of the first cycle, we have already converted 125 new users! Those in turn get re-entered into the viral coefficient formula.

Be careful not to include your full user base when calculating future cycles. It's a dangerous and false assumption that your current users will share your app at the same rate indefinitely.

A cycle is most commonly a campaign that is ran to share or spread virality within your product. This could be in weeks, months, or days. It really depends on the time frame that fits well with your specific situation, and will likely vary case by case.

Now let's adjust a few of the parameters and watch what happens. We'll have the same 100 users, but on average they'll only tell 3 friends. That makes a 20% conversion rate. (Figure 4.9.4)

Figure 4.9.4

Users	Friends Shared to	Users Converted			
100	300	60	i (Average # of users friends that were shared to)		3
160	180	36	Conversion %		20%
196	108	22	k (Viral Coefficient)		0.6
218	65	13			
231	39	8			
238	23	5			
243	14	3			
246	8	2			
247	5	1			
248	3	1			
249	2	0			
249	1	0			
250	1	0			
250	0	0			
250	0	0			
250	0	0			

You will notice three things right off the bat. **Our viral coefficient falls below 1, and eventually our converted users diminish to 0, which means our growth came to a screeching halt.** Bummer.

So we can safely conclude that we need to keep our viral coefficient above 1 to maintain steady growth. (Figure 4.9.5)

Figure 4.9.5

Users	Friends Shared to	Users Converted			
100	500	100	i (Average # of users friends that were shared to)		5
200	500	100	Conversion %		20%
300	500	100	k (Viral Coefficient)		1
400	500	100			
500	500	100			
600	500	100			
700	500	100			
800	500	100			
900	500	100			
1,000	500	100			
1,100	500	100			
1,200	500	100			
1,300	500	100			
1,400	500	100			
1,500	500	100			
1,600	500	100			

So how do we increase our viral coefficient?

1. Increasing how many friends your app is shared to by your current user base

2. Increasing the conversion rate

3. Do both because you're a ROCKSTAR

Increasing invites is a great way to increase your viral coefficient. Getting your current user base to share your awesome app with their friends becomes increasingly easier with technology. A common technique is giving discount or coupon codes for sharing. **(ie Get 15% off your purchase by sharing to Facebook or Twitter)**.

Increasing conversion rates are also extremely efficient. If you know your app is being shared by friends who trust each other, increasing the conversion rate could result in tremendous returns.

Often, techniques will be used hand in hand with increasing invites.
For example, when you share Uber with a friend, Uber rewards both you and your friend with 20% off your next ride (if your friend signs up). We've just killed two birds with one stone. We have incentivized sharing, usage, and new user adoption.

There are many more ways to use the viral coefficient and a number of hybrid formulas for specific use cases. If you are interested, I encourage you to look further into them. It can significantly impact the driving forces for better decision making.

User Behavior

In the last part of this Chapter, I'd like to touch on behavior. What makes a user take action? What are the driving forces behind these actions? B.J. Fogg, a behavioral scientist from Stanford University, breaks it down into the following:

Behavior = Motivation + Ability + Trigger

Motivation for all intent and purposes refers to how motivated the user is to complete an action.
For example, a scenario in which someone might have a high motivation to act, would be paying an electricity bill. By paying an electricity bill, one can avoid late dues, and maintain power in their home.
Motivation can vary case by case. For our next example, a 10 year old child might have less motivation to do his or her household chores than adult keeping up with their bills (As much as we'd like to go back to being a kid doing chores).

Ability refers to how capable one is to complete an action. In our electricity bill example, if one is struggling to make ends meet, they might have less ability to pay their bills vs their next door millionaire neighbor.
Ability becomes extremely important because if your user does not have the ability to

complete an action, the behavioral model is lost. Conversely, if someone is easily able to complete an action it makes all the other levers involved easier to pull.

A **Trigger** refers to something that prompts you to take action. For example, your bill sent to your mailbox, or a push notification on your phone would be a prompt for you to take action.

So how does this all piece together?

If you want your users to do something, it will depend on their level of motivation and ability, which will be prompted by a trigger. Prompting triggers with low motivation and difficult ability, have an extremely low success rate.
Where as aiming to combine high motivation with ease of execution, results in higher success rate with your trigger.

Furthermore, you can have success with a highly motivating action and a mediocre ability level, and conversely, a lower motivating action with a higher ability level.

Imagine a trigger for a 15% discount coupon upon emailing 5 of your friends about the app. I would imagine motivation would be relatively low depending on the original price, and the ability might be difficult if you have to manually email 5 people, and carefully select those you send it to.
Now imagine if the trigger prompted a **free item** (high motivation), with a mid to high ability level. Now you might start seeing some results!

Wrapping up

You might be thinking, "Okay this is great, but what is the point of all this?"

These principles are imperative from the moment you start brainstorming your minimum viable product, and will continue as long as your app is still alive and kicking. These principles are intertwined into the fabric of all great products in some capacity, and are not merely a check mark on the path to success.
I encourage you to incorporate all these in your future applications, and I'm excited to see what amazing products you crank out because of it. :)

Exercise

Use a current app you have built, or one that you are planning on building, and create a model for your viral coefficient. Think about how many of your friends and family can get to use your product from the jump, and what tactics you could use to increase your viral coefficient. I encourage you to actually implement your ideas and quantify the results so you know where you can improve, and what tactics performed the best.

SECTION 5 - Intermediate iOS

Chapter 35: In-App Purchases

Monetizing your apps is a common way to create wealth as a developer. Apple has made it easy to do this by integrating In-App Purchases.

What you will learn

- How to create a Collection View

- Navigating iTunes Connect for IAP's

- Registering a App Id for IAP's

- Creating multiple IAP tiers

- Sandbox testing IAP's

Key Terms

- **IAP (in-app purchase)**

- **UICollectionView**

- **UICollectionCell**

- **SKPayment**

- **Non-Consumable**

- **Restore Purchases**

- **Sandbox**

Resources

Download here:

Setting up **in-app purchases** is easier than you'd think. I'll take you through it step by step.

First, we need to make products in iTunes Connect * *__This requires a paid developer account__*.

Once we have them set up we need to request those products to see if they are available. Once we know they are available we can display the product info. Then the purchase can be made by creating an **SKPayment** and add that to the queue.

We'll set up a system to handle all the responses we get from Apple, such as successful or declined. Once a payment is successful, we provide the user with the purchase. We are going to make a simple Collection View with custom cells and a purchase **restore** button. That will recover all your purchases if you ever delete the app or get a new device.

Your **IAP** iOS App (Figure 5.1.0) will have a **UICollectionView**, five **UICollectionCells** and one UIButton.

Figure 5.1.0

Creating an Xcode Project

Open Xcode and, from the File menu, select New and then New Project.... A new
workspace window will appear, and a sheet will slide from its toolbar with several
application templates to choose from.

On the left-hand side, select Application from the iOS section.

From the choices that appear, select Single View Application and press the Next button
(Figure   5.1.1).

(Apple changes these templates and their names often.)

Figure 5.1.1

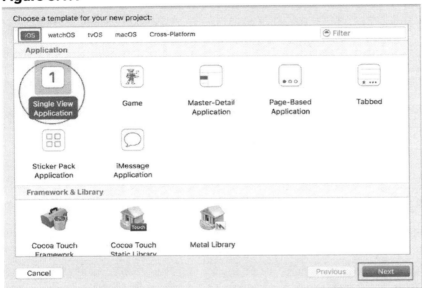

Under Product Name enter the name of your project, I named mine *InAppPurchases*. Then
press Next.

(Figure 5.1.2)

Figure 5.1.2

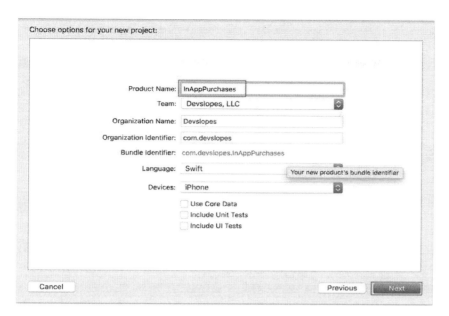

Okay, so we are going to get straight to the purchase screen.

Click on `Main.Storyboard` and lets place a **UICollectionView** on it. Let's leave some space on the bottom for our restore purchase button.

Now `pin` it to the margins **0** to the **top**, **0 left** and **right** and **40** from the **bottom**. (Figure 5.1.3)

Figure 5.1.3

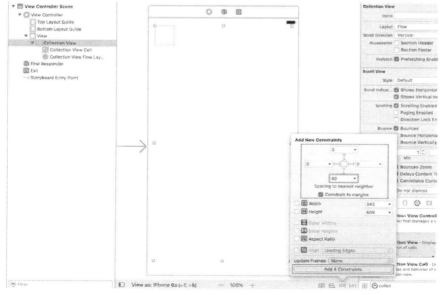

Because this is not a tutorial on how to set up a **UICollectionView** or constraints, I'm going to go through it pretty quickly and just explain what we did.

Figure 5.1.4

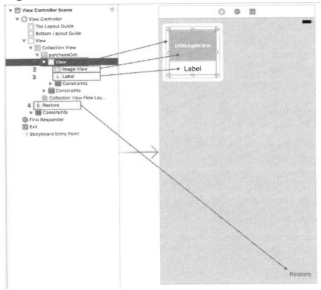

Okay, so I made the cell **160** x **160 points** big. I added a UIView to the cell and constrained it to the margins (so I can round the corners and add a shadow later on to make it prettier).

Second,I added a UIImage view and a label inside the view that was just added and pinned them **8** points all the way around and **4** points from the label (we can always adjust these as needed once we have real images in them).
Lastly, I added the restore button under the Collection View and pinned it to the corner.

Lets add the assets now.
I added *Arcade Time Background*, *Arcade-1*, *Arcade-2*, *Arcade-3*, *Arcade-4*, and *Bear-1*. (Figure 5.1.5)

Figure 5.1.5

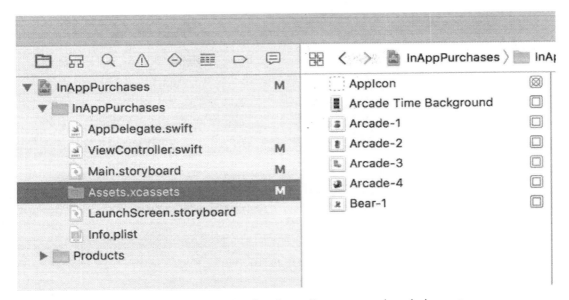

We can now add a image placeholder for the cell we created and also set up a UIImageView for a background.

First select the UIImageView inside the cell.

Then select the `Attributes inspector`, where it says Image select the `dropdown menu` and select *Arcade-1*.

Then for Content Mode select the `dropdown menu` and select `Aspect Fit`.

(Figure 5.1.6)

Figure 5.1.6

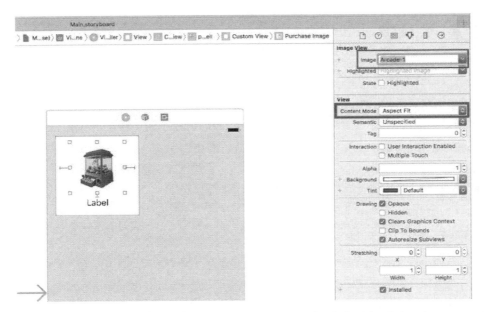

Drag a UIImageView from the `Object Library` to the left side right above our Collection View, this will insure that the background image will be behind the Collection View. Once its there and still selected lets `pin` it right away.

Uncheck `Constrain to margins` and lets put **-20** from the **top**, and **0** from **left**, **right** and **bottom**.

(Figure 5.1.7)

Figure 5.1.7

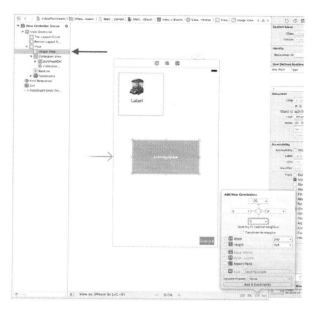

The Collection View needs to be clear so we can see our background when we set a image to it.

Select your *Collection View* on the left side. Then select the `Attributes inspector` on the right and set the background color to **clear**.

(Figure 5.1.8)

Figure 5.1.8

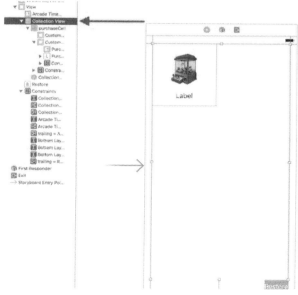

473

Select the UIImageView on the left side that we placed above our Collection View. Select Attributes inspector again and where it says *Image*, select the dropdown menu and select *Arcade Time Background*.

Then for Content Mode select the dropdown menu and select Scale To Fill. (Figure 5.1.9)

Figure 5.1.9

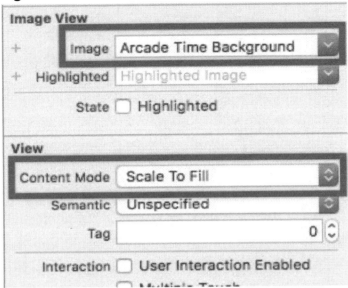

Our Storyboard should now resemble something like this. We will get our Collection View functioning so we can see it in the simulator before we beautify it like Figure 5.1.0.

Figure 5.1.10

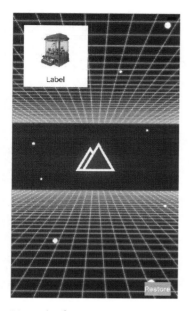

Now, before we can get the **UICollectionView** all set up and have the ViewController inherit from the **UICollectionView** Data source and delegate, we need to make a *UICollectionViewCell* file to customize the cell.

Right click the *InAppPurchases* folder and select New file.

Make sure you select iOS, then select Cocoa Touch Class and click Next.

Figure 5.1.11

Make sure the subclass selected is `UICollectionViewCell` and name the class
PurchaseCell, click `Next`.

Make sure your project is selected on the next screen and click `Create`.

We'll come back to this file later to add more to it, this is good for now.

(Figure 5.1.12)

Figure 5.1.12

Now, you need to click on the `Identity inspector` on the right side and select the
`PurchaseCell` class for the Collection View cell.

(Figure 5.1.13)

Figure 5.1.13

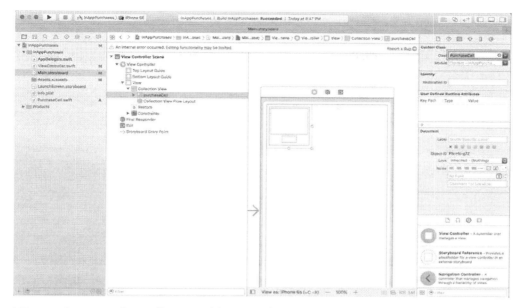

We need to give this cell a reusable identifier as well.

Click on the `Attributes inspector` and type *purchaseCell* in the identifier text field. (Figure 5.1.14)

Figure 5.1.14

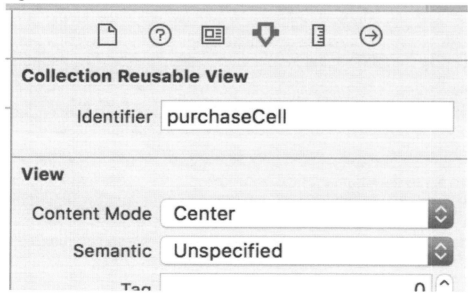

We are now ready to set up our `ViewController` and connect all of our IBOutlets.

Let's add the UICollectionViewDelegate and UICollectionViewDataSource to our `ViewController`.

We also need to set the delegate and data source and add the required methods to allow the UICollectionView protocols to work.

These are **numberOfItemsInSection**, **cellForItemAt indexPath**, and **didSelectItemAt indexPath**.

For sizing purposes so our *Collection View* cells look nice on all screen sizes, lets inherit from one more protocol, add UICollectionViewDelegateFlowLayout next to UICollectionViewDelagate and DataSource at the top.

Then add one more method to our class called *collectionViewLayout*.

```
import UIKit

class ViewController: UIViewController, UICollectionViewDelegate,
UICollectionViewDataSource, UICollectionViewDelegateFlowLayout {

    @IBOutlet weak var collectionView: UICollectionView!

    override func viewDidLoad() {
        super.viewDidLoad()
        collectionView.delegate = self
        collectionView.dataSource = self
    }

    func collectionView(_ collectionView: UICollectionView, numberOfItemsInSection
section: Int) -> Int {
        //This is a temporary value, just to show us some cells
        return 6
    }

    func collectionView(_ collectionView: UICollectionView, cellForItemAt
indexPath: IndexPath) -> UICollectionViewCell {
        if let cell = collectionView.dequeueReusableCell(withReuseIdentifier:
"purchaseCell", for: indexPath) as? PurchaseCell {
            return cell
        }else {
            return UICollectionViewCell()
        }
    }

    func collectionView(_ collectionView: UICollectionView, layout
collectionViewLayout: UICollectionViewLayout, sizeForItemAt indexPath: IndexPath) -
> CGSize {
```

```
        //This is so the cells look good on any screen size
        return CGSize(width: self.collectionView.bounds.size.width/2 - 20, height:
160)
    }


    func collectionView(_ collectionView: UICollectionView, didSelectItemAt
indexPath: IndexPath) {
        //This gets called when cell is tapped
        //We will add to this later
    }
}
```

Lets connect our Collection View `IBOutlet` to our Storyboard.

Open `Assistant Editor` and click the + next to the `IBOutlet` and drag it to the *Collection View*.

(Figure 5.1.15)

Figure 5.1.15

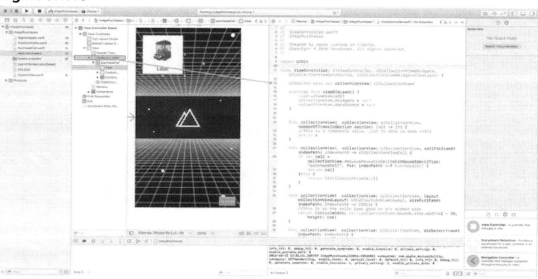

Now, that this is finished we can test and run our app. We should see 6 cells with our claw machine image. (Figure 5.1.16)

Figure 5.1.16

We need to configure the cell with data so we can change the image and also update the image and label.

So first, at the top of `ViewController.swift`, right under the `CollectionView IBOutlet`; declare an array of strings called *products* with the proper purchase item names you want to use.

```
let products = ["tier1","tier2","tier3","tier4","tier5"]
```

Select the `PurchaseCell.swift` file we created earlier, it is now time to add a configuration method and IBOutlets.

We need two *IBOutlets*. One we will call *purchaseImage* of type UIImageView and the second one is *purchaseLbl* of type UILabel.

Lastly, lets create a function called *configureCell* and pass in a variable called *imageName* of type String for now.

We'll use a *switch case* and manually set the label name and image for now.
We'll come back and refactor this code to work with our **IAP** stuff later.
This is enough to get everything set up and tested to make sure all our images work and look good.

```
import UIKit

class PurchaseCell: UICollectionViewCell {
```

```
@IBOutlet weak var purchaseImage: UIImageView!
@IBOutlet weak var purchaseLbl: UILabel!

func configureCell(imageName: String){
    switch imageName {
    case "tier1":
        purchaseImage.image = UIImage(named: "Arcade-1")
        purchaseLbl.text = "$2,500"
        break
    case "tier2":
        purchaseImage.image = UIImage(named: "Arcade-2")
        purchaseLbl.text = "$5,000"
        break
    case "tier3":
        purchaseImage.image = UIImage(named: "Arcade-3")
        purchaseLbl.text = "$10,000"
        break
    case "tier4":
        purchaseImage.image = UIImage(named: "Arcade-4")
        purchaseLbl.text = "$25,000"
        break
    case "tier5":
        purchaseImage.image = UIImage(named: "Bear-1")
        purchaseLbl.text = "$50,000"
        break
    default:
        break
    }
}
}
```

Time to connect those *IBOutlets* to our Storyboard.

Open `Assistant Editor` and click the + next to the *IBOutlet* and drag *purchaseLbl* to the Label in the cell, and *purchaseImage* to the *UIImageView*.
(Figure 5.1.17)

Figure 5.1.17

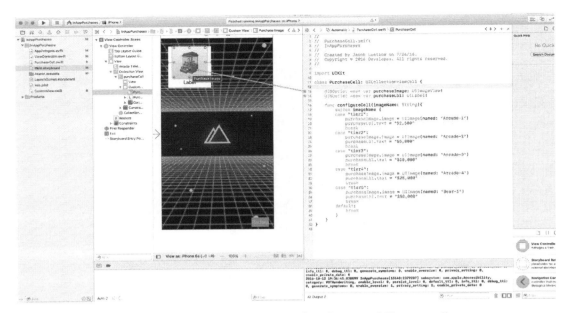

Alright, we are almost ready to test this to see if we have 5 different cells.
We need to refactor our `ViewController.swift` file a little, so select that.
Lets change the `return 6` in the `numberOfItemsInSection` to the count of our `products` array.

```swift
    func collectionView(_ collectionView: UICollectionView, numberOfItemsInSection section: Int) -> Int {
        return products.count
    }
```

One more code addition, we have to call our new *configureCell* method we created in our cell view and pass in one of our String values in our `products` array.

```swift
func collectionView(_ collectionView: UICollectionView, cellForItemAt indexPath: IndexPath) -> UICollectionViewCell {
        if let cell = collectionView.dequeueReusableCell(withReuseIdentifier: "purchaseCell", for: indexPath) as? PurchaseCell {

            cell.configureCell(imageName: products[indexPath.row])

            return cell
        }else {
            return UICollectionViewCell()
        }
}
```

Okay, lets run this in our simulator and we should have something that looks like this. (Figure 5.1.18)

Figure 5.1.18

The cells are really boring and just don't look great.

Lets create a custom view that will round the corners and put a shadow around the edge.

Right click the *InAppPurchases* folder and select **new file** -> select **iOS**, then select **Cocoa touch class** and click **Next**.

Make sure the subclass selected is **UIView** and name the class *CustomView*.

Click **Next**.

Make sure your project is selected on the next screen and click **Create**.

Add the code shown below to this new swift file.

```
import UIKit

class CustomView: UIView {

    override func awakeFromNib() {
        layer.cornerRadius = 2.0
        layer.shadowColor = UIColor(red: 157.0 / 255.0, green: 157.0 / 255.0, blue: 157.0 / 255.0, alpha: 0.5).cgColor
        layer.shadowOpacity = 0.8
        layer.shadowRadius = 5.0
        layer.shadowOffset = CGSize(width: 0.0, height: 2.0)
```

```
    }
}
```

We need to add another *UIView* to our cell, so lets go to the Storyboard and drag a UIView right above our view that contains our UIImageView and UILabel. (Figure 5.1.19)

Figure 5.1.19

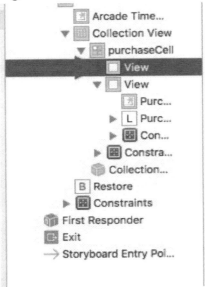

Once thats there, select both the new view and the one that was there and `pin` the view to the **leading**, **trailing**, **top** and **bottom** edges of the view thats already there. (Figure 5.1.20)

Figure 5.1.20

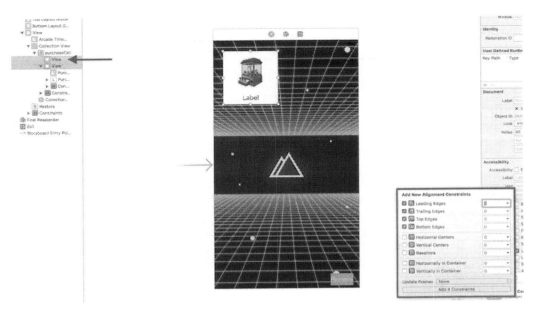

Go to your Main.Storyboard and select the view we placed in the cell and go to your
`Attributes inspector` and select `CustomView` for the class.
(Figure 5.1.21)

Figure 5.1.21

Select the *CustomView* we just placed in the cell and go to your `Attributes inspector`
and change the alpha to *0.6*.
(Figure 5.1.22)

Figure 5.1.22

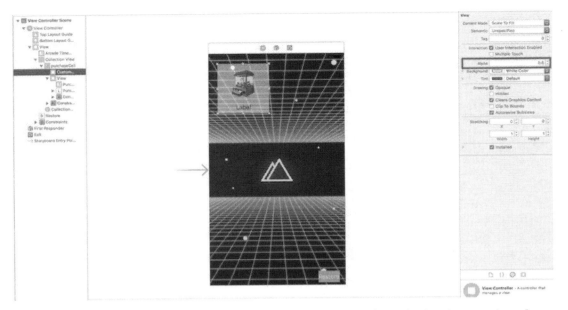

Select View that contains our UIImageView and UILabel and set the background to **clear**. (Figure 5.1.23)

Figure 5.1.23

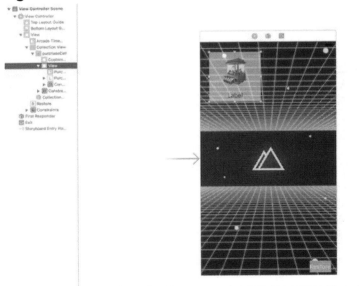

Lastly, select the `Restore` button and change the font to anything you like and make sure you change the background color to **clear**.

(Figure 5.1.24)

Figure 5.1.24

Now build and run your project and your cells will have slightly rounded corners and a little bit of a shadow (it is hard to see since the background is so dark).
It should look just like figure 5.1.0 at the beginning of this section.

Time to setup In App Purchases!

First, we need to go to our iTunes Connect page and Click on My Apps.
Then click the + symbol on the left side and select New App.
(Figure 5.1.25 & 5.1.26)

Figure 5.1.25

Figure 5.1.26

We then need to create a bundle ID for our app if you haven't already done so. Just click on the `developer portal` link.

(Figure 5.1.27)

Figure 5.1.27

On the left side of the page under `Identifiers` select the `App IDs` link.

Now you just need to name your app, in our case I named it *InAppPurchases*.

Then create a bundle identifier, ours is *com.devslopes.inAppPurchaseExample*.

This should use your own custom domain, it can only be used once.

Click `continue`, you will notice that **in-app purchases** is selected by default. Once you are on the next page just click `register`.

(Figure 5.1.28 & Figure 5.1.29)

Figure 5.1.28

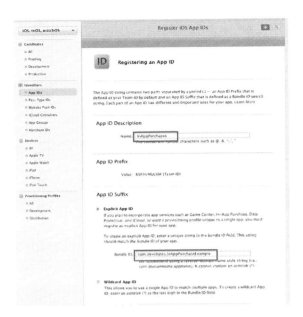

Figure 5.1.29

Now we can go back and refresh our iTunes connect account and our bundle ID should be available.

Once you see your bundle ID, fill everything else out.
(note: the name of the app needs to be unique and if it's already taken you'll have to

rename it). Click Create.
(Figure 5.1.30)

Figure 5.1.30

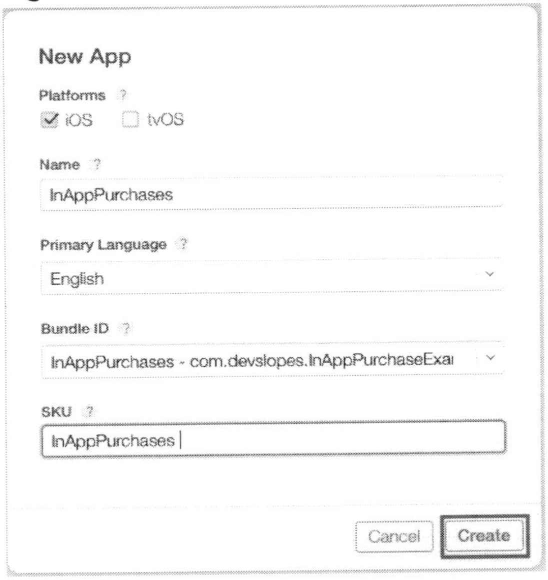

Select Features at the top and then press the + next to **In-App Purchases** to begin adding them.
(Figure 5.1.31)

Figure 5.1.31

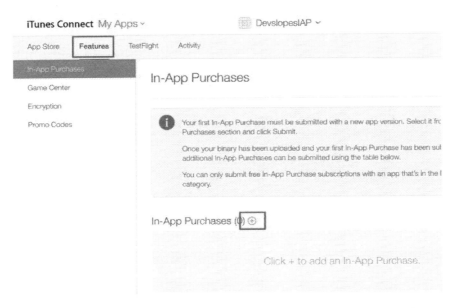

Select non-consumable for the type for this exercise. If you'd like to know what the other types are, the descriptions are very clear.

We are working with non-consumables because we can demonstrate the **restore** purchases feature this way.

(Figure 5.1.32)

Figure 5.1.32

We now need to name this **in-app purchase** and give it a unique product ID and select a pricing tier.

I wont be going through this process for every tier (5), so for the other items we'll have in our app, I will be naming them *tier1* through *tier5* and copying the pricing tier to match their name.
(Figure 5.1.33)

Figure 5.1.33

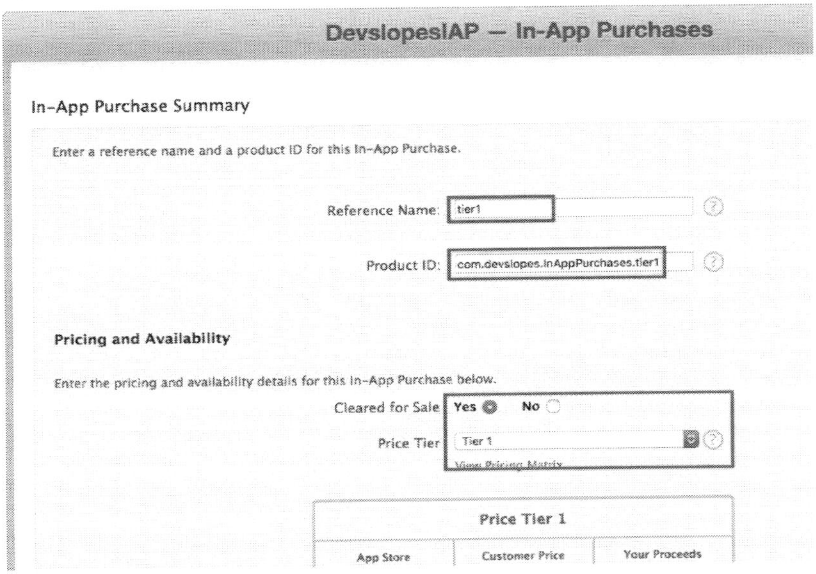

We need to have a language selected. For now, just add English and name the item whatever you'd like with a short description. Then press save.
(Figure 5.1.34)

Figure 5.1.34

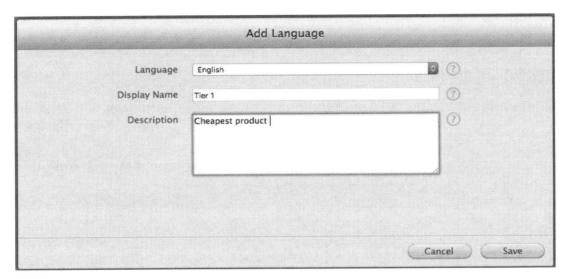

Now click **save** to finish entering the first item, and repeat this for tiers 2 through 5. (Figure 5.1.35)

Figure 5.1.35

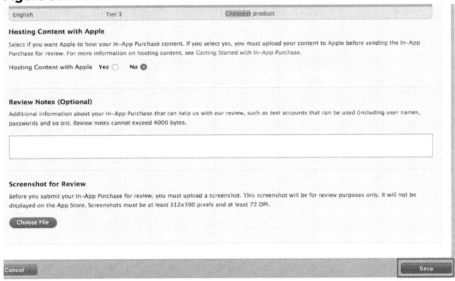

When you finish adding all 5 items, your **In-App Purchases** should look like this. (Figure 5.1.36)

Figure 5.1.36

Reference Name ^	Type	Product ID	Status
tier1	Non-Consumable	com.devslopes.InAppPurchases.tier1	● Waiting for Screenshot
tier2	Non-Consumable	com.devslopes.InAppPurchases.tier2	● Waiting for Screenshot
tier3	Non-Consumable	com.devslopes.InAppPurchases.tier3	● Waiting for Screenshot
tier4	Non-Consumable	com.devslopes.InAppPurchases.tier4	● Waiting for Screenshot
tier5	Non-Consumable	com.devslopes.InAppPurchases.tier5	● Waiting for Screenshot

Request Available Products

Now that all of our products are entered into iTunes connect, we now need to request our products from Apple to make sure they are available to buy.
First, we need to `import StoreKit` in our class and also inherit **SKProductsRequestDelegate**.

Once we do that, we need to create a *requestProducts function*.
Inside this function we need a Set of strings with the bundle ID's for all the products we added to iTunes Connect and then do a **SKProductsRequest** and wait for a response and hope we're told they're ready.

```
import UIKit
import StoreKit

class ViewController: UIViewController, UICollectionViewDelegate,
UICollectionViewDataSource, UICollectionViewDelegateFlowLayout,
SKProductsRequestDelegate {

    @IBOutlet weak var collectionView: UICollectionView!

    var products = ["tier1","tier2","tier3","tier4","tier5"]

    override func viewDidLoad() {
        super.viewDidLoad()
        collectionView.delegate = self
        collectionView.dataSource = self
        requestProducts()
    }
```

```swift
    func requestProducts() {
        let ids: Set<String> =
["com.devslopes.InAppPurchases.tier1","com.devslopes.InAppPurchases.tier2","com.dev
slopes.InAppPurchases.tier3","com.devslopes.InAppPurchases.tier4","com.devslopes.In
AppPurchases.tier5"]
        let productsRequest = SKProductsRequest(productIdentifiers: ids)
        productsRequest.delegate = self
        productsRequest.start()
    }
```

Above, you see that we set the `SKProductsRequest` delegate.

Now we need to add a required function called *productsRequest didReceive response*. This is where we know if our products are available to sell or not.

```swift
    func productsRequest(_ request: SKProductsRequest, didReceive response:
SKProductsResponse) {
        print("Products ready: \(response.products.count)")
        print("Products not ready: \(response.invalidProductIdentifiers.count)")
}
```

Build and run your project. If your *products ready* doesn't show all the items you've added, make sure your bundle ID's on your project match the ones on iTunes Connect.

Okay, now that we are receiving products ready to sell from the App Store, let's create a new array of **SKProduct** type. Replace the `products` array.

```swift
var products = [SKProduct]()
```

Then, inside our `productRequest` function we can set the `products` array equal to our `response.products` array with the items that are ready to sell.
Be sure to reload the Collection View after this and also update the array name.

```swift
swift
func productsRequest(_ request: SKProductsRequest, didReceive response:
SKProductsResponse) {
        print("Products ready: \(response.products.count)")
        print("Products not ready: \(response.invalidProductIdentifiers.count)")
        products = response.products
        collectionView.reloadData()
        for product in response.products {
            print(product.productIdentifier)
        }
}
```

Alright, we are almost done with this. We need to inherit one more protocol in our class, called `SKPaymentTransactionObserver`.

Place this next to the `SKProductsRequestDelegate` at top, next to the class name.

We will need to add the *paymentQueue function* to abide by this protocol and also set the observer.

Inside the *paymentQueue function* we will add a switch statement that takes care of all the cases that can be returned from Apple.

These are *purchased, failed, restored, purchasing* and *deferred*.

* *Purchased* gets called when the item is successfully processed.

* *Failed* is called if payment transaction fails.

* *Purchasing* is called when the payment is being processed, this is called before the purchase is successful or not.

* *Restored* is an option for non-consumable products like our products, that will restore all purchases automatically if you delete the app or get a new device.

* *Deferred* means something happened and it will be tried again at a later time.

```
    func paymentQueue(_ queue: SKPaymentQueue, updatedTransactions transactions:
[SKPaymentTransaction]) {
        for transaction in transactions {
            switch transaction.transactionState {
            case .purchased:
                print("purchased")
                SKPaymentQueue.default().finishTransaction(transaction)
                break
            case .failed:
                print("failed")
                let errorMsg: String! = transaction.error?.localizedDescription
                showErrorAlert(title: "Oops! Something went wrong.", msg: "Unable
to make purchase.  Reason: \(errorMsg).")
                SKPaymentQueue.default().finishTransaction(transaction)
                break
            case .restored:
                print("restored")
                showErrorAlert(title: "Purchases Restored.", msg: "Your purchases
have been restored.")
                SKPaymentQueue.default().finishTransaction(transaction)
                break
            case .purchasing:
                print("purchasing")
                break
            case .deferred:
                print("deferred")
```

```
            break
        }
    }
}
```

Also, add a *UIAlert function* that can be called so the user knows what is happening.

```
func showErrorAlert(title: String, msg: String) {
    let alert = UIAlertController(title: title, message: msg, preferredStyle:
.alert)
    let action = UIAlertAction(title: "Ok", style: .default, handler: nil)
    alert.addAction(action)
    present(alert, animated: true, completion:nil)
}
```

We need to update our `configureCell` method in our `PurchaseCell.swift` file.

The image name we pass in is going to be the `Product ID` we created for our IAP's in iTunes Connect.

We'll also want to pass in the price, because we can now get this from Apple and this allows us to use the correct price associated with the *tier* that was selected.

```
func configureCell(imageName: String, price: String){
    switch imageName {
    case "com.devslopes.InAppPurchases.tier1":
        purchaseImage.image = UIImage(named: "Arcade-1")
        purchaseLbl.text = price
        break
    case "com.devslopes.InAppPurchases.tier2":
        purchaseImage.image = UIImage(named: "Arcade-2")
        purchaseLbl.text = price
        break
    case "com.devslopes.InAppPurchases.tier3":
        purchaseImage.image = UIImage(named: "Arcade-3")
        purchaseLbl.text = price
        break
    case "com.devslopes.InAppPurchases.tier4":
        purchaseImage.image = UIImage(named: "Arcade-4")
        purchaseLbl.text = price
        break
    case "com.devslopes.InAppPurchases.tier5":
        purchaseImage.image = UIImage(named: "Bear-1")
        purchaseLbl.text = price
        break
    default:
        break
    }
```

}

Okay, so because we added another parameter `price` of type String to our `configureCell` method we'll need to get our price from our `products` array.

We are going to format the number to currency and also use a nifty built in tool that will change the currency displayed to whatever country the user is in.

Then we'll convert it to a String and send it into our `configureCell` method.

```
func collectionView(_ collectionView: UICollectionView, cellForItemAt indexPath:
IndexPath) -> UICollectionViewCell {
        var cellPrice = ""
        if let cell = collectionView.dequeueReusableCell(withReuseIdentifier:
"purchaseCell", for: indexPath) as? PurchaseCell {
            let product = products[indexPath.row]
            let formatter = NumberFormatter()
            formatter.numberStyle = NumberFormatter.Style.currency
            formatter.locale = product.priceLocale
            if let price = formatter.string(from: product.price){
                cellPrice = "\(price)"
            }

            cell.configureCell(imageName:
products[indexPath.row].productIdentifier, price: cellPrice)
            return cell
        }else {
        return UICollectionViewCell()
        }
}
```

Let's make our Collection View cells selectable now, we'll need to add an *observer* here, and also send the payment to the queue.

```swift
func collectionView(_ collectionView: UICollectionView, didSelectItemAt indexPath:
IndexPath) {
        SKPaymentQueue.default().add(self)
        let payment = SKMutablePayment(product: products[indexPath.row])
        payment.simulatesAskToBuyInSandbox = true
        SKPaymentQueue.default().add(payment)
}
```

One thing you need to remember is that we can't test **in-app purchases** without using our device. You will also need to create a **Sandbox** tester in your iTunes Connect account. This cannot be your apple ID you already use.

(Figure 5.1.37)

Figure 5.1.37

Select `Users and Roles` and then select `Sandbox Testers` and add a tester.

Next, you need to log out of your apple ID in your **General** settings on your iPhone. Do not log in to your **Sandbox** account here, you will need to do this from inside the app when it prompts you. You are now ready to test your **in-app purchases**! (Figure 5.1.38)

Figure 5.1.38

One last thing to do is connect an *IBAction* to your restore button and add one line of code to it and that's it! All your purchases will be restored.

```
@IBAction func restoreBtnPressed(_ sender: AnyObject) {
    SKPaymentQueue.default().restoreCompletedTransactions()
}
```

Congratulations!

That's all you need to do, to set up **in-app purchases**. Obviously, wherever I printed *purchase* and called a *UIAlert* view, you can add more code to maintain and change your data whether you are using Firebase or core data to keep track of purchases.

Wrapping up

That is all it takes to make in-app purchases. We covered a lot in this section. First we learned how to navigate through iTunes Connect and register our app ID for in-app purchases. Then we got multiple tiers set up and connected the app store with our app. Lastly, we learned how to create a sandbox user to test our in-app purchases so we don't actually get charged in our testing phases.

Exercise

I am going to leave you with a final challenge. Implement in-app purchases into one of your apps. Make it possible to track users' purchases and start making money with your apps!

Chapter 36: Protocol-Oriented Programming

*If you like Object-Oriented Programming, then you will **love** Protocol-Oriented Programming. Prepare your mind to drive down an exciting new avenue in the programming world.*

What you will learn

- Overview of Swift Types

- Writing your first Protocol

- Conforming to a Protocol

- Reference types & protocols

- Protocol Extensions

Key Terms

- **Protocol**

- **Extension**

- **Value Type**

- **Reference Type**

- **Struct (Structure)**

In 2015, there was a talk given at Apple's WWDC event simply called "Protocol-Oriented Programming in Swift" by Dave Abrahams, professor of "Blowing Your Mind". His confident title ended up working in his favor because over the duration of that 45 minute talk, he proceeded to blow the minds of every developer in attendance. This talk is known as the "Crusty" talk based on the imaginary old-school developer named Crusty who doesn't like newfangled programming technologies or "fads". Throughout the talk, Dave proceeds to show Crusty the benefits of using **protocols** and how Swift truly is a protocol-oriented programming language.

In this chapter, you will read a brief overview of Protocol-Oriented Programming (POP) and learn how it can be useful as a developer.

Overview of Swift Types

The Swift programming language uses named and compound types as you'd expect. Figure 5.2.1 shows these types:

Figure 5.2.1

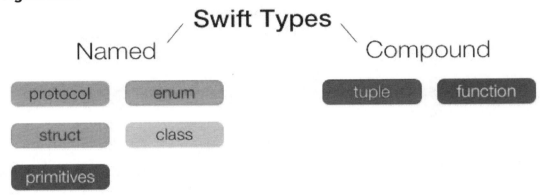

In addition to being named types, Primitives like `Int`, `String`, and `Float` in addition to **structures (structs)** and enums (enumerations) are also **value types**. This means that if you create a value of one of these types, that value is copied when it is assigned to a constant or variable. It is also copied when passed to a function or method. Every time a new copy of that value is created, the new copy is used not the original version. Multiple unique copies can be made.

This is in stark contrast to a **reference type**. Classes are **reference types**. If we create a class, that value is saved and if we assign the reference to a variable or constant we actually copy in the original value. If we modify the value in the variable we made, we modify the original value. After we copy it, we've made a shared instance of the same value.

Figure 5.2.2 shows this in action:

Figure 5.2.2

Reference Type Class	Value Type Struct
`var car1 = Car()`	`var car1 = Car()`
`var car2 = car1`	`var car2 = car1`
`car2.color = UIColor.red` 🚗 `car1.color == UIColor.red` 🚗	`car2.color = UIColor.red` 🚗 `car1.color == UIColor.blue` 🚙

As you can see on the left, there is a class named `Car` which is a **reference type**. There is also a variable called `car1` and it is instantiated as a copy of the class `Car`. Beneath that, a variable called `car2` is created and instantiated as a copy of `car1`. At the bottom of the image, `car2`'s color property is set to be red and `car1`'s color property is also set to red. This is because we've used a **reference type** and by changing the color of `car2`, we also change the color of `car1`.

On the right-hand side, there is a struct which is a **value type**. You can see the same code is used to create `car1` and `car2`, but if you look at the bottom you can see that I set the color property of `car2` to be red, while the color property of `car1` is blue. With **value types**, each copy is a unique copy that exists independently. This allows us to give each copy different values.

As you can imagine, the more complex our code becomes, the more room there is for error with **reference types** since you need to remember that any copy you make will modify the original. **Value types** have their problems as well, but **reference types** need much more maintenance. Apple reccomends that developers use **value types** (i.e. **struct**, enum, etc.) whenever possible.

Getting Started

With that topic under our belt, we now have a foundation to begin unpacking POP. We will be doing this lesson in a Playground, simply because this is an introductory chapter to POP and we could go into many chapters about how to implement this into your apps. But really, dig in to this stuff. If you find it as interesting as I do, that won't be a challenge.

Okay, let's get down to business.

First, open Xcode if you haven't already and click `Create New Playground`. Give it a name like *Protocol-Oriented Fun* and click `Next`. Choose somewhere to save this .playground file and click `Create` to save it. You should see a screen like the one in Figure 5.2.3.

Figure 5.2.3

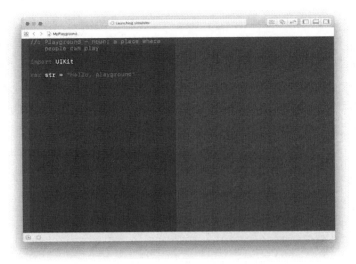

Delete all the boilerplate code on the left side but leave `import UIKit` as it is necessary.

Writing Your First Protocol

We're going to write a **protocol** for a spaceship. At the bottom of your Playground file, type the following:

```
protocol Spaceship {
    var isFlying: Bool { get set }
}
```

In this **protocol**, we declared a property called `isFlying` of type `Boolean`. In **protocols**, you need to define whether it is read/write or read-only. We've set it to be read/write because we've used `{ get set }`. If we wanted to make it a read only property, we could have simply used `{ get }`.

We will now define a few functions, but there is a bit of a caveat when it comes to

506

protocols. Think of any functions we choose to include in our **protocol** as part of a contract meaning anything that conforms to the **protocol** will need to implement all of the functions in the "contract". We won't include any implementation code or even a set of brackets. We are simply telling our **protocol** what functions to require of anything that conforms to it.

Add the following functions for our spaceship:

```
protocol Spaceship {
    var isFlying: Bool { get set }
    func launch()
    func land()
}
```

The code above actually won't work just yet. Another thing to know is that when working with **value types**, we need to specify that our functions can mutate the properties inside a class, **structure**, or even other **value types**. To make this change, simply add the keyword `mutating` before the function's declaration:

```
protocol Spaceship {
    var isFlying: Bool { get set }
    mutating func launch()
    mutating func land()
}
```

Conforming To A Protocol

So now we have a **protocol** that contains the property `isFlying` in addition to two functions for launching and landing. But what good is it if nothing is going to use it? Let's create a **structure** called `TIEFighter` that will conform to our **protocol**. Beneath the Spaceship **protocol**, write the following:

```
...

struct TIEFighter: Spaceship {

}
```

You probably noticed that your Playground window threw an error. The error says, "Type 'TIEFighter' does not conform to **protocol** 'Spaceship'"

Interesting! How do we make it conform? Simple. We need to honor the contract we wrote in the **protocol** which included `isFlying`, `launch()`, and `land()` by adding them into our **structure**.

```swift
struct TIEFighter: Spaceship {
    var isFlying: Bool = false

    mutating func launch() {
        if isFlying {
            print("Already launched!")
        } else {
            isFlying = true
            print("BLAST OFF!")
        }
    }

    mutating func land() {
        if isFlying {
            isFlying = false
            print("Silence...")
        } else {
            print("Already landed!")
        }
    }
}
```

As you can see, our error has vanished! We have now conformed to all of the requirements of the contract we set in the protocol `Spaceship`.

A place you've already used **protocols** is in apps with UITableView. We actually conform to the **protocols** `UITableViewDelegate` and `UITableViewDataSource` for using UITableView. You will encounter errors unless you honor the contract set in the UITableView **protocols** by conforming to certain functions.

Reference Types Can Conform, Too!

Why should **value types** have all the fun? **Reference types** like classes can conform to **protocols** as well. To illustrate this point, write the following code at the bottom of your Playground file:

```swift
class MilleniumFalcon: Spaceship {
    var isFlying: Bool = false

    func launch() {
```

508

```
        if isFlying {
            print("Great, kid. Don't get cocky.")
        } else {
            isFlying = true
            print("Punch it!")
        }
    }

    func land() {
        if isFlying {
            isFlying = false
            print("You know, sometimes I amaze even myself...")
        } else {
            print("Chewie, we're home.")
        }
    }
}
```

Our class `MilleniumFalcon` conforms to the `Spaceship` protocol by implementing the properties and functions required by it. But that doesn't mean we can't add in extra functionality. Let's put the **fun** in functionality and add in the following function to the `MilleniumFalcon` class:

```
class MilleniumFalcon: Spaceship {
    var isFlying: Bool = false

    func launch() {
        if isFlying {
            print("Great, kid. Don't get cocky.")
        } else {
            isFlying = true
            print("Punch it!")
        }
    }

    func land() {
        if isFlying {
            isFlying = false
            print("You know, sometimes I amaze even myself...")
        } else {
            print("Chewie, we're home.")
        }
    }

    func fireLasers() {
        print("PEW PEW PEW!")
```

```
    }
}
```

Cool, so now we have a **struct** called `TIEFighter` and a class called `MilleniumFalcon` both of which conform to the protocol `Spaceship`. Let's create an instance of each. At the bottom of your Playground file add the following code:

```
var tieFighter = TIEFighter()
var milleniumFalcon = MilleniumFalcon()
```

Now let's call some of the functions declared in these instances to see how they work:

```
var tieFighter = TIEFighter()
var milleniumFalcon = MilleniumFalcon()

tieFighter.launch() // isFlying set to true / prints "BLAST OFF!"
milleniumFalcon.launch() // isFlying set to true / prints "Punch it!"
milleniumFalcon.fireLasers() // prints "PEW PEW PEW!"
```

As you can see, our functions work as expected. We could have also called our `land()` function for both the TIE Fighter and the Millenium Falcon, but we didn't.

Next, we are going to create an array and fill it with things that conform to our `Spaceship` protocol. Then we will loop through the array and print each element. Add the following to the bottom of your Playground file:

```
var spaceshipArray: Array<Spaceship> = [tieFighter, milleniumFalcon]

for spaceship in spaceshipArray {
    print("\(spaceship)")
}

/* Prints:
TIEFighter(isFlying: false)
MilleniumFalcon
*/
```

As you can see, it doesn't print the same thing for the **struct** and the class. We have yet to set a description and by default we don't have one. To add a description we can actually set our `Spaceship` protocol to conform to another protocol called `CustomStringConvertible`, which can give it the extra functionality we want. Let's conform to it now!

Protocolception: A Protocol Within A Protocol

OK, so we aren't really putting a **protocol** *inside* of another **protocol**, so to speak, but we will be conforming to another **protocol** so that we can add some functionality.

Go to the very top of your Playground file and in the `Spaceship` **protocol**, set it to conform to `CustomStringConvertible` like so:

```
protocol Spaceship: CustomStringConvertible {
    var isFlying: Bool { get set }
    mutating func launch()
    mutating func land()
}
```

Now any **structure** or class that conforms to the **protocol** `Spaceship` **also** has to conform to the **protocol** CustomStringConvertible which has one required property: `description`.

You should be seeing two errors. One in the **struct** `TIEFighter` and one in the class `MilleniumFalcon`. Both have to do with the fact that we have not yet conformed to the **protocol** `CustomStringConvertible`. To do so, we are going to enter the `TIEFighter` **struct**, create a variable called `description`, and set return values like so:

```
struct TIEFighter: Spaceship {
    var isFlying: Bool = false

    var description: String {
        if isFlying {
            return "TIE Fighter is flying"
        } else {
            return "TIE Fighter is not flying"
        }
    }

    mutating func launch() {
        if isFlying {
            print("Already launched!")
        } else {
            isFlying = true
            print("BLAST OFF!")
        }
    }

    mutating func land() {
        if isFlying {
            isFlying = false
            print("Silence...")
        } else {
```

```
            print("Already landed!")
        }
    }
}
```

Do the same in the `MilleniumFalcon` class:

```
class MilleniumFalcon: Spaceship {
    var isFlying: Bool = false

    var description: String {
        if isFlying {
            return "The Millenium Falcon is flying"
        } else {
            return "The Millenium Falcon is not flying"
        }
    }

    func launch() {
        if isFlying {
            print("Great, kid. Don't get cocky.")
        } else {
            isFlying = true
            print("Punch it!")
        }
    }

    func land() {
        if isFlying {
            isFlying = false
            print("You know, sometimes I amaze even myself...")
        } else {
            print("Chewie, we're home.")
        }
    }

    func fireLasers() {
        print("PEW PEW PEW!")
    }
}
```

Since our **struct** and class both conform to the **protocol** Spaceship, they are also required to conform to CustomStringConvertible. Now both the class and **struct** have a description property thanks to CustomStringConvertible.

Back before we created a loop and walked through our array of spaceships, two different description values were printed to the console because there was no specific description set and it was printing the default description.

Let's change our loop at the bottom of our Playground window to print our new descriptions:

```swift
var spaceshipArray: Array<Spaceship> = [tieFighter, milleniumFalcon]

for spaceship in spaceshipArray {
    print("\(spaceship.description)")
}

/* Prints:
TIE Fighter is not flying
The Millenium Falcon is not flying
*/
```

It works! Pretty cool. So far, we've learned the basics of how **protocols** work in Swift 3. But where **protocols** become very powerful is in **protocol extensions**. Announced in Swift 2, they expanded the capabilities of **protocols** for added functionality and more. You're about to read a brief overview of **protocol extensions** and how to use them in code.

Protocol Extensions in Swift 3

This is where the real magic happens.   **Protocol Extensions** were introduced in 2015 when Apple launched Swift 2 and they are so powerful. Not only can you extend functionality in your own **protocols**, but you can even extend the **protocols** predefined in the Swift Standard Library. **Protocol extensions** were introduced to help soothe the pains of working with value types, since there is no inheritance like in **reference types**. In a **protocol extension**, you can write implementation code which can be used by any class or **struct** that conforms to it's related **protocol**.

Let's dive back in where we left off above in this chapter.

Extending The Spaceship Protocol

Before we begin, we're going to add two new properties (make and model) to our **protocol**. We will use these later in our **protocol extension**. Write the following code inside of the `Spaceship` **protocol**:

```
protocol Spaceship {
    var isFlying: Bool { get set }
    var make: String { get set }
    var model: String { get set }
    mutating func launch()
    mutating func land()
}
```

Now we have two properties for `make` and `model`. We will now create the body of our **protocol extension**. It is as simple as using the keyword `extension` and calling the name of the **protocol** that you want to extend. This is similar to writing a type **extension** if you've done that before. Beneath the closing bracket of the `Spaceship` **protocol**, write the following:

```
extension Spaceship {

}
```

BOOM. Done. We will come back to adding in code to this later. Now, just like before, we have some errors in our `TIEFighter` and `MilleniumFalcon` class. This is because we are no longer conforming properly to `Spaceship` as we have added some new properties. We need to create properties for `make` and `model` in both the **struct** and class.

Do so like this:

```
struct TIEFighter: Spaceship {
    var isFlying: Bool = false
    var make: String
    var model: String

    // Other code redacted for spacing purposes.
}
```

Notice how a **struct** doesn't require the variables to be instantiated as they are initialized when a new copy of `TIEFighter` is created. And now add the same thing to our class:

```
class MilleniumFalcon: Spaceship {
    var isFlying: Bool = false
    var make: String
    var model: String

    // Other code redacted for spacing purposes.
}
```

AHH!   Another error. We fixed one and made another. If you look at the error description, you will see that it is because we have no initializers. The class `MilleniumFalcon` doesn't have any initializers, so we will need to create one. Add the following code beneath where you just created `make` and `model`:

```
class MilleniumFalcon: Spaceship {
    var isFlying: Bool = false
    var make: String
    var model: String

    init(isFlying: Bool, make: String, model: String) {
        self.isFlying = isFlying
        self.make = make
        self.model = model
    }

    // Other code redacted for spacing purposes.
}
...
```

Because we have changed so much in our class and **struct**, you will see a lot of other errors near the bottom of the Playground file. We will come back to this later on, so for now just comment out the following code:

```
/*
var tieFighter = TIEFighter()
var milleniumFalcon = MilleniumFalcon()

tieFighter.launch() // isFlying set to true / prints "BLAST OFF!"
milleniumFalcon.launch() // isFlying set to true / prints "Punch it!"
milleniumFalcon.fireLasers() // prints "PEW PEW PEW!"

var spaceshipArray: Array<Spaceship> = [tieFighter, milleniumFalcon]

for spaceship in spaceshipArray {
    print("\(spaceship.description)")
}
*/
```

Alright, with those errors silenced for the moment, we need to go add some implementation code to our **protocol extension**. Scroll back up to the top of your Playground file and inside of the `Spaceship` **extension**, write the following:

```
extension Spaceship {
    mutating func launch() {
```

```
    if isFlying {
        print("Already flying!")
    } else {
        isRunning = true
        print("\(self.description) blasted off!")
    }
}

mutating func land() {
    if isFlying {
        isFlying = false
        print("\(self.description) landed.")
    } else {
        print("Already landed!")
    }
}
}
```

The reason we added these functions into our **protocol extension** is because we're actually implementing them twice which is bad programming. We used the same code inside the `launch()` and `land()` functions within our **struct** and class. By placing this code in our **protocol extension**, now both `TIEFighter` and `MilleniumFalcon` can access this function and implement it without it needing to be repeated. This also means that if we add any other **structs** or classes, we can easily use the `launch()` and `land()` functions with them.

Now that we've added these functions to our **protocol extension**, we need to clean up our **struct** and class. Remove the functions `launch()` and `land()` from both the **struct** `TIEFighter` and the class `MilleniumFalcon`.

Even though the functions are no longer within our class or **struct**, they still have access to them via the **protocol extension**. As you can imagine, being able to extend **protocols** becomes extremely useful when wanting a certain functionality that the Swift Standard Library doesn't offer.

Making Our Description Property More Descriptive

Earlier in this chapter, we created a property for our spaceship's `make` and `model`. Let's put those to use. We're going to add a property to our **protocol** extension and change up the way we used `description` in both our class and **struct**.

At the top of the extension, add the following property:

```
extension Spaceship {
    var makeModel: String {
        return "\(make) \(model)"
    }

    mutating func launch() {
        if isFlying {
            print("Already flying!")
        } else {
            isRunning = true
            print("\(self.description) blasted off!")
        }
    }

    mutating func land() {
        if isFlying {
            isFlying = false
            print("\(self.description) landed.")
        } else {
            print("Already landed!")
        }
    }
}
```

Since `TIEFighter` and `MilleniumFalcon` have to conform to the properties and functions in our **protocol/extensions**, we can use the `make` and `model` properties to construct a value of `makeModel`. `makeModel` is a String value that combines both `make` and `model`.

Now all we need to do to create a specific `description` property for both the **struct** and class, we simply need to return `makeModel`. Inside of the `description` property for `TIEFighter` and `MilleniumFalcon`, delete all current code and replace it with this:

```
var description: String {
    return self.makeModel
}
```

Now, using our extension's functionality, we can return the make and model values that we set when we instantiate our class/**struct**.

Re-Instantiating Our Structs & Classes

Let's go ahead and uncomment the code we commented earlier. We're going to need to change how we instantiate `tieFighter` and `milleniumFalcon`, though. When we first wrote this code, we didn't have any initializer or a need to initialize any values. Since we added a make and model property the way we did, we need to initialize their values now.

For `tieFighter`, we initially wrote:

```
var tieFighter = TIEFighter()
```

But we need to change this to:

```
var tieFighter = TIEFighter(isFlying: false, make: "TIE", model: "Fighter")
```

Likewise, in our `milleniumFalcon` variable, we first wrote:

```
var milleniumFalcon = MilleniumFalcon()
```

We need to update it to say:

```
var milleniumFalcon = MilleniumFalcon(isFlying: false, make: "Millenium", model: "Falcon")
```

If you look at the code beneath these variables where we called our `launch()` and `fireLasers()` functions earlier, you should see that they are working again! You'll also notice that on the right-hand side of the Playground window where the console prints, the names of the ships we've made based on their `description` property. The `description` property is being created by combining the `make` and `model` property passed in when we instantiate the class/**struct**.

You should also see in the bottom console panel that our `launch()` and `fireLasers()` functions are successfully using the description to print:

```
TIE Fighter blasted off!
Millenium Falcon blasted off!
PEW PEW PEW!
```

Pretty amazing! We've written an **extension** implementing a couple functions and a property to build the make and model of our spaceship and it's working great!

We can also modify our for loop so that it uses `makeModel` from our **extension** like so:

```
var spaceshipArray: Array<Spaceship> = [tieFighter, milleniumFalcon]

for spaceship in spaceshipArray {
    print("\(spaceship.makeModel)")
```

```
}
```

As you should be able to see, this for loop should print out the make and model name in the console. We have access to the `makeModel` property thanks to our handy dandy **protocol extension**!

Wrapping up

This chapter has been a brief overview of Protocol-Oriented Programming in Swift. Although there were probably a lot of new ideas and concepts in this chapter, it is really only the tip of the iceberg. POP is a deep and wide topic and is actually an entirely new way to approach programming. While there are still places where classes and **reference types** are useful, POP aims to reduce the use of classes and increase the use of **value types** and **protocols**.

There are lots of fantastic ways to use POP in your apps and I highly suggest that you research and dig deeper into this topic. It's new and fascinating and I only foresee it's popularity increasing from here on out.

Exercise

Create a class named `StarKillerBase` and set it to conform to the `Spaceship` protocol. Ensure that it conforms to `Spaceship` by adding in the necessary properties and methods. Add any extra functions you think StarKiller Base might need such as `obliteratePlanets(planetName:_)`.

Add it as an item into your `spaceshipArray` and ensure that it is printed via it's `makeModel` property.

Chapter 37: SimpleWeather

Learn all about communicating with APIs and using CoreLocation in this app that will provide current weather details in a beautiful UI.

What you will learn

- Communicate with an API

- Use URLSession to make web requests

- How to use closures

- How to work with JSON

- How to use LocationServices

Key Terms

- **Closure**

- **API**

- **JSON**

- **URLSession**

Resources

Download here: https://github.com/devslopes/book-assets/wiki

In this chapter, we are going to build a simple weather app called SimpleWeather. It will display the weather at your current location with a beautiful UI that communicates with the open weather **API** system.

Here is a sneak peak at the finished product!

Figure 5.3.1

Creating an Xcode Project

Open Xcode and, from the File menu, select New and then New Project.... A new workspace window will appear, and a sheet will slide from its toolbar with several application templates to choose from. On the top, make sure to select iOS, and then look in the 'Application' section. From the choices that appear, select Single View Application and press the Next button (Figure 5.3.2). (Note that Apple changes these templates and their names often. But it should be very similar to what is shown here)

Figure 5.3.2

Then fill out the product name. I am calling mine 'SimpleWeather'. You can select a Team and Organization Name. The organization identifier is usually in reverse DNS format. Make sure the language is Swift and select which devices you want your app to run on. We'll keep it simple for this app and just do iPhone. We do not need Core Data, Unit or UI Tests for this chapter, so you can leave those unchecked (Figure 5.3.3).

Figure 5.3.3

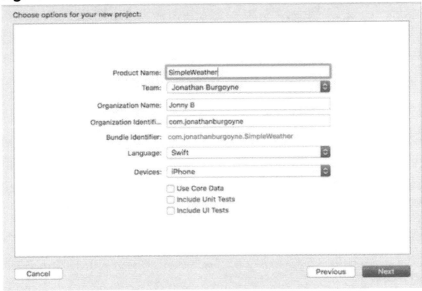

Finally choose a location for your app to be saved to, and I recommend checking the 'Create Git repository' so that you can push your project to your Github (or Bitbucket) account and show off your awesome app to friends and potential employees!

Once the project loads, you will be looking at a brand new project that is just waiting to be turned into something great!

Setting up the Interface

With this app we are actually going to start out building the interface first since it is pretty simple. So go to your Main.storyboard file and first thing we are going to do is give the background a nice blue color. Select the ViewController in the interface builder, and change the background color to **#51A4FF** as seen below:

Figure 5.3.4

Next, referring back to figure 5.3.4 it looks like we have several labels and one image view. They are all lined up vertically, so I think this would be a good time to use our old friend stack views. So lets add the three labels on top of each other, then an image view, then one more label. They don't have to be placed exactly or anything, since we'll be dropping them in a stack view.

Figure 5.3.5

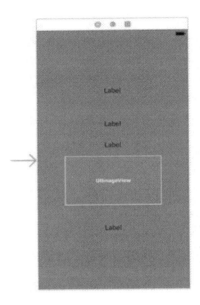

Next, we'll style the labels a little. Select all 4 labels and change the color to white, the font to Avenir Next, and the style to medium.

Figure 5.3.6

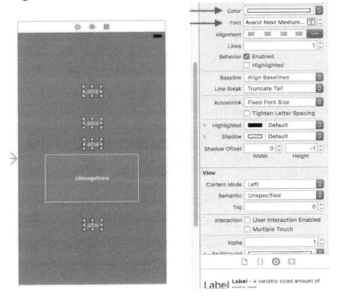

Next add titles to the labels as follows in Figure 5.3.7. This is just placeholder text to let us know how to space things out. Change the size of the second from top label to 64 and make the style bold. Change the size of the image view to 100 x 100.

Figure 5.3.7

Next select all elements, and add them to a stack view by clicking on the button indicated in Figure 5.3.8.

Figure 5.3.8

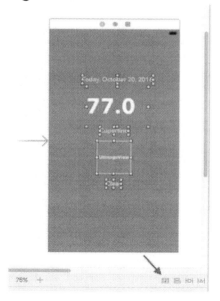

Next, with the stack view selected, make sure the Axis is Vertical, Distribution is Fill Proportionally, and Spacing is 10. Then give it alignment constraints of Horizontally and Vertically in container to center it.

Figure 5.3.9

And that's our whole UI!

Now lets jump over to ViewController.swift file and make some IBOutlets and hook up those elements to our code. Just above the `viewDidLoad` function add the following:

```
@IBOutlet weak var dateLabel: UILabel!
@IBOutlet weak var currentTempLabel: UILabel!
@IBOutlet weak var locationLabel: UILabel!
@IBOutlet weak var currentWeatherImage: UIImageView!
@IBOutlet weak var currentWeatherTypeLabel: UILabel!
```

Then as we have done so many times, go back into storyboard, and right-click on the ViewController in the project navigator and drag from the IBOutlets to the corresponding UI elements.

Figure 5.3.10

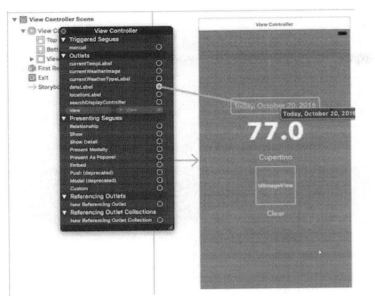

Now all our labels and elements are hooked up and we are ready to start talking about **APIs**!

OpenWeather API

What is an **API**? **API** stands for "Application Programming Interface" and provides a way for programmers to communicate with a certain application.
There are many many useful **APIs** available. Some are from well known companies like Facebook, Google, Twitter and YouTube.

There are ones for getting information about StarWars, Pokemon, and the weather. What's important to know is that, whatever **API** you use, you have to follow they rules. An **API** is able to provide only the specific information that it was built to provide, and the programmer must communicate with the **API** in a very specific way to get the results they want.

In this app we are going to be working with an **API** that can be found at 'OpenWeatherMap.org'
Go ahead and check out the website, as we will be creating an account and using it extensively.
On the website homepage you will see the Current weather data service description which includes:

527

- Access current weather data for any location including over 200,000 cities
- Current weather is frequently updated based on global models and data from more than 40,000 weather stations
- Data is available in JSON, XML, or HTML format
- Available for Free and all other paid accounts

That is the one we want. But first we need to sign up, so click the sign up button and follow the instructions:

Figure 5.3.11

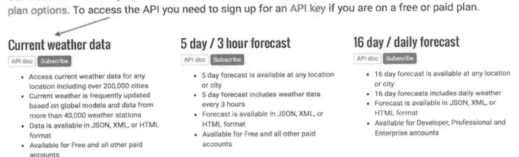

Figure 5.3.12

Figure 5.3.13

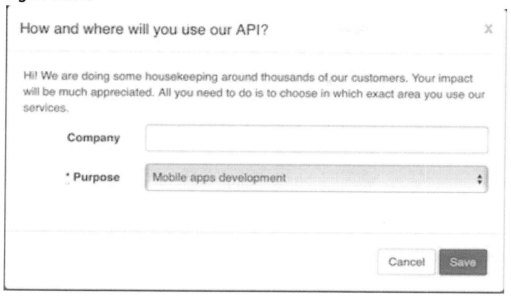

You will land on a dashboard, then select the **API** keys menu option. Your **API** key is very important, without it, you would not be able to use the service. This is a common practice with **APIs** and is used to track usage for **API**s that charge. Don't worry though, unless you switch to a paid plan you will not be charged for your account. Now copy your **API** key and navigate back to the **API** Page:

Figure 5.3.14

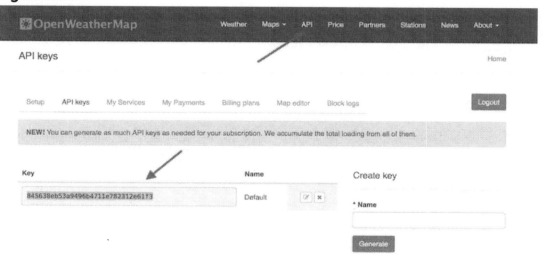

Find the 'Current Weather data' section and click on the 'API doc' button.

Figure 5.3.15

Current weather data

- Access current weather data for any location including over 200,000 cities
- Current weather is frequently updated based on global models and data from more than 40,000 weather stations
- Data is available in JSON, XML, or HTML format
- Available for Free and all other paid accounts

Then scroll down to the header 'By city name' and click on the first example link.

Figure 5.3.16

By city name

Description:

You can call by city name or city name and country code. API responds with a list of results that match a searching word.

API call:

api.openweathermap.org/data/2.5/weather?q={city name}

api.openweathermap.org/data/2.5/weather?q={city name},{country code}

Parameters:

q city name and country code divided by comma, use ISO 3166 country codes

Examples of API calls:

api.openweathermap.org/data/2.5/weather?q=London

api.openweathermap.org/data/2.5/weather?q=London,uk

You will get an error saying "{"cod":401, "message": "Invalid API key. Please see http://openweathermap.org/faq#error401 for more info."}" This means that the **API** key is not valid. Thats to be expected, because that is just the default **API** key open weather uses. Go ahead and click on the URL in your browser and at the end of the url you will see a long string of numbers. This is the bad **API** key.

Figure 5.3.17

Go ahead and replace that **API** key (everything after '&appid=') with your **API** key we copied earlier, and reload it. You should now see a bunch of information that may seem difficult to read. If you look in the URL you will 'london,uk'. If you want, you can change the city and get different results.

Figure 5.3.18

{"coord":{"lon":-0.13,"lat":51.51},"weather":[{"id":803,"main":"Clouds","description":"broken clouds","icon":"04n"}],"base":"stations","main":{"temp":283.15,"pressure":1026.25,"humidity":78,"temp_min":283.15,"temp_max":283.15,"sea_level":1033.96,"grnd_level":1026.25},"wind":{"speed":4.36,"deg":351.503},"clouds":{"all":68},"dt":1477004929,"sys":{"message":0.1733,"country":"GB","sunrise":1476945318,"sunset":1476982439},"id":2643743,"name":"London","cod":200}

So what you are looking at here, is what is called **JSON**, which stands for JavaScript Object Notation. It is defined as a "lightweight data-interchange format. It is easy for humans to read and write. It is easy for machines to parse and generate."

Now it says its easy for humans to read, but let's make it a little easier shall we. Copy everything, and google '**JSON** formatter' and I like this first one at https://jsonformatter.curiousconcept.com

Figure 5.3.19

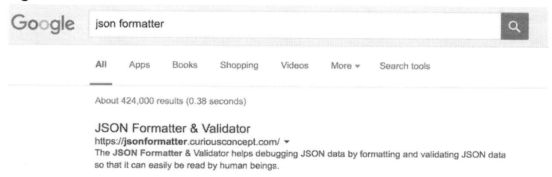

Paste the raw **JSON** data into the **JSON** Formatter window and press Process:

Figure 5.3.20

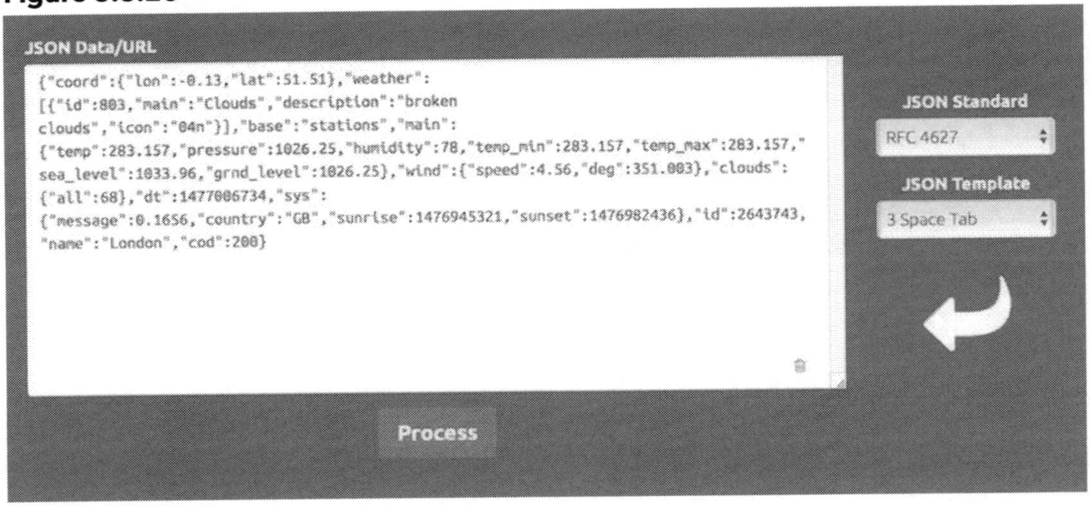

This will take you down to the formatted **JSON** view as seen below:

Figure 5.3.21

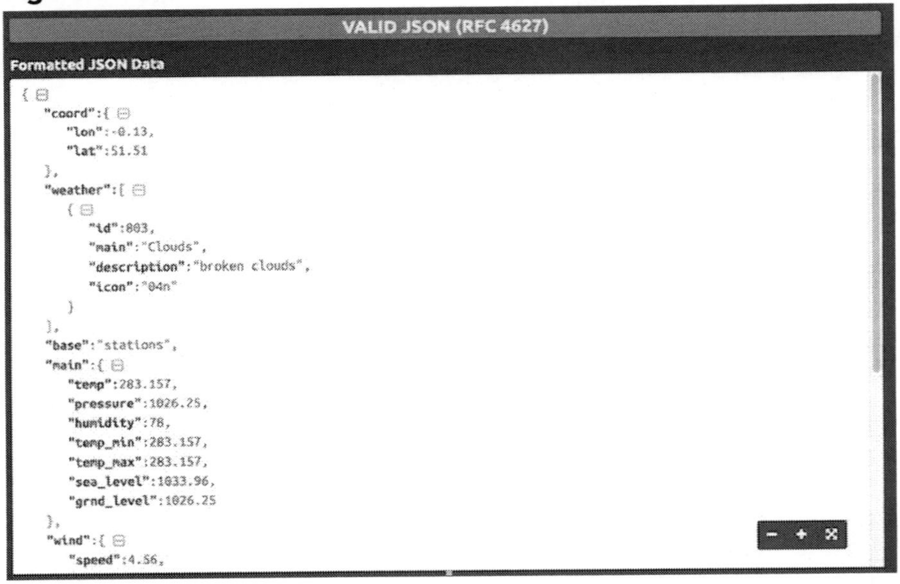

Now let's take a closer look here. **JSON** is arranged with keys and values. The keys are strings, and the values could be objects like strings, ints, or bools.

So taking a look at Figure 21 you see that it is arranged in a kind of nested format. There is an opening parentheses that contains the entirety of the data. Then within that there are other groups of data. For instance, there is a key of "weather" that has a value of type array. That array has within it keys with values. Among which is the key "main" and the value of "clouds". A little further down is the key "main" with a dictionary of keys and values. One of which is "temp". BINGO! We have located our temperature within this jumble of **JSON**.

You can kind of think of **JSON** like a Russian nesting doll, only instead of one doll in each, there may be many. The outermost doll is the entire data set. Then you open it up and you might find the doll called "main" and you find a bunch of other dolls inside it, then you find the doll named "temp" open it and find the value of 283.157. And thats what you do for every value you are looking for.

Scroll through the formatted **JSON** and familiarize yourself with it. Most **APIs** these days will return **JSON** data. And the way to request that data is through a web request. Just like you entered the url with your key into the web browser to get this data, we are going to make a web request from your app to retrieve this **JSON** data, extract the necessary information, then display the data in our UI.

Remember in the URL you included the city information? You can imagine how you could have a variable for a city, then include that in the **API** request to retrieve the information for a specific city. We are going to actually use your current location to do that, but we'll get into that later.

So let's jump back into Xcode and get working on it! Create a new Swift file and name it CurrentWeather. This is going to be our custom class that contains all the class properties and **API** call. So what are we going to need? We will need private variables and getters for the city name, the date, the weather type, and the current temperature. Add this to the CurrentWeather file:

```
class CurrentWeather {
    fileprivate var _cityName: String!
    fileprivate var _date: String!
    fileprivate var _weatherType: String!
    fileprivate var _currentTemp: Double!

    var cityName: String {
        if _cityName == nil {
            _cityName = ""
        }
        return _cityName
    }
```

```swift
var date: String {
    if _date == nil {
        _date = ""
    }

    let dateFormatter = DateFormatter()
    dateFormatter.dateStyle = .long
    dateFormatter.timeStyle = .none
    let currentDate = dateFormatter.string(from: Date())
    self._date = "Today, \(currentDate)"
    return _date
}

var weatherType: String {
    if _weatherType == nil {
        _weatherType = ""
    }
    return _weatherType
}

var currentTemp: Double {
    if _currentTemp == nil {
        _currentTemp = 0.0
    }
    return _currentTemp
}
}
```

The city name, weather type, and temperature are straight forward. We declare the properties, and then create the getters and do a check to see if the value is nil, and if so, we set it equal than empty string so we don't get any crashes.

The date is a little more involved so lets break that down. First we create a `DateFormatter()`. This is a class that helps create string representations of NSDate objects. It has a number of functions as seen in the next two lines. First we set the `.dateStyle = .long` which specifies a long style, typically with full text, such as "October 23, 2016". Then since we are not really interested in the time we set `.timeStyle = .none`. Then we create the date by using `dateFormatter.string(from: Date())` where we take the current date as created by `Date()` and turn it into a string based on the `dateFormatter` parameters we set.

Setting up the API Call

Now that we have our current weather properties we need some way to get the data and assign it to our class properties.

But first we need to think about how this is going to work. We could put the **API** call directly in the ViewController file, assign the properties, then update the UI. But it is not considered best practice to have the controller also be retrieving and managing data. So we want the **API** call to be in the CurrentWeather custom class.

But that introduces a new challenge. Web requests are asynchronous. For example, suppose I have three lines of code A, B, and C. And B is a web request that retrieves information, and C is the function that takes that information and updates the UI. But because B is asynchronous, we don't know when that information will be available. It could be milliseconds, it could be minutes, depending on connection speed and the service or site being contacted. So then, B fires off the web request, and C immediately tries to use information that may or may not be there, potentially causing crashes.

So what we need is a way to know when a web request has completed, and we do that by way of **closures**. A **closure** is basically a block of code, that is self contained and can be passes around in your code, and that we can call at a pre-determined time. And we are going to create a custom **closure** that we can use to determine when the download is complete.

So create a new Swift file, and call it Constants. And add the following:

```
typealias DownloadComplete = () -> ()
```

The syntax to create a **closure** is `var closureName: (ParamterTypes) -> (ReturnType)`

Our custom **closure**, does not have any parameter types, nor are we returning anything hence the empty parentheses. And `typealias` is just a way of renaming an existing type.

Now we are ready to create our function that we will eventually call in the ViewController file that will update the UI. So go back to CurrentWeather.swift and add the following below your getters:

```
func downloadWeatherDetails(completed: @escaping DownloadComplete) {

}
```

We name our function, then we name our **closure** `completed` and then we include our custom **closure** DownloadComplete. But first we have the @escaping. An escaping **closure** is often used in asynchronous operations like the web request we are going to

535

be dealing with.

So lets build that web request!

First we need to have a URL to point to. At this point we are just going to call it
`CURRENT_WEATHER_URL`. This will go inside the `downloadWeatherDetails` function we just
created. Later on we will add the URL to the Constants file when we are ready.

```
let url = URL(string: CURRENT_WEATHER_URL)!
```

Then add `let session = URLSession.shared`. The **URLSession** class is the Apple class
that provides the **API** for downloading content. It provides all the necessary delegate
methods we will need later on such as serializing **JSON** data and capturing the data and
error responses.

Then we need to call a `dataTask` which retrieves the contents of our URL, and supplies the
data, response, and error in a completion handler. When you auto complete
`session.dataTask` there will be code completion prompts, press return, then rename the
data, response, and error parameters. The `.resume()` is necessary to kick off the desk of
making the request.

So our `downloadWeatherDetails` function should now look like this:

```
func downloadWeatherDetails(completed: @escaping DownloadComplete) {

    let session = URLSession.shared
    let url = URL(string: CURRENT_WEATHER_URL)!

    session.dataTask(with: url) { (data, response, error) in


    } .resume()
}
```

Next we need to take the response from the web request, and turn it into useable **JSON**
data. So we are going to use the `JSONSerialization.jsonObject` method as follows.

```
session.dataTask(with: url) { (data, response, error) in
    if let responseData = data {
        do {
            let json = try JSONSerialization.jsonObject(with: responseData,
options: JSONSerialization.ReadingOptions.allowFragments)
            print(json)
        } catch {
            print("Could not serialize")
```

```
        }
    }
} .resume()
```

The `JSONSerialization.jsonObject` can fail, so it needs a `do-catch` block. If it fails, we'll simple print out that it could not serialize. Now we have an object **JSON** that contains all the information from the point of **API** call and can start drilling down into the **JSON** to acquire the information we need.

But first we need an actual url. If you recall `CURRENT_WEATHER_URL` was just a placeholder. So lets go back to our **API** website `http://openweathermap.org/api` and return to the 'Current weather data' **API** docs.

Figure 5.3.22

Current weather data

- Access current weather data for any location including over 200,000 cities
- Current weather is frequently updated based on global models and data from more than 40,000 weather stations
- Data is available in JSON, XML, or HTML format
- Available for Free and all other paid accounts

Then scroll down to the 'By geographic coordinates' section. If you recall, we want our app to give us the weather based on our current location. This section provides us with the information we need to make that type of call. It provides the base **API** call:

`api.openweathermap.org/data/2.5/weather?lat={lat}&lon={lon}`

Tells us what parameters we need, `lat` and `lon` (latitude and longitude).

And gives an example of an **API** call:

`api.openweathermap.org/data/2.5/weather?lat=35&lon=139`

Go ahead and plug that into your browser, and remember to replace the invalid **API** key at the end with your own.

This will provide the following **JSON** data:

```
{
    "coord": {
        "lon": 138.93,
        "lat": 34.97
    },
    "weather": [{
        "id": 803,
        "main": "Clouds",
        "description": "broken clouds",
        "icon": "04n"
    }],
    "base": "stations",
    "main": {
        "temp": 295.139,
        "pressure": 1021.33,
        "humidity": 100,
        "temp_min": 295.139,
        "temp_max": 295.139,
        "sea_level": 1030.63,
        "grnd_level": 1021.33
    },
    "wind": {
        "speed": 2.11,
        "deg": 68.0001
    },
    "clouds": {
        "all": 68
    },
    "dt": 1477077361,
    "sys": {
        "message": 0.1611,
        "country": "JP",
        "sunrise": 1476996953,
        "sunset": 1477036867
    },
    "id": 1851632,
    "name": "Shuzenji",
    "cod": 200
}
```

So let's copy the base **API** call and paste it into our Constants file as follows, including the required `http://` portion of a URL.

```
let CURRENT_WEATHER_URL = "http://api.openweathermap.org/data/2.5/weather?lat={lat}&lon={lon}"
```

Then from playing with the URLs in the browser, we know we need to end with `&appid=` then your **API** key.

So now your URL should look something like:

```
let CURRENT_WEATHER_URL = "http://api.openweathermap.org/data/2.5/weather?lat={lat}&lon={lon}&appid=42a1771a0b787bf12e734ada0cfc80cb"
```

We're getting closer now. But you see that we now need to know the longitude and latitude parameters to pass into the URL. So lets work on that next.

Getting Current location

Our location anywhere on the planet can be determined by latitude and longitude. Your phone has GPS (global positioning system) and our app can take advantage of the phone GPS by using the Apple library CoreLocation.

Let's create another custom class that will hold our current location. Create a new Swift file and name it `Location` and add the following:

```
import CoreLocation

class Location {
    static var sharedInstance = Location()
    private init() {}

    var latitude: Double!
    var longitude: Double!
}
```

First we import the CoreLocation library that is necessary to provide the required methods and delegates we will need.

The we create a static `sharedInstance` of the `Location` class and set up an initializer. And the only two properties we need in this class are latitude and longitude. So we are good here!

Next we need to go to our ViewController.swift file and get ready to calculate our current location when the app opens.

First up, import the CoreLocation library and add the 'CLLocationMnagerDelegate'.

```
import CoreLocation

class WeatherVC: UIViewController, CLLocationManagerDelegate {
```

Then we need to instantiate and declare a `locationManager` and a `currentLocation`. Add these right below the IBOutlets and above the `viewDidLoad` function.

```
let locationManager = CLLocationManager()
var currentLocation: CLLocation!
```

So, what is a locationManager? Apple defines it as "the central point for configuring the delivery of location- and heading-related events to your app. You use an instance of this class to establish the parameters that determine when location and heading events should be delivered and to start and stop the actual delivery of those events. You can also use a location manager object to retrieve the most recent location and heading data."

So basically it is in charge of all the location acquisition, parameters like accuracy, requesting permission to use GPS, and more.

`currentLocation` is a variable of class `CLLocation` which represents the location data generated by the `locationManager`

Next we need to add some settings for our `locationManager` so in `viewDidLoad` add the following:

```
locationManager.delegate = self
locationManager.desiredAccuracy = kCLLocationAccuracyBest
locationManager.requestWhenInUseAuthorization()
locationManager.startMonitoringSignificantLocationChanges()
```

First we are setting the delegate like we are used to doing, then we are choosing the desired accuracy which we are selecting the best available. The next line `locationManager.requestWhenInUseAuthorization()` generates the pop up that asks the user if they will allow our app to access their location. Then we have `locationManager.startMonitoringSignificantLocationChanges()` which monitors location changes and will update the locationManager delegates as needed.

Next we need to add two more functions. The first one is a method of `locationManager` and tells the delegate whether or not the app has permission to use the location services.

```
func locationManager(_ manager: CLLocationManager, didChangeAuthorization status:
CLAuthorizationStatus) {
    locationAuthStatus()
}
```

We also want to call this function whenever the view appears in `viewDidAppear(_ animated:)`, so that the temperature will be updated:

```
override func viewDidAppear(_ animated: Bool) {
    super.viewDidAppear(animated)
    locationAuthStatus()
}
```

`locationAuthStatus()` is a function we create that checks whether or not the app has permission to use location services. If it does, then we will set the current location, extract the latitude and longitude and set those equal to the custom class `Location` properties for latitude and longitude. If we do NOT have access, then we will request access.

```
func locationAuthStatus() {
    if CLLocationManager.authorizationStatus() == .authorizedWhenInUse {
        currentLocation = locationManager.location
        Location.sharedInstance.latitude = currentLocation.coordinate.latitude
        Location.sharedInstance.longitude = currentLocation.coordinate.longitude

    } else {

        locationManager.requestWhenInUseAuthorization()

    }
}
```

We also need to add permissions to our info.plist so head over there, hover over the last entry until a '+' sign pops up. Click on it to create a new entry and start typing 'Privacy-Location' and select the one that says 'Privacy - Location When In Use Usage Description' and then to the right, under 'Value' add a message that will be displayed to the user when it opens, something like "We need your location to give you relevant, up-to-date weather information."

While we are in the `info.plist` we also need to add permissions for web requests to non-https websites, as OpenWeather is. So again, hover over the last entry in the plist, and press the '+' button. Select "App Transport Security Settings" then click the small arrow on the left that is pointing to the right, so that it points down, and click on the '+' button again, which will create a sub entry. Here select 'Allow Arbitrary Loads' and set the value to YES. Now our app is able to communicate with any website.

So, remember where we were when we started down this rabbit hole? Let's recap. We created a custom class for CurrentWeather, we started implementing the **API** call using **URLSession**, and we got to the point we are ready to make the call, so then we went to our **API** documentation and saw we need to know a longitude and latitude, so we created a Location custom class, then implemented the code to request access to location services, and if granted, set the current location latitude and longitude to our instance of custom class Location.

Whew! So now, we can circle back to our Constants file and insert the longitude and latitude parameters from our Location instance, and it should now look something like this:

```
let CURRENT_WEATHER_URL = "http://api.openweathermap.org/data/2.5/weather?lat=\
(Location.sharedInstance.latitude!)&lon=\
(Location.sharedInstance.longitude!)&appid=42a1771a0b787bf12e734ada0cfc80cb"
```

except with your **API** key at the end.

Lets head back to our CurrentWeather file. We have our URL and the next thing to do is extract the desired values from it. So lets take a look at the example result we had earlier, only I'm going to throw it into the **JSON** formatter we talked about earlier:

```
{
    "coord":{
        "lon":138.93,
        "lat":34.97
    },
    "weather":[
        {
            "id":803,
            "main":"Clouds",
            "description":"broken clouds",
            "icon":"04n"
        }
    ],
    "base":"stations",
    "main":{
        "temp":295.139,
        "pressure":1021.33,
        "humidity":100,
        "temp_min":295.139,
```

```
        "temp_max":295.139,
        "sea_level":1030.63,
        "grnd_level":1021.33
    },
    "wind":{
        "speed":2.11,
        "deg":68.0001
    },
    "clouds":{
        "all":68
    },
    "dt":1477077361,
    "sys":{
        "message":0.1611,
        "country":"JP",
        "sunrise":1476996953,
        "sunset":1477036867
    },
    "id":1851632,
    "name":"Shuzenji",
    "cod":200
}
```

We want the name of the city, the temperature, and the weather conditions. Remember our analogy of the Russian nesting dolls? We open the first doll and we see all this, inside it is a doll with the label "name" on it and inside it is the value of the city. In this case "Shuzenji". For the weather type we have to go down two levels, first to the key "weather" then to the key "main" which has the value of 'Clouds'.

So are you seeing how you drill down to the values you want?

Lastly we need the temperature which is in 'Main' then down one more level to 'Temp' with the value of 295.139.

So that is the path you take looking at it visually, but what does that look like in code. Inside our `downloadWeatherDetails` function we have created our session, data task, and serialized the response data into **JSON**. So the next step is to turn that **JSON** into a dictionary, then use implicit unwrapping to unwrap and cast to dictionaries one layer at a time until we get the values we need. So modify your `downloadWeatherDetails` as follows. These additions are inside the **do** block.

```
if let dict = json as? Dictionary<String, AnyObject> {
```

```swift
    if let name = dict["name"] as? String {
        self._cityName = name.capitalized
    }

    if let weather = dict["weather"] as? [Dictionary<String, AnyObject>] {

        if let main = weather[0]["main"] as? String {
            self._weatherType = main.capitalized
        }

    }

    if let main = dict["main"] as? Dictionary<String, AnyObject> {
        if let currentTemperature = main["temp"] as? Double {
            let kelvinToFarenheitPreDivision = (currentTemperature * (9/5) - 459.67)
            let kelvinToFarenheit = Double(round(10 *
kelvinToFarenheitPreDivision/10))
            self._currentTemp = kelvinToFarenheit
        }
    }
}
```

We start out by converting the **JSON** into a dictionary of type `<String, AnyObject>`. Then just like we discussed above, we drill down to each level, implicitly unwrapping as we go, until we reach the desired value, at which point we set it equal to the CurrentWeather property.

The temperature is a little more involved as it requires some math to convert Kelvin to Fahrenheit. Next we need to add one last thing related to the **closure**.

Remember how we named the **closure** `completed`? This is what determines when the asynchronous call is done. When we call this function from the ViewController it is going to look for when it reaches `completed()` then execute the next block of code. So we need to place it inside the request and after all the **JSON** has been assigned to the class properties. One level inside the `.resume()` should be good. So your final `downloadWeatherDetails` function should look like this:

```swift
    func downloadWeatherDetails(completed: @escaping DownloadComplete) {

        let session = URLSession.shared
        let url = URL(string: CURRENT_WEATHER_URL)!

        session.dataTask(with: url) { (data, response, error) in
```

```swift
            if let responseData = data {

                do {
                    let json = try JSONSerialization.jsonObject(with: responseData,
options: JSONSerialization.ReadingOptions.allowFragments)

                    print(json)
                    if let dict = json as? Dictionary<String, AnyObject> {

                        if let name = dict["name"] as? String {
                            self._cityName = name.capitalized
                        }

                        if let weather = dict["weather"] as? [Dictionary<String,
AnyObject>] {

                            if let main = weather[0]["main"] as? String {
                                self._weatherType = main.capitalized
                            }

                        }

                        if let main = dict["main"] as? Dictionary<String,
AnyObject> {
                            if let currentTemperature = main["temp"] as? Double {
                                let kelvinToFarenheitPreDivision =
(currentTemperature * (9/5) - 459.67)
                                let kelvinToFarenheit = Double(round(10 *
kelvinToFarenheitPreDivision/10))
                                self._currentTemp = kelvinToFarenheit
                            }
                        }
                    }

                    print(json)
                } catch {
                    print("Could not serialize")
                }
            }
            completed()
        }.resume()
    }
```

It's a big one!

Now lets go back to our ViewController.swift file and add the final touches.

Above the `viewDidLoad` function declare a `currentWeather` variable:

`var currentWeather: CurrentWeather!`

Inside `viewDidLoad` instantiate it:

`currentWeather = CurrentWeather()`

And the inside the `locationAuthStatus` function modify as follows:

```
    func locationAuthStatus() {
        if CLLocationManager.authorizationStatus() == .authorizedWhenInUse {
            currentLocation = locationManager.location
            Location.sharedInstance.latitude = currentLocation.coordinate.latitude
            Location.sharedInstance.longitude =
currentLocation.coordinate.longitude
            currentWeather.downloadWeatherDetails {

                DispatchQueue.main.async {
                    self.updateMainUI()

                }

            }
        } else {

            locationManager.requestWhenInUseAuthorization()

        }
    }
```

We are adding `currentWeather.downloadWeatherDetails` which will then call an async task that will then call a function `updateMainUI` which we will create next. And we don't have to worry about crashes due to trying to assign variables that don't exist, all because of our use of **closures**!

In our `updateMainUI` function, all we are going to do is assign our UI elements IBOutlets to the properties of the custom class. The current weather image is assigned based on the image title, which we cleverly named the same as the weather type returned by the **API** call. So find those images in the resources, and drop them into your Assets folder.

Figure 5.3.23

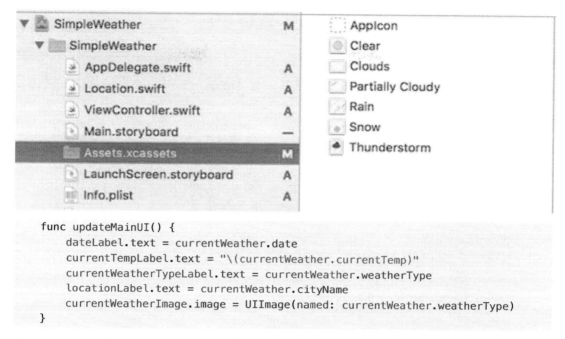

```
func updateMainUI() {
    dateLabel.text = currentWeather.date
    currentTempLabel.text = "\(currentWeather.currentTemp)"
    currentWeatherTypeLabel.text = currentWeather.weatherType
    locationLabel.text = currentWeather.cityName
    currentWeatherImage.image = UIImage(named: currentWeather.weatherType)
}
```

And that seals the deal. Run it, and if you are on the simulator it will probably default to Cupertino. If you are not getting anything, check that there is a location set in the menu Debug > Location while in the simulator. If you are on device it should give your current location temperature and weather conditions.

Wrapping up

So let's recap what we've learned in this chapter. We have learned a little about how **API**s work, how to contact them using **URLSession** to make web requests, how to work with **JSON** and how to use CoreLocation. Quite a lot for such a simple app! Now I want to give you a challenge to think of some ways you could expand on this app and make it even more awesome! The OpenWeather **API** has more options for getting a ten day forecast, high and low temperatures, and much much more.

Exercise

Sometimes you don't want to know the weather conditions in your current location, but want to check the weather in a different city. You exercise is to add a button that takes you to a new view controller where you can enter in a city and return the weather details for that city. The weather API we have been dealing with allows you to do this quite easily. You will just need to modify the existing API call slightly.

By city name

Description:

You can call by city name or city name and country code. API responds with a list of results that match a searching word.

API call:

api.openweathermap.org/data/2.5/weather?q={city name}

api.openweathermap.org/data/2.5/weather?q={city name},{country code}

Parameters:

q city name and country code divided by comma, use ISO 3166 country codes

Examples of API calls:

api.openweathermap.org/data/2.5/weather?q=London

api.openweathermap.org/data/2.5/weather?q=London,uk

Screen Shot 2016-12-01 at 9.50.39 AM.png

Happy coding!

Chapter 38: Firebase Chat App

Introduction and Building a Realtime Chat App

What you will learn

- What Firebase is

- Components that make up Firebase

- Firebase Limitations

- Set up a Firebase Project

- Using the Firebase Console

- Build an Authentication Service

- Build a Realtime Data Service

- Displaying Realtime Data in a TableView

Key Terms

- **API**

- **Firebase**

- **(BaaS) Backend as a Service**

- **Authentication Service**

- **Data Service**

- **Data Model**

- **UITableView**

Introduction to Firebase

Firebase is a **Backend as a service (BaaS)** company offering a robust collection of cloud services geared toward making backend services easier for developers.

Firebase was founded in 2011 and released with a realtime database component in April of 2012. Firebase was subsequently purchased by Google in 2014 and has since reached version 3, in which several new components were introduced.

With the version 3 release of Firebase, the service now includes several individual components that make up the service as a whole: Analytics, Authentication, Cloud Messaging, Realtime Database, Storage, Hosting, Remote App Configuration, Test Lab for Android, Crash Reporting, Notifications, App Indexing, Dynamic Links and Invites. Many times when people refer to Firebase, they may just be referring to the realtime database component, however, by including Firebase into your project, all of these individual services are included right out of the box.

Firebase has native SDKs for iOS, Android and Web. One of the drawbacks with Firebase is that, as of Oct 2016, they do not offer native SDKs for tvOS, MacOS or Windows. If your app will be available on any of those platforms, then you may have to find an alternate solution. If, however, your app will only target one of the 3 platforms that has a native SDK, it is hard to beat Firebase for its ease of setup and cost to get started.

Firebase Chat App

In the following sections, we will walk through the process of creating a realtime chat app for iOS 10 in Swift 3 using Firebase. We will be using the Authentication and Realtime Database components of Firebase. This is a full-featured app, but fairly basic. After we build it, I will offer a challenge for you to customize it and take it in your own direction. I really look forward to see where you can take this project.

As with all projects I work on, I like to break it down into smaller components. The components we will build out are as follows:

- Creating the Firebase project

- Creating the Xcode project

- Installing the Firebase SDK with Cocoapods

- Creating our Authentication Service

- Creating our Data Service

- Adding View Controllers in Interface Builder

- Adding the Authentication UI

- Adding the code for the SignInVC

- Adding the Chat TableView UI

- Adding the code for the MainVC

- Custom UITableViewCell

- Custom UIView for our header

- Wiring things up

Creating the Firebase project

For the first part of our project, we need to log into Firebase and set up our project. In your web browser, head over to https://firebase.google.com. If you are not signed into your Google account, the first thing to do is sign in. In the upper right corner, click on Sign in and log in with your credentials.

Figure 5.4.1

After signing in, you should see a link in the upper right corner that says `Go to console`.
Go ahead and click that to go the the Firebase console to set up our project.

Figure 5.4.2

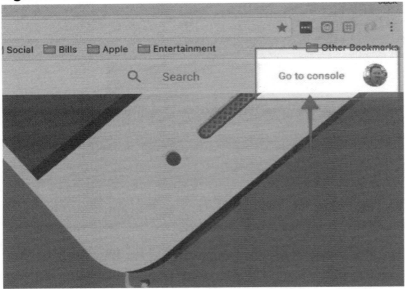

After going to the console, you will see a list of any of your existing projects, if you have
any. You will also see a Button that says `CREATE NEW PROJECT`. We will click this button to
add our new project.

Figure 5.4.3

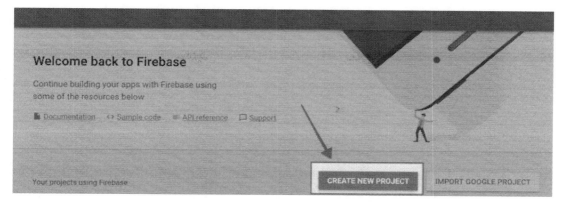

Once the new project popup form comes up, choose a name for your project. In this case we chose **Devslopes-Chat**. Once you fill that in, be sure the correct country is selected and then click CREATE PROJECT.

Figure 5.4.4

Once the dialog box disappears, you will be greeted once again with your list of projects. There should now be a card for your new project we just created.

Figure 5.4.5

Next, we need to create our Xcode iOS project so that we can get the **bundle id** and add that to our project in the Firebase console.

Creating the Xcode project

Go ahead and open up Xcode. When the welcome screen appears, click on `Create a new Xcode Project`.

Figure 5.4.6

Welcome to Xcode

Version 8.0 (8A218a)

Get started with a playground
Explore new ideas quickly and easily.

Create a new Xcode project
Create an app for iPhone, iPad, Mac, Apple Watch or Apple TV.

Check out an existing project
Start working on something from an SCM repository.

☑ Show this window when Xcode launches

When the template dialog appears, make sure the project type is set to iOS, choose
`Single View Application` and click `Next`.

Figure 5.4.7

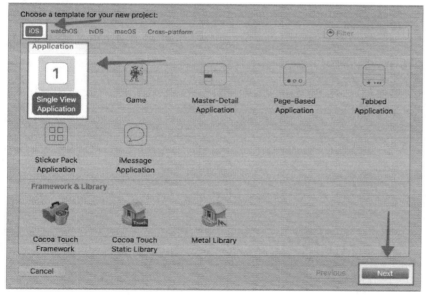

In the Project options dialog that appears next, choose a name for your project,
`devslopes-chat` in my case.

Make sure you have an organization identifier specified. The *organization identifier* is usually your company's domain name in reverse.

In the case of Devslopes, our organization identifier is **com.devslopes**. If you do not have a domain, just use something that would be unique, like *com.yourname* or something similar.

The **bundle identifier** will be listed below the organization identifier. Take note of this, because you will need it when you set up your iOS app in Firebase. Also, be sure you specify **Swift** for the Language and *iPhone* in this case for our app as this will be for iPhone only.

I have also checked the box to include unit tests which I will add in the **unit testing** chapter. Go ahead and click Next.

Figure 5.4.8

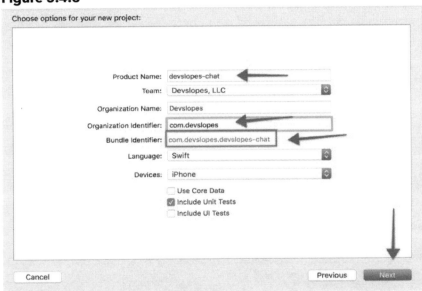

In the save project dialog, choose a location to save your project. In my example, I am saving to my desktop.

Also go ahead and check Create Git repository on My Mac to set up the git repo and click Create.

Figure 5.4.9

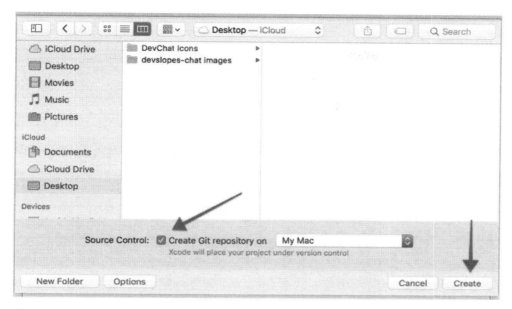

Once our project is created in Xcode and saved, the *General* project page should be shown. Again, take note of the *bundle id* here in the project settings and uncheck **landsape left** and **landscape right**. The only option that should be checked is **portrait**.

Figure 5.4.10

At this point, we need to quit Xcode and move on to installing the Firebase SDK with

Cocoapods in the next section.

Installing the Firebase SDK with Cocoapods

Now that we have our Xcode project set up, it is time to set up the Firebase SDK with Cocoapods.

I am currently using a Mac without Cocoapods installed, so we will quickly walk through the process. If you already have it installed, you can skip through the first part of this section.

Installing Cocoapods

To check to see if you have Cocoapods already installed, simply open up a terminal window and type `which pod`. If Cocoapods is installed, you should see a path to the executable. If not, follow on.

Figure 5.4.11

To install Cocoapods, simply type `sudo gem install cocoapods` followed by `return` in a terminal window.

You will have to enter your password and then hit `return` again.

Figure 5.4.12

It will take Cocoapods a few minutes to install based on your internet connection, but it should finally finish up and report a success message similar to the following:

Figure 5.4.13

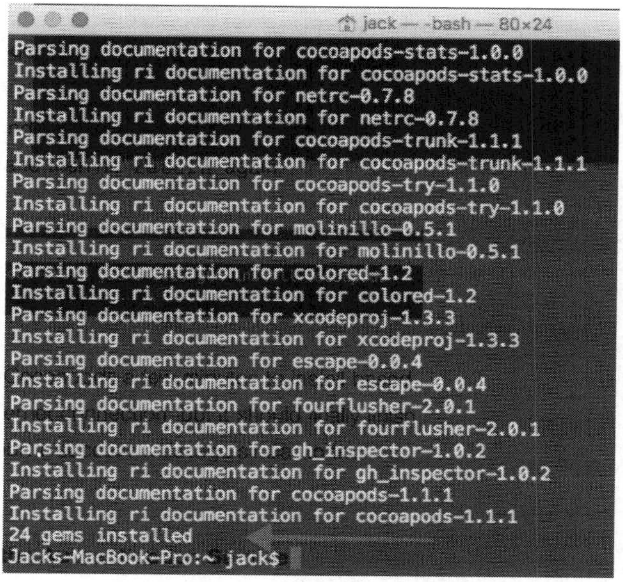

```
                              jack — -bash — 80×24
Parsing documentation for cocoapods-stats-1.0.0
Installing ri documentation for cocoapods-stats-1.0.0
Parsing documentation for netrc-0.7.8
Installing ri documentation for netrc-0.7.8
Parsing documentation for cocoapods-trunk-1.1.1
Installing ri documentation for cocoapods-trunk-1.1.1
Parsing documentation for cocoapods-try-1.1.0
Installing ri documentation for cocoapods-try-1.1.0
Parsing documentation for molinillo-0.5.1
Installing ri documentation for molinillo-0.5.1
Parsing documentation for colored-1.2
Installing ri documentation for colored-1.2
Parsing documentation for xcodeproj-1.3.3
Installing ri documentation for xcodeproj-1.3.3
Parsing documentation for escape-0.0.4
Installing ri documentation for escape-0.0.4
Parsing documentation for fourflusher-2.0.1
Installing ri documentation for fourflusher-2.0.1
Parsing documentation for gh_inspector-1.0.2
Installing ri documentation for gh_inspector-1.0.2
Parsing documentation for cocoapods-1.1.1
Installing ri documentation for cocoapods-1.1.1
24 gems installed
Jacks-MacBook-Pro:~ jack$
```

Adding the Firebase pod to our app

Now that cocoapods is installed, we can move on and add Firebase to our project. From your terminal window, `cd` to our app project folder.

In my case, I had to type `cd /Users/jack/Desktop/devslopes-chat`.

Adjust your path accordingly. Once there, type `pod init` to initialize Cocoapods for our project.

Figure 5.4.14

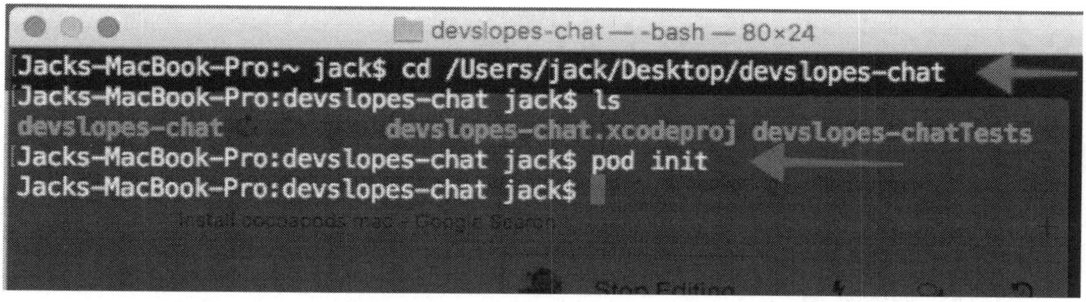

```
                           devslopes-chat — -bash — 80×24
Jacks-MacBook-Pro:~ jack$ cd /Users/jack/Desktop/devslopes-chat
Jacks-MacBook-Pro:devslopes-chat jack$ ls
devslopes-chat            devslopes-chat.xcodeproj devslopes-chatTests
Jacks-MacBook-Pro:devslopes-chat jack$ pod init
Jacks-MacBook-Pro:devslopes-chat jack$
```

We should now have our project set up and ready to go. We need to edit our **Podfile** to add Firebase and then install it.

With a text editor, open up the **Podfile** file in your project folder to edit it. I use Vim, but you can use whatever flavor of editor you like.

Make sure that the `Platform` line is uncommented, and then add `pod 'Firebase'`, `pod 'Firebase/Auth'` and `pod 'Firebase/Database'` under the *use frameworks* line.

Figure 5.4.15

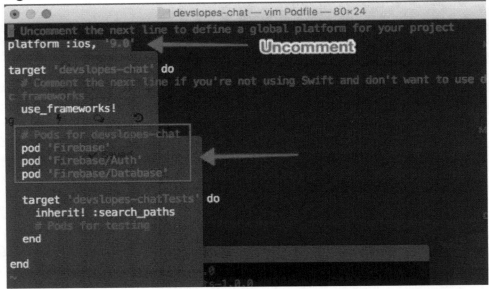

Out of the many features Firebase has to offer, Authentication and Realtime Database are the only two services we will be using in this project.

We could always incorporate some of the other Firebase services in our project, but for now, these two are what we need.

Once you have your **Podfile** in shape, go ahead and type `pod install` followed by `return`.

This will start the ball rolling and begin installing our SDKs. If this is the first time you have used Cocoapods on your Mac, it may take some time because it has to update the master repo on your machine.

Once complete, you should see a message advising you to no longer use the **.xcproject** file to open your project, but instead to use the new **.xcworkspace** file.

Figure 5.4.16

```
Jacks-MacBook-Pro:devslopes-chat jack$ pod install  ◀─────
Setting up CocoaPods master repo
Setup completed
Analyzing dependencies
Downloading dependencies
Installing Firebase (3.7.1)
Installing FirebaseAnalytics (3.4.4)
Installing FirebaseAuth (3.0.5)
Installing FirebaseCore (3.4.3)
Installing FirebaseDatabase (3.0.3)
Installing FirebaseInstanceID (1.0.8)
Installing GoogleInterchangeUtilities (1.2.2)
Installing GoogleNetworkingUtilities (1.2.2)
Installing GoogleSymbolUtilities (1.1.2)
Installing GoogleUtilities (1.3.2)
Generating Pods project
Integrating client project

[!] Please close any current Xcode sessions and use `devslopes-chat.xcworkspace`
    for this project from now on.

Sending stats
Pod installation complete! There are 3 dependencies from the Podfile and 10 total
  pods installed.
```

You can now open the new **.xcworkspace** file from within finder or from **file->open** within Xcode.

From here, we need to create the iOS App in the Firebase Console and import the `Google Service plist` file in our Xcode project.

Back over in the **Firebase Console**, click on the card for your app and you will be taken to a *Getting Started* page.

We are setting up an iOS app, so click on the **Add Firebase to your iOS App** option.

Figure 5.4.17

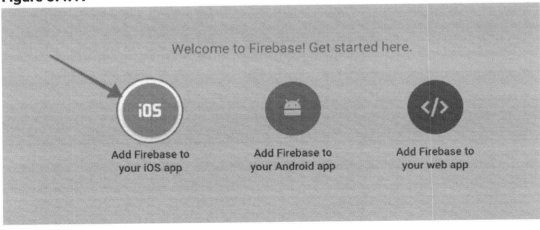

Once you do this, you are greeted with a series of steps to get your app set up. In the

561

first dialog, you are asked to enter the **bundle id** of your app.

This is the *bundle id* that I asked you to remember earlier. Type or paste that into the box and then enter a nickname for your app if you wish. Once you complete these steps, click `continue`.

Figure 5.4.18

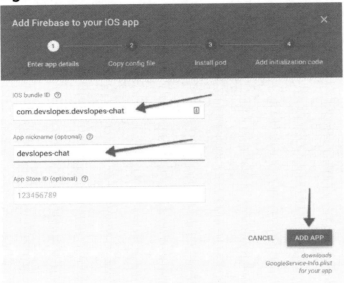

Once you click `continue`, a file should download called **GoogleService-info.plist**.

This is the file we will import into your project in just a minute as we configure it. For now, just hang on to that in a safe place.

Figure 5.4.19

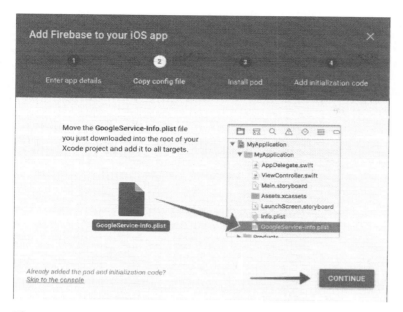

This screen, as well as the next two, give you some information about how to set up your project. Go ahead and glance through them, even though we are going to do all of that here in this text.

When you click Continue, you are advised on the procedure for installing the SDK via Cocoapods. We have already done this, so go ahead and click Continue to carry on.

Figure 5.4.20

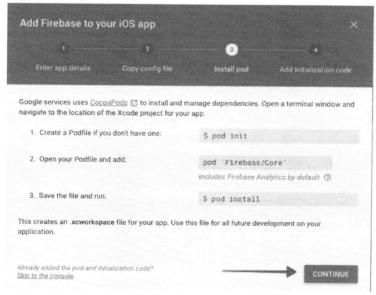

On the fourth and final dialog, we are shown the initialization code to add to our app to connect the SDK. We cover that next, so go ahead and click `Finish`.

Figure 5.4.21

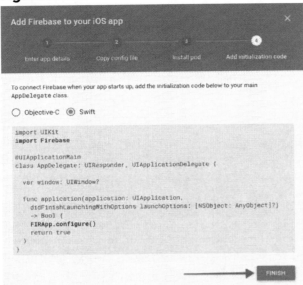

Now that we have our project set up, let's move on to writing some code.

The first thing we need to do is add a call inside our `AppDelegate.swift` file. Click on the `AppDelegate.swift` file in the *Project Navigator*.

Figure 5.4.22

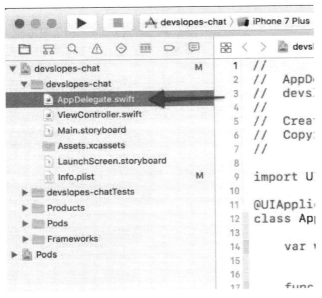

The first thing is to add `import Firebase` in our import statements (just below `import UIKit`).

In the code editor, find the `application(application:didFinishLaunchingWithOptions)` method.

Inside the body of this method, before the `return true` statement, We need to add `FIRApp.configure()`. The full method should look like the following code:

Figure 5.4.23

```
import UIKit
import Firebase

func application(_ application: UIApplication, didFinishLaunchingWithOptions
launchOptions: [UIApplicationLaunchOptionsKey: Any]?) -> Bool {

    FIRApp.configure()
    return true
}
```

I almost got ahead of myself. We still need to import our `GoogleService-info.plist` file into our project.

Open a finder window and navigate to the location where you saved the `plist` file.

Click and drag that file into your project navigator *on the same level as your app delegate.*

An *Add File dialog* will appear.

Make sure that **copy items if needed** is checked as well as the **devslopes-chat** target option and click `Finish`.

Figure 5.4.24

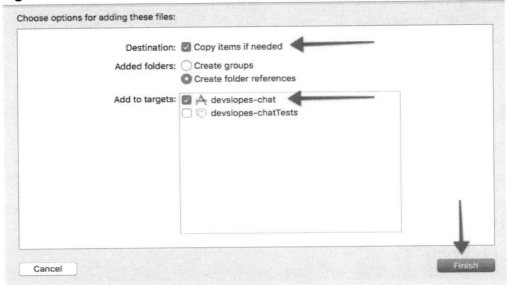

The `GoogleService-info.plist` file should now be in your *Project Navigator* similiar to the following image.

Figure 5.4.25

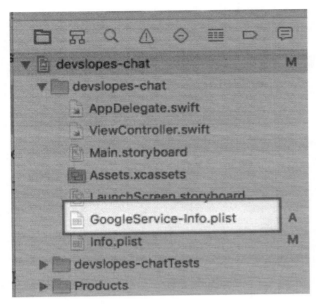

Now that we have Firebase configured in our `AppDelegate` and our `plist` file imported, we can move on to creating our *Authentication Service* in the next section.

Creating the Authentication Service

In this section we are going to create our *Authentication Service* in code to be sort of a middle-man between our app and the Firebase Auth system.
Before writing our code, we need to do one more thing in the **Firebase Console**.

In the console, click `Authentication` in the left menu bar. Near the top of the page, you should see `Sign In Method`, go ahead and click that.
Finally, under `Email/Password`, click the little *edit pencil* out to the right to edit that method.

Figure 5.4.26

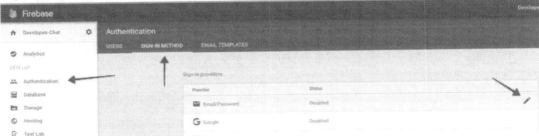

In the dialog box that appears, *toggle* the `Enable` switch and click `Save`.

Figure 5.4.27

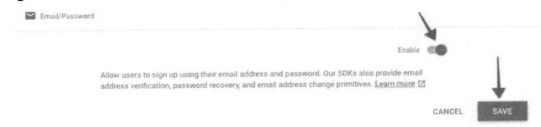

With these steps complete, we have enabled *Email/Password* authentication with Firebase. Now time to move on to code...I promise.

Our *Authentication Service* will be a single file and structured as a **singleton**. A *singleton* is code that is instantiated one time and one time only in your app and is available everywhere within your app.

There can only ever be **ONE** instance of a *singleton* throughout an app. Services are great candidates for *singletons* and in fact, our *Auth Service* as well as our *Data Service* will both be singletons.

First, let's create some groups. To do this, **right-click** on your *project folder* inside the *Project Navigator* and choose `New Group`.

Figure 5.4.28

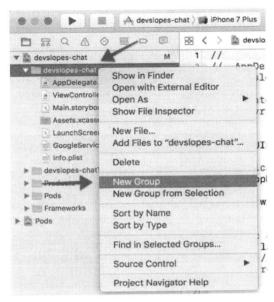

Once the new group is added (which looks like a folder), go ahead and rename it *Services*.

While we're at it, add three more groups and name them *Model*, *View* and finally *Controller*.

Figure 5.4.29

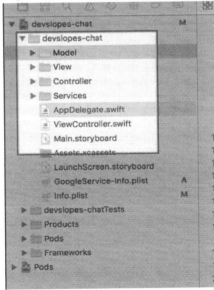

Next, time to create our **AuthService.swift** file. Right click on the *Services* group and then click on `New File`.

Figure 5.4.30

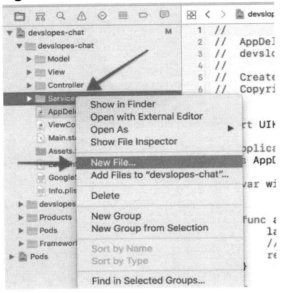

In the dialog that appears, be sure iOS is selected at the top, click on **Swift File** and then click `Next`.

Figure 5.4.31

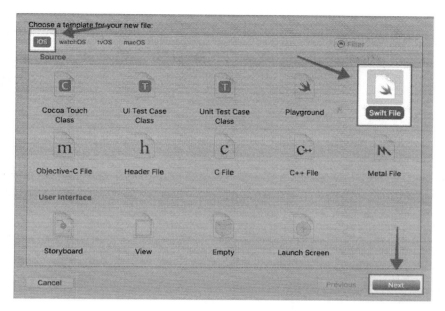

In the *save as* dialog, type `AuthService.swift` in the *Save As:* box, make sure the `devslopes-chat` target is checked and click `Create`.

Figure 5.4.32

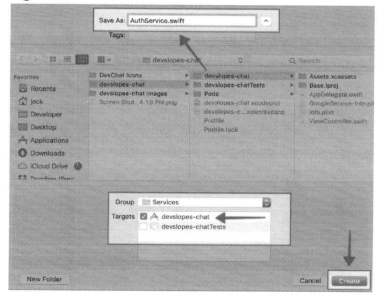

After saving the file, you should now see our newly created `AuthService.swift` file in the *Project Navigator* under the *Services group*.

Figure 5.4.33

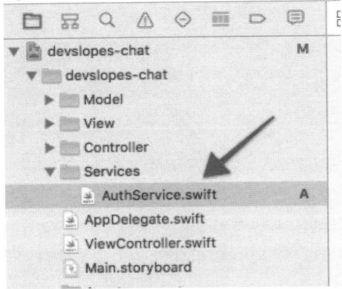

With our `AuthService.swift` file open in our Xcode editor, let write some code. First we need to import Firebase. At the top of the file underneath `import Foundation`, add the line `import Firebase`.

Next add the *singleton* structure to the file.

Figure 5.4.34

```
class AuthService {
    static let instance = AuthService()

}
```

Next, we will set up a couple of variables to store some data. First we need an optional variable for a username and second we need a *Boolean* variable to keep track of the *logged in* state.

Figure 5.4.35

```
class AuthService {
    static let instance = AuthService()

    var username: String?
    var isLoggedIn = false
}
```

Finally, the meat of our *Auth Service* comes down to one single function. Here is the code and we will walk through it below.

Figure 5.4.36

```
class AuthService {
  static let instance = AuthService()

  var username: String?
  var isLoggedIn = false

  func emailLogin(_ email: String, password: String, completion: @escaping (_
Success: Bool, _ message: String) -> Void) {

    FIRAuth.auth()?.signIn(withEmail: email, password: password, completion: {
(user, error) in
      if error != nil {
        if let errorCode = FIRAuthErrorCode(rawValue: (error?._code)!) {
          if errorCode == .errorCodeUserNotFound {
            FIRAuth.auth()?.createUser(withEmail: email, password: password,
completion: { (user, error) in
              if error != nil {
                completion(false, "Error creating account")
              } else {
                completion(true, "Successfully created account")
              }
            })
          } else {
            completion(false, "Sorry, Incorrect email or password")
          }
        }
      } else {
        completion(true, "Successfully Logged In")
      }
    })
  }
}
```

First we declare our function. It takes a String username and String password as parameters and includes a completion handler.

First up, we try to sign in to Firebase with our `FIRAuth.auth()` function call here. We first check for the presence of an error.

If there was an error, we check to see if the error we received was that the user was not found. If it was, then we attempt to create a new user via the

573

`FIRAuth.auth()?.createUser(withEmail:password:completion)` method.

With this method, again, we are either successful or we receive an error. If we receive an error, then we pass in `false` (not successful) and an error message to our completion handler.
If we did not receive an error, creating the new user was successful, so we pass in `true` and a success message to our completion handler.

If the error received in our `signIn` method was not `.errorCodeUserNotFound`, the we know that the user exists, but the password was wrong.
For this case, we pass `false` and another message to our completion handler.

Finally, if we did not receive an error on `signIn`, we are successfully authenticated. We pass in `true` and 'Successfully Logged In' to our completion handler.

This is all we need for our *Auth Service*, so let's move on to our *Data Service* next

Creating our Data Service

Right click on your **Services** group once again and add another iOS Swift file as we did above.
Name this file `DataService.swift`. As above, under `import Foundation`, add your `import Firebase` statement.
We are going to start off here by adding a protocol. Under your import statements, add the following:

Figure 5.4.37

```
import Foundation
import Firebase

protocol DataServiceDelegate: class {
  func dataLoaded()
}
```

This is our delegate protocol which will let us fire a delegate method any time our data is loaded. Next, go ahead and set up our singleton class structure.

Figure 5.4.38

```
import Foundation
import Firebase
```

574

```
protocol DataServiceDelegate: class {
  func dataLoaded()
}

class DataService {
  static let instance = DataService()
}
```

We will need a total of 3 variables for this file, a *constant* for our **Firebase Database** reference, a variable for storing our *array* of messages and a *weak* variable for our delegate. Let's add those now:

Figure 5.4.39

```
import Foundation
import Firebase

protocol DataServiceDelegate: class {
  func dataLoaded()
}

class DataService {
  static let instance = DataService()

  let ref = FIRDatabase.database().reference()
  var messages: [Message] = []

  weak var delegate: DataServiceDelegate?
}
```

Before continuing, we really need to create our **Data Model** for a **Message**. This being a *chat* app, it wouldn't be structured very well if we didn't have a *Message model*.

Message Data Model

Right click on your **Models** group and add a new file.
Make this a *Swift* file and name it Message.swift.
This model will be a **structure** or **struct**.
At the top of the file, let's go ahead and set it up:

Figure 5.4.40

```
import Foundation
```

575

```
struct Message {
  fileprivate let _messageId: String
  fileprivate let _userId: String?
  fileprivate let _message: String?
}
```

Here, we have declared our *struct* and set up three private properties, a message ID, a user ID and a message.

Since these are private, next we need to create some public accessors for them:

Figure 5.4.41

```
import Foundation

struct Message {
  fileprivate let _messageId: String
  fileprivate let _userId: String?
  fileprivate let _message: String?

  var messageId: String {
    return _messageId
  }

  var userId: String? {
    return _userId
  }

  var message: String? {
    return _message
  }
}
```

Now we have three private properties and three *getters* for those properties. We didn't include any *setters* as these will only be set through initializers. In fact, we will have two initializers, one to init with all three parameters and another to init with a *messageId* and *Firebase Data*.

We are also going to add a static method (a method that is called on the struct itself and not an instance of the struct) to load and return a message array from passed in *Firebase Data*.

Let's start with the two initializers; first up, *Firebase Data*:

Figure 5.4.42

576

```
init(messageId: String, messageData: Dictionary<String, AnyObject>) {
    _messageId = messageId
    _userId = messageData["user"] as? String
    _message = messageData["message"] as? String
}
```

This initializer is fairly straightforward. We pass in the `messageId` and our *Firebase data* as a dictionary of type `<String, AnyObject>`.

The `messageId` is set to the passed in `messageId` and the other two properties are set by pulling the corresponding value out of our dictionary.

Next up, our initializer with all properties passed in:

Figure 5.4.43

```
init(messageId: String, userId: String?, message: String?) {
    _messageId = messageId
    _userId = userId
    _message = message
}
```

This initializer is even more straightforward than the first. We simply set each property equal to the passed in value of the same name. Now let's look at the code for our static function and then we will discuss it:

Figure 5.4.44

```
static func messageArrayFromFBData(_ fbData: AnyObject) -> [Message] {

    var messages = [Message]()
    if let formatted = fbData as? Dictionary<String, AnyObject> {

        for (key, messageObj) in formatted {
            let obj = messageObj as! Dictionary<String, AnyObject>
            let message = Message(messageId: key, messageData: obj as
Dictionary<String, AnyObject>)
            messages.append(message)
        }
    }
    return messages
}
```

First up here, we create a new empty array of type `Message` to store our messages in. Next, we grab our passed in *Firebase Data* `fbData` and store it in a variable `formatted` as a *Dictionary* of type `<String, AnyObject>`.

Next, we loop through each element in the *dictionary* and grab the key (which is the `messageId`) and the object which is in turn formatted as another *Dictionary* of type `<String, AnyObject>`.

We then call our init method from above that takes *Firebase Data* to create a new, properly initialized `Message`.

Once we have a `Message` for that iteration, we append it onto our `messages` array.

Finally, after we have looped through every element, we return our `messages` array. The code for the entire file should look like the following:

Figure 5.4.45

```
import Foundation

struct Message {
  fileprivate let _messageId: String
  fileprivate let _userId: String?
  fileprivate let _message: String?

  var messageId: String {
    return _messageId
  }

  var userId: String? {
    return _userId
  }

  var message: String? {
    return _message
  }

  init(messageId: String, messageData: Dictionary<String, AnyObject>) {
    _messageId = messageId
    _userId = messageData["user"] as? String
    _message = messageData["message"] as? String
  }

  init(messageId: String, userId: String?, message: String?) {
    _messageId = messageId
    _userId = userId
    _message = message
  }

  static func messageArrayFromFBData(_ fbData: AnyObject) -> [Message] {
```

```swift
    var messages = [Message]()
    if let formatted = fbData as? Dictionary<String, AnyObject> {

        for (key, messageObj) in formatted {
            let obj = messageObj as! Dictionary<String, AnyObject>
            let message = Message(messageId: key, messageData: obj as
Dictionary<String, AnyObject>)
            messages.append(message)
        }
    }
    return messages
  }
}
```

Back to our Data Service

Now that we took care of our **Message Data Model**, let's get back to work on our *Data Service*. We will have two methods in this service.

One to load all messages from Firebase and a second to *save* a message to *Firebase*. Take note of the pattern here, we are keeping our data totally separate from our UI which is **always** a great idea.

Our first method will load up our messages from *Firebase* and store them in our `messages` array:

Figure 5.4.46

```swift
  func loadMessages(_ completion: @escaping (_ Success: Bool) -> Void) {
    ref.observe(.value) { (data: FIRDataSnapshot) in
      if data.value != nil {
        let unsortedMessages = Message.messageArrayFromFBData(data.value! as
AnyObject)
        self.messages = unsortedMessages.sorted(by: { $0.messageId < $1.messageId
})

        self.delegate?.dataLoaded()
        if self.messages.count > 0 {
          completion(true)
        } else {
          completion(false)
        }
      } else {
        completion(false)
      }
```

```
    }
  }
```

This method takes no parameters, but includes a completion handler.

First up, we call the `observe` method on our *Firebase Reference* `ref`. We are observing the *value* of that *Firebase* location and will receive a `FIRDataSnapshot`.

We check to make sure `data.value` if not nil, otherwise we pass in `false` to our completion handler (*not successful*).

If `data.value` is not nil, we call our static method in our **Message** struct, passing it in as type `AnyObject`.

We assign the value returned from that method to a constant called `unsortedMessages`.

Next up, we take the `unsortedMessages` array and sort by the `messageId`.

We then assign that *sorted* array to our messages array. Since we will be using **AutoId** keys that *Firebase* provides, this will keep our messages sorted in chronological order.

We fire off our delegate method to notify any subscribers that our data has loaded and then check to make sure our messages array actually contains data. If so, we pass `true` to our completion handler and `false` otherwise.

Finally, let's turn to our last method in this service:

Figure 5.4.47

```
func saveMessage(_ user: String, message: String) {
  let key = ref.childByAutoId().key
  let message = ["user": user,
                 "message": message]
  let messageUpdates = ["/\(key)": message]
  ref.updateChildValues(messageUpdates)
}
```

This method simply saves a message to *Firebase*. We pass in the *user* as a *String* and the *message* as a *String*. We make the key by using the *Firebase* `childByAutoId().key` method.

By using this, our messages will be sorted in chronological order because the *autoId* provided by *Firebase* incorporates a timestamp in it.

We create a message *Dictionary* using the passed in values and then create another Dictionary containing our key and the message dictionary.

Finally we call the *Firebase* method `updateChildValues` and pass in our data to be saved to *Firebase*. To try and clarify just a little, what we are passing to `updateChildValues` would look something like this:

Figure 5.4.49

```
["-KUedAHaUiD9rx2BR1gY":["user":"jack","message":"What's going on?"]]
```

The full file for our **DataService.swift** file should look as follows:

Figure 5.4.48

```swift
import Foundation
import Firebase

protocol DataServiceDelegate: class {
  func dataLoaded()
}

class DataService {
  static let instance = DataService()

  let ref = FIRDatabase.database().reference()
  var messages: [Message] = []

  weak var delegate: DataServiceDelegate?

  func loadMessages(_ completion: @escaping (_ Success: Bool) -> Void) {
    ref.observe(.value) { (data: FIRDataSnapshot) in
      if data.value != nil {
        let unsortedMessages = Message.messageArrayFromFBData(data.value! as
AnyObject)
        self.messages = unsortedMessages.sorted(by: { $0.messageId < $1.messageId
})
        self.delegate?.dataLoaded()
        if self.messages.count > 0 {
          completion(true)
        } else {
          completion(false)
        }
      } else {
        completion(false)
      }
    }
  }

  func saveMessage(_ user: String, message: String) {
    let key = ref.childByAutoId().key
    let message = ["user": user,
```

```
            "message": message]
    let messageUpdates = ["/\(key)": message]
    ref.updateChildValues(messageUpdates)
  }
}
```

Now that our *Data Service* is complete, we need to make a quick addition to our
AppDelegate.

After our app is *configured*, we need to set up an **observer** to "watch" the data and
update it if it changes.

Update your *AppDelegate*'s `application(application:didFinishLaunchingWithOptions)`
method like so:

Figure 5.4.48.1

```
    func application(_ application: UIApplication, didFinishLaunchingWithOptions
launchOptions: [UIApplicationLaunchOptionsKey: Any]?) -> Bool {

        FIRApp.configure()

        DataService.instance.loadMessages({ Success in
            if !Success {
                print("Load Firebase data FAILED!")
            } else {
                print("Success!")
            }
        })

        return true
    }
```

All we are doing here is calling our `loadMessages` method in our `DataService` singleton. It
sets up the observer to make updates when the data changes.

By calling this method in the *AppDelegate*, we insure that the data gets downloaded on
application launch and updates as necessary.

Adding View Controllers in Interface Builder

Now that we have our **Data Model** and **Data Service** set up and totally disconnected
from our UI, let's turn our attention to the UI.

Let's start by ditching the **ViewController.swift** file in our project. Right click on the file in the *Project Navigator* and choose delete.

Figure 5.4.49

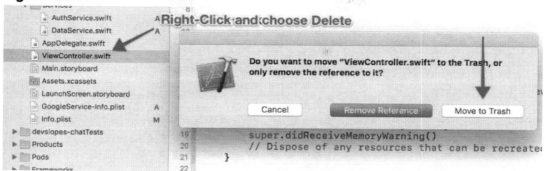

Now that our default *ViewController* is gone, let's make a new one. Right click on the **Controller group** and choose New File.

Figure 5.4.50

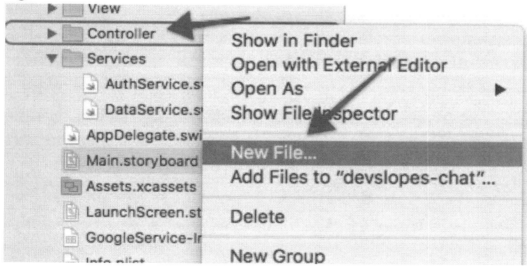

In the *New File Dialog*, choose iOS, Cocoa Touch Class and click Next.

Figure 5.4.51

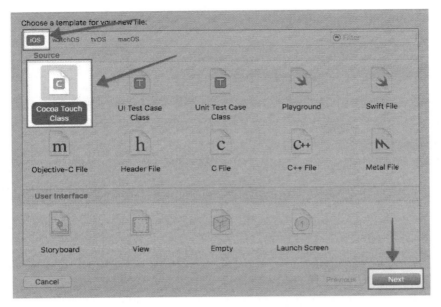

In the *New File Options* dialog, Name the class `SignInVC` and change *Subclass of* to `UIViewController` if is not that already.

Make sure the language is `Swift` and click `Next`.

Figure 5.4.52

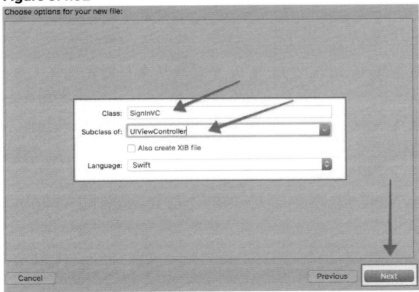

Click on `Main Storyboard` and locate your main View Controller.

Click on the **File Owner** button at the top and the in th **Identity Inspector** on the right, change the class in the dropdown to `SignInVC`.

Figure 5.4.53

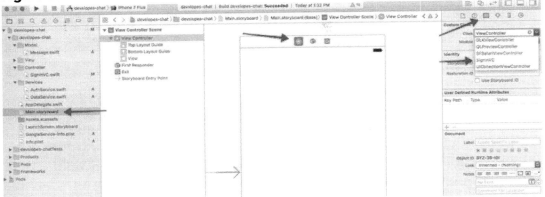

While still in the **Main Storyboard**, drag out a new *View Controller* from the **Object Library** into **interface builder**.

Place it to the right of our existing *SignInVC*.

Figure 5.4.54

Now, repeat the process for creating a new *ViewController Swift* file.

Right click on the *Controller* group and choose *New File*.

Make the class name `MainVC` and make sure it is a subclass of `UIViewController`. Also make sure the language is set to *Swift*. Once you have that file saved, click the *file owner* button at the top of the new *View Controller* you dragged into *interface builder* and set the class to `MainVC` in the **identity inspector** the way you did above.

Figure 5.4.55

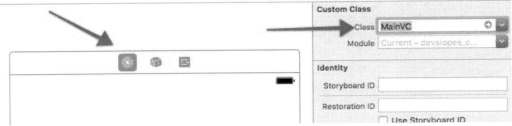

The only thing left before we move on to controls is to add a couple of segues. There are multiple ways to do this, but for this example, we are going to hold down `ctrl` on our keyboard and click and drag from `SignInVC` to `MainVC` in our **document outline**.

Figure 5.4.56

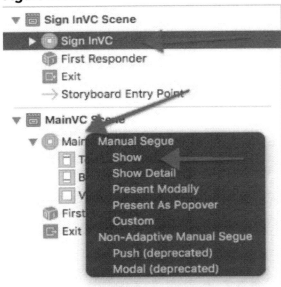

Once you drag this connection, you should see a small dialog box appear asking what type of manual segue you would like.

Go ahead and choose `Show`. Once this is done, you should see the *segue* connecting the two *view controllers* in *interface builder*.

Click on the small circle in between the two *view controllers* on the *segue* line and in the

attributes inspector on the right, add the identifier showMainVC.

Figure 5.4.57

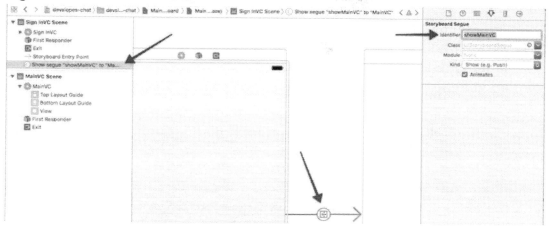

We also need a segue back to the **SignInVC** from our **MainVC**.

To do this, just reverse the order. Hold down ctrl and click and drag from MainVC to SignInVC in the **document outline**.

Select that new *segue* and in the **attributes** inspector, set the *segue identifier* to showSignInVC.

Figure 5.4.58

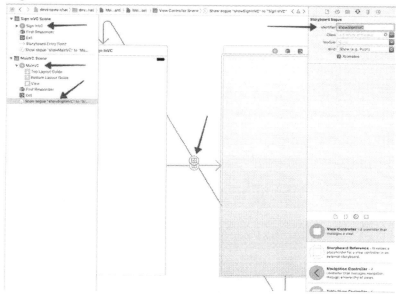

This wraps up the basics of adding our two *View Controllers* and hooking up our *segues*. In the next section, we will start adding controls to our *View Controllers* and finally conclude by hooking everything up.

Adding the Authentication UI

Our *SignInVC* is fairly straightforward, just a Label, Image, two Text Fields and one Button.

To get started, click on the *SignInVC* and in the **attributes inspector**, click the drop down box next to `Background`.

Choose `other` to bring up our *color picker*.

Figure 5.4.59

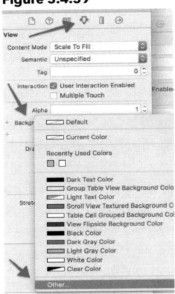

The color I am going to use for the background is hex value `FFB234`.

In the *color picker*, choose **color sliders** at the top and pull down the drop down box to choose **RGB Sliders**.

Add our *hex value* `FFB234` to the `Hex Color #` box.

Figure 5.4.60

Next, let's drag out a **UILabel** from our **Object Library** onto our *SignInVC*.

Figure 5.4.61

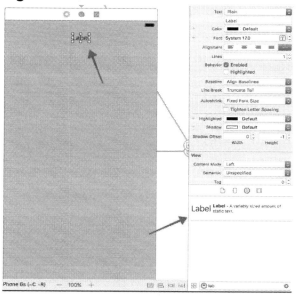

Place the label near the top and change the text property in the **attributes inspector** to
Devslopes Chat or whatever you want to call your app. I also changed the font color to
white, the font to *Futura Medium 28* and set the alignment to *center*.

Adjust these values to what you would like. One thing to note here is that I am placing the controls fairly high on this sign in VC so that when the keyboard appears, it will not cover anything.

In the next section when we are dealing with our table view, the message input text field is at the bottom. In that case, we will add code to move the entire view up so that the keyboard does not interfere with the user experience.

Figure 5.4.62

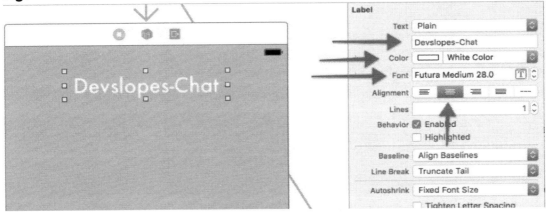

The next thing to do is add a **UIImageView** to our VC. This will be for our app icon image.

Click on the **Assets.xcassets** folder in the *Project Navigator*.

In the *Document Outline*, click the plus sign at the bottom and then click New Image Set.

Figure 5.4.63

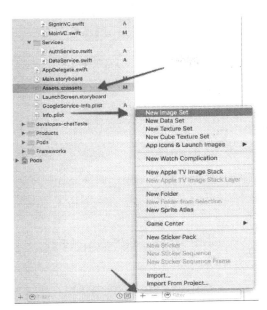

Double click the name of the new image set you just added and rename it to `DevslopesChat` or whatever you would like it to be.

Find your image you want to use and drag it into the *1x* location in the image set you just made. Your image is now ready to be used.

Figure 5.4.64

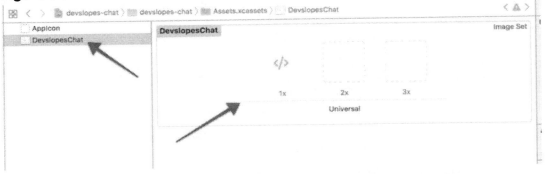

Go back to your `Main.storyboard` and let's get back to work. Drag an *Image View* from the *Object Library* onto your *SignInVC*. Place it right under your label and center it. In the *attributes inspector* pull down the *Image* drop down box and choose your image you just added.

Figure 5.4.65

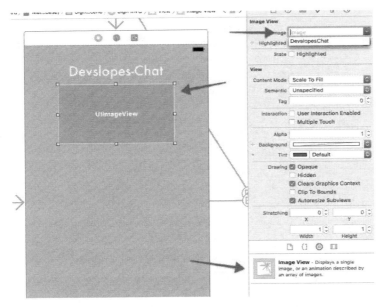

I changed my *Content Mode* to `Aspect Fit` and then used the resize handles on the image view to adjust the size.

Figure 5.4.65

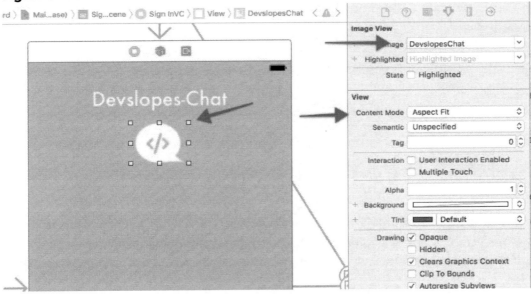

Next up, drag out two **Text Fields** from the *object library* and center those underneath your new image.

In these two Text Fields, I went ahead and added *placeholder text* in the attributes inspector, as well as a custom font and keyboard options.

For the password field, I also ticked the box next to **secure text entry**.

Figure 5.4.66

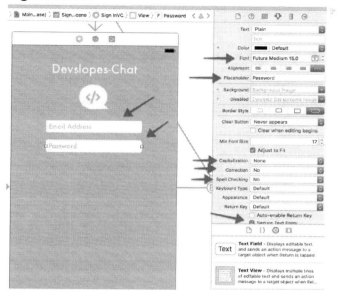

The only thing left to do here is to add a sign in button. Go ahead and drag out a button from the *object library* and center it up underneath our text fields.

In the attributes inspector, I changed the text to `Sign In/Up` since we will be able to do either from this single button.

I also changed the font color to *white*, the font style to *Futura Medium 18* and the background to hex value `22A685`.

We will round the corners a little when we get to the code.

Figure 5.4.67

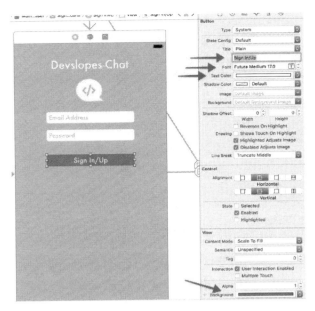

All that is left at this point is to add constraints to all of my controls. I will start by giving my label at the top a fixed width, pinning it to the top and centering it horizontally.

Figure 5.4.68

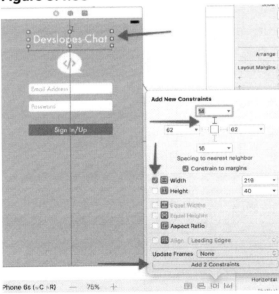

Figure 5.4.69

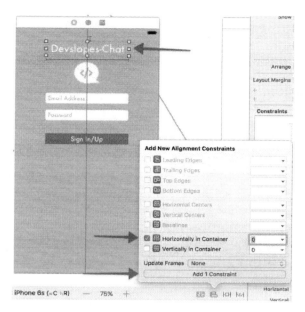

For our image, I am going to pin it to the label above, give it a fixed width and height and center it horizontally with the label above.

Figure 5.4.70

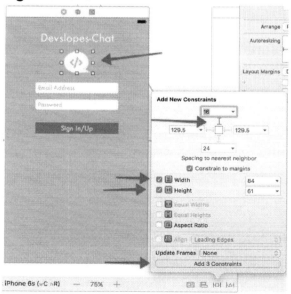

To center the image with the label above, I held down `ctrl`, clicked and dragged from the image view up to the label above. I was then presented with a popup where I chose

center horizontally.

Figure 5.4.71

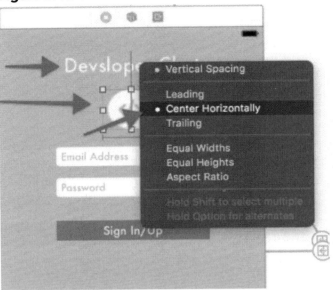

I will repeat these steps for the remaining controls. The final version should look like this:

Figure 5.4.72

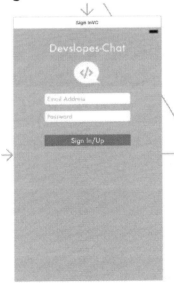

That wraps up adding controls to our `SignInVC`, so let's now turn to the code behind it.

Adding the code for the SignInVC

To begin, we need to `import Firebase` and we need three `@IBOutlets` for our controls.

Figure 5.4.73

```
import UIKit
import Firebase

class SignInVC: UIViewController {

    @IBOutlet weak var emailTextField: UITextField!
    @IBOutlet weak var passwordTextField: UITextField!
    @IBOutlet weak var signInButton: UIButton!
}
```

We obviously need the text field outlets so we can grab the text out of them. The reason we added an outlet for our button is that we are going to round the corners of it now. In `ViewDidLoad`, add the following:

Figure 5.4.74

```
override func viewDidLoad() {
    super.viewDidLoad()

    signInButton.layer.cornerRadius = 8
}
```

Since we are configuring our **Firebase** SDK in our *AppDelegate*, there is a chance that since this is the first screen to load that the app will not be configured by the time `viewDidLoad` is called.

To make sure our app is configured before we move on, I am going to add an *override* of `viewDidAppear`.

Here is the code in `viewDidAppear`...we will discuss it in one second.

Figure 5.4.75

```
override func viewDidAppear(_ animated: Bool) {

    setUsername()
    if AuthService.instance.isLoggedIn {
        performSegue(withIdentifier: "showMainVC", sender: nil)
    }
}
```

In this code, we are calling a function we will create in just a moment. It is just basically checking to see if a user is logged in, and if so, it grabs the username portion of their email address and hangs onto it for later use and then immediately segues to our `MainVC`. It might be a better idea to have our `MainVC` as the *initial View Controller* and display a login popup if there is no user logged in, but for our example app, this will work for now.

Next we are going to create a new `showAlert` function.
This function takes a *title* and a *message* and just displays an alert if we encounter a problem in our code.

Figure 5.4.76

```
func showAlert(title: String, message: String) {
    let alertController = UIAlertController(title: title, message: message,
preferredStyle: .alert)
    let okAction = UIAlertAction(title: "OK", style: .default, handler: nil)
    alertController.addAction(okAction)
    self.present(alertController, animated: true, completion: nil)
}
```

Now on to our `setUsername()` function. As I explained above, we are just storing the username for the logged in user if one is available. This way we can display that in our chat *TableView* instead of displaing the entire email address.
It also sets the `isLoggedIn` Boolean variable in our *AuthService*. Note that if a user is loggged in, `FIRAuth.auth()?.currentUser` will have a value; otherwise it will be `nil`.

Figure 5.4.77

```
func setUsername() {
    if let user = FIRAuth.auth()?.currentUser {
        AuthService.instance.isLoggedIn = true
        let emailComponents = user.email?.components(separatedBy: "@")
        if let username = emailComponents?[0] {
            AuthService.instance.username = username
        }
    } else {
        AuthService.instance.isLoggedIn = false
        AuthService.instance.username = nil
    }
}
```

The last bit of code to add for this file is for our *Sign in* button.

Figure 5.4.78

```
@IBAction func signInTapped(sender: UIButton) {

        // unwraps the textfields and stores them in constants
        guard let email = emailTextField.text, let password =
passwordTextField.text else {
            showAlert(title: "Error", message: "Please enter an email and
password")
            return
        }
        // check to make sure they are not an empty string
        guard email != "", password != "" else {
            showAlert(title: "Error", message: "Please enter an email and
password")
            return
        }

        AuthService.instance.emailLogin(email, password: password) { (success,
message) in
            if success {
                self.setUsername()
                self.performSegue(withIdentifier: "showMainVC", sender: nil)
            } else {
                self.showAlert(title: "Failure", message: message)
            }
        }
    }
}
```

This code is very straightforward. We are making sure that our text fields have values in them, or we are calling our `showAlert()` function and displaying an alert on the screen. If they do contain values, we call our `emailLogin` function we created in our *Auth Service*.

If the authentication was successful, we again call `setUsername()` and then immediately *segue* to our `MainVC`.

If authentication was unsuccessful, we display an alert. Remember here that we are attempting to authenticate first and if a user with that email doesn't exist, then we try to create the account. We should only receive a failure if either the password was incorrect for an existing account, or there was a system error creating the account. The full code for this file:

Figure 5.4.79

```
import UIKit
import Firebase
```

```swift
class SignInVC: UIViewController {

    @IBOutlet weak var emailTextField: UITextField!
    @IBOutlet weak var passwordTextField: UITextField!
    @IBOutlet weak var signInButton: UIButton!

    override func viewDidLoad() {
        super.viewDidLoad()

        signInButton.layer.cornerRadius = 8
    }

    override func viewDidAppear(_ animated: Bool) {

        setUsername()
        if AuthService.instance.isLoggedIn {
            performSegue(withIdentifier: "showMainVC", sender: nil)
        }
    }

    func showAlert(title: String, message: String) {
        let alertController = UIAlertController(title: title, message: message,
preferredStyle: .alert)
        let okAction = UIAlertAction(title: "OK", style: .default, handler: nil)
        alertController.addAction(okAction)
        self.present(alertController, animated: true, completion: nil)
    }

    func setUsername() {
        if let user = FIRAuth.auth()?.currentUser {
            AuthService.instance.isLoggedIn = true
            let emailComponents = user.email?.components(separatedBy: "@")
            if let username = emailComponents?[0] {
                AuthService.instance.username = username
            }
        } else {
            AuthService.instance.isLoggedIn = false
            AuthService.instance.username = nil
        }
    }

    @IBAction func signInTapped(sender: UIButton) {

        // unwraps the textfields and stores them in constants
        guard let email = emailTextField.text, let password =
passwordTextField.text else {
```

600

```
            showAlert(title: "Error", message: "Please enter an email and
password")
            return
        }
        // check to make sure they are not an empty string
        guard email != "", password != "" else {
            showAlert(title: "Error", message: "Please enter an email and
password")
            return
        }

        AuthService.instance.emailLogin(email, password: password) { (success,
message) in
            if success {
                self.setUsername()
                self.performSegue(withIdentifier: "showMainVC", sender: nil)
            } else {
                self.showAlert(title: "Failure", message: message)
            }
        }
    }
}
```

Adding the Chat UITableView UI

Next up, we can create our `UITableView` to contain our messages. Let's start off by
clicking on `Main.storyboard` and scrolling over to our `MainVC`.
In the *Object Library*, search for `UIView` and then drag that onto the Storyboard.
Anchor it at the top of our `MainVC` and resize it so that it stretches from edge to edge.
Change the background color of the view to our yellow/orange hex value `FFB234`.
In the **size inspector**, set the *height* to **75**.

Figure 5.4.80

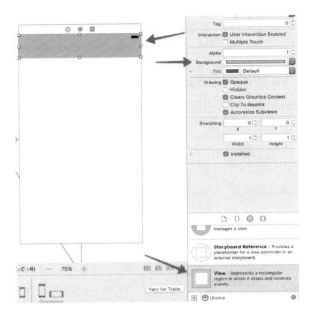

Figure 5.4.81

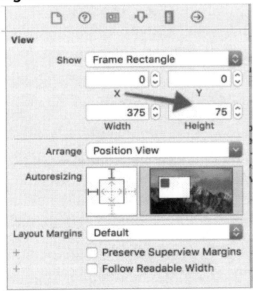

In the *Object Library*, find a **Table View** and drag one out onto our *View Controller*. Leave just a little space between the *Table View* and the *UIView* we added at the top because we are going to add a small drop shadow under the *UIView*.

Also leave some space at the bottom, because we have to add our message *Text Field* and *Send Button*.

Figure 5.4.82

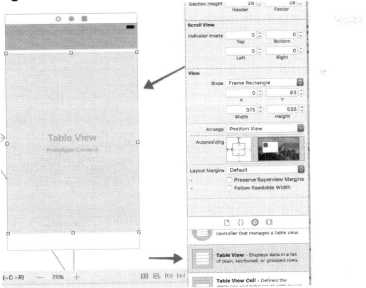

Add a **UITextField** and **UIButton** in the empty space at the bottom similar to the following screenshot.

Figure 5.4.83

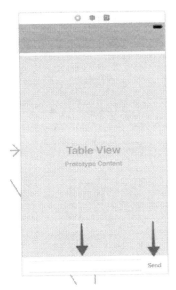

Let's turn our attention back to our *header view*. Add a **UIImageView** and a **UIButton**

inside the view we added at the top. Resize the image as needed, select our icon and set the *Content Mode* to **aspect fit**. Add the button on the right, change the color to white and the text to **Log Out**.

Figure 5.4.84

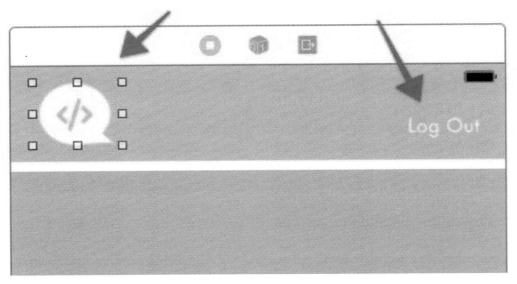

Click on your *table view* and then in the **attributes inspector**, make sure **prototype cells** is set to *1*. If not, change it to 1. This adds a *prototype cell* on your *view control* to lay out your UI. In the prototype cell, add two labels, one for the username and the other for the message.

Figure 5.4.85

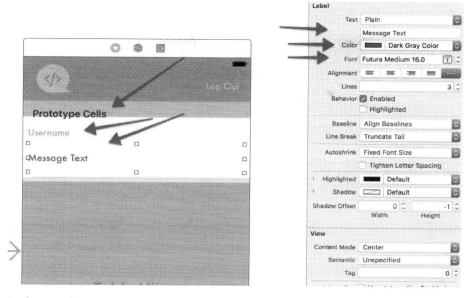

In the *attributes inspector*, I changed the label text as well as the font color and font style. For the font color, I used *light gray* for the username and *dark gray* for the message.

Next up, we need to add constraints. To get started, I am going to pin the header *view* to the left, right and top, as well as add a fixed height of **75**.

Figure 5.4.86

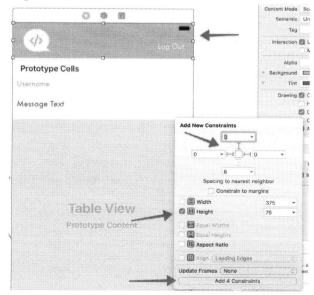

605

I will pin our logo image to the left, the bottom of the header view and give it a fixed height and width.

I will do the same for the *Log Out* button with the exception that it will be pinned to the right instead of the left. You get the idea here. I will leave it as an exercise for you to add in the other constraints.

Just be sure you leave a little room between the *table view* and *header view*.

After laying all of the controls out and adding constraints, your completed `MainVC` should look something like the following:

Figure 5.4.87

We are almost there...let's move on, shall we?

Adding the code for the MainVC

To start, we need two `@IBOutlets`; one for our **table view** and one for our **message text field**.

Figure 5.4.88

```
import UIKit
import Firebase
```

```
class MainVC: UIViewController {

    @IBOutlet weak var tableView: UITableView!
    @IBOutlet weak var messageTextField: UITextField!
}
```

I like to keep my code organized by using extensions for any protocols I need to conform to. We are going to be conforming to our `DataServiceDelegate` that we created earlier, so skip to the bottom of the file after the last curly brace and add our extension.

Figure 5.4.89

```
extension MainVC: DataServiceDelegate {
    func dataLoaded() {
        tableView.reloadData()
        if DataService.instance.messages.count > 0 {
            let indexPath = IndexPath(row: DataService.instance.messages.count - 1,
section: 0)
            tableView.scrollToRow(at: indexPath, at: .bottom, animated: true)
        }
    }
}
```

In this extension, we implement our one required method `dataLoaded()`.
In this method, we reload our *table view* data, and then check to see if the messages array in our *Data Service* actually contains any messages. If it does, we grab the index of the last item in our array and finally scroll the tableView to the bottom. This way, it will be similar to iMessage and other messaging apps in that the newest messages will be on bottom and the view automatically scrolls to the bottom.

Moving back up in our code, let's take a look at `viewDidLoad()`.

Figure 5.4.90

```
    override func viewDidLoad() {
        super.viewDidLoad()

        DataService.instance.delegate = self

        tableView.delegate = self
        tableView.dataSource = self

        NotificationCenter.default.addObserver(self, selector:
#selector(keyboardWillShow), name: NSNotification.Name.UIKeyboardWillShow, object:
nil)
```

```
        NotificationCenter.default.addObserver(self, selector:
#selector(keyboardWillHide), name: NSNotification.Name.UIKeyboardWillHide, object:
nil)

        let tap = UITapGestureRecognizer(target: self, action:
            #selector(dismissKeyboard))

        view.addGestureRecognizer(tap)
    }
```

Here, we set up our `DataService` and `tableView` delegates to be self (this object). We add a couple of **NSNotificationCenter** *observers* so we will be notified when the keyboard appears, as well as when it disappears.

When we receive those messages, a new function that we will create shortly gets called to take some action. We also set up and add a `tapGestureRecognizer` to our view so that when our view is tapped, it will dismiss the keyboard, if present.

Our next bit of code is our first `@IBAction` in this vc.

Figure 5.4.91

```
    @IBAction func logOutButtonTapped(sender: UIButton) {
        do {
            try FIRAuth.auth()?.signOut()
            performSegue(withIdentifier: "showSignInVC", sender: nil)
        } catch {
            print("An error occurred signing out")
        }
    }
```

If our `Log Out` button is tapped, we simply log out of **Firebase** with the `signOut()` method and then immediately segue back to our *SignInVC*.

This particular method can `throw`, so we set up the appropriate `catch` block to handle that if the need arises.

Our next and final `@IBAcion` is for our *send* button.

Figure 5.4.92

```
    @IBAction func sendMessageButtonTapped(sender: UIButton) {
        guard let messageText = messageTextField.text else {
            showAlert(title: "Error", message: "Please enter a message")
            return
        }
        guard messageText != "" else {
```

```
            showAlert(title: "Error", message: "No message to send")
            return
        }
        if let user = AuthService.instance.username {
            DataService.instance.saveMessage(user, message: messageText)
            messageTextField.text = ""
            dismissKeyboard()
            tableView.reloadData()
        }
    }
}
```

In this function, we **guard** against our text field being *nil* or empty once again. We check to make sure we have a good username, and if so, pass that as well as our message to our saveMessage method in our **DataService** singleton we set up earlier.

Finally, we clear out our *text field*, dismiss the keyboard and reload our *tableView* data.

Next up, we have three functions that deal with the keyboard.

The first two are functions that get called by our NSNotificationCenter observers we set up above. The third just simply dismisses the keyboard.

Figure 5.4.93

```
    func keyboardWillShow(notif: NSNotification) {
        if let keyboardSize = (notif.userInfo?[UIKeyboardFrameBeginUserInfoKey] as?
NSValue)?.cgRectValue {
            if self.view.frame.origin.y == 0 {
                self.view.frame.origin.y -= keyboardSize.height
            }
        }
    }

    func keyboardWillHide(notif: NSNotification) {
        if let keyboardSize = (notif.userInfo?[UIKeyboardFrameBeginUserInfoKey] as?
NSValue)?.cgRectValue {
            if self.view.frame.origin.y != 0 {
                self.view.frame.origin.y += keyboardSize.height
            }
        }
    }

    func dismissKeyboard() {
        view.endEditing(true)
    }
```

Our first observer function gets called when the keyboard is about to be shown. We get the size of the keyboard and then move the entire view up the size of the height of the keyboard if the view isn't already moved up.

The second function gets called when the keyboard is about to close. We simply reverse the process in this method. The `dismissKeyboard` function simply ends editing in the view and thus triggers the keyboard to hide.

The only remaining code before getting to our *tableView* methods is a `showAlert` function which is identical to the one we set up in `SignInVC`.

Figure 5.4.94

```swift
func showAlert(title: String, message: String) {
    let alertController = UIAlertController(title: title, message: message,
preferredStyle: .alert)
    let okAction = UIAlertAction(title: "OK", style: .default, handler: nil)
    alertController.addAction(okAction)
    self.present(alertController, animated: true, completion: nil)
}
```

Finally, we get to our `tableView` code. Here again, I like to put this in an extension to keep my code organized.

Figure 5.4.95

```swift
extension MainVC: UITableViewDelegate, UITableViewDataSource {
    func numberOfSections(in tableView: UITableView) -> Int {
        return 1
    }

    func tableView(_ tableView: UITableView, numberOfRowsInSection section: Int) ->
Int {
        return DataService.instance.messages.count
    }

    func tableView(_ tableView: UITableView, cellForRowAt indexPath: IndexPath) ->
UITableViewCell {

        let msg = DataService.instance.messages[(indexPath as NSIndexPath).row]
        if let cell = tableView.dequeueReusableCell(withIdentifier: "MessageCell")
as? MessageCell {
            if let user = msg.userId, let message = msg.message {
                cell.configureCell(user: user, message: message)
            }
            return cell
```

```
        } else {
            return MessageCell()
        }
    }
}
```

Here, we set our `numberOfSections` to 1.

Next up, we set `numberOfRowsInSection` to the count of our messages array in our **DataService**.

Finally I call `cellForRow` where I set up each individual cell. I am calling a custom `UITableViewCell` here, which we will create in just a second.

We grab the message located at the *index* in question and then call `dequeueReusableCell(withIdentifier:)` to configure the cell.

We are done with our `MainVC`, so let's create our custom `UITableViewCell` now.

Custom UITableViewCell

Right click on your `View` group in *Project Navigator* and add a new file.
This will be a **Cocoa Touch Class**.
Name the class `MessageCell` and make it a subclass of `UITableViewCell`. Open that file up in your editor and add the following code.

Figure 5.4.96

```
import UIKit

class MessageCell: UITableViewCell {

    @IBOutlet weak var userLabel: UILabel!
    @IBOutlet weak var messageLabel: UILabel!

    func configureCell(user: String, message: String) {
        userLabel.text = user
        messageLabel.text = message
    }
}
```

Here we have two outlets for our labels we added to our *prototype cell*. The configure cell method takes a *user* and a *message*. This is the method we called from `dequeueReusableCell` over in `MainVC`. It simply sets the labels text properties equal to the values passed in. Pretty simple, right?

There are just a couple of things left to do before we call this a wrap.

First I want to create a custom *Header View* so that we can add a slight drop shadow on our header UIView.

After that, it's just a matter of connecting all of our outlets and specifying our cell reuse identifier. Let's go ahead and create our custom header view now.

Custom UIView for our header

Right click on your `View` group once again and create a new file. This should be a **Cocoa Touch Class** class named **HeaderView** and a subclass of **UIView**.

The code is very simple.

Figure 5.4.97

```
import UIKit

class HeaderView: UIView {

    override func awakeFromNib() {
        layer.shadowColor = UIColor.black.cgColor
        layer.shadowOpacity = 0.7
        layer.shadowOffset = CGSize.zero
        layer.shadowRadius = 2
    }
}
```

In this file we simply adjust the layer shadow properties on our view. With this, we can set the custom class for our header and have a nice little shadow right under the header. This is a nice touch that makes it more appealing visually.

To set the class on the header, click on the *identity inspector* and set the class to `HeaderView`.

Figure 5.4.98

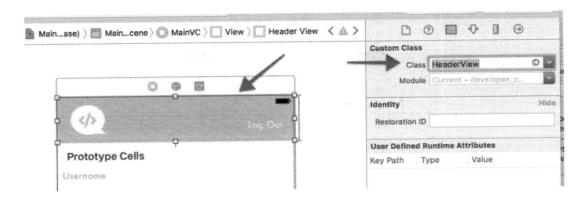

Wiring things up

At this point, all that is really left to do is to make all of our `IBOutlet` and `IBAction` connections as well as specify our `cell reuse identifier`.

For our cell reuse identifier, go back to the Storyboard and click on our table view cell in the *Document Outline*.

In the *Attributes Inspector*, type in `MessageCell` in the box for the reuse identifier.

Figure 5.4.99

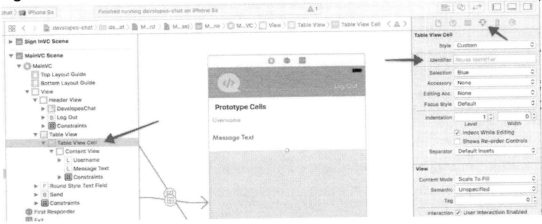

I normally don't like to make assumptions, however with this being an intermediate topic, I am going to make one here. I am going to assume that you are familiar with hooking up outlets and actions.

Lets go ahead and walk through one and then I'll leave the rest for you to connect.

If I *right-click* on the *file owner* of my view controller in the *document outline*, I am

presented with a dialog of all my actions and outlets.
I can then click the circle next to the item and "drag" a connection to the control in the Storyboard.

If it is just an outlet, that is all you have to do.
If it is an action, you are presented with one more dialog asking which action to connect it to. In the case of the button in my example here, that action would be `touch up inside`.

Figure 5.4.100

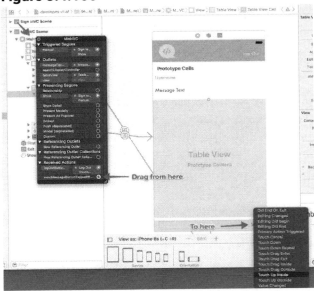

Take your time and make sure you have all of the outlets and actions connected. Be sure not to forget to connect the outlets in our custom *TableViewCell*.
Once you are sure, go ahead and fire it up in the simulator or run it on your device. Put the app through its paces and see how it works. Log in with one session in your simulator and another session of your device with a different email address...talk to yourself.

Figure 5.4.101

Conclusion

Firebase is a really nice Backend as a Service (BaaS) for quickly and cost effectively setting up services for your apps to connect with. It would require a large amount of resources and time to set up your own realtime database, and yet Firebase offers that plus a lot more right out of the box.

Realtime Database, built in authentication, Cloud Messaging, Storage, Hosting, Notifications and other services are offered as a part of the package. As long as you are using one of the platforms which has a native SDK, it is hard to beat Firebase for setting up your backend services. The chat app we built in this chapter is a perfect example of the power and ease of use that Firebase offers.

Exercise

This is obviously a simplistic app, but it showcases the power of the *Firebase Realtime Database and Authentication System.*

As an Exercise, extend your version by adding/completing the following:

- Currently, all chats are left justified in the tableView. Add a second prototype cell so that your messages can be justified to the right and others messages can be justified to the left.

- Add the necessary code to your tableView to make the rows variable height. *hint* look into estimatedRowHeight and UITableViewAutomaticDimension.

- Do some custom drawing to make chat "bubbles" similar to what a standard messages app might have.

Come up with some other cool ideas and extend it any way you see fit. All we ask is that if you do, send us an email or post something in our forums letting us know what you came up with...we would love to see it.

Chapter 39: DreamLister

Learn all about CoreData in this app that will let you make a wish list of all your most coveted items.

What you will learn

- How to use Core Data

- How to use NSFetchedResultsController

- How to sort Core Data results

- How to use PickerViews

Key Terms

- **Core Data**

- **NSFetchedResultsController**

- **Picker View**

Resources

Download here: https://github.com/devslopes/book-assets/wiki

In this chapter you will be building the DreamLister app. Figure 5.6.0 shows what this app will look like. The main goal of this app is to do a deep dive on **CoreData**, learning about when to use it and how to use it.

You will learn about how to use the **NSFetchedResultsController** which facilitates displaying data in a Table View while using **CoreData**. You will also learn about how to use **Picker Views**: So let's get started!

Figure 5.6.0 A, B

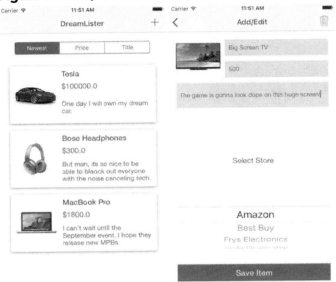

When and Why to Use Core Data

In the **myHood** app we learned about saving data using UserDefaults. The other common way is using **CoreData**. You may have heard about how scary and complex **Core Data** is, and a lot of programmers get scared off by that. And it is a little bit complex.

But thanks to the recent changes in iOS 10, it is a little easier than it was before, and I am going to do my very best to break it down and simplify it for you.

But first, WHAT is **Core Data**, and when would you use it?

Core Data is a framework provided by Apple that allows you to persist, or save, complex data to your device so it can be accessed offline. The keywords here being complex and offline.

If you are just saving simple things like user settings, or login name, then you are totally fine using UserDefaults. Or if you don't need data off line, then you may not need **Core Data**.

These days just about everywhere you go you have Internet connection in some form, so these are things you need to think about when deciding whether or not to use **Core**

Data.

Just because you need to save something, doesn't always mean **Core Data** is the right option. Another thing to think about is now days you have some services like **Firebase** that provide both on and off line syncing.

So just to reiterate, you want to use **Core Data** when you have complex data you need to save off line. And I should clarify, its not just for offline use, you can also download data from the Internet, and save to **Core Data**, then fetch it and serve it up locally. And this provides for a very fast experience in serving up the data.

So what are some other benefits to using **Core Data**?

Core Data is set up to manage a lot of things for you:

- Like Save and Undo functionality, sorting and filtering based on customizable attributes. (Apple claims Core Data typically decreases 50 to 70 percent the amount of code you would write)

- **Core Data** tracks changes for you. Better memory management. (when you have changed or updated objects you don't have to change the entire data set, just the objects being modified)

- Makes it easy to display your data (i.e. `NSFetchResultsController`)

- Provides a graphical user interface to manage:

  1. Your entities

  2. Attributes

  3. Relationships
     And other details related to your model data.

So, now that you know WHEN and WHY to use **Core Data**, lets go over HOW **Core Data** works at a high level, as well as the changes made in iOS 10.

How Core Data Works

Here, we have a model of the **Core Data** stack based on versions by Apple and the site objc.io. This is the entire **Core Data** stack basically. The whole framework boiled down.

Figure 5.6.1

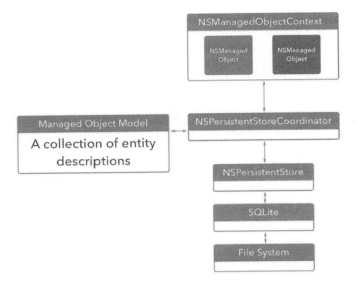

So, lets talk about storage and databases. With **Core Data** or really any storage, you have a database. And the most common one for iOS and **Core Data** is SQLite.
In the past, you used to have to work with SQLite directly. And thats a huge pain. So **Core Data** was born, to help ease data management. It was introduced in April 2005 and has been making improvements ever since, and with iOS 10 is easier now more than ever.

So how does it work. You are familiar with custom classes by now. In the **myHood** app we worked with a custom Post class with properties like *title* and *description*, etc. With **Core Data** we have entities that have attributes. These entities are NSManagedSubclasses, and reside in the NSManagedContext.

Figure 5.6.2

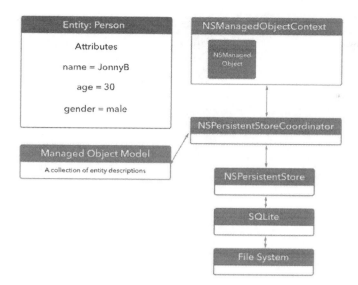

Think of the context like a scratch pad. When you create or insert an entity into the context, it is created in memory. You can modify it and display it, but it is not yet persisted (or saved) to memory.

Once you are ready to save it, the persistent store coordinator and managed object model work to send it down to the persistent store and then to the database, where it is stored. That data is now there permanently, until it is deleted.

With the changes in iOS 10, the NSManagedObject context, managed object model and persistent store coordinator that were previously separate functions in the app delegate are all now combined under the NSPersistentContainer.

Figure 5.6.3

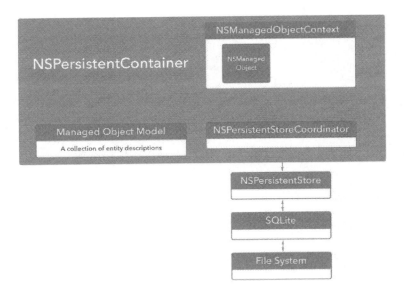

Now the nice thing about **Core Data**, is that you don't actually need to worry about most of this chart. Most of this is handled behind the scenes by **Core Data**.

What you need to understand is how to create `NSManagedObject` entities, define attributes, relationships, and how insert into the context, save, and fetch those results to be used at a later point in time.

That's basically **Core Data** from a very high level. It's really not too bad once it is broken down. So, remember this terminology and the flow chart, because that will really help you get a handle on things quickly.

In fact, once you're done reading this for the first time. Go back and read this a couple times just to get the high level terminology and flow ingrained. Then, we'll be ready to start our project!

Creating an Xcode Project

Open `Xcode` and, from the `File` menu, select `New` and then `New Project...`.
A new workspace window will appear, and a sheet will slide from its toolbar with several application templates to choose from.
On the top, make sure to select `iOS`. In the **Application** section, select `Single View Application` and click `Next`. (Figure 5.6.4). (Note that Apple changes these templates and their names often. But it should be very similar to what is shown here)

Figure 5.6.4

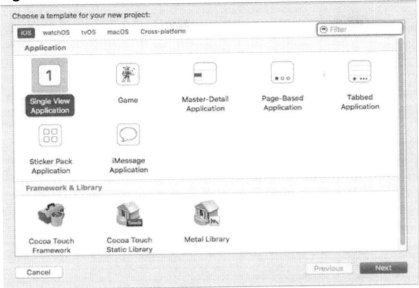

Then fill out the product name. I'm calling mine *DreamLister*.

You can select a Team and Organization Name.

The organization identifier is usually in reverse DNS format. Make sure the language is *Swift* and select which devices you want your app to run on.

We'll keep it simple for this app and just do iPhone.

We **DO** need **Core Data** so make sure that is checked! We do not need Unit or UI Tests for this chapter, so you can leave those unchecked (Figure 5.6.5).

Figure 5.6.5

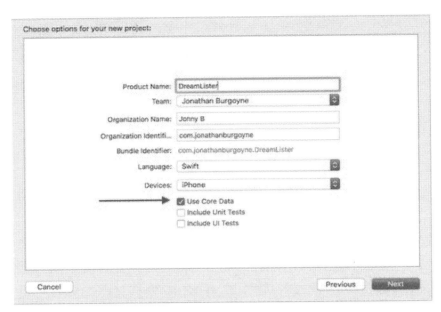

Finally choose a location for your app to be saved to, and I recommend checking the
Create Git repository so that you can push your project to your Github (or Bitbucket)
account and show off your awesome app to friends and potential employees!

Once the project loads, you will be looking at a brand new project that is just waiting to
be turned into something great!

Exploring a CoreData project

First lets take a look into the `AppDelegate` file. Because we selected to include **Core Data**
when we created our project, the app delegate was created with the following functions:

```
// MARK: - Core Data stack

    lazy var persistentContainer: NSPersistentContainer = {
        /*
         The persistent container for the application. This implementation
         creates and returns a container, having loaded the store for the
         application to it. This property is optional since there are legitimate
         error conditions that could cause the creation of the store to fail.
        */
        let container = NSPersistentContainer(name: "DreamLister")
        container.loadPersistentStores(completionHandler: { (storeDescription,
error) in
```

```
                if let error = error as NSError? {
                    // Replace this implementation with code to handle the error
appropriately.
                    // fatalError() causes the application to generate a crash log and
terminate. You should not use this function in a shipping application, although it
may be useful during development.

                    /*
                    Typical reasons for an error here include:
                    * The parent directory does not exist, cannot be created, or
disallows writing.
                    * The persistent store is not accessible, due to permissions or
data protection when the device is locked.
                    * The device is out of space.
                    * The store could not be migrated to the current model version.
                    Check the error message to determine what the actual problem was.
                    */
                    fatalError("Unresolved error \(error), \(error.userInfo)")
                }
            })
        return container
    }()

    // MARK: - Core Data Saving support

    func saveContext () {
        let context = persistentContainer.viewContext
        if context.hasChanges {
            do {
                try context.save()
            } catch {
                // Replace this implementation with code to handle the error
appropriately.
                // fatalError() causes the application to generate a crash log and
terminate. You should not use this function in a shipping application, although it
may be useful during development.
                let nserror = error as NSError
                fatalError("Unresolved error \(nserror), \(nserror.userInfo)")
            }
        }
    }
}
```

As we saw in Figure 5.6.3 the NSPersistenContainer now includes the
NSManagedObjectContext, the Managed Object Model, as the
NSPersistentStoreCoordinator.

We will mostly only be working directly with the Context.

Then we have the `saveContext()` function at the bottom.
This is a nice baked in function that we call when we're ready to save an entity to the database.

Next, look in the **Project Navigator** on the left, and you will see a new file we have not yet encountered call `DreamLister.xcdatamodelid` as seen in Figure 5.6.6.

Figure 5.6.6

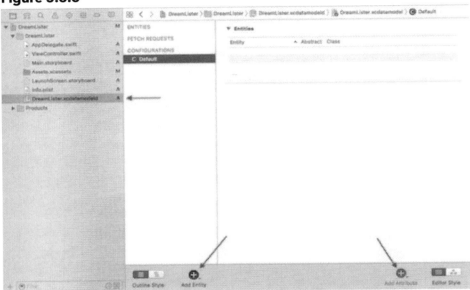

When you click on it you will see + buttons for adding an Entity and Attribute. Remember that an **Entity** is equivalent to a custom class, and an **Attribute** is equivalent to a property of a custom class.

So let's think about our app. We have a Table View that displays some information about an item we want. It has an image, a name, description, and a store we can select from a Picker View.

Let's go ahead and create our first entity. The first entity we create will be for the Item itself.
Click on the plus button to Add Entity. The entity will then appear under the Entities header. Double click on it to rename it to **Item**.

Figure 5.6.7

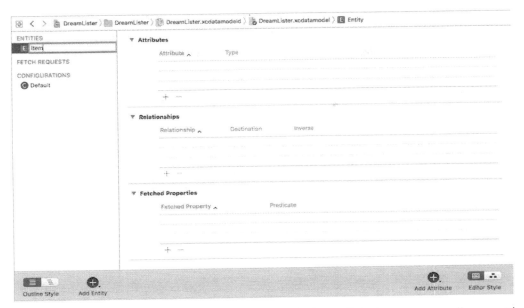

We are going to be managing our NSManagedObject Subclasses manually, so with the Entity selected, in the right hand pane select the Data Model Inspector, and find the drop down menu `Codegen` option and set it to `Manual/None`.

Then to the right there is a header called **Attributes**. There is a small + sign to add attributes.

Click the + and set the name of the attribute to *title*.

Then there is an option to set the type. The same way we declare the type of a property in a custom class, for example `var name: String!`. Here we also set the type. Since our title is a *String*, go ahead and select **String** as the type. Good job, you just created your first **CoreData** entity with an attribute!

Figure 5.6.8

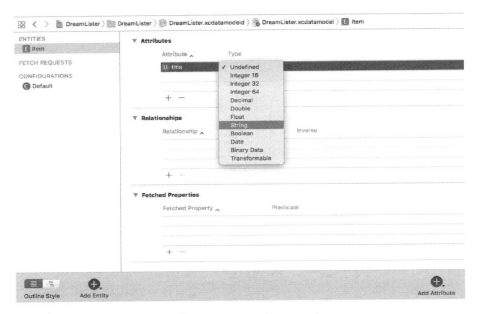

Now add the following attributes to your Item entity.

`details` of type **String**
`created` of type **Date**
`price` of type **Double**

It should end up looking like this:

Figure 5.6.9

Next we want to add some more entities. We are going to need an Image, a Store, and an ItemType. Create each of those Entities, and add the Attributes as follows:

For Image, make an attribute titled *image* of type **Transformable**.
For Store, make an attribute titled *name* of type **String**
For ItemType, make an attribute titled *type* of type **String**

Remember to set the `Codegen` option to `Manual/None` for each entity.

Your end result should look like the following.

Figure 5.6.10

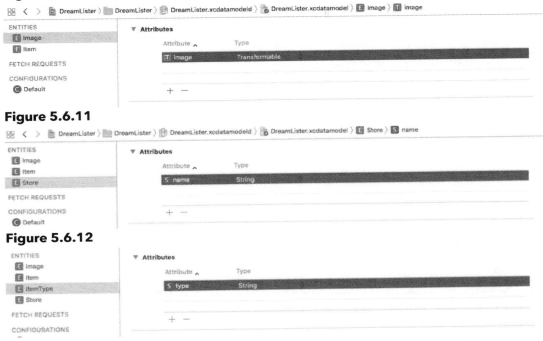

Figure 5.6.11

Figure 5.6.12

Now you may be wondering, why are we having separate entities for things like Image and ItemType? Couldn't those just be Attributes of the Item entity itself?
Yes, they could be. But, I want to teach you about data relationships as well.

For instance, if we wanted the Store to also be able to have an Image, instead of both the Item AND the Store having Image attributes; instead you have them both reference an Image entity.

So what are relationships? In life we have relationships. In your family, lets say you have a Mom, brothers, sisters and a house.
There's relationships between all of these. Now lets pretend that your Mother is an instance of the entity **Parent**.

You and your siblings are instances of the entity **Child**.
And your house is an instance of the entity **House**.
There is a relationship between you and your Mother. But what kind is it?

For you (a Child entity) it is *one to one*. Meaning that you have one Mother. But for your Mother, who has several children, the relationship of a **Parent** entity to a **Child** entity is *one to many*.

And the relationship of both the **Child** and **Parent** entity to the **House** is *one to one*, while the relationship of the **House** to both **Parent** and **Child** entity is *one to many*.

So looking at our data set of entities, how do we want our relationships to look?

For each Item there should be one Store.
But for each Store there could be many associated Items.
For each Item there will be one type, but for each type there potentially could be many Items.
For each Item and Store there will be one Image, and for each Image there will be one Store or Item.

So lets see how to make this work in Xcode.

Lets start with the *Item* entity.
Below **Attributes**, you will see a section under **Relationships**.
Click the + button to add a relationship and then select a destination value.

So, to start out lets create the relationship that goes from the *Item* to the *Image*.

Click the + button to create a relationship, then name that relationship **image**.
Select the **Destination** as *Image*. At this point we will not add the *Inverse* value.
On the right hand **Utilities Pane**, in the **Data Model Inspector**, you will see a dropdown menu with **Type**.
You can choose *To One* or *To Many*. For the Item to the Image relationship, we want it to be *To One*.

Figure 5.6.13

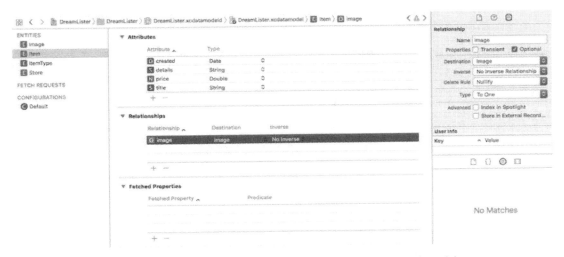

Now add relationships for the remaining entities. We want **Item** to be able to connect as follows, and each of them should be of Type: To One.

Figure 5.6.14

Next lets add relationships to the **Image** entity.

We will add relationships to the **Item** and **Store** entities, titled *item* and *store* with destinations to their respective entities.

The relationship type will be To One for both of these. Also, now that we have added a relationship from **Image** to **Item**, and we already have a relationship from **Item** to **Image**, we can select the *Inverse* relationship from the dropdown, which is image. This won't be available yet for the **store** relationship. It should appear as follows:

Figure 5.6.15

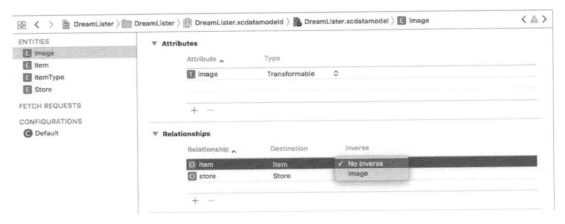

Next add relationships for **Store**.

We will create two relationships of title *image* and *item*, supply their Destinations, and at this point the *Inverse* will be available for both.

This time though, for the **item** relationship type, it will be `To Many`.

This is because we want a **Store** type to be able to be applied to many different types of Items. I buy tons of stuff from Amazon. So Amazon has to have a relationship type of `To Many` to **Items**.

Figure 5.6.16

Lastly we need to add the relationships for the ItemType. The relationship is titled *item* and has the type of `To Many`.

Again, you could have many **Items** of ItemType: *electronics* or *cars* or whatever you want!

It should appear as follows:

Figure 5.6.17

Now that all the relationships have been defined, do a quick run through of your entities, to make sure the *inverse* values have been set for all relationships.

Now for those of you that are visual learners, there is a graphical representation of the Entities and the Relationships between them that can be seen by clicking in the bottom right and toggling the Editor Style.

You may need to drag the Entities around a little the first time you open it, and you will see the arrows that represent the relationships. The arrows that end with a single arrow represent `To One` relationship. The double arrows represent `To Many` relationships.

Figure 5.6.18

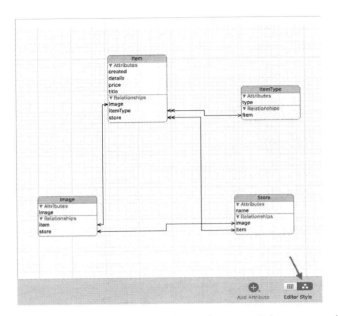

Now that we have created our data models, we need to create our NSManagedObjects (refer back to Figure 5.6.1).

Select all 4 of our entities, then go to Editor and select Create NSManagedObject Subclass. (Figure 6.7.19)

A window will pop up (Figure 5.6.20) with the project selected, click Next.

Then a second window will pop up with the entities selected (Figure 5.6.21), and we do want all entities selected, so click Next, then click Create.

Figure 5.6.19

634

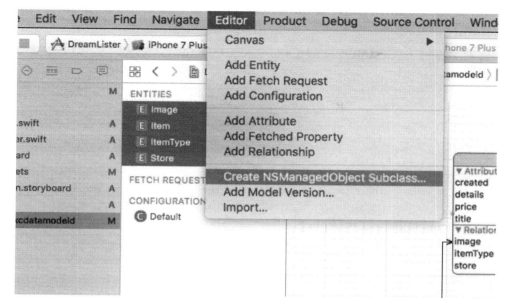

Figure 5.6.20

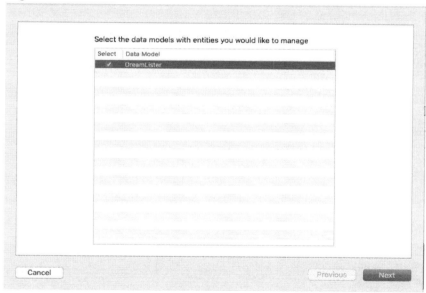

Figure 5.6.21

Select the entities you would like to manage

Select	Entity
✓	Item
✓	Image
✓	Store
✓	ItemType

Cancel   Previous   Next

This will create two files for each Entity as shown below:

Figure 5.6.22

Let's clean up our file system a little. Create a new group called Model.
Within that group create another one called Generated. Then place the four new files that
end with Class in the Model group.

Then select the four new files that end in `Properties` in the `Generated` folder.

Figure 5.6.23

Now lets take a look at these files, and talk about them a little. Lets look at the file called `Item+CoreDataClass.swift`.

```
import Foundation
import CoreData


public class Item: NSManagedObject {


}
```

This is the class for the **Item** entity that we created in our `.xcdatamodelid`.
If we need to implement any code for these classes, this is where you would do that.
Now let's look at the extension file called `Item+CoreDataProperties.swift`.

```
import Foundation
import CoreData
import

extension Item {

    @nonobjc public class func fetchRequest() -> NSFetchRequest<Item> {
        return NSFetchRequest<Item>(entityName: "Item");
    }
```

```
    @NSManaged public var title: String?
    @NSManaged public var price: Double
    @NSManaged public var created: NSDate?
    @NSManaged public var details: String?
    @NSManaged public var image: Image?
    @NSManaged public var itemType: ItemType?
    @NSManaged public var store: Store?

}
```

At the time of writing this, Xcode still has a bug (even though its the official release!) where it adds an extra empty `import` statement.
If you are getting an error, that is probably why, if there is no empty import statement then don't worry about this.

So this file is an extension of the previous **Item** class we looked at.
You don't want to change anything here. This is auto generated code that manages the relationships and `fetchRequests`. If you do need to make a change to the data model, make the change in the `.xcdatamodelid` file, then re-generate this file.

Now lets go back to the `Item+CoreDataClass` file and add just a little custom code. You remember that one of the attributes of the **Item** entity is `created` of type 'Date'.
We want to know the time and date that an item is created so that later on, we can add sorting by date added. So we are going to add some code to set the `created` attribute equal to the time the Item was created in the Context (or scratchpad).

```
public class Item: NSManagedObject {

    public override func awakeFromInsert() {
        super.awakeFromInsert()
        self.created = NSDate()
    }
}
```

So all we're doing here is saying when the **Item** is inserted into the Context, set the `created` attribute equal to the current date and time.

I also want to make a quick change by renaming the `ViewController.swift` file to `MainVC.swift` just to eliminate confusion when I am referencing this file and not a generic ViewController.
So just make the changes as shown in Figure 5.6.24.
You will rename the file in the Project Navigator, rename the class, and rename the

commented part at the top.

Figure 5.6.24

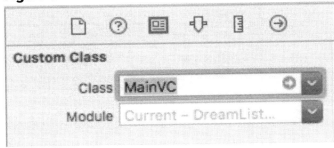

Lastly, we need to change the class of the View Controller in the Storyboard to our newly renamed file `MainVC`

Figure 5.6.25

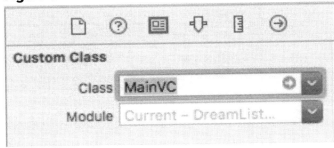

Building the User Interface

Now we are ready to start building the user interface for the `MainVC` screen.

Open the `Main.storyboard` file and select the **View Controller** and go to `Editor` then `Embed In` and select `Navigation Controller`.

We have learned about Navigation Controllers in previous chapters, but basically it provides some built in functionality for menu bars, and moving between screens.

Lets start putting our view together. If we go back to Figure 5.6.1 A, we see we need a Table View, a Segmented Control, a Title, and a + button to add new posts.

Lets start from the top and add that + button. In the object library search for **bar button** item and drag it into the top right of your View Controller and it will snap into place. Select the button, and open the **Attribute Inspector** in the **Utilities** pane and set the **System Item** to Add. Change the **Tint** to Dark Gray Color.

Figure 5.6.26

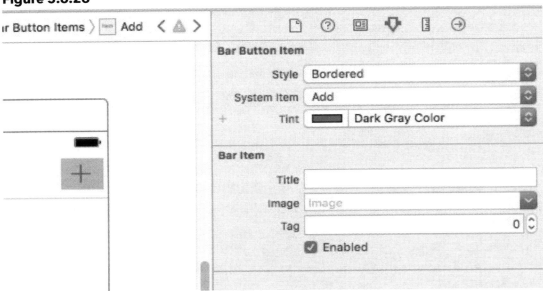

Then select the Navigation Item and set the title to *Dream Lister*.

Figure 5.6.27

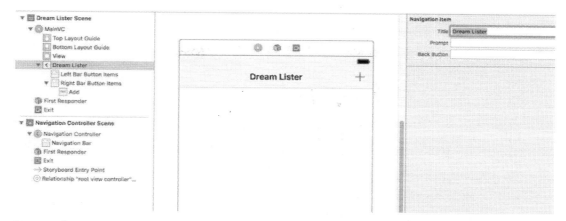

Next, select the Navigation Bar and set the Bar Tint to `White`, and the Title Color to `Dark Gray Color`.

Figure 5.6.28

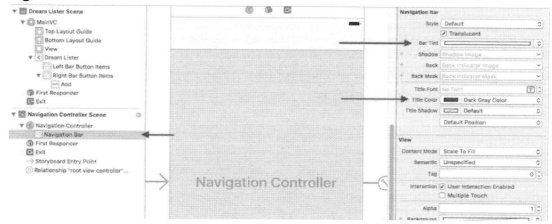

Now we need to add the segmented control. Search for *segmented control* in the object library and drag it to the top below the navigation bar.

Set the constraints with `Constrain to margins` checked **0** from the left, **20** from the top, and **0** from the right and *check* the height.

We also need to set the number of segments to *3*.

Figure 5.6.29

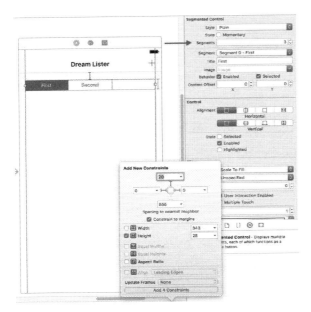

To change the name of the segment sections select the drop down menu by Segment that you want to change the name for, then just change the Title. We want segment 0 to be 'Newest', segment 1 to be 'Price' and segment 2 to be 'Title'. Then scroll down a little and change the Tint to Dark Gray Color.

Figure 5.6.30

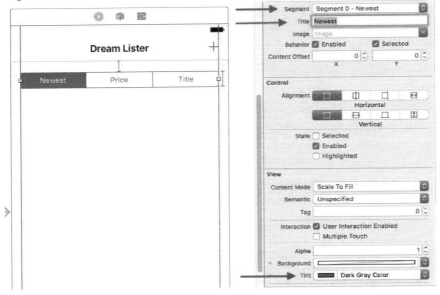

Next we need to add our Table View. Search for Table View in the object library and drag it into the View Controller under the segmented control.

Add constraints with `Constrain to margins` checked, **0** from the right, **20** from the top, **20** from the left, and **0** from the bottom.

Click `add constraints`.

Figure 5.6.31

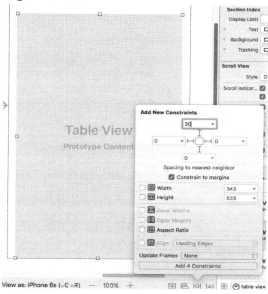

Now drag in a Table View Cell and with the Table View Cell selected, set the Row Height to **150** in the Size Inspector.

Also set the background color to a different color to help visualize the size of the cell.

With the Table View Cell selected, go to the **Attributes Inspectors** and set `Selection` to **none**.

Figure 5.6.32 A

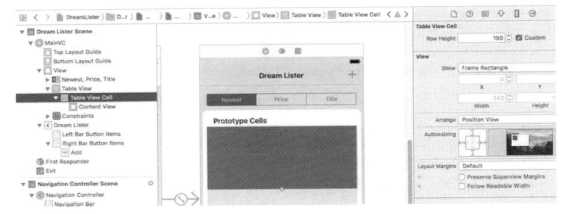

Figure 5.6.32 B

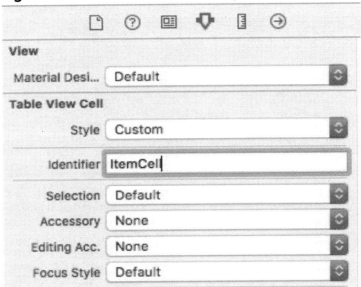

Figure 5.6.33

Next we want to add another view INSIDE the Table View Cell that will contain the information. We do this so that we have separation between the cells.

Search for `uiview` in the object library and drag it into the Table View Cell

Add constraints with `Constrain to margins` checked and set left, top, right, and bottom to **zero**. The height of the inner view should then be **133**.

Figure 5.6.33

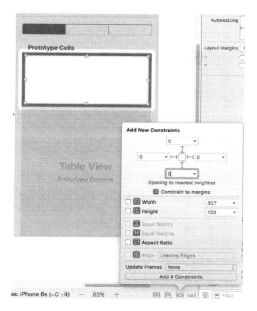

Next add the image view on the left of the inner view we just added.

Make it **100** x **100** and set constraints **8** from the right.

Set height and width and click `add constraints`.

Then add alignment constraint `Vertically in Container`.

Figure 5.6.34

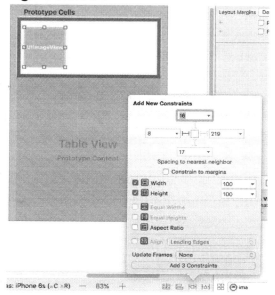

Figure 5.6.35

Now we need to add three labels for the title, price, and description.

Lets add them now.

For the top Title label, set the constraints to **8** from the top, left and right.

Check height, and click `add constraints`.

For the Price label, add constraints **8** from the top, left, and right.

Check height and click `add constraints`.

For the bottom label, set left, top, right, and bottom constraints to **8** and click `add constraints`.

Figure 5.6.36

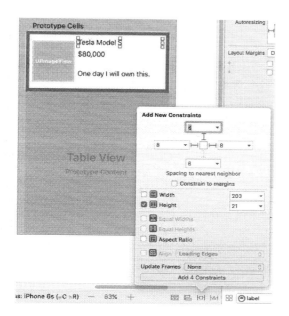

Now select all three labels, and change the color to `Dark Gray Color` and change the font to *Helvetica Neue*.

Set the style for the top Title label to `Medium`. And change the **Lines** to **3** for the bottom description label, and drop the font size to **15**.

Figure 5.6.37

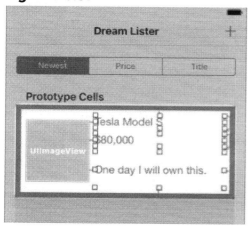
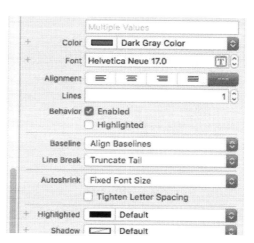

Now lets remove the blue background by selecting the **Content View** and changing the **Background** to `Clear Color`. Then do the same thing for the Table View.

Figure 5.6.38

 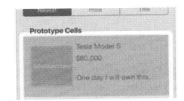 

Now to make the prototype cell look nicer while we are working on this, I am going to drag in a test image of a Tesla into the `Assets.xcassets` and set the image view to the file name (you can choose any image you like, or you can go with the Tesla image that can be found in the assets folder) then change the **Content Mode** to `Aspect Fit`.

Figure 5.6.39

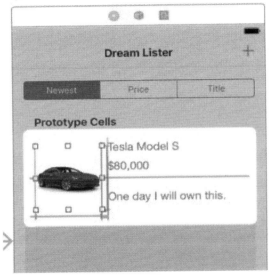 

View Styling

Now that we have the Table View Cell all set up with constraints, we're going to add a little styling to it to make it really pop.

So with your left Navigator pane open, select your project folder, right-click and select `New Group` and name it **View**.
Then right click on that new folder and select `New File`, Select `Cocoa Touch Class` and click `Next`.
Make the subclass inherit from `UIView`, and name it `MaterialView`.
Then go ahead and delete the auto generated comments in green. And we are ready to

get started.

First off change the class to an extension:

Was: `class MaterialView: UIView {`
Change to: `extension UIView {`

What we're doing here is instead of creating a class that inherits from **UIView**, we are making an extension of the **UIView** that will be available to anything that inherits from it. We'll then be able to toggle the **MaterialView** properties we add on and off depending on whether we want it to apply. Since pretty much all the UI elements inherit from **UIView**, this styling will be available to all of them.

Next modify the file as follows:

```
private var materialKey = false

extension UIView {

    @IBInspectable var materialDesign: Bool {

        get {
            return materialKey
        }
        set {
            materialKey = newValue
        }

    }
}
```

First we define a variable `materialKey` outside the extension and initialize it to `false`. This is the variable that will determine whether the view is using this styling.
Then we create an `IBInspectable`. This is what actually creates the interface to select in Storyboard.
Next we create a `getter` and `setter` for the `materialKey`.

Then under the `materialKey = newValue` add this `if` statement.

```
if materialKey {

                self.layer.masksToBounds = false
                self.layer.cornerRadius = 3.0
                self.layer.shadowOpacity = 0.8
                self.layer.shadowRadius = 3.0
```

649

```
                self.layer.shadowOffset = CGSize(width: 0.0, height: 2.0)
                self.layer.shadowColor = UIColor(red: 157/255, green: 157/255,
blue: 157/255, alpha: 1.0).cgColor

            } else {

                self.layer.cornerRadius = 0
                self.layer.shadowOpacity = 0
                self.layer.shadowRadius = 0
                self.layer.shadowColor = nil
        }
```

All we're doing here is saying, "if the user has selected to use this `MaterialView` styling, then this is the styling we will implement, followed by the corner radius, shadow, shadow color etc. If the user does **NOT** select the `MaterialView` option, then we remove any styling to return it to the default state."

So now, when we head back over to the `Main.storyboard` file and select the inner view of the Table View Cell, we'll see the option for **Material Design**. Set it to On.

Figure 5.6.40

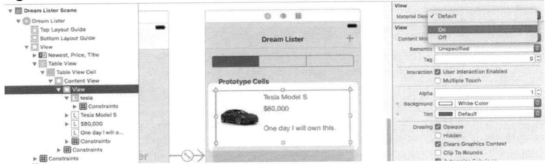

Now that you can see the behavior of the code you wrote, it should make a little more sense. So lets quickly revisit what we did.

The `IBInspectable` is what implements the ability to view a property in the Storyboard. We initialized the default behavior to be `off`, and then checked for the `newValue` that the user enters (on, off). Then we set the styling depending on which is selected.

Creating the Custom Cell

Next up is creating the custom cell. Hopefully you remember how to do this from the **myHood** app.

650

Right-click on the *View* group and select `New File`, then select `Cocoa Touch Class`. Set the subclass to `UITableViewCell` and name it `ItemCell` then click `Next` and then `Create`.

We are creating this custom class that inherits from `UITableViewCell` so that we can have outlets that hook up to the UI elements we created in the Table View Cell in the Storyboard.

Replace the contents of the `ItemCell.swift` file with the following:

```
class ItemCell: UITableViewCell {

    @IBOutlet weak var thumb: UIImageView!
    @IBOutlet weak var title: UILabel!
    @IBOutlet weak var price: UILabel!
    @IBOutlet weak var details: UILabel!

    func configureCell(item: Item) {

        title.text = item.title
        price.text = "$\(item.price)"
        details.text = item.details

    }

}
```

Here we have written out our `IBOutlets` and created our `configureCell` function. Let's come back to the `configureCell` function and hook up our `IBOutlets`.

Go to the Storyboard and the first thing we need to do is change the Class to `ItemCell` in the **Identity Inspector**.

Figure 5.6.41

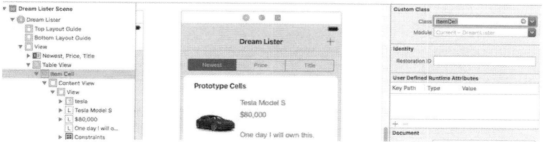

Then right-click on `ItemCell` in the **Document Outline** and drag over from the `IBOutlet` labels to the corresponding UI element.

`thumb` goes to the Image.

`title` to the top label.

`price` to the second label.

`details` to the bottom label.

Figure 5.6.42

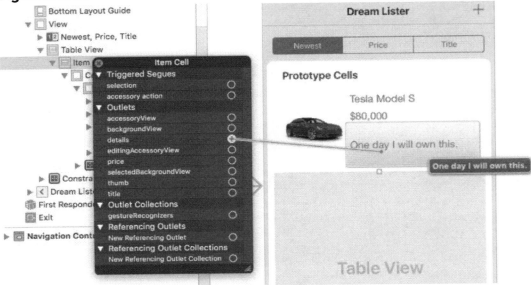

Now lets talk a little about the `configureCell` function.

This function will be used in the `MainVC` View Controller.

What it does is accept an **Item** object, then set the attributes of the Table View Cell to the the corresponding properties of the item that is passed into the `configureCell` function. We are not going to worry about the image at this point.

Next we are going to hook up the Table View to the `MainVC`.

Open up the `MainVC` file and create an `IBOutlet` for the Table View as follows:

```
@IBOutlet weak var tableView: UITableView!
@IBOutlet weak var segment: UISegmentedControl!
```

and place this above the `viewDidLoad()` file.

Then in Storyboard, right-click on the **Dream Lister** view and connect the `tableView` outlet to the table view. Then connect the `segment` outlet to the segmented control.

Figure 5.6.43

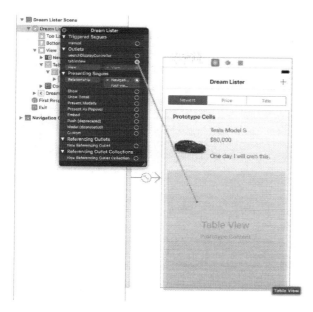

Lets head back to the `MainVC` file and start implementing the code we will need to work with the Table View. We need to add two protocols, and set the delegates. So add the following code:

```
class MainVC: UIViewController, UITableViewDelegate, UITableViewDataSource {
```

then in viewDidLoad() add:

```
override func viewDidLoad() {
        super.viewDidLoad()

        tableView.delegate = self
        tableView.dataSource = self

    }
```

What we've done here is add the two protocols to our class that will allow us to work with the Table View. We then set the delegate and dataSource to `self`, meaning that this class will handle both of those.

Now you will probably be getting an error that says "Type `MainVC` does not conform to protocol `UITableViewDataSource`".

This means that we have not yet implemented the required **Methods** that go along with these protocols. For the Table View Protocols, those methods are the following:

```
    func tableView(_ tableView: UITableView, cellForRowAt indexPath: IndexPath) ->
```

```
UITableViewCell {

        return UITableViewCell()
    }

  func tableView(_ tableView: UITableView, numberOfRowsInSection section: Int) ->
Int {


        return 0
    }

    func numberOfSections(in tableView: UITableView) -> Int {

        return 0
    }

    func tableView(_ tableView: UITableView, heightForRowAt indexPath: IndexPath) ->
CGFloat {
        return 150
    }
```

We're familiar with these Methods.

The first one is used to dequeue and fill the cells. The second returns the number of rows. The next one returns the number of sections in our Table View. And the last one sets the height of the row to **150**.

Right now, its still pretty boiler plate stuff.

NSFetchedResultsController

We are finally ready to start working with some **CoreData** code. First thing to do is at the top of the `MainVC.swift` file, import **CoreData**.

Next we need to add a new protocol for the `NSFetchedResultsController`.
Lets modify the class declaration as follows:

```
class MainVC: UIViewController, UITableViewDelegate, UITableViewDataSource,
NSFetchedResultsControllerDelegate
```

So what is an **FRC**? From the Apple documentation: "You configure an instance of this class using a fetch request that specifies the entity, optionally a filter predicate, and an array containing at least one sort ordering. When you execute the fetch, the instance efficiently collects information about the results without the need to bring all the result

654

objects into memory at the same time.

As you access the results, objects are automatically faulted into memory in batches to match likely access patterns, and objects from previous accessed disposed of. This behavior further serves to keep memory requirements low, so even if you traverse a collection containing tens of thousands of objects, you should never have more than tens of them in memory at the same time."

So basically, it is a handy dandy class Apple has made for us to make it easier to connect the data in **CoreData** with displaying it in a Table View (or Collection View).
It has built in functionality for things like memory saving, filtering, saving and deleting entries, and more. It's really pretty cool once you get it all set up. So lets keep trucking.

First we will declare the variable for our **FRC** right under the `IBOutlets` in the `MainVC.swift` file. Add the following:

```
var controller: NSFetchedResultsController<Item>!
```

We're declaring our **FRC**, but what is important to note here is that we are required to state what Entity we will be working with, so thats why we have `<Item>`.

Now I gotta warn you, that we're going to be writing a LOT of code here without being able to test anything. So strap in tight!

Next thing I think we will do is head into the `AppDelegate` file, and at the very bottom, even outside of the last curly brace, add the following:

```
let ad = UIApplication.shared.delegate as! AppDelegate
let context = ad.persistentContainer.viewContext
```

What we did is created a constant called `ad` that is a path to the app delegate. So for instance, now when we want to access the `saveContext()` function that lives in the `appDelegate`, all we have to do is say `ad.saveContext()`.
We also made it easier to call the context from the app delegate by creating the constant `context`.
Now press `save`, so that these constants will be available in other files.

Now lets go back into `MainVC.swift` file. We're going to add a BIG function called `attemptFetch()`. This can be placed at the bottom of the file, but still inside the class as follows:

```
func attemptFetch() {
```

```swift
    let fetchRequest: NSFetchRequest<Item> = Item.fetchRequest()
    let dateSort = NSSortDescriptor(key: "created", ascending: false)
    fetchRequest.sortDescriptors = [dateSort]

    let controller = NSFetchedResultsController(fetchRequest: fetchRequest,
managedObjectContext: context, sectionNameKeyPath: nil, cacheName: nil)

    controller.delegate = self

    self.controller = controller

    do {

        try controller.performFetch()

    } catch {

        let error = error as NSError
        print("\(error)")

    }

}
```

Lets break this down line by line.

First we create a `fetchRequest`. This is like saying, "hey, go down into the database and see what you can find that's of the type entity, Item"

Then we have a *sort descriptor*. This class allows you to compare attributes of an entity. In this case we have put "created" because we're going to sort on **Newest** as default.

Then we create the controller and pass in the fetch request and the context from the app delegate. We can then put `nil` for the last two parameters.

Next we set the Controller variable we declared at the beginning to the Controller we just instantiated.

Last, we attempt the fetch, using the **do-catch** method.

Next we are going to add a few more methods below the `attemptFetch()` function as follows:

```swift
  func controllerWillChangeContent(_ controller:
NSFetchedResultsController<NSFetchRequestResult>) {
        tableView.beginUpdates()
   }
```

656

```
    func controllerDidChangeContent(_ controller:
NSFetchedResultsController<NSFetchRequestResult>) {
      tableView.endUpdates()
    }
```

What these methods do is listen for when changes are about to be made and when they
have been made, respectively.

When they're about to be made, they get ready to update the Table View with the
`beginUpdates()` function. This is analogous to the `tableView.reloadData()` you should be
familiar with.

Next we have another big function to write. This one you can get to auto generate by
typing `didChange` and finding the method as shown in following figure:

Figure 5.6.44

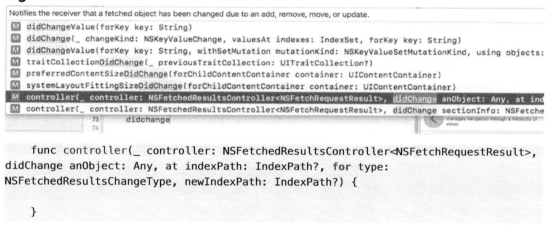

```
    func controller(_ controller: NSFetchedResultsController<NSFetchRequestResult>,
didChange anObject: Any, at indexPath: IndexPath?, for type:
NSFetchedResultsChangeType, newIndexPath: IndexPath?) {


    }
```

This is another helper method that we get with **CoreData** and the **FRC**. It listens for
specific changes and can perform actions based on the type of change. If you command
click on the `NSFetchedResultsChangeType` you will see the following types of changes:

```
case insert

case delete

case move

case update
```

We need to write code to handle each of those cases so lets get to it. Modify the function
as follows:

657

```
func controller(_ controller: NSFetchedResultsController<NSFetchRequestResult>,
didChange anObject: Any, at indexPath: IndexPath?, for type:
NSFetchedResultsChangeType, newIndexPath: IndexPath?) {

    switch(type) {

    case.insert:
        if let indexPath = newIndexPath {
            tableView.insertRows(at: [indexPath], with: .fade)
        }

    case.delete:
        if let indexPath = indexPath {
            tableView.deleteRows(at: [indexPath], with: .fade)
        }

    case.update:
        if let indexPath = indexPath {
    let cell = tableView.cellForRow(at: indexPath) as! ItemCell
    //come back later
        }

    case.move:
        if let indexPath = indexPath {
            tableView.deleteRows(at: [indexPath], with: .fade)
        }
        if let indexPath = newIndexPath {
            tableView.insertRows(at: [indexPath], with: .fade)
        )

    }
}
```

It may seem like a lot, but it is mostly repetitive and self explanatory. We have a switch statement and cases that represent each type of possible changes.
Then for each type, we have the suitable action.

For `insert`, we grab a new index path (since it is new) and insert a new row.
If the case is `delete` we grab the `indexPath` that we want to delete, and delete it!
The `update` case is an interesting one, we'll come back later to it.
Finally we have the case of `move`, where we take the row at one location, delete it, and then insert it at another location.

Next we are ready to start updating some of our Table View methods. Now in the past while working with Table Views, you would usually have an array with data in it and return the `.count` value for number of rows in the section. You would also manually select the number of sections. Since we are working with the **FRC**, the number of rows and sections depends on what the `FetchRequest` returns.

We use the following code:

```swift
func numberOfSections(in tableView: UITableView) -> Int {

    if let sections = controller.sections {
        return sections.count
    }

    return 0
}

func tableView(_ tableView: UITableView, numberOfRowsInSection section: Int) ->
Int {
    if let sections = controller.sections {
        let sectionInfo = sections[section]
        return sectionInfo.numberOfObjects
    }
    return 0
}
```

Next we want to update the `cellForRowAt` function. We're going to do something a little different than we're used to doing.

Remember in our `ItemCell.swift` file, we created a `configureCell` function.

Normally we'd call that directly in the `cellForRowAt` function. But we actually need to use that function twice in the `MainVC` file.

So what we're going to do is create a secondary `configureCell` function inside the `MainVC` file right below the `cellForRowAt` function as follows:

```swift
func configureCell(cell: ItemCell, indexPath: NSIndexPath) {

    let item = controller.object(at: indexPath as IndexPath)
    cell.configureCell(item: item)

}
```

This function accepts a cell and an index path, then calls the original `configureCell` function in ItemCell.swift.

Now we can update the `cellForRowAt` function as follows:

```
    func tableView(_ tableView: UITableView, cellForRowAt indexPath: IndexPath) ->
UITableViewCell {

        let cell = tableView.dequeueReusableCell(withIdentifier: "ItemCell", for:
indexPath) as! ItemCell
        configureCell(cell: cell, indexPath: indexPath as NSIndexPath)
        return cell
    }
```

Here we are creating a cell from a dequeued cell, then passing that cell into our secondary `configureCell` function, which is then passed to the ItemCell `configureCell` function that actually updates the cell.

And we can also return to our `case.update` function down at the bottom of MainVC that we said we would return to. So go ahead and update it as follows:

```
case.update:
            if let indexPath = indexPath {
                let cell = tableView.cellForRow(at: indexPath) as! ItemCell
                configureCell(cell: cell, indexPath: indexPath as NSIndexPath)

            }
```

When we update a cell, it will grab that cell, and send it to the **MainVC** `configureCell` function which then sends it to the **ItemCell** `configureCell` function that makes the updates to the modified cell.

With a final addition to our code we will be ready to run it for the first time! In `viewDidLoad` under the `tableView` delegate and data source add:

`attemptFetch()`

And run it! It won't be very exciting yet because we don't have any data, but it should look something like this.

Figure 5.6.45

Let's make a quick change to the `TableView` in Storyboard. With the `TableView` selected, go into the **Attributes Inspector** in the right **Utilities** pane, find **Separator** and change it from `Default` to `None`.

Then un-check both the **Scroll Indicators** `Shows Horizontal Indicator` and `Shows Vertical Indicator`.

Lets go back to our `MainVC` and put in some test data so that we can actually test that our **FRC** is working correctly.

At this point we finally get to save something to the database using **CoreData**. Create a new function called `generateTestData()` and create it as follows:

```
func generateTestData() {

    let item = Item(context: context)
    item.title = "MacBook Pro"
    item.price = 1800
    item.details = "I can't wait until the September event, I hope they release
new MPBs"

    let item2 = Item(context: context)
    item2.title = "Bose Headphones"
    item2.price = 300
    item2.details = "But man, its so nice to be able to blaock out everyone
with the noise canceling tech."
```

```
        let item3 = Item(context: context)
        item3.title = "Tesla Model S"
        item3.price = 110000
        item3.details = "Oh man this is a beautiful car. And one day, I willl own
it"

        ad.saveContext()

    }
```

Let's look at one of these items. To create an item in the Context, or our *scratchpad*, all we have to do is `let item = Item(context: context)`.

You create the name of the variable, the type of Entity, then pass in the Context we created the path too in the appDelegate.

Now that entity has been created in the context and we can assign values to its attributes. We did that three times.

Last but most important, we add `ad.saveContext()`.

If we did not have the `ad.saveContext()` and then generate the test data, it would still show up in our simulator.

BUT if you stopped the simulator, removed the test data, and ran it again, the Table View would return nothing because the `ad.saveContext()` command was not included. Just because you have an entity created in the context, does not mean it is saved to disc!

Add `generateTestData()` to `viewDidLoad` above the `attemptFetch()` command and run the simulator.

Ta-da! You should have three items displaying in your simulator as follows:

Figure 5.6.46

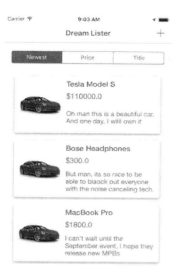

If you run it again, you will see there are now 6 entries. This is because each time you run `generateTestData()` it will add three more entries to your database. If you don't want to keep adding entries, you can just comment out the `generateTestData()` function. So go ahead and do that.

Create Second ViewController

In the **Project Navigator** on the left, create a new group by right-clicking on your project and select `New Group` and name it **Controller**.
Then right-click on the group **Controller** and select `New File`, select `Cocoa Touch Class` and click `Next`.
Name the file **ItemDetailsVC** and set the subclass to `UIViewController` then click `Next` and `Create`.

Then head over to Storyboard and drag a new View Controller into the Storyboard next to the initial screen. Now make sure to go to the **Identity Inspector**, and change the class to `ItemDetailsVC`. Don't forget it!

So what do we need? We have a + button on the **MainVC** screen, so we will need a segue from the button to the **ItemDetailsVC** screen.
But we also want to be able to tap a cell that will open a second screen for editing that cell. So we are going to have two segues, one from the '+' button and one from the

MainVC View Controller to the **ItemDetailsVC** View Controller.

Control click and drag from the + button to the new View Controller and select show for the segue type. Then name the identifier `ItemDetailsVCNew`.

Figure 5.6.47

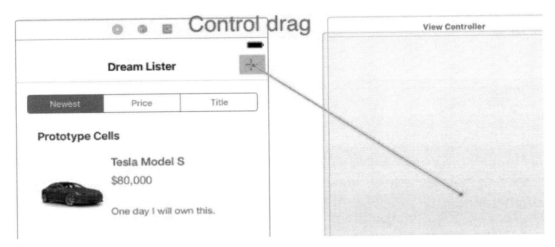

Figure 5.6.48

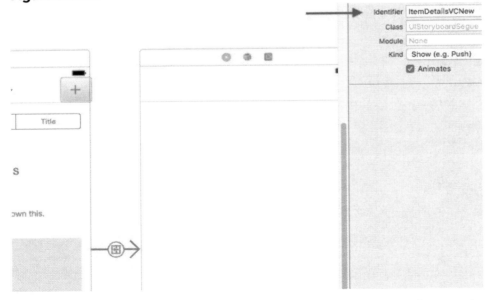

Next control click and drag from the initial View Controller icon to the new View

Controller and select show for the segue type. Then name the identifier `ItemDetailsVC`.

Figure 5.6.49

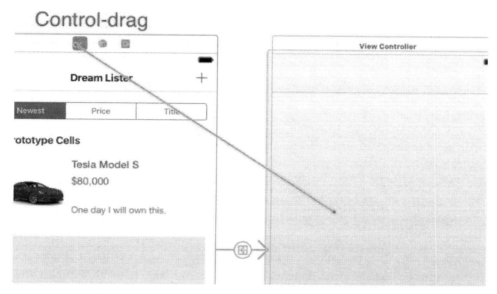

Figure 5.6.50

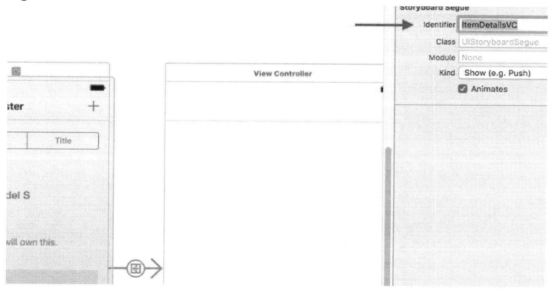

Now lets start adding our UI elements. Below is a reference to our end goal.

Figure 5.6.51

So we need an image view that we will add to the top left, and make it 100 x 100, and constrain it 8 from the top, 0 from the left and set the width and height. At this point, drag in the imagePick.png file to the Assets.xcassets folder and set the image to 'imagePick.png'.

Figure 5.6.52

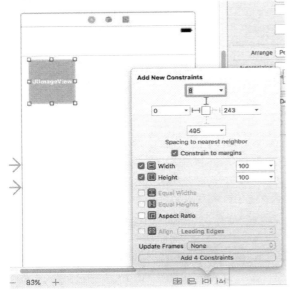

Figure 5.6.53

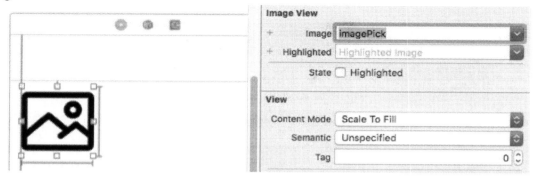

Drag a button over the Image View, and set the same size of **100** x **100** and the same constraints as the image, **0** from the left, and **8** from the top. With `Constrain to margins` set.

Next we need to add three text fields. Make sure you are adding text fields and not text views or labels.

Place two, to the right of the image/button and one below the image as shown below. For all three text fields remove the border, and set the **Background** to a `light gray color`. Change the height to **40**.

Quick note: *at this point in the book we will not be having screenshots for every single step. You should have the experience by now to know how to do things like setting height, changing background colors etc.*

Add placeholder text to *Title*, *Price*, and *Details* as seen in the following figure. Change the font of all three to *Helvetica Neue* and drop the size to **15**.

Add constraints to the *Title* field: **8** from the left, **20** from the top, and **0** from the right, with `Constrain to margins` checked. Set height, click `Add Constraints`.

Figure 5.6.54

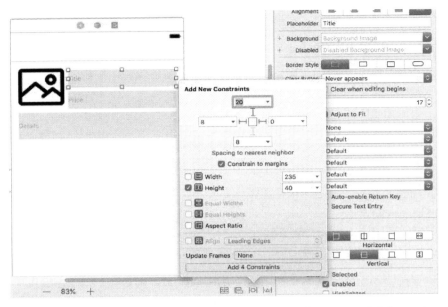

Add constraints to the *Price* field of **8** from the left, top, and **0** from the right. Set height, and `add constraints`.

Add constraints to the *Details* field of **0** from the left and right, **8** from the top, and set height = **60** and `add constraints`.
The details field is a little taller because it may hold more text.

Next we are going to add a file called `CustomTextField` that is available in the resources, or you can create a new file in the **View** group of `Cocoa Touch Class`, name it `CustomTextField` and set subclass to `UITextField` and paste the following code into it.

```swift
import UIKit
/** extension to UIColor to allow setting the color
 value by hex value */
extension UIColor {
    convenience init(red: Int, green: Int, blue: Int) {
        /** Verify that we have valid values */
        assert(red >= 0 && red <= 255, "Invalid red component")
        assert(green >= 0 && green <= 255, "Invalid green component")
        assert(blue >= 0 && blue <= 255, "Invalid blue component")

        self.init(red: CGFloat(red) / 255.0, green: CGFloat(green) / 255.0, blue:
CGFloat(blue) / 255.0, alpha: 1.0)
    }

    /** Initializes and sets color by hex value */
```

```swift
    convenience init(netHex:Int) {
        self.init(red:(netHex >> 16) & 0xff, green:(netHex >> 8) & 0xff,
blue:netHex & 0xff)
    }

}


@IBDesignable
class CustomTextField: UITextField {


    // MARK: - IBInspectable
    @IBInspectable var tintCol: UIColor = UIColor(netHex: 0x707070)
    @IBInspectable var fontCol: UIColor = UIColor(netHex: 0x707070)
    @IBInspectable var shadowCol: UIColor = UIColor(netHex: 0x707070)


    // MARK: - Properties
    var textFont = UIFont(name: "Helvetica Neue", size: 14.0)

    override func draw(_ rect: CGRect) {
        self.layer.masksToBounds = false
        self.backgroundColor = UIColor(red: 230, green: 230, blue: 230)
        self.layer.cornerRadius = 3.0
        self.tintColor = tintCol
        self.textColor = fontCol
        self.layer.borderWidth = 1
        self.layer.borderColor = UIColor(red: 255, green: 255, blue: 255).cgColor

        if let phText = self.placeholder {
            self.attributedPlaceholder = NSAttributedString(string: phText,
attributes: [NSForegroundColorAttributeName: UIColor(netHex: 0xB3B3B3)])
        }

        if let fnt = textFont {
            self.font = fnt
        } else {
            self.font = UIFont(name: "Helvetica Neue", size: 14.0)
        }
    }

    // Placeholder text
    override func textRect(forBounds bounds: CGRect) -> CGRect {
        return bounds.insetBy(dx: 10, dy: 0)
    }
```

```
// Editable text
override func editingRect(forBounds bounds: CGRect) -> CGRect {
    return bounds.insetBy(dx: 10, dy: 0)
}

}
```

I'm not going to go over this file in detail, simply because it is outside the scope of our purpose in this chapter which is learning **CoreData**. Also, we already went over a styling section in detail for the `MaterialView file`. But basically, it just supplies some nice styling to text fields.

So select all three text fields, and go to the **Identity Inspector**, and change the Class to `CustomTextField`. And then you will see the Storyboard rebuild, and you will see some subtle shifts in the text field appearance.

The text is slightly indented, and the corners are slightly rounded.

Figure 5.6.55

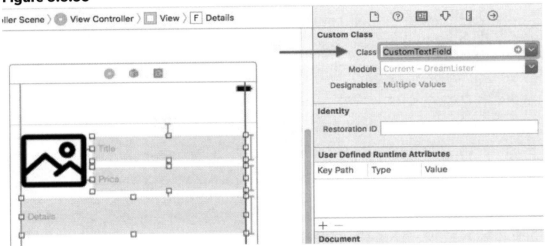

Now for the bottom half of the screen we need a label, **picker view**, and a button. Lets start from the bottom with the button.

Add the following constraints, **0** from the left, bottom, and right. And set the height to **40**. Click `Add constraints`.

Figure 5.6.56

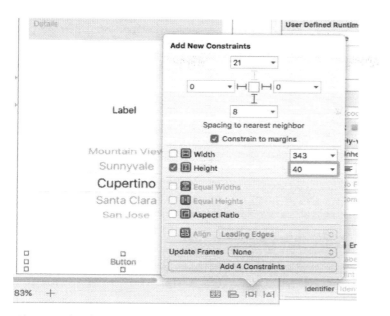

Change the font to *Helvetica Neue*, bump up the text size to **20** with style of **Medium**. Change the font color to `light gray`, and the **background** color to `dark gray`. Change the button title to `Save Item`

Figure 5.6.57

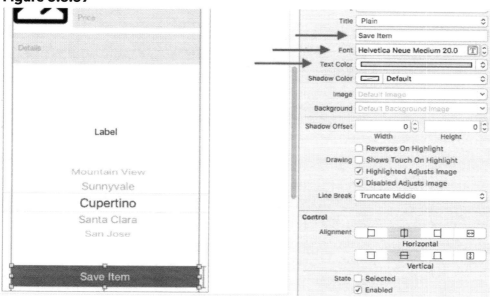

For the **picker view**, set constraints with `Constrain to margins` checked, **0** from the right and left, **8** from the bottom and a height of **216** is fine. And set margins.

Figure 5.6.58

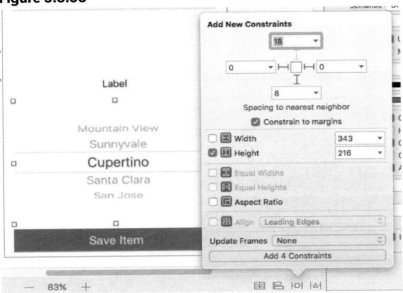

Finally set the text of the label to **Select Store**, change the color to `dark gray`, change the font to *Helvetica Neue*, and center the label `horizontally` with the alignment constraint. Pin it **8** for the bottom and set height and width.

Figure 5.6.59

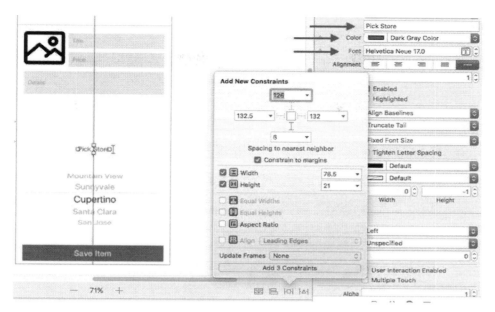

Now let's work on the menu. From the object library, search for `navigation item` and drag it into the top of the View Controller. Change the title to **Add/Edit**.

Figure 5.6.60

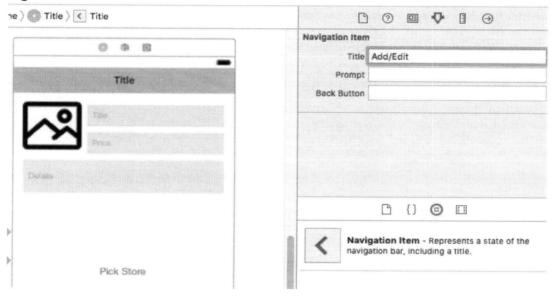

Next we need a way to delete entries, so drag in a **Bar Button Item** from the object library, change the `System item` to **Trash** and the **Tint** to a red color.

Figure 5.6.61

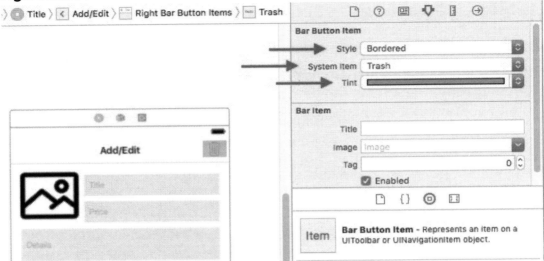

Now go ahead and run it and make sure the segue from the plus button is working to take you to the new screen.

The Table View segue wont work quite yet. You should see the following:

Figure 5.6.62

It's looking pretty good... except I don't like that ugly blue back button with the prior VC title. So lets get rid of that.

To fix the blue tint, select the **Navigation Bar** in the Navigation Controller Scene VC and set the **Tint** to Dark Gray Color.

Figure 5.6.63

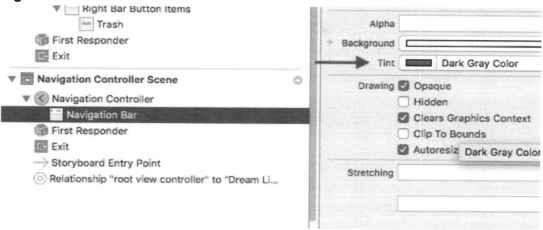

Then open the `ItemDetailsVC.swift` file and modify the `viewDidLoad()` function as follows:

```swift
override func viewDidLoad() {
        super.viewDidLoad()

        if let topItem = self.navigationController?.navigationBar.topItem {
            topItem.backBarButtonItem = UIBarButtonItem(title: "", style:
UIBarButtonItemStyle.plain, target: nil, action: nil)
        }
    }
```

All we are doing here, is programmatically changing the title of the existing `backBarButtonItem` to not have a title, leaving just the back arrow. It should look like this:

Figure 5.6.64

Now lets hook up all our UI elements to the code. Open the `ItemDetailsVC.swift` file and delete the `didReceiveMemoryWarning()` function and any commented code. Then right below the class declaration add the following code:

```
@IBOutlet weak var storePicker: UIPickerView!
@IBOutlet weak var titleField: CustomTextField!
@IBOutlet weak var priceField: CustomTextField!
@IBOutlet weak var detailsField: CustomTextField!
@IBOutlet weak var thumgImg: UIImageView!
```

Then below the rest of the functions add the `IBAction` for the `Save Post` button, the `Add Picture` button and the `Trash` button.

```
@IBAction func savePressed(_ sender: UIButton) {

    }


@IBAction func addImage(_ sender: UIButton) {

    }


@IBAction func deletePressed(_ sender: UIBarButtonItem) {

    }
```

Head back to the Storyboard and right click the View Controller **Add/Edit** with the yellow circle, and drag it to hook up the IBOutlets created in code for the UI elements as shown in below figures.

For the buttons, you will be asked to select a type of event, choose Touch Up Inside.

Figure 5.6.65

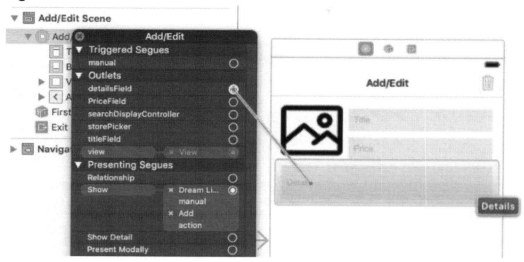

Figure 5.6.66

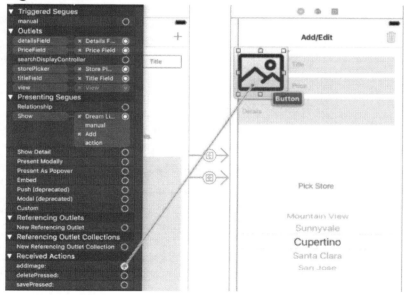

Next, we are going to make it so that when you press Return in the keyboard, after selecting a text field the keyboard will remove so that you can select the save button and store picker. So first thing we need to do is add a Protocol to our ItemDetailsVC view controller. Add `UITextFieldDelegate` so now you should have `class ItemDetailsVC: UIViewController, UIPickerViewDelegate, UIPickerViewDataSource, UITextFieldDelegate {`.

Next, we need to set the delegate of each text field, so anywhere in `viewDidLoad()` add the following:

```
titleField.delegate = self
priceField.delegate = self
detailsField.delegate = self
```

This is simply setting the delegates for each of our text fields. This is required to use certain delegate methods that relate to the UITextFieldDelegate protocol. And one of those methods we are going to use is the following:

```
func textFieldShouldReturn(_ textField: UITextField) -> Bool {
      textField.resignFirstResponder()
      return true;
}
```

This function is called when the `Return` button is pressed in the keyboard, and the `textField.resignFirstResponder()` line of code, dismisses the keyboard.

Now, when you use any of the textfields and the keyboard opos up, pressing return will close it! Nifty eh??

Picker View

Now we have everything hooked up to our code, lets get to work on making that Picker View work. There is more than one way to work with **CoreData**, you don't have to only use an **NSFetchedResultsController**. You can use regular Yable Views, or you can simply save data into arrays and display them in a **Picker View** like we are going to do here.

So first off, like Table Views, **Picker View** has protocols and methods we must implement. So modify the class declaration as follows:

```
class ItemDetailsVC: UIViewController, UIPickerViewDataSource, UIPickerViewDelegate {
```

Then just like we do with table views, add the following to `viewDidLoad`:

```
storePicker.delegate = self
storePicker.dataSource = self
```

And before we forget, go ahead and add `import CoreData` to your file. Next, we are going to create an array of objects of entity **Store** eventually, so lets create that variable now, underneath the `IBOutlets`:

```
var stores = [Store]()
```

Now we need to add the methods to conform with the protocols and those are as follows:

```
    func pickerView(_ pickerView: UIPickerView, titleForRow row: Int, forComponent
component: Int) -> String? {

        let store = stores[row]
        return store.name
    }
```

This function is in charge of displaying the row information. So we create a store from our array of stores that corresponds to the picker row, then display the name of that store at that specific row.
And remember, the `store.name` comes from the attribute that you created in the `.xcdatamodelid` at the very very beginning.

```
    func pickerView(_ pickerView: UIPickerView, numberOfRowsInComponent component:
Int) -> Int {
        return stores.count
    }
```

This method simply counts the number of objects in the stores array and returns that number to be the number of rows in the **Picker View**.

```
    func numberOfComponents(in pickerView: UIPickerView) -> Int {
        return 1
    }
```

This method determines how many columns there are in the **Picker View**. For instance if you have a date picker, you'll usually have a few columns for month, day, year. In that case you would return 3.

So lets create some **stores** so that we can populate the **Picker View**.
Create a function down at the bottom of your file as follows:

```
func generateStores() {
```

```
        let store = Store(context: context)
        store.name = "Best Buy"
        let store2 = Store(context: context)
        store2.name = "Tesla Dealership"
        let store3 = Store(context: context)
        store3.name = "Frys Electronics"
        let store4 = Store(context: context)
        store4.name = "Target"
        let store5 = Store(context: context)
        store5.name = "Amazon"
        let store6 = Store(context: context)
        store6.name = "K Mart"

        ad.saveContext()
    }
```

Just like we did with the test data for the items in `MainVC.swift`, we create store objects of entity **Store**, insert them into the context, then assign values to the `store.name` attribute. Then most importantly, we call the built in `saveContext()` function that is found in the app delegate.

We need a way to fetch those object we just saved to **core data**, so create the following function:

```javascript
func getStores(){
```

```
    let fetchRequest: NSFetchRequest<Store> = Store.fetchRequest()

    do {

        self.stores = try context.fetch(fetchRequest)
        self.storePicker.reloadAllComponents()

    } catch {

        // handle error
    }
}
```
```
```

This is a little different from what we saw with the **FetchedResultsController**, so lets break it down.
We create a `fetchRequest` which we've seen before.

680

Then since a fetch request can fail, we have our **do-catch** block.

We are directly assigning the result of the fetch to the stores array in this line `self.stores = try context.fetch(fetchRequest)`.

Then we tell the store picker to `reloadAllComponents`. This is analogous to the Table View `reloadData` function.

When changes have been made to the **Picker View**, it will reload and show the data. If there is an error, you can write some code to handle it.

Next add those two functions to `viewDidLoad` and run it!

```
generateStores()
getStores()
```

Once you have run it once, go ahead and comment out the `generateStores()` function in `viewDidLoad` or it will continually add those stores to the `stores` array and you're Picker View will be really long!

Figure 5.6.67

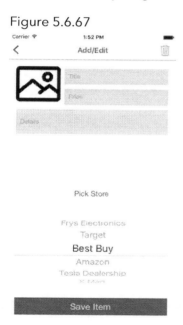

Saving an Item

We are now ready to implement the **Save Item** button. So let's think about what we need to have happen for that to work.

First we are going to create an item of entity type **Item**, then we are going to check to see if there is anything written in each of the text fields.

If there is, we are going to assign the item attributes to those values.

To assign the store for the item, we need to use the relationship to the store, so we say `item.store` is equal to the store that is picked.

At this point we need to clarify something. We are not assigning the name of the store we picked to the item. We are connecting two independent entities to each other. If you wanted to access the name of the store we just associated with the item (which we will do later), you would need to say something like `item.store.name`, or in other words, get the name (attribute) of the store (entity) that is associated with this item (entity).

Then we'll save it and segue back to initial screen.

So here it goes, modify the `savePressed` function as follows:

```
@IBAction func savePressed(_ sender: UIButton) {

    let item = Item(context: context)

    if let title = titleField.text {
        item.title = title
    }

    if let price = priceField.text {
        item.price = Double(price)!
    }

    if let details = detailsField.text {
        item.details = details
    }

    item.store = stores[storePicker.selectedRow(inComponent: 0)]

    ad.saveContext()

    _ = navigationController?.popViewController(animated: true)
}
```

Now that should work! Run it! Add an item, save it, and watch it pop up in the Table View!

Edit existing items

682

We can already add new items. But now we want to make it so we can edit existing items by clicking on them and changing their values.

So what we are going to need is a way to pass the item that was clicked on in the first screen, to pass that item to the second screen for editing. We'll create a function that loads the items information into the second screen.

So first, we're going to create a variable in `ItemDetailsVC` called `var itemToEdit: Item?` and place it right under the `stores` array variable.

We are saying it is optional, because a user could create a new item via the + button instead of editing an item.

So we will do a check in `viewDidLoad()` to see if there actually is an item to edit.

So in `viewDidLoad` add the following:

```
if itemToEdit != nil {
    loadItemData()
}
```

And if you don't remember creating a function called `loadItemData` you would be correct, so lets create it now, beneath the `savePressed` function.

```
func loadItemData() {

    if let item = itemToEdit {

        titleField.text = item.title
        priceField.text = "\(item.price)"
        detailsField.text = item.details


        if let store = item.store {

            var index = 0
            repeat {

                let s = stores[index]
                if s.name == store.name {

                    storePicker.selectRow(index, inComponent: 0, animated: false)

                    break
                }
                index += 1
```

```
        } while (index < stores.count)
      }
    }
  }
```

We have checked in `viewDidLoad` to make sure that there is an `itemToEdit`, meaning that we can be sure we have arrived at this screen by selecting an item from the Table View.

So what we want to happen when we call this function, is load into the text fields and set the **picker view** to the data of that item, so they can then be edited as desired.
The text fields are pretty straight forward. All we have to do is retrieve the values of the attributes of the item and set the text fields to those values.
Getting the title of the store is bit trickier.

What we do is create a `repeat while` loop that loops through the stores in our `stores` array, and compares the name of the store of our item with that in the `stores` array. If it matches, it grabs the index and sets the `storePicker` row to that index.

Now we're ready to receive the item in **ItemDetailsVC** from the **MainVC** screen. We start by implementing the `didSelectRowAt` method in **MainVC**.
Be careful when you get this function, many many people accidentally grab the `didDEselectRowAt`. So add the following function under the `cellForRowAt` function:

```
func tableView(_ tableView: UITableView, didSelectRowAt indexPath: IndexPath) {
    if let objs = controller.fetchedObjects , objs.count > 0 {
        let item = objs[indexPath.row]
        performSegue(withIdentifier: "ItemDetailsVC", sender: item)
    }
}
```

This method is called whenever the user taps on a cell. So what we are doing, is checking first to make sure that there is in fact an object in the `fetchedObjects`. That way we don't get a crash.
Then we're assigning the item object at the row that is connected to the constant `item`.
Next we are going to perform the segue, and send `item`.

To actually send `item`, we need to use another function called `prepareForSegue`:

```
override func prepare(for segue: UIStoryboardSegue, sender: Any?) {
    if segue.identifier == "ItemDetailsVC" {
        if let destination = segue.destination as? ItemDetailsVC {
            if let item = sender as? Item {
                destination.itemToEdit = item
            }
```

```
            }
        }
    }
```

So lets break this one down. This function is called in preparation to change screens. So the first thing we do is check which segue we are going to use, then we assign what the destination screen is going to be.

Next we assign what the item we are sending is.

And lastly we assign the item we are sending to the variable in the **destination** View Controller that it will be assigned to.

So that inner most assignment is saying, "that variable over in the next screen called `itemToEdit`, we're assigning the `item` we created in this screen to that one."

Let's run it and make sure everything we have written so far is working.

What we should expect to see is that when we click on an item, it will segue to the next screen and fill in the text fields and select the correct store on the **picker view**. You can then edit the text fields and store selection, save it, and it will update the table view accordingly! Pretty cool!

But there is a catch, it didn't **actually** update the existing entry, it simply created a new entry with the updated info, so lets fix that.

What we need to do in the `savePressed` function is implement another check as to whether we are saving a new item, or saving an edited item. At the top of the function replace `let item = Item(context: context)`

with:

```
    var item: Item!

    if itemToEdit == nil {

        item = Item(context: context)

    } else {

        item = itemToEdit

    }
```

Here we are declaring an item of entity type **Item**.

Then we do a check to see if we have received an item from the first screen to edit. If not,

685

then we continue as before, creating a new item in the context and saving it. However, if we have an item to edit, all we do is set the item we declared equal to that item. Then **CoreData** actually knows what to do with it and will update the cell accordingly when we press save! Pretty cool right? And that is part of the big `didChangeFunction` in **MainVC** where we check for `.update` changes.

Deleting an Item

Now that we can add and edit, its time to delete. Make sure you're still in the `ItemDetailsVC.swft` file and go to the `deletePressed` function and modify it as follows:

```
@IBAction func deletePressed(_ sender: UIBarButtonItem) {

    if itemToEdit != nil {
        context.delete(itemToEdit!)
        ad.saveContext()
    }

    _ = navigationController?.popViewController(animated: true)
}
```

How easy is that?? All we have to do is check that we have an `itemToDelete`. Then say `context.delete()` and pass in the item to be deleted and save. That is the power of using the **NSFetchedResultsController** with **CoreData**. Imagine if you had to write all the code to do that yourself.

So try and run it, select an existing item and try to delete it. It should pop you back to the table view and watch it disappear.

Adding Images

Lets get to adding images. Just like we did with the **myHood** app we are going to start out by adding the necessary protocols for working with `UIImagePickers`. So add the following to your class declaration:

```
class ItemDetailsVC: UIViewController, UIPickerViewDelegate,
UIPickerViewDataSource, UIImagePickerControllerDelegate,
UINavigationControllerDelegate {
```

Then declare a variable for our `imagePicker` along with the `stores` array and `itemToEdit` called: `var imagePicker: UIImagePickerController!` The UIImagePickerController is a class that manages taking pictures and video, and accessing user media. Next in the `viewDidLoad` instantiate the `imagePicker` and set the delegate.

```
imagePicker = UIImagePickerController()
imagePicker.delegate = self
```

Now we need to implement the `imagePickerController` method as follows, you can add this at the bottom of the file:

```
    func imagePickerController(_ picker: UIImagePickerController,
didFinishPickingMediaWithInfo info: [String : Any]) {

        if let img = info[UIImagePickerControllerOriginalImage] as? UIImage {

            thumgImg.image = img
        }

        imagePicker.dismiss(animated: true, completion: nil)
    }
```

This method tells the delegate that the user picked a still image or movie.
Next we grab the picked image and set it equal to the thumbnail image, and then dismiss the picker view.

Now we are ready to present the `imagePickerController` when the `addImage` button is pressed. So modify the `addImage` function as follows:

```
    @IBAction func addImage(_ sender: UIButton) {
        present(imagePicker, animated: true, completion: nil)
    }
```

Last thing we need to do before we can just test that the **imagePicker** is working is provide permissions in the `info.plist`.

Open the `info.plist` from the left hand pane and in the last entry, when you hover over there should be a + sign that pops up. Click on it and type **Privacy**.
You should get some auto completed entries, and we are looking for "Privacy - Photo Library Usage Description". On the right there is space available to enter a message to the user why you would like to access their photos. Say something like "DreamLister needs to access your photos."

Figure 5.6.68

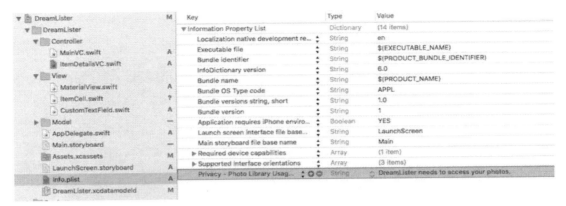

Go ahead and run it, and verify that when you click the "Add Pic" button, you are asked to allow access to photos. Then when you click a photo, it returns to the `ItemDetailsVC` and the image you selected is now displayed as seen in following figure:

Figure 5.6.69

(the waterfall is from Amazon.... get it?)

Next thing we need to do is save the image to **CoreData**.
So go to the `savePressed` function and create a new Image entity. Then set the image attribute of that entity equal to the image we just selected.
Add the following under `var item: Item!`

```
let picture = Image(context: context)
```

688

```
picture.image = thumgImg.image
```

So we are creating `picture` of entity **Image** then setting the attribute of `image` to the thumbnail image we picked using our ImagePicker.

Right below we do our check to see whether we are editing or creating a new entity:

```
if itemToEdit == nil {

    item = Item(context: context)

} else {

    item = itemToEdit

}
```

add:

```
item.image = picture
```

And again, just reiterating the fact that here we are associating two independent entities. And when we access the image to load it upon editing, we do it as seen in the `loadItemData()` function by adding:

```swift
thumgImg.image = item.image?.image as? UIImage
```

When an edited cell is loaded, we simply access the image entity associated with our item, grab the image out of it and set it equal to the thumbnail image.

And finally, to enable the images being set in the Table View, let's modify the `ItemCell.swift` `configureCell` function as follows, just add:

```
thumb.image = item.image?.image as? UIImage
```

Now if you run it, you will see that any existing test data or entries you had will not have any images in the Table View. That's because there had not been any image associated with the item before. But now you should be able to either edit one of the existing cells, or add a new one and add an image. It should work!
And if you don't add an image, it will use the placeholder image instead.

Sorting

Next up is sorting. Open the `MainVC.swift` file and find your `attemptFetch()` function. We currently have only one **SortDescriptor**, which compared the `created` attributes. We want to add a few more in order to sort by price and alphabetically.
So right under the current **SortDescriptor** add these two:

```
let priceSort = NSSortDescriptor(key: "price", ascending: true)
let titleSort = NSSortDescriptor(key: "title", ascending: true)
```

Then we need to write some logic to determine which **SortDescriptor** to use when the segmented controller is changed. Replace the `fetchRequest.sortDescriptors = [dateSort]` with:

```
if segment.selectedSegmentIndex == 0 {

    fetchRequest.sortDescriptors = [dateSort]

} else if segment.selectedSegmentIndex == 1 {

    fetchRequest.sortDescriptors = [priceSort]

} else if segment.selectedSegmentIndex == 2 {

    fetchRequest.sortDescriptors = [titleSort]

}
```

All we're doing here is checking which segment is selected, and depending on which one is selected, we'll apply a different **sortDescriptor**.

But the problem is, we don't currently have any way of knowing when a user chooses a different sort method.
So we need to add a listener for that.
Add the following `IBAction` below the `attemptFetch` function:

```
@IBAction func segmentChange(_ sender: AnyObject) {

    attemptFetch()
    tableView.reloadData()

}
```

Go into Storyboard and right-click the **MainVC** View Controller and hook up the segmented control.
When you do, it is going to ask what type of event to select, and we want `Value changed`. What this action does, is listen for whenever a different segment is selected, then runs

690

the code inside the method.

In this case, we are going to run the `attemptFetch` function. This will reload the **CoreData**, then we will reload the **tableView**. Give it a try!

Add some items that are different in price and name, and see how the sorting goes. Play with the `ascending` value in the **SortDescriptor** declaration to learn how it works.

Wrapping up

And that's a wrap for DreamLister! This has been a huge section and we have gone over a LOT. We have learned all about core data, NSFetched Results Controller, picker views, sorting, and tons more.

Exercise

I am going to leave you with a final challenge, and that is to implement `ItemType`. Come up with a way to assign an item type and then sort by item type. Possibly a second picker view that has item types such as electronics, games, etc. Then like you did with store, you would save that item entity and associate it with a specific item. Happy coding!

Chapter 40: Submitting to the App Store

There is nothing more exciting than taking your project which has taken your sleep, sweat, and tears and uploading it to the App Store to be seen by the masses. Let's learn how to submit an app to the App Store.

What you will learn

- Overview of Provisioning

- Adding your development account

- Creating & installing Development Certificates/Profiles

- Creating & installing Production Certificates/Profiles

- Adding an App to iTunes Connect

- Archiving a release build

- Submitting an App to the App Store

Key Terms

- **Certificate**

- **App ID**

- **Provisioning Profile**

Congratulations! You've finally made it to the point in your development career when you're ready to show the world what you've done. It's time to change the world with your killer app! Let's learn how to upload it to the App Store and release it to the masses.

First let's begin with a flyover of the provisioning process and I will explain what some new terms and concepts mean.

Overview of Provisioning

Provisioning is simply a way of providing something (ie. your app) or making something available to a group of people. The process of making our app available to others via provisioning can cause some headaches. But thankfully Apple has done lots of great work to make this process easier than ever before. The amount of steps needed to get your app on the App Store may seem overwhelming at first, but don't worry – we'll take it step by step.

Checking Out Our Apple Developer Account

First, go to developer.apple.com and click 'Account' on the top right (Figure 5.7.1). Log in with your Apple ID and if you haven't already bought an Apple Developer subscription ($99/yr.) now would be the time to do so because what I will show you in this chapter requires you to have a paid Apple Developer account.

Figure 5.7.1

Click on 'Certificates, Identifiers, & Profiles' and on the following screen you will see several sections. On the left, there is a menu with the major sections Certificates, Identifiers, Devices, and Provisioning Profiles. Within each section are more specific options that we won't go over until that section is covered in more detail later on in this chapter.

Figure 5.7.2

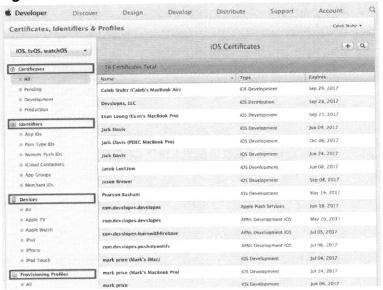

We will now talk about some of the main components inside these sections.

Certificates

A certificate is basically a security measure that allows you to develop and deploy apps. A certificate is provided by Apple and it links your specific computer to your developer account. Any app that you create on your computer gets signed with your certificate (Figure 5.7.3).

Figure 5.7.3

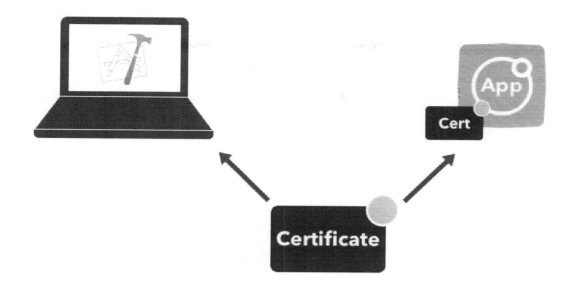

App IDs

An App ID is a unique identifier that helps to set your app apart from any other app. When you submit your app to the App Store, Apple requires it to have this identifier so that it can be separate from all other apps in it's marketplace.

The **App ID** we use in Xcode will need to be the same as the one we use in our Apple Developer account when trying to submit it to the App Store. Figure 5.7.4 shows an imaginary App ID "a9R39Fe" being shared by Xcode and an app in an Apple Developer account.

Figure 5.7.4

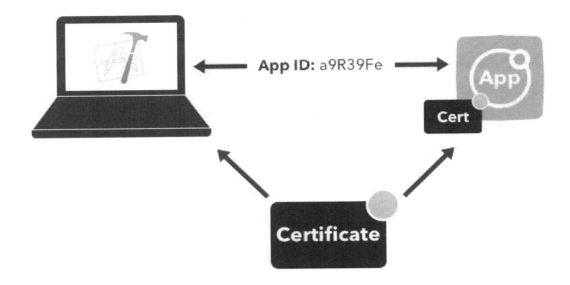

An App ID also informs Apple of what features your app uses (i.e. Push Notifications, Apple Pay, SiriKit, etc.).
When you go to create one in your Apple Developer account, you can tick boxes to enable these features. More on that later.

Devices

This section is for your test devices. The ones you can register in your Apple Developer account for development purposes. You may be wondering, "Do I need to register my iPhone or iPad to test my own apps?" The answer, thankfully, is now "No" as of Xcode 7. You actually don't even need a paid developer account to test apps on a local device via Lightning cable, but that is beside the point! If you want to build an app over the Internet to many test devices (i.e. beta testing via TestFlight) or via Ad-Hoc, the devices must be registered here.

Provisioning Profiles

A **provisioning profile** has two main types – Development and Distribution.

A Development **provisioning profile** allows for us to code-sign an app so that it can be installed and tested on various devices via TestFlight or via an Ad-Hoc server. A

Distribution **provisioning profile** allows for an app to be submitted to the App Store.

When we create a **provisioning profile**, it will take in our app and allow us to either work towards development or towards distribution.

We will create a profile like this in our Apple Developer account. It will pass through the certificate we created for verification and then will be usable by Xcode (Figure 5.7.5). For uploading to the App Store, it works similarly but in reverse. We can use a production **provisioning profile** to send our project from Xcode through our certificate, then through our **provisioning profile**, and to Apple.

Figure 5.7.5

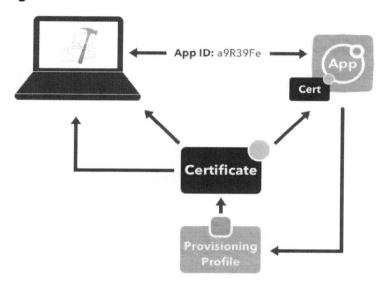

This section has served as a very general overview of what we can do in our Apple Developer account. In following the sections, we will go into specific details about each section and how it applies to us as a developer.

Setting Up A Project

Creating A New Xcode Project

First, open Xcode if you haven't already and click Create New Project. Click Single View Application. Click Next.

You should see a screen like the one in Figure 5.7.6. Give your project a name like *ProvisioningDemo*. Below the name field, there are a few drop down menus but for the sake of this chapter, you won't need to change any of them. Click `Next`. Choose somewhere to save this project file and click `Create` to save it.

Figure 5.7.6

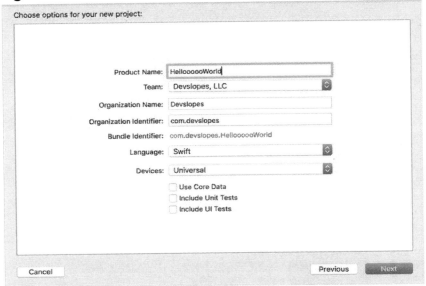

We will use this project for the duration of this chapter to help us in installing certificates, provisioning profiles, and submitting to the App Store.

Adding Your Developer Account

Now that we have a project set up, we need to add a development account via our Apple ID so that we can connect Xcode to our developer account. Go to `Xcode` > `Preferences` > `Accounts` and click the + button at the bottom left-hand side of the window. Click `Add Apple ID...` and log in to your Apple ID connected with your Apple Developer account (Figure 5.7.7).

Figure 5.7.7

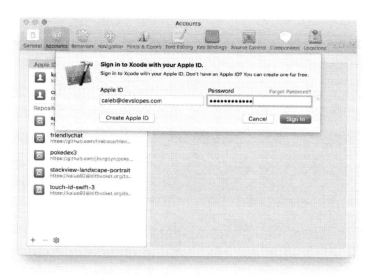

After logging in, you should see your Apple ID show up in the **Apple IDs** section on the left. If you click on it, you will see your role under that account. Most likely, you will see **Admin** or **Member** depending if you're working alone or with a team. As you can see from my account, I am considered a **User** on my personal account *Caleb Stultz*, but am a **Member** for *Devslopes, LLC* (Figure 5.7.8).

Figure 5.7.8

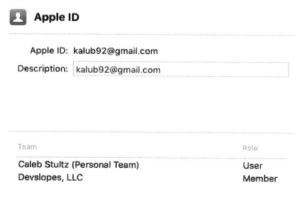

🔲 **Apple ID**

Apple ID: kalub92@gmail.com

Description: kalub92@gmail.com

Team	Role
Caleb Stultz (Personal Team)	User
Devslopes, LLC	Member

View Details...

According to Apple's documentation, the roles operate as shown in Figure 5.7.9:

Figure 5.7.9

Apple Developer Program Team Roles

- **Team Agent**
  Available to developers enrolled as an individual or an organization
  The person who completes enrollment automatically becomes the Team
  Agent. There can only be one Team Agent.

- **Admin**
  Available only to developers enrolled as an organization
  Admins serve as a secondary contact for teams and have many of the same
  responsibilities as Team Agents.

- **Member**
  Available only to developers enrolled as an organization
  Members have access to membership benefits, but have limited
  responsibilities.

The **User** role basically means that my personal account is not linked to a paid developer account, but my link to Devslopes, LLC is.

If we go back into our Xcode project settings, we can see that under `General` > `Signing` there is a new drop-down menu where you can select a development team (Figure 5.7.10):

Figure 5.7.10

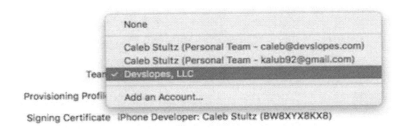

Installing Development Certificates & Provisioning Profiles

Let's set up our project to be available to developers on our team or to beta testers with a Development **provisioning profile**.

Setting Up

First, while in the `Signing` settings notice that there is a check box selected which says, "Automatically manage signing".

Beneath it, there is a message – "Xcode will create and update profiles, app IDs, and certificates." This means that Xcode can and will manage everything we need to do in this chapter, but as it can be a bit buggy, we can't always trust that it will work perfectly. You are learning the manual method to provisioning in case the automatic method doesn't work properly.

Now, look up at the **Identity** section and notice that our app has a field for `Display Name`, `Bundle Identifier`, `Version`, and `Build` (Figure 5.7.11). We want to pay attention to the `Bundle Identifier` because that is what we will actually paste into our Apple Developer account in a moment so that we can link our app to our Apple Developer account.

Figure 5.7.11

▼ Identity

Display Name	ProvisioningDemo
Bundle Identifier	com.stultzapps.ProvisioningDemo
Version	1.0
Build	1

Copy the **Bundle Identifier** from Xcode. We will use it in a moment.

Creating an App ID

Go to developer.apple.com and click `Account` at the top. Sign in to your Apple Developer account if you haven't already.

Click on `Certificates, Identifiers, and Profiles` just as we did before. Under the **Identifiers** section, click `App IDs`. Then click the + sign on the top right. You will see the screen as shown in Figure 5.7.12:

Figure 5.7.12

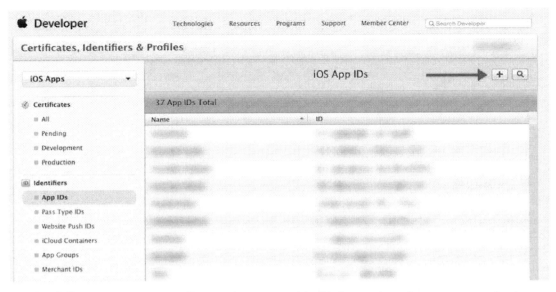

On the following page, we will enter in some critical information about our app. Let's start with the Name field. Enter in the app name as you'd like it to appear. For our app, we will enter in "Provisioning Demo" (Figure 5.7.13):

Figure 5.7.13

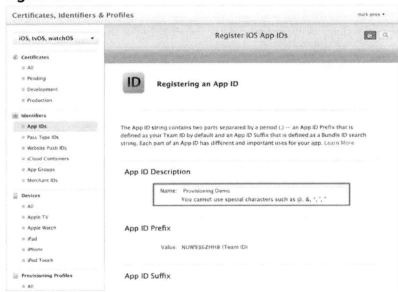

We also need to select the Explicit App ID button under the **App ID Suffix** section. This is where you get to paste in that **Bundle Identifier** you copied from Xcode – get

702

excited!

Figure 5.7.14

App ID Suffix

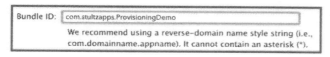

Explicit App ID

If you plan to incorporate app services such as Game Center, In-App Purchase, Data Protection, and iCloud, or want a provisioning profile unique to a single app, you must register an explicit App ID for your app.

To create an explicit App ID, enter a unique string in the Bundle ID field. This string should match the Bundle ID of your app.

Bundle ID: com.stultzapps.ProvisioningDemo

We recommend using a reverse-domain name style string (i.e., com.domainname.appname). It cannot contain an asterisk (*).

Wildcard App ID

This allows you to use a single App ID to match multiple apps. To create a wildcard App ID, enter an asterisk (*) as the last digit in the Bundle ID field.

Bundle ID:

Example: com.domainname.*

Next, if you want an app to use any of the services in Figure 5.7.15, you need to tick those boxes. As you can see, I have ticked **Push Notifications** as that is a commonly used service in mobile apps. Note: You can always edit your App ID later on and add/remove services.

Figure 5.7.15

App Services

Select the services you would like to enable in your app. You can edit your choices after this
App ID has been registered.

Enable Services: ☐ App Groups
                   ☐ Apple Pay
                   ☐ Associated Domains
                   ☐ Data Protection
                      ○ Complete Protection
                      ○ Protected Unless Open
                      ○ Protected Until First User Authentication

                   ☑ Game Center
                   ☐ HealthKit
                   ☐ HomeKit
                   ☐ iCloud
                      ○ Compatible with Xcode 5
                      ○ Include CloudKit support
                        (requires Xcode 6)

                   ☑ In-App Purchase
                   ☐ Inter-App Audio
                   ☐ Personal VPN
                   ☑ Push Notifications
                   ☐ SiriKit
                   ☐ Wallet
                   ☐ Wireless Accessory Configuration

After you've filled out the `Name` and `Explicit App ID` fields and have ticked the boxes for the services that you want, click the `Continue` button at the bottom.

The page that follows simply is a confirmation of your choices. Look it over carefully and make sure that you've entered everything as you have planned. If you need to change something, there is an `Edit` button at the bottom of the page. Note that **Game Center** and **In-App Purchases** are always enabled and ready for use (with the proper configuration) and **Push Notifications** are shown as configurable by default. If everything is good to go, click `Register` to create and save your App ID.

Creating A Development Certificate

Now that we have a unique identifier set up for our app, we need to create a certificate which will allow us to securely send our app to other developers within our team or deploy it to beta testers.

We need to create what is called a Development certificate. You should see the menu containing the sections **Certificates**, **Identifiers**, **Devices**, and **Provisioning Profiles**.

Within the **Certificates** section, click `Development`, then click the + button in the top right. Make sure you tick the box **iOS App Development**. Your screen should look like the screen shown in Figure 5.7.16:

Figure 5.7.16

 What type of certificate do you need?

Development

◉ **iOS App Development**
Sign development versions of your iOS app.

Intermediate Certificates
To use your certificates, you must have the intermediate signing certificate in your system keychain. This is automatically installed by Xcode. However, if you need to reinstall the intermediate signing certificate click the link below:

▨ Worldwide Developer Relations Certificate Authority

Click `Continue` and on the next screen you will see that you need to create a `CSR` file. CSR stands for "Certificate Signing Request" and we can create one using an app already on our Mac.

To do so, press ⌘ + `Space` to use Spotlight Search and search for `Keychain Access`. You can also find it by going to `Applications` > `Utilities` > `Keychain Access`.

Creating a CSR File

The whole point of creating a development certificate is to link our physical machine to our Apple Developer account, so we need to request that our certificate be signed by the **Certificate Authority**.

To do this, click `Keychain Access` > `Certificate Assistant` > `Request a Certificate From a Certificate Authority...` (Figure 5.7.17):

Figure 5.7.17

On the following screen (Figure 5.7.18), our information has been auto-filled but we need to tick the box entitled `Saved to disk`. Ensure that your Apple ID linked with your Apple Developer account is entered in the `User Email Address` field then click `Continue`.

Choose a place to save this file (I chose the Desktop), and click `Save`.

Figure 5.7.18

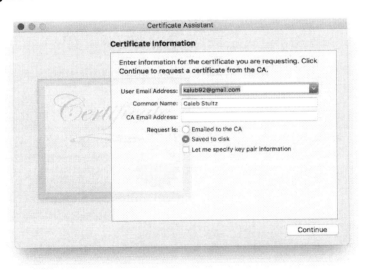

Back in your web browser, click `Continue` so that we can upload the file we just created called `CertificateSigningRequest.certSigningRequest`.
Click `Choose File...` and select the file from wherever you saved it (Figure 5.7.19).

Figure 5.7.19

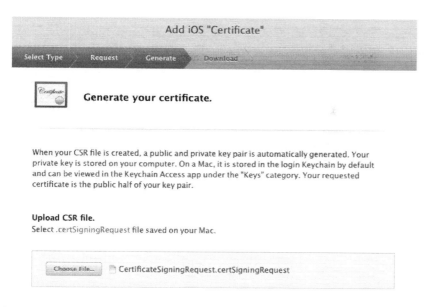

Click Continue to finish making your Development certificate.

Downloading and Installing a Development Certificate

Go back into Certificates > Development and click on the Development certificate you just created. You will see a Download button (Figure 5.7.20). Click it to download the certificate, then double-click the downloaded file to install it into Xcode.

Figure 5.7.20

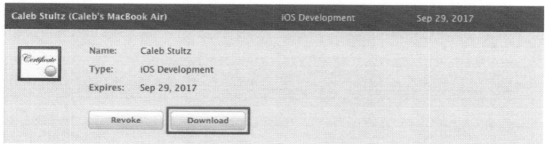

Creating a Development Provisioning Profile

Now that we have a certificate linking our physical computer to our Apple Developer account, we need to create a **provisioning profile** so that we can actually send our project to a development test device.

Go back into your Apple Developer account, scroll down to the **Provisioning Profiles** section, and click on Development.

Next, click the + button in the top right (Figure 5.7.21):

Figure 5.7.21

Select iOS App Development and click Continue. Next, we need to select the App ID we created earlier for our *Provisioning Demo* project. Select it from the drop-down menu if it isn't selected already (Figure 5.7.22):

Figure 5.7.22

Select App ID.

If you plan to use services such as Game Center, In-App Purchase, and Push Notifications, or want a Bundle ID unique to a single app, use an explicit App ID. If you want to create one provisioning profile for multiple apps or don't need a specific Bundle ID, select a wildcard App ID. Wildcard App IDs use an asterisk (*) as the last digit in the Bundle ID field. Please note that iOS App IDs and Mac App IDs cannot be used interchangeably.

Click Continue and on the following screen select the appropriate development certificate for your device which we made earlier (Figure 5.7.23). Click Continue to move on.

Figure 5.7.23

Select certificates.

Select the certificates you wish to include in this provisioning profile. To use this profile to install an app, the certificate the app was signed with must be included.

The following screen (Figure 5.7.24) prompts you to select devices which you want your project to be able to be built to. If you want to register team members devices, you can do that back in the **Devices** section on the main screen of your Apple Developer account. Select all devices that are there and click `Continue`.

Figure 5.7.24

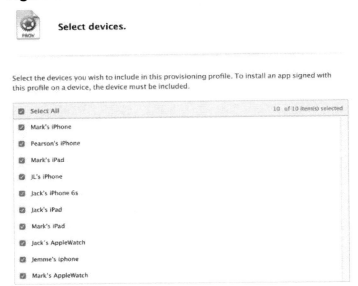

Select devices.

Select the devices you wish to include in this provisioning profile. To install an app signed with this profile on a device, the device must be included.

☑ Select All	10 of 10 item(s) selected
☑ Mark's iPhone	
☑ Pearson's iPhone	
☑ Mark's iPad	
☑ JL's iPhone	
☑ Jack's iPhone 6s	
☑ Jack's iPad	
☑ Mark's iPad	
☑ Jack's AppleWatch	
☑ Jemme's iphone	
☑ Mark's AppleWatch	

Lastly, we need to give a name to our profile which will be seen in the main menu. I named mine `ProvisioningDemoProfileDev` to be specific and clear about the type of profile that it is (Figure 5.7.25):

Figure 5.7.25

Name this profile and generate.

The name you provide will be used to identify the profile in the portal.

Profile Name: | ProvisioningDemoProfileDev

Type: **iOS Development**

App ID: **Ultra Energy (NUW936ZHH8.com.devslopes.ultraenergy)**

Certificates: **1 Included**

Devices: **10 Included**

Click `Continue` again and you will be brought to a page where you can download your development **provisioning profile**. So, click `Download` and double-click the file to install it into Xcode.

Checking Build Settings

Now that our profile is installed, we need to check our build settings in Xcode to make sure that it's configured properly for development.

With the **ProvisioningDemo** project open, navigate to your project's settings and in the menu select `Build Settings`, then scroll down and find `Signing` (Figure 5.7.26):

Figure 5.7.26

Notice that for **Debug** and **Release**, the option **Don't Code Sign** is selected.
his may or may not be the case for your project, but what it means is that Xcode can only work with development devices.

You can't submit an app to the App Store without code-signing and we can't even send the build to other developers this way, because code-signing is a way to ensure that our project is being accessed by only those whom we've given access.

It is best practice to select either the generic `iOS Developer` profile or our explicit development profile like the one we just created. In Figure 5.7.27 below, I selected `iOS Developer` under the **Debug** menu for development:

Figure 5.7.27

Installing Production Certificates & Provisioning

712

Profiles

A Production certificate and production provisioning profiles are what allow us to submit our app to the App Store for the world to download and enjoy!

Creating & Installing A Production Certificate

To create one, we need to start back at the Apple Developer portal like before. The process to create certificates and provisioning profiles for *Production* is basically the same as making one for development with a few key differences.

In the **Certificates** menu, click `Production`, then click the + sign at the top right to create a new production certificate (Figure 5.7.28):

Figure 5.7.28

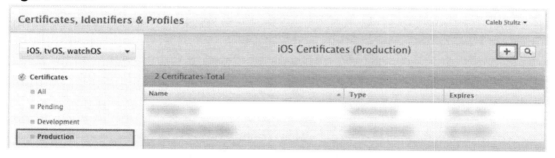

On the screen that follows, select `App Store and Ad Hoc` under the **Production** category (Figure 5.7.29). This is so we can connect our project to the App Store or to beta testers via *TestFlight* or an *Ad Hoc* network later on.
Click `Continue` to move on.

Figure 5.7.29

What type of certificate do you need?

Development

- **iOS App Development**
  Sign development versions of your iOS app.

- **Apple Push Notification service SSL (Sandbox)**
  Establish connectivity between your notification server and the Apple Push Notification service sandbox environment to deliver remote notifications to your app. A separate certificate is required for each app you develop.

Production

- **App Store and Ad Hoc**
  Sign your iOS app for submission to the App Store or for Ad Hoc distribution.

- **Apple Push Notification service SSL (Sandbox & Production)**
  Establish connectivity between your notification server, the Apple Push Notification service sandbox, and production environments to deliver remote notifications to your app. When utilizing HTTP/2, the same certificate can be used to deliver app notifications, update ClockKit complication data, and alert background VoIP apps of incoming activity. A separate certificate...

Now we need to create a **CSR** request just like before. If you'd like, you can actually use the same .certSigningRequest file you saved before.

Click Continue. On the following screen click Choose File... and select the same .certSigningRequest file from earlier.

Click Continue to upload that file and finish up making our **Production** certificate.

Now we can download that certificate just like before by clicking on the name of the certificate then the Download button in the menu Certificates > Production like in Figure 5.7.30:

Figure 5.7.30

Double-click the downloaded file to install the certificate.

Creating & Installing A Production Provisioning Profile

Now that we have a certificate in place, we need to create a **provisioning profile** for the distribution of our app.

In the Apple Developer portal, scroll down to **Provisioning Profile** and click `Distribution`.

hen click the + button to create a new **provisioning profile** (Figure 5.7.31).

Figure 5.7.31

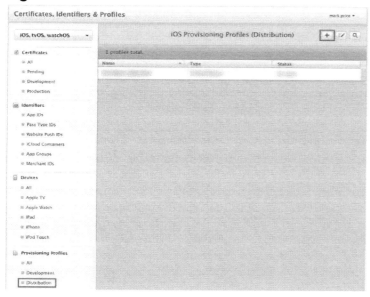

On the page that follows, tick the box **App Store** under the **Distribution** section. Then click `Continue` (Figure 5.7.32):

Figure 5.7.32

What type of provisioning profile do you need?

Development

○ **iOS App Development**
  Create a provisioning profile to install development apps on test devices.

○ **tvOS App Development**
  Create a provisioning profile to install development apps on tvOS test devices.

Distribution

◉ **App Store**
  Create a distribution provisioning profile to submit your app to the App Store.

○ **tvOS App Store**
  Create a distribution provisioning profile to submit your tvOS app to the App Store.

○ **Ad Hoc**
  Create a distribution provisioning profile to install your app on a limited number of registered devices.

○ **tvOS Ad Hoc**
  Create a distribution provisioning profile to install your app on a limited number of registered tvOS devices.

Next, select the App ID for the app you want to submit (i.e. ProvisioningDemo) and click `Continue` once more.

Select the appropriate **iOS Distribution** certificate on the next page. You should be able to see the one you just made in the last section (Figure 5.7.33):

Figure 5.7.33

 Select certificates.

Select the certificates you wish to include in this provisioning profile. To use this profile to install an app, the certificate the app was signed with must be included.

○ **Devslopes, LLC** (iOS Distribution)
  Jun 20, 2017

Click `Continue` and give your profile a name. I named mine **ProvisioningDemoDistribution** which is specific to our app and describes the type of profile.

Click `Continue` one last time and click the `Download` button to download your distribution

716

provisioning profile. Double-click the downloaded file to install it.

Checking Build Settings

We are now going to modify the build settings in our Xcode project. Earlier, we set up our project's build settings for Development and now we're going to set it up for Production.

In your Xcode project, navigate back to the project settings and click on `Build Settings`, then find the **Signing** section.

Under the **Release** section, select `iOS Distribution` from both the **Release** and **Any iOS SDK** drop-down menus (Figure 5.7.34):

Figure 5.7.34

At this point, we have set up Xcode as far as we need to. Let's move on.

Submitting an App to the App Store

Using iTunes Connect to Create An App Project

To submit our app to the App Store, we must first create an app project on a website called **iTunes Connect**.
This site is linked with your Apple ID already, so we don't need to create a new account or anything.

Go to https://itunesconnect.apple.com in your web browser and log in with your Apple ID. Upon logging in, you should be presented with the following page (Figure 5.7.35):

Figure 5.7.35

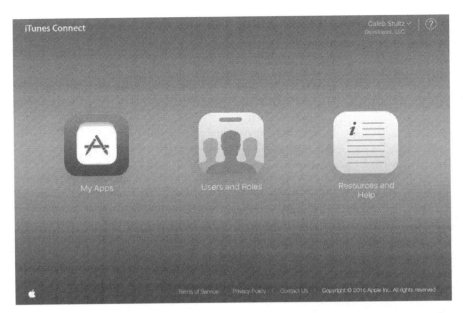

Click My Apps, click the + sign in the top left-hand side of the window, then click New App (Figure 5.7.36):

Figure 5.7.36

You should see a pop-up appear asking for information regarding this new app. Ensure that the iOS box is ticked and then look at the text fields beneath it. You must enter the

Name, `Primary Language`, `Bundle ID`, and SKU fields.

For the `Name` enter the app name that you would like to appear in the App Store. Bear in mind that your app name has the **most** significance to your app being discovered. This is why when you go to download an app like **YouTube**, the actual title of the **YouTube** app at the moment is "YouTube - Watch and Share Videos, Music & Clips".

This is because the **YouTube** team knows that most people search for those kinds of terms when they are looking for an app like **YouTube**. It actually has the most weight out of anything else that you do to optimize your app, so use your app name to your advantage.

Choose the **Primary Language** your app will use.

our `Bundle ID` is the one we made earlier. If you're following this example, it will be called `ProvisioningDemo`.

The SKU of an app is a unique identifier which sets your app apart. Think of it like a barcode for your app. I chose `ProvisioningDemoFunTimes` just to have a little fun with it.

Figure 5.7.37a

After all the required information is entered, click `Create`.

The screen that follows is where you need to enter in any relevant information about your app (Figure 5.7.37b).

First, ensure that the name is correct and that the Bundle ID matches the one you created earlier. It should, but it's best to be safe here.

The `Privacy Policy URL` field is where you need to link to your app's Privay Policy. If you don't yet have one, do some research on how to write one and throw it up on a website. You can either buy a domain and design a website for your app (probably a good idea in the long run), or just create a free website using something like Google Sites or Wix.

Figure 5.7.37b

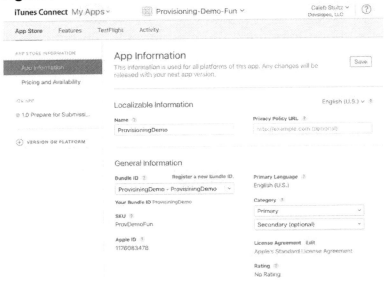

The reason for needing a Privacy Policy is stated by Apple on this page:

> A URL that links to your organization's privacy policy. Privacy policies are required for apps that are Made for Kids or offer auto-renewable or free subscriptions. They are also required for apps with account registration, apps that access a user's existing account, or as otherwise required by law. Privacy policies are recommended for apps that collect user- or device-related data.

So if your app is described in any way by the following statement, you need a Privacy Policy.

Next, you should select a **Category** for your app.
Click on the `Primary` drop down (this one is required) and select the category that best fits your app. If you'd like, select a secondary category as well.

Click `Save` at the top to save your progress thus far.

Setting Up Our App's Price

Click on `Pricing and Availability` on the left-hand side of the window and you will see the following page appear:

Click on the drop-down menu that says `Choose...` to select a pricing tier (Figure 5.7.38). f you want your app to be free, simply select `USD 0 (Free)` as you'd expect. If you'd like to set a fixed price, do so by clicking on the price in the drop-down menu.

Figure 5.7.38

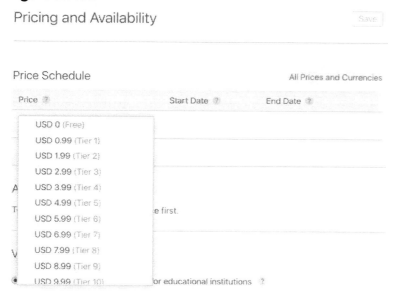

Once you've saved your changes, you can even set up price staggering which allows you to set a launch promo price or even schedule a discounted price for your app.

Now we need to add some super critical stuff to our app project – **metadata**!

Adding App Metadata

On the left-hand side, click on `1.0 Prepare for Submission` (Figure 5.7.39) and you should see this screen appear (Figure 5.7.40):

Figure 5.7.39

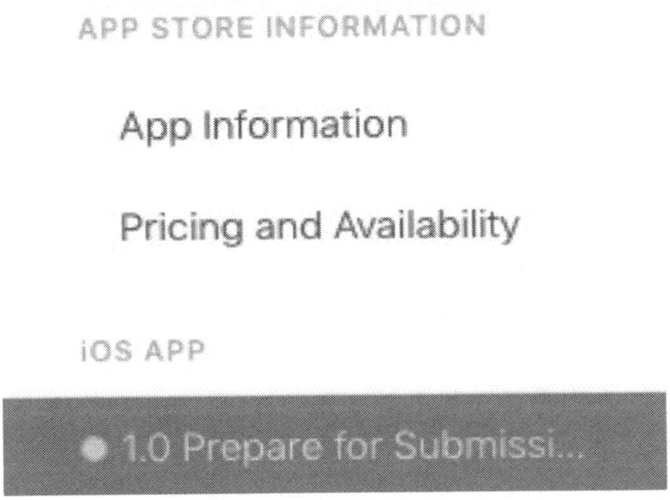

APP STORE INFORMATION

App Information

Pricing and Availability

iOS APP

● 1.0 Prepare for Submissi...

Figure 5.7.40

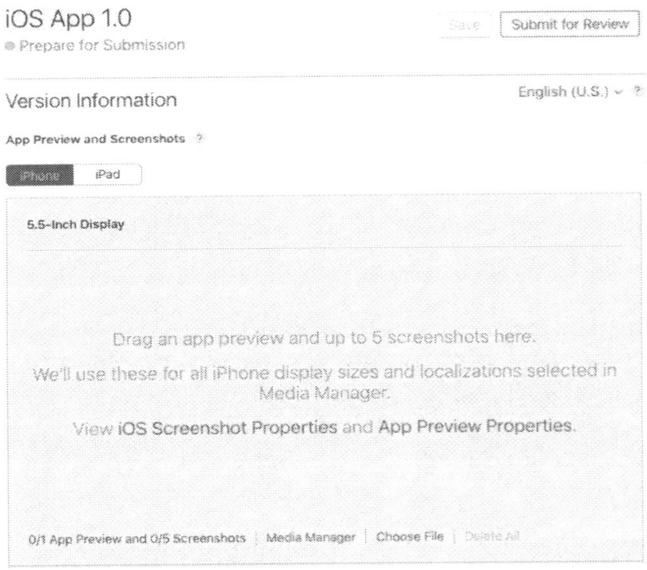

iOS App 1.0
● Prepare for Submission

Save   Submit for Review

Version Information   English (U.S.) ∨ ?

App Preview and Screenshots ?

iPhone   iPad

5.5-Inch Display

Drag an app preview and up to 5 screenshots here.

We'll use these for all iPhone display sizes and localizations selected in
Media Manager.

View iOS Screenshot Properties and App Preview Properties.

0/1 App Preview and 0/5 Screenshots | Media Manager | Choose File | Delete All

Apple requires that you include an app preview video and up to 5 screenshots of your
app.

If you look at the most successful apps on the App Store, they are doing an amazing job
at utilizing this space.

Helpful Hint:

An app preview video can easily be created by using QuickTime's Movie Recording feature. Connect your iPhone via Lightning cable and change cameras from your Mac's FaceTime camera to your iPhone! You can then record input from your iPhone and save it as a video file for editing later on.

The best practice is to create a set of five App Store screenshots at each device resolution (iPhone 4, iPhone SE, iPhone 7, & iPhone 7 Plus) however Apple only requires you to upload 5 screenshots at iPhone 7 Plus resolution.

Whenever your screenshots are created, upload them to **iTunes Connect** by dragging them on the grey rectangle in Figure 5.7.41.

Figure 5.7.41

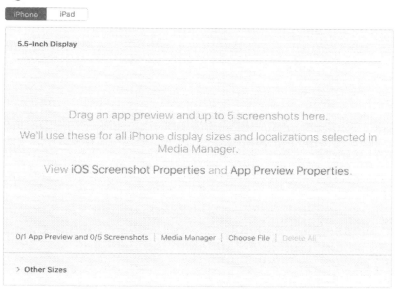

Scroll down and we can add our app *description*, *keywords*, *support URL*, and *marketing URL*.

Your app description is important and I suggest that you research what the big guys are doing and seek to emulate them. Find an app on the App Store like Uber, Instagram, Snapchat, etc. and see how they've formatted and written their app description.

Your keywords are also important as they are used to show your app when a person searches for certain keywords. Your keywords should be specific and relevant to your app. Think of what your prospective user would search for to find your app. Your support URL can be a website you own or a free website as long as it is a legitimate website where users can find more information about your app. The marketing URL is optional but if you have a URL with marketing information about your app (perhaps a press kit, etc.) you should include it here (Figure 5.7.42):

Figure 5.7.42

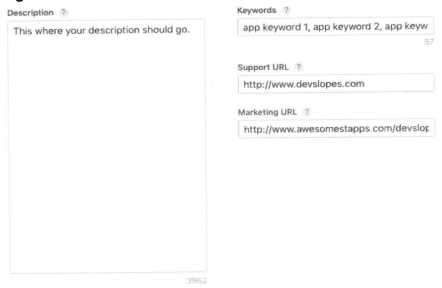

Once that's all squared away and filled out nicely, we need to keep scrolling down the page. Scroll past **Build** for now and move on to **General Information** (Figure 5.7.43):

Figure 5.7.43

General App Information

App Icon ?

Choose File

Version ?

1.0

Rating   Edit

No Rating

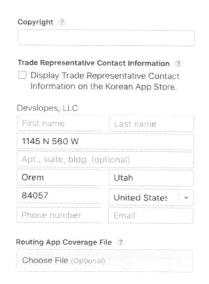

Copyright ?

Trade Representative Contact Information ?

☐ Display Trade Representative Contact
Information on the Korean App Store.

Devslopes, LLC

First name	Last name
1145 N 560 W	
Apt., suite, bldg. (optional)	
Orem	Utah
84057	United States ⌄
Phone number	Email

Routing App Coverage File ?

Choose File (Optional)

This is where you need to enter in all relevant information for your app like copyright information and your address. You also need to upload an app icon with these requirements:

This icon will be used on the App Store and must be in the JPG or PNG format, with a minimum resolution of at least 72 DPI, and in the RGB color space. It must not contain layers or rounded corners.

You also need to choose a version number. This number needs to match the version number in your project settings in Xcode. If you aren't sure what to put here, go to your Xcode app project and open the project settings.
The version number is in a text field directly beneath the `Bundle Identifier` field. Make sure that this number matches what is in **iTunes Connect**.

After uploading and entering in all required data, scroll down to the **App Review Information** section.
You need to give Apple a your *name*, *phone number*, *email address*, and a demo account (should your app require any type of authentication). There is also a field for notes which, according to Apple, is meant for:

Additional information about your app that can help during the review process. Include information that may be needed to test your app, such as app-specific settings.

Once you've entered that, we have finally reached the bottom of the page. We need to decide when to release.

The options are shown in Figure 5.7.44. As you can see, **Automatically release this version** is selected by default:

Figure 5.7.44

○ Manually release this version

◉ Automatically release this version

○ Automatically release this version after App Review, no earlier than   ?

Your local date and time.

⊞ Nov 14, 2016   🕐 12:00 AM

Alright, phew! We made it! Almost there... Click Save at the top of the page because now it's time to upload a build to **iTunes Connect** so that we can submit it once and for all! Woohoo!

Archiving and Submitting a Release Build to the App Store

Now that we have our certificates and profiles installed as well as our app metadata entered in iTunes Connect, we are finally ready to submit our app to the App Store! Yaass...

Switch on over to Xcode and open `ProvisioningDemo.xcodeproj` if it isn't already open. Make sure that you are in the project settings then click on `Build Settings` and find the **Code Signing** section just like before.

Under the **Provisioning Profile** menu, select the Distribution provisioning profile we created earlier in this chapter called `ProvisioningDemoDistribution`.
You also need to select your iPhone Distribution certificate from the **Release** and **Any iOS SDK** drop-down menus (Figure 5.7.45):

Figure 5.7.45

Bear in mind, this will disable you from building your project to a device or the Simulator until you switch this setting back to your development profile.

Changing Our Build Scheme

In the top-left of your Xcode window, click on your project name and click `Edit Scheme` (Figure 4.7.46):

Figure 5.7.46

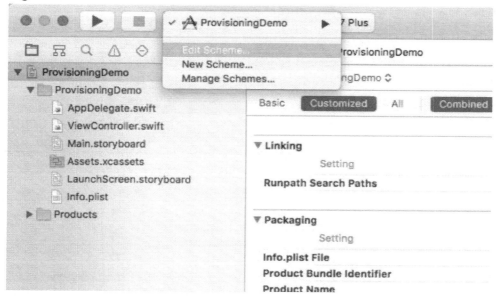

On the screen that pops up you need to click on `Archive` from the menu on the left-hand side.

When submitting a build of our app to the App Store, we need to archive it. Imagine that you're sealing off this build of your project so that it is uploaded to **iTunes Connect**, just the way it is.

On the **Archive** screen, we need to verify that `Archive` is selected from the `Build Configuration` drop-down menu. Afterward, click `Close` to close out and change our Build Scheme.

Archiving A Release

Next, at the top-left of the Xcode window, we need to switch from a Simulator device to either:
(1) Our actual device plugged via Lightning cable.
(2) `Generic iOS Device`.

Choose one of those options and click to select it (Figure 5.7.47):

Figure 5.7.47

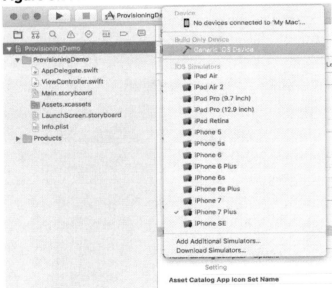

Here comes the exciting part! In the menu bar at the top of Xcode, click `Product > Archive` and allow for Xcode to do it's thing. It will appear as if it's building as normal, but when it's finished it will open up a new application called **Organizer**. It can take quite a while for your app to successfully archive and copy into **Organizer**, so give it some time.

Once **Organizer** has opened, you will see the following screen (Figure 5.7.48):

Figure 5.7.48

Before we do anything, we should validate our app. This will basically run our app through an automated version of some of Apple's tests they run on our app to make sure it's good to go to the App Store.

This is a huge time-saver because in the good ol' days, you had to submit your app to Apple and wait 7 days just to tell you that you needed to fix some really minor things. Being able to validate it ourselves means that we don't have to waste our time.

Click the `Validate...` button and on the pop-up that follows, you need to select the appropriate development team.

Choose the one you've been using, then click `Continue`.

The pop-up will show the progress of the preparation of our archive. After the archive is ready to be validated, you will see a confirmation screen like in Figure 5.7.49:

Figure 5.7.49

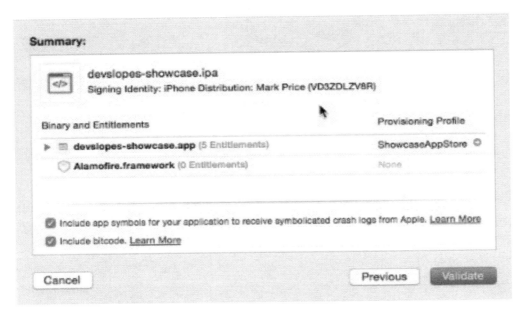

When you're ready to validate your project, click `Validate` and Xcode will do it's thing. After a while, your archive will be uploaded. Should there be any warnings or errors, they will be displayed afterwards (Figure 5.7.50):

Figure 5.7.50

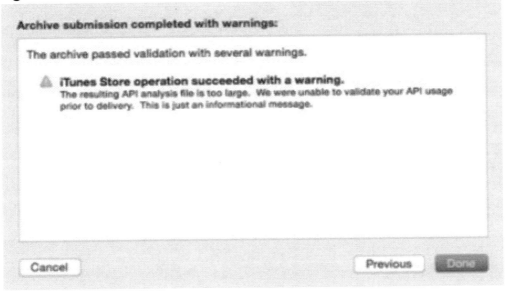

Since I was only shown a warning, I'm going to move forward by clicking Done.

Believe it or not, our build has been uploaded to **iTunes Connect**. Go back into your **iTunes Connect** account and open up the app project we started earlier. Click `1.0 Prepare for Submission`.

If you scroll to the **Build** section, you should now see the build we just validated and uploaded. It should have a status of **Processing** at the moment.

To officially submit your build to the App Store, ensure that all of the information from above is completed in full. Click `Save` to save all changes then click `Submit for Review` and your app will be sent to Apple for review!

WOOHOO!

You finally did it. You've uploaded your first app to the App Store! You will need to wait a few days to hear back from Apple and to be honest, expect that your app won't be approved at first.

Apple is very picky about the apps on their App Store. It is how they ensure they have a top-of-the-line marketplace.

Of course, make sure you refer to Apple's documentation and guidelines for uploading to the App Store which can be found in their developer documentation online. Remember, Google is your friend.

Wrapping up

Wow, so as you can see there are TONS of steps in order to get your app onto the App Store. Apple has helped with a lot of this actually by enabling automatic signing, app ID, and certificate creation, but you now know the entire process.

You can now upload apps to the App Store manually if the automatic features aren't working. As a developer, it is good to learn how these things work behind the scenes.

But seriously, pat yourself on the back. Amazing work.

Chapter 41: @IBDesignable & @IBInspectable

Interface Builder is an amazing platform for building app UIs. But, in this chapter, you will learn how to make it even more useful.

What you will learn

- Use @IBInspectable to allow for customization of properties in Interface Builder.

- Use @IBDesignable to view your changes live in Interface Builder without running your app.

Key Terms

- **@IBInspectable**

- @IBDesignable

When building apps in Xcode, developers take one of two routes: **1)** using Interface Builder and Storyboards or **2)** creating everything from code.

Apple has done a lot of the hard work to bring us Interface Builder and Storyboards so that we can easily and visually create an amazing UI/UX for users. There are certainly upsides to creating user interfaces from code – such as making your code decisions very explicit and readable or preventing tiny, frustrating inconsistencies which can arise when working with numerous Storyboards.

But regardless of the potential nuisances of working with Interface Builder, it ultimately is a powerful tool that we can supercharge with the help of **@IBInspectable** and **@IBDesignable**.

In this chapter, we will create part of an onboarding experience where a user will need to grant permissions for certain device services. We will use

@IBInspectable/@IBDesignable to customize and modify our design directly within Interface Builder – all without needing to build or run our app.

Creating a New Project and Set Up User Interface

To begin, open up Xcode and double-click `Single View Application` to create a new project. Name it whatever you'd like and save it anywhere.

Next, open up `Main.storyboard` and click on the `ViewController` in Interface Builder (Figure 5.8.1) and change the Background Color property to any color. I used #FFCC66.

Figure 5.8.1

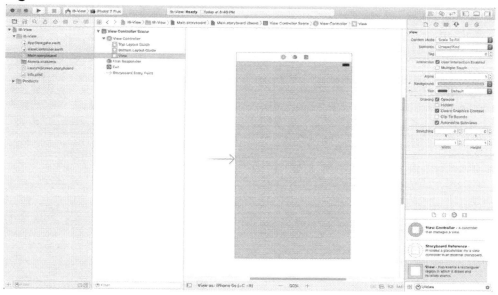

To start building our UI, drag a UIView into the ViewController. This will eventually house several buttons for granting permissions for location, camera, and notification access.

Select the view you've dragged in and position it so that it looks like the view in Figure 5.8.2 below.

Figure 5.8.2

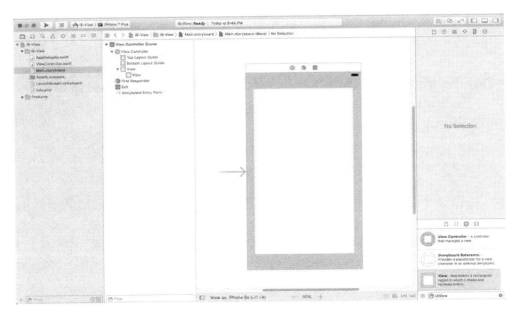

We want this view to stay in the center of our ViewController and to maintain it's distance from the edges of the screen, so click on our white UIView to select it and then click the

Pin button( ) at the bottom of the Xcode window.

Give the UIView constraints to ensure that it maintains its height and width on any screen size (Figure 5.8.3) and click `Add 2 Constraints`.

Figure 5.8.3

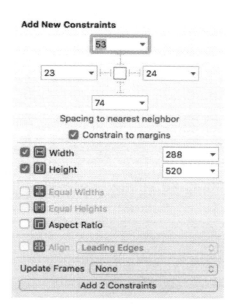

Afterward, click the Align button () to the left of the Pin button and select
Horizontally in Container and Vertically in Container to force our UIView to stay in the
center of the ViewController (Figure 5.8.4). Click Add 2 Constraints to set them in place.

Figure 5.8.4

Once you have set up constraints on our view, the base interface for this app is now complete. We will now move on to create a custom class for this view and customize it with **@IBInspectable** and **@IBDesignable**.

Creating a Custom View Class

To allow us to modify our UIView we need to create a custom class which will house the default properties we want our view to adopt.

Right-click on your project's folder in the **Navigator** and click on `New File...` (Figure 5.8.5).
Click `iOS` and then select `Cocoa Touch Class`. Click `Next` and name your class *RoundedShadowView*.

Pay attention to how the class is named with capital letters for each word – this is best practice when naming classes.
In the **Subclass** section, delete whatever text is there and type **UIView**. It should auto-complete, but in case it doesn't ensure that you have typed it with the appropriate capital letters.
Leave the **Language** drop-down menu with `Swift` selected. Click `Next` and click `Create` as this will save a new `Swift` file in your project directory.

Figure 5.8.5

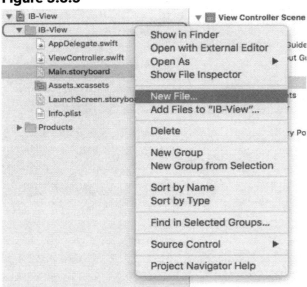

You now should have a new file called `RoundedShadowView.swift` in your project folder (Figure 5.8.6) which is a custom class we will use to customize our view.

Figure 5.8.6

Delete all commented-out boilerplate code as we will not be needing it.

@IBInspectable

First, we want our view to have rounded corners so we will need properties for that. Create an **@IBInspectable** for the corner radius and a variable to store it's value like so:

```swift
import UIKit

class RoundedShadowView: UIView {

    @IBInspectable var cornerRadius: CGFloat = 0.0 {
        didSet {


        }
    }

}
```

We use `didSet` because it is a property observer meaning that it executes our view code when the `cornerRadius` property has been set by Interface Builder. Inside of `didSet`, add code to set the `cornerRadius` property of our view's layer to whatever value is set in **Interface Builder**.

```swift
import UIKit
```

```
class RoundedShadowView: UIView {

    @IBInspectable var cornerRadius: CGFloat = 0.0 {
        didSet {
            layer.cornerRadius = cornerRadius
        }
    }
}
```

Just like that, we can now modify the corner radius of our view in **Interface Builder**! Don't believe me? Check it out!

Go to `Main.storyboard` and click on the white view you created earlier.

Click on the **Identity Inspector** (🔲) and change the class by typing *RoundedShadowView* and pressing the `Return` key as in Figure 5.8.7 below.

Figure 5.8.7

Click on the `Attributes Inspector` icon (🔽) and you will see that – *ouila!* – there is now a customizable property for Corner Radius!

Screen Shot 2016-10-07 at 9.37.45 PM.png

We now have an easy way to modify the `cornerRadius` of our view without needing to change the code inside `RoundedShadowView.swift`.

Enter a value (like 25) into the **Corner Radius** text field and press `Enter` to set it. You probably noticed that nothing has changed in **Interface Builder**. That is because we

738

have not yet implemented **@IBDesignable**.

In the next section, we will do just that.

@IBDesignable

Click on RoundedShadowView.swift and above the class declaration add @IBDesignable.

```swift
import UIKit

@IBDesignable
class RoundedShadowView: UIView {

    @IBInspectable var cornerRadius: CGFloat = 0.0 {
        didSet {
            layer.cornerRadius = cornerRadius
        }
    }
}
```

Next, you need to override the method prepareForInterfaceBuilder() by adding the following code to your RoundedShadowView class.

```swift
import UIKit

@IBDesignable
class RoundedShadowView: UIView {

    @IBInspectable var cornerRadius: CGFloat = 0.0 {
        didSet {
            layer.cornerRadius = cornerRadius
        }
    }

    override func prepareForInterfaceBuilder() {

    }
}
```

The method prepareForInterfaceBuilder() allows our view code to run inside of Interface Builder. But in order to do this, we must run the same code in two places.
Once in our @IBInspectable and once in prepareForInterfaceBuilder().

So we don't violate the DRY principle (Don't Repeat Yourself), create a function called *setupView()* beneath `prepareForInterfaceBuilder()` like so:

```swift
import UIKit

@IBDesignable
class RoundedShadowView: UIView {

    @IBInspectable var cornerRadius: CGFloat = 0.0 {
        didSet {
            layer.cornerRadius = cornerRadius
        }
    }

    override func prepareForInterfaceBuilder() {

    }

    func setupView() {

    }
}
```

We want to add our custom view code to be inside of `setupView()` instead of being inside of **@IBInspectable** like so:

```swift
import UIKit

@IBDesignable
class RoundedShadowView: UIView {

    @IBInspectable var cornerRadius: CGFloat = 0.0 {
        didSet {

        }
    }

    override func prepareForInterfaceBuilder() {

    }

    func setupView() {
        layer.cornerRadius = cornerRadius
    }
}
```

Finally, to allow for **@IBInspectable** to access our `cornerRadius` property and to allow for the changes to be viewable in **Interface Builder** (with the help of **@IBDesignable**) call the function `setupView()` in both places like so:

```
import UIKit

@IBDesignable
class RoundedShadowView: UIView {

    @IBInspectable var cornerRadius: CGFloat = 0.0 {
        didSet {
            setupView()
        }
    }

    override func prepareForInterfaceBuilder() {
        setupView()
    }

    func setupView() {
        layer.cornerRadius = cornerRadius
    }
}
```

Return back to `Main.storyboard` and allow for your app to build.
Interface Builder is basically running your custom view code and seeing if there are any changes that need to be displayed.

Click on the white view we created earlier and in the **Attributes Inspector** (), set the Corner Radius property to **25**.

Screen Shot 2016-10-07 at 9.59.32 PM.png

You should see the corners become rounded in **Interface Builder** without needing to run our app on a device (Figure 5.8.8)!

Figure 5.8.8

Adding A Shadow to RoundedShadowView

Now that you understand the basic principles of adding an **@IBInspectable** to a custom view class, we will add several more lines of code to handle creating a shadow for our view.

Click on RoundedShadowView.swift and add the following lines of code to the RoundedShadowView class.

```
import UIKit

@IBDesignable
class RoundedView: UIView {

    @IBInspectable var cornerRadius: CGFloat = 0.0 {
        didSet {
            setupView()
        }
    }

    @IBInspectable var shadowColor: UIColor? {
        didSet {
            setupView()
        }
```

```
    }

    @IBInspectable var shadowRadius: CGFloat = 0.0 {
        didSet {
            setupView()
        }
    }

    @IBInspectable var shadowOffset: CGSize = CGSize(width: 0.0, height: 0.0) {
        didSet {
            setupView()
        }
    }

    @IBInspectable var shadowOpacity: Float = 0.0 {
        didSet {
            setupView()
        }
    }

    func setupView() {
        layer.cornerRadius = cornerRadius
        layer.shadowColor = shadowColor?.cgColor
        layer.shadowRadius = shadowRadius
        layer.shadowOpacity = shadowOpacity
    }

    override func prepareForInterfaceBuilder() {
        setupView()
    }
}
```

As you can see, we can create **@IBInspectable** properties for values of type UIColor, Float, CGSize, & CGFloat.

Helpful Tip:

You can also modify values of type(s): Int, CGFloat, Double, String, Bool, CGPoint, CGSize, CGRect, UIColor, & UIImage.

Return to Main.storyboard and click on our white RoundedShadowView.

In the **Attributes Inspector** (⬇), you should now see various properties to modify our view's shadow (Figure 5.8.9).

Figure 5.8.9

Rounded Shadow View

Corner Radius	25
Shadow Color	Default
Shadow Radius	--
Shadow Offset	Width / Height
Shadow Opac...	--

Set the following values to give our view a shadow (Figure 5.8.10):

* **Shadow Color:** Dark Gray Color
* **Shadow Radius:** 10
* **Shadow Opacity:** 0.3

Figure 5.8.10

Adding UIButtons & UILabels To Our

RoundedShadowView

To add some interactivity to our pop-up view, we need to add a couple **UIButtons** and **UILabels** to allow our user to grant permissions for the camera, location services, and notifications.

Drag a **UIButton** onto our white **RoundedShadowView** and size it to fit as in Figure 5.8.11 below. My example has a height of **50** and a width of **250**.

Figure 5.8.11

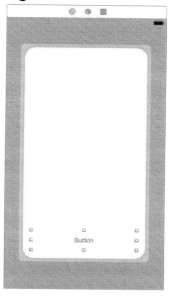

Drag on two more **UIButtons**, resize them to match the first, and position them to have a bit of spacing as in Figure 5.8.12 below.

Figure 5.8.12

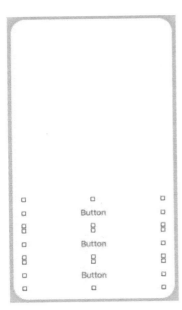

To provide a message asking the user for permissions, drag on two **UILabels** positioned as in Figure 5.8.13 and make sure that the text is center aligned for both labels. Choose a font other than the System font (yuck).

Figure 5.8.13

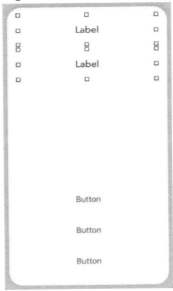

The top-most label should have a friendly, personal greeting like, "Hey! We need your help!" to give our app some personality. Feel free to change the font size to something larger or bolder to help it stand out.

The bottom label should say something about what the app needs to do like, "We need your permission to move forward. This lets our app work nicely for you."
Typing a message that long will cause our label to stretch out beyond the bounds of our screen, so click and drag to resize the label so it fits back into our white **RoundedShadowView** (Figure 5.8.14).
You will also need to change the **Lines** property of the **UILabel** to something like **3** or **4** so that it can fit inside nicely.

Screen Shot 2016-10-08 at 9.09.06 AM.png

Figure 5.8.14

We haven't set up any constraints yet to keep our **UIButtons** or **UILabels** in place. Let's do that now. We will make this process much easier on ourselves by using a **UIStackView**.

Hold the Shift key and click on both **UILabels** and all three **UIButtons**.

Then click the Stack button ( ) at the bottom of the Xcode window to put all five elements into a **UIStackView**.

When we do this, our design becomes really messy (Figure 5.8.15). It doesn't look like it should, but don't worry! We will fix that.

Figure 5.8.15

Select your **UIStackView** from the **Document Outline** on the left side of the **Interface Builder** window (Figure 5.8.16).

It is easier to select it from here than inside the **Interface Builder** at times.

Figure 5.8.16

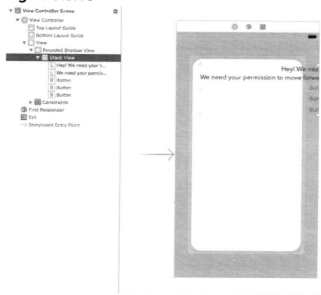

Now we need to constrain our **UIStackView** to fit nicely within **RoundedShadowView**.

While it is still selected click the `Pin` button (⊡) and set up your constraints to match mine in Figure 5.8.17 below:

Figure 5.8.17

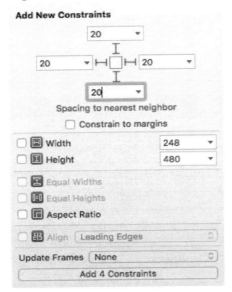

Now our **UIStackView** is looking better, but not exactly how we want it.

Ensure that the **UIStackView** is selected and in the `Attributes Inspector` () click on the drop-down menu for the `Distribution` property.

Select `Fill Proportionally` to give each element in the **UIStackView** a proportional fill determined by it's size.

After that, change the `Spacing` property to be equal to **50** (Figure 5.8.18).

Figure 5.8.18

One thing to note is when creating a **UIStackView**, any constraints on any of the items placed inside the **UIStackView** are removed.

So we need to re-add constraints for each of our **UIButtons**.

Hold Shift and select all three buttons. Then click the `Pin` button ( ) and give each button a height constraint of **50** as in Figure 5.8.19a/b.

Figure 5.8.19a

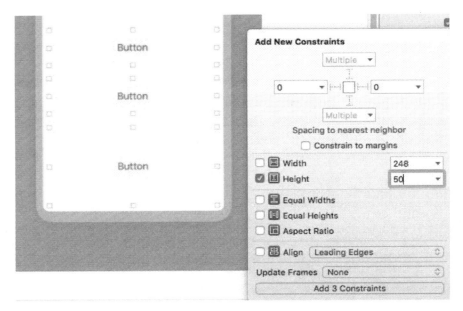

Figure 5.8.19b

Once that is complete, we can now create a custom class for our buttons to modify the view properties.

Creating a RoundedButton Class

In the **Navigator**, right-click on your project folder and click `New File...` (Figure 5.8.20a). Double-click `Cocoa Touch Class` and give the class a name of *RoundedButton*. Set it to subclass **UIButton** (Figure 5.8.20b). Click `Next` then click `Create` to save the class into your project directory.

Figure 5.8.20a

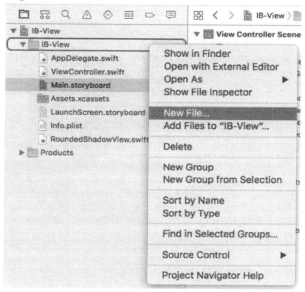

Figure 5.8.20b

Click on `RoundedButton.swift` and delete the commented out boilerplate code. We want this class to operate very similarly to our `RoundedShadowView` class, so we actually can copy and paste the **@IBInspectable**'s, `setupView()` function, and `prepareForInterfaceBuilder()` function we already wrote from `RoundedShadowView.swift` to `RoundedButton.swift`.

The code inside of our class in `RoundedButton.swift` should now look identical to `RoundedShadowView.swift` (Figure 5.8.1a).
But we need to add **@IBDesignable** to the top of our class.
Now, add two extra **@IBInspectable**'s. Create an **@IBInspectable** for both of **UIButton's** `borderWidth` and `borderColor` properties (Figure 5.8.1b).

Figure 5.8.21a

```swift
import UIKit

@IBDesignable
class RoundedButton: UIButton {

    @IBInspectable var cornerRadius: CGFloat = 0.0 {
        didSet {
            setupView()
        }
    }

    @IBInspectable var shadowColor: UIColor? {
        didSet {
            setupView()
        }
    }

    @IBInspectable var shadowRadius: CGFloat = 0.0 {
        didSet {
            setupView()
        }
    }

    @IBInspectable var shadowOffset: CGSize = CGSize(width: 0.0, height: 0.0) {
        didSet {
            setupView()
        }
    }

    @IBInspectable var shadowOpacity: Float = 0.0 {
        didSet {
```

754

```
            setupView()
        }
    }

    func setupView() {
        layer.cornerRadius = cornerRadius
        layer.shadowColor = shadowColor?.cgColor
        layer.shadowRadius = shadowRadius
        layer.shadowOpacity = shadowOpacity
    }

    override func prepareForInterfaceBuilder() {
        setupView()
    }
}
```

Figure 5.8.1b

```
//
//  RoundedButton.swift
//  IB-View
//
//  Created by Caleb Stultz on 10/8/16.
//  Copyright © 2016 Caleb Stultz. All rights reserved.
//

import UIKit

@IBDesignable
class RoundedButton: UIButton {

    @IBInspectable var borderWidth: CGFloat = 0.0 {
        didSet {
            setupView()
        }
    }

    @IBInspectable var borderColor: UIColor? {
        didSet {
            setupView()
        }
    }

    ...

    func setupView() {
```

```
        layer.borderWidth = borderWidth
        layer.borderColor = borderColor.cgColor
        ...
    }


    override func prepareForInterfaceBuilder() {
        setupView()
    }
}
```

Modifying UIButton Properties in Interface Builder

Now that we have our `RoundedButton` class finished, let's head over to `Main.storyboard` and set our buttons to inherit from the `RoundedButton` class.

With the Shift key held, click on all three buttons, then click on the **Identity Inspector** (

) and in the **Class** field, type *RoundedButton* and press `Enter`.

All three buttons now have access to customizable properties in **Interface Builder**! Hold

Shift and select all three **UIButtons** then open up the **Attributes Inspector** (   ).
Set the following properties below (Figure 5.8.22). The yellow color used is the same as before (#FFCC66).

Figure 5.8.22

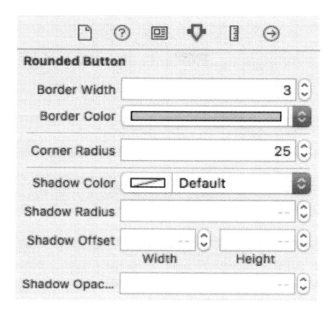

Our buttons now have a rounded yellow border. But we want to change the text to look nice as well.

Set the font to something other than the System font. I tend to favor *Avenir*. Next if you're looking for ideas, change the words to say something about the permissions you want to request. Set the font color to the same yellow color as the `borderColor` as in Figure 5.8.3.

Figure 5.8.23

I went on to add an extra **Done** button (and added a shadow with our custom controls) at the bottom of `RoundedShadowView` to give the user a way to tell the app they were finished granting permissions (Figure 5.8.24). But that is entirely optional. I also had to reduce the **UIStackView** spacing value to **30** instead of **50** because of spacing issues.

Figure 5.8.24

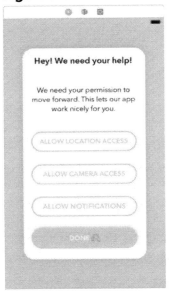

Wrapping Up

In this chapter, you've learned how to make your UI customizations show up in Interface Builder as well as give them custom controls in the Attributes Inspector. I'm sure you can see how powerful this can be for designing beautiful and custom UI controls. This is a really nice way for you to see what your UI will look like without needing to build and run your app over and over again to see small design changes.

Exercise

Create a new Xcode project and in Interface Builder, do your best to recreate this app's User Interface with the knowledge you now have regarding @IBDesignable and @IBInspectable. You should be able to complete this all without having to build the app once.

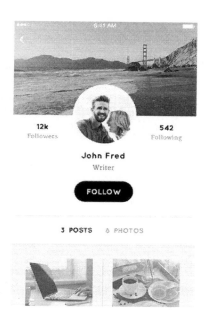

Slack for iOS Upload (3).jpg

Chapter 42: Touch ID

In 2013, Apple launched the iPhone 5S which included the Touch ID fingerprint sensor. Since then, many popular apps have adopted the use of Touch ID to secure content, perform fast re-authentication, and more.

What you will learn

- LocalAuthentication

- UIAlertController

- UIAlertAction

- Storyboard IDs

- Error Handling

- DispatchQueue

Key Terms

- **LAContext:** a programmatic interface for evaluating authentication policies and access controls, managing credentials, and invalidating authentication contexts.

- **LAError:** a list of errors that can occur within an LAContext.

- **Thread:** a section of code that can be run independently of the main program.

Resources

Download here: https://github.com/devslopes/book-assets/wiki

Before fingerprint sensors came to smartphones, I thought of them in terms of what a deep-cover CIA operative would use to gain access to places in spy movies. But Apple brought that magic and security to everyone when they integrated the Touch ID sensor into the iPhone home button.

Touch ID is ultra-secure (though it does have it's weaknesses), as it stores all fingerprint data locally on a secured portion of the device CPU, inaccessible by iCloud or other servers. This makes it an amazing way to secure content of all kinds on Apple devices.

In this chapter, we will be building an app called **Touchy** that utilizes Touch ID. After authenticating our identity in the app via fingerprint, a new ViewController will load showing some secured content.

Setting Up Xcode

To begin, download and open up the **Touchy** starter project from the link above.

This starter project includes a pre-built UI, custom UIButton class called RoundedOutlineButton with @IBDesignable/@IBInspectable properties, and our intial ViewController called AuthenticationVC which you can see in Figure 5.10.1 below:

Figure 5.10.1

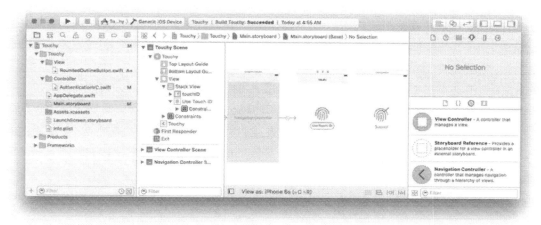

Importing LocalAuthentication

In order to use Touch ID in our app, we need to import the framework **LocalAuthentication**.

To do this, select the **Touchy** project settings (Figure 5.10.2) then scroll to the bottom of the screen until you see **Linked Frameworks and Libraries** (Figure 5.10.3)

Figure 5.10.2

Figure 5.10.3

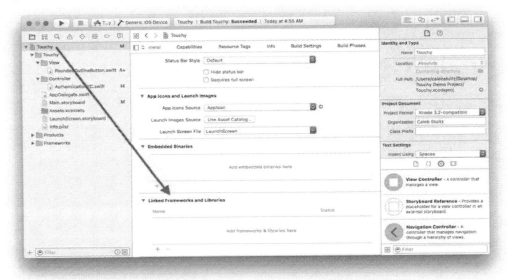

Next, click the + button to add a framework. Search on the resulting pop-up for **LocalAuthentication** and double-click to add it to your project (Figure 5.10.4).

Figure 5.10.4

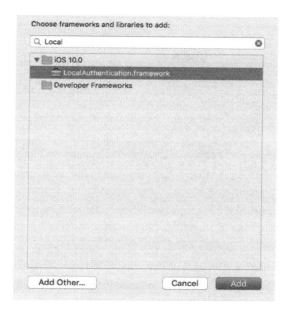

We are now ready to begin coding our app.

Adding an @IBAction to our Touch ID Button

Let's set the button in our UI to be able to respond to input.

Open up `Main.storyboard`, click on AuthenticationVC, and open the **Assistant Editor** (

).

Right-click on the rounded **Touch ID** button and drag to `AuthenticationVC` within the brackets of our `AuthenticationVC` class.

A blue line will pop up showing where you dragged from. Release the mouse once you have entered the code side of the **Assistant Editor** (Figure 5.10.5).

Figure 5.10.5

Click on the drop down menu that says **Outlet** and select Action to create an@IBAction.

In the **Name** field, type *onTouchIDButtonPressed*.

We always want to be descriptive about what our @**IBAction** does.

Click Connect to add an @IBAction (Figure 5.10.6).

Figure 5.10.6

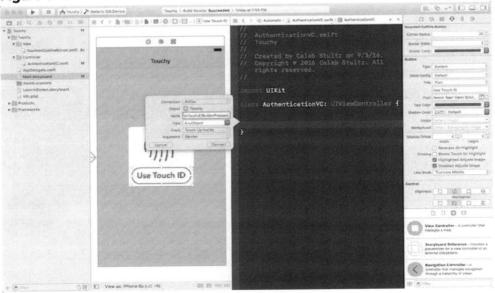

Building Out AuthenticationVC

Now switch over to `AuthenticationVC` and, we need to import `LocalAuthentication` into our `AuthenticationVC`.

Beneath `import UIKit`, add `import AuthenticationVC`:

```
import UIKit
import LocalAuthentication

class AuthenticationVC: UIViewController {

    @IBAction func onTouchIDButtonPressed(_ sender: AnyObject) {

    }

}
```

Now we have access to the framework which will allow us to use Touch ID.

The first thing we need to do to integrate Touch ID is to define an **LAContext**. "LA" stands for LocalAuthentication, in case you were wondering.

We also need to create a variable to handle and hold the value for any errors we may encounter.

Inside of the brackets of our `@IBAction`, add the following:

```
...

@IBAction func onTouchIDButtonPressed(_ sender: AnyObject) {
    let authenticationContext = LAContext()
    var error: NSError?
}
```

LAContext is going to allow us to check if our device has a Touch ID sensor. We're going to use one of LAContext's built-in delegate methods called `canEvaluatePolicy(policy:error:)` to check this.

```
...

@IBAction func onTouchIDButtonPressed(_ sender: AnyObject) {
    let authenticationContext = LAContext()
    var error: NSError?
```

```
    if
authenticationContext.canEvaluatePolicy(.deviceOwnerAuthenticationWithBiometrics,
error: &error) {


    }


}
```

.deviceOwnerAuthenticationWithBiometrics is a **LocalAuthentication** policy that, according the the Xcode documentation, "indicates that the device owner authenticated using Touch ID" – just what we need!

We use the ampersand (&), to indicate that we are passing in *error* as an input value so that we can modify it directly. I will explain why later on in this chapter.

Now that we have checked to see if we have a Touch ID sensor, we need to actually authenticate with it. To do this add the following code inside the brackets of .canEvaluatePolicy(policy:error:):

```
...

@IBAction func onTouchIDButtonPressed(_ sender: AnyObject) {
    let authenticationContext = LAContext()
    var error: NSError?

    if
authenticationContext.canEvaluatePolicy(.deviceOwnerAuthenticationWithBiometrics,
error: &error) {

authenticationContext.evaluatePolicy(.deviceOwnerAuthenticationWithBiometrics,
localizedReason: "We need your fingerprint to authenticate.", reply: { (success,
error) in


        })
    }
}
```

So basically what we have now done is allowed our app to perform authentication since it now knows that we have a Touch ID sensor.
We used .deviceOwnerAuthenticationWithBiometrics as our policy.

We declared a String value for *localizedReason*, which is the messaging that is shown beneath the stock iOS Touch ID popup (Figure 5.10.7).
We then determined our reply which is a closure statement.

Within our reply to the Touch ID sensor, we have two things to think about – what to do if we are successful and what to do if not.

There are two values we can use to manage this – success and error right at the end of our closure statement.

We're going to add some conditional code to operate if we are successful or not:

```
...

@IBAction func onTouchIDButtonPressed(_ sender: AnyObject) {
    let authenticationContext = LAContext()
    var error: NSError?

    if
authenticationContext.canEvaluatePolicy(.deviceOwnerAuthenticationWithBiometrics,
error: &error) {

authenticationContext.evaluatePolicy(.deviceOwnerAuthenticationWithBiometrics,
localizedReason: "We need your fingerprint to authenticate.", reply: { (success,
error) in
            if success {
                // Navigate to locked content
            } else {
                if let error = error as? NSError {
                    // Display a specific error
                }
            }
        })
    }
}
```

Great! So now, if we have success in verifying Touch ID, then we will navigate to the locked content we have created. If not, we will display a specific error so the user knows what is wrong.

If you're wondering why error is followed by as? NSError that's because the error value passed in via our closure is of type Error not NSError.
We are casting the value this way because NSError has property called code which returns an integer based on an error code.
Later on we will use these error codes to display specific error information.

Let's now write the function to navigate to our **Success ViewController** once we have successfully authenticated.

Below the last bracket of the @IBAction, add the following function:

```
...

@IBAction func onTouchIDButtonPressed(_ sender: AnyObject) {
    ///Code redacted for spacing purposes.
}

func navigateToSuccessVC() {

}
```

Now let's instantiate a ViewController and give it a Storyboard ID, then push it onto our **Navigation Controller** so that we can navigate to the **Success ViewController** with the green success image:

```
...

func navigateToSuccessVC() {
    if let successVC = storyboard?.instantiateViewController(withIdentifier:
"SuccessVC") {
        self.navigationController?.pushViewController(successVC, animated: true)
    }
}
```

We created a conditional by writing if, then we added a constant called *successVC* and instantiated a ViewController on it.
We gave it an identifier – in this case a Storyboard ID – of "SuccessVC".
Then, inside the conditional we told our **Navigation Controller** to push successVC onto our navigation stack as the next ViewController inside it.

Now wherever we call navigateToSuccessVC() it will push our **Success ViewController** onto the **Navigation Controller**.

Let's call it in the success condition block inside of our @IBAction:

```
  @IBAction func onTouchIDButtonPressed(_ sender: AnyObject) {
      let authenticationContext = LAContext()
      var error: NSError?

      if
authenticationContext.canEvaluatePolicy(.deviceOwnerAuthenticationWithBiometrics,
error: &error) {

authenticationContext.evaluatePolicy(.deviceOwnerAuthenticationWithBiometrics,
```

```
localizedReason: "We need your fingerprint to authenticate.", reply: { (success,
error) in

            if success {
                self.navigateToSuccessVC()
            } else {
              if let error = error as? NSError {
                    // Display a specific error
                }
            }

        })
    }
  }
```

You may be wondering why we needed to type `self` before we called our navigation function. This is because we are inside of a closure.

We are using `navigateToSuccessVC()` as an unowned reference. We're doing this since we know that our reference to `navigateToSuccessVC()` can't ever be nil (or empty) once we have initialized it.

Our function has code that **must** run and has no option but to work. If you don't understand this yet, that's okay. For the curious, you could do some research on *strong*, *weak*, and *unowned* references in Swift.

In many closures, you will need to use `self` keyword before calling *functions*, *variables*, *constants*, *etc.*

Errors: Creating An Alert Pop-Up

Now that we've handled what should happen if we are successful, we should handle what should happen in case of an error.

To begin, let's create a function that will create a stock iOS alert pop-up. Beneath `navigateToSuccessVC()` add the following:

```
...

func showAlertWithTitle(title: String, message: String) {
    let alertVC = UIAlertController(title: title, message: message, preferredStyle:
.alert)
    let okAction = UIAlertAction(title: "OK", style: .default, handler: nil)
}
```

We created a function called `showAlertWithTitle(title:message:)` and have declared two constants `alertVC` and `okAction`.

The constant `alertVC` is of type `UIAlertController` and we have passed in the title, message, and set a style (alert).
Our `okAction` is of type `UIAlertAction` and we passed it a title, style (default), and made it's handler `nil` because we don't need to do anything after our error pop-up displays.

Now let's add our action to `alertVC` and ask our ViewController to present it:

```
func showAlertWithTitle(title: String, message: String) {
    let alertVC = UIAlertController(title: title, message: message, preferredStyle:
.alert)
    let okAction = UIAlertAction(title: "OK", style: .default, handler: nil)

    alertVC.addAction(okAction)

    self.present(alertVC, animated: true, completion: nil)
}
```

Okay, awesome.   We now have added `okAction` to `alertVC` and asked to present the alert pop-up whenever our function is called. So let's call it.
We will create a function to display an error message for a device that doesn't have a Touch ID sensor.

Beneath `showAlertWithTitle(title:message:)` write the following:

```
...

func showAlertForNoBiometrics() {
    showAlertWithTitle(title: "Error", message: "This device does not have a Touch
ID sensor.")
}
```

We're written a function inside a function. Aside from any Inception-related jokes, we now can call `showAlertForNoBiometrics()` in the else clause of `canEvaluatePolicy(policy:error:)` above.
Remember that we've been writing code inside of the `if` clause so far, meaning if we have a Touch ID sensor. We want the following code to be written in case the device doesn't have what it needs.
Add an `else` clause at the bottom of `canEvaluatePolicy(policy:error:)` like so:

```
if
authenticationContext.canEvaluatePolicy(.deviceOwnerAuthenticationWithBiometrics,
```

```
error: &error) {
    authenticationContext.evaluatePolicy(.deviceOwnerAuthenticationWithBiometrics,
localizedReason: "We need your fingerprint to authenticate.", reply: { (success,
error) in

            if success {
                self.navigateToSuccessVC()
            } else {
                if let error = error as? NSError {
                    // Display a specific error
                }
            }
        })
    } else {
    showAlertForNoBiometrics()
    }
}
```

Awesome, so we now can display an error if our app is run on a device without a Touch ID sensor.

Build & Run

We should now check to see if what we've done works. Make sure that you set the active scheme to an iPhone/iPad of choice.

Click the triangular `Build & Run` button from the top left corner of Xcode and wait for the app to build (Figure 5.10.7).

Figure 5.10.7

Once it launches in Simulator, click on the **Touch ID** button on the screen.

We should see an error message pop up saying we don't have a Touch ID sensor (Figure 5.10.8)!

Figure 5.10.8

This is because we have not yet enabled the virtual Touch ID sensor in Simulator. To do this, go to the macOS menu bar and click `Hardware` > `Touch ID` > `Toggle Enrolled State`.

Now, try clicking on the **Touch ID** button again. You should see a nice stock iOS Touch ID pop-up with our custom **localizedReason** for why we need Touch ID (Figure 5.10.9).

Figure 5.10.9

We can now pass in a successful or unsuccessful fingerprint scan by selecting `Hardware >` `Touch ID > Matching Touch` or `Non-matching Touch` from the macOS menu bar.

Select `Matching Touch` and you'll probably notice that nothing happens. Actually, something is happening. Our app works and after about 10 seconds you should see that the app successfully transitions to our locked content, but it takes forever. This is a terrible user experience! Why is this happening?

Certain functions in Swift (and all other programming languages) can be performed on what are called "threads". Think of them as different channels where code is run.

There is a main thread where most code is run, but there are also background threads where other code is run. Threading allows for a much more efficient running of our apps because the work the CPU needs to do is split up into several sections (threads).

Touch ID happens to be run on a background thread. So is the pushing of ViewControllers onto a NavigationController.
Since they are both happening simultaneously, the background thread they're running on is full and therefore causes a serious memory issue and delay of our app. Let's save it!

Inside `navigateToSuccessVC`, we pushed a ViewController onto our NavigationController. We need to add the following code to bring this animation up to the main thread using `DispatchQueue`:

```
func navigateToSuccessVC() {
    if let successVC = storyboard?.instantiateViewController(withIdentifier:
"SuccessVC") {
        DispatchQueue.main.async {
            self.navigationController?.pushViewController(successVC, animated:
true)
        }
    }
}
```

`DispatchQueue` is like a thread manager and it can move code around and place it on different threads. In our case, we moved some code up onto the main thread of our app, then called `async`, which stands for "asynchronously".
This just means that the code runs from top to bottom as you'd expect.

Now, build and run the app once more. If we tap the **Touch ID** button and then send in a successful fingerprint by selecting `Hardware > Touch ID > Matching Touch` it should push

`SuccessVC` and animate the transition instantly! Huzzah!

Specific Error Handling

Next, let's create a function to handle the variety of errors that could occur for issues with Touch ID. Perhaps our user tapped cancel. Maybe they closed the app after the Touch ID pop-up appeared. Regardless, we should have a way of handling these errors. We will write one function to handle all errors with a message.

Beneath `showAlertForNoBiometrics()` write:

```
func showAlertViewAfterEvaluatingPolicyWithMessage(message: String) {
    showAlertWithTitle(title: "Error", message: message)
}
```

Wow, this function has a huge name. But it is specific and leaves other developers with no question as to what it does.
This function is basically going to create a pop-up alert with a title of "Error" and a message that will change.
Whenever we call `showAlertViewAfterEvaluatingPolicyWithMessage(message:)` we will pass in a message value of type `String`. This way we can display a number of different errors with a single function.

Now we need to create the function beneath this one to handle what error has occurred and passing the message into the message parameter of `showAlertViewAfterEvaluatingPolicyWithMessage(message:)`.

```
func errorMessageForLAErrorCode(errorCode: Int) -> String {

}
```

Before we dive into adding anything to the above function, I want you to see all possible errors, so you know what type of errors to add to it. I borrowed this from inside of the `LAError` class:

```
        /// Authentication was not successful, because user failed to provide valid
credentials.
        case authenticationFailed

        /// Authentication was canceled by user (e.g. tapped Cancel button).
        case userCancel
```

```
        /// Authentication was canceled, because the user tapped the fallback
button (Enter Password).
        case userFallback

        /// Authentication was canceled by system (e.g. another application went to
foreground).
        case systemCancel

        /// Authentication could not start, because passcode is not set on the
device.
        case passcodeNotSet

        /// Authentication could not start, because Touch ID is not available on
the device.
        case touchIDNotAvailable

        /// Authentication could not start, because Touch ID has no enrolled
fingers.
        case touchIDNotEnrolled

        /// Authentication was not successful, because there were too many failed
Touch ID attempts and Touch ID is now locked.
        case touchIDLockout

        /// Authentication was canceled by application (e.g. invalidate was called
while authentication was in progress).
        case appCancel

        /// LAContext passed to this call has been previously invalidated.
        case invalidContext
```

After reading the above errors, it is easy to see that there is a lot that can go wrong with Touch ID. To make sure we are covering all of these potential errors, we are going to write a **switch** that can sift through them based on the error code associated with them and pass in the message we want.

Return back to the function we just created called
`errorMessageForLAErrorCode(errorCode:)`.
We need to create a variable to store the message provided by each error.
Then we need to write a **switch statement** to handle all the potential cases. Finally, we need to return our message as a `String` as required by our function. Add the following:

```
func errorMessageForLAErrorCode(errorCode: Int) -> String {
    var message = ""
```

```
    switch errorCode {
    case LAError.appCancel.rawValue:
        message = "Authentication was cancelled by application"

    case LAError.authenticationFailed.rawValue:
        message = "The user failed to provide valid credentials"

    case LAError.invalidContext.rawValue:
        message = "The context is invalid"

    case LAError.passcodeNotSet.rawValue:
        message = "Passcode is not set on the device"

    case LAError.systemCancel.rawValue:
        message = "Authentication was cancelled by the system"

    case LAError.touchIDLockout.rawValue:
        message = "Too many failed attempts."

    case LAError.touchIDNotAvailable.rawValue:
        message = "TouchID is not available on the device"

    case LAError.userCancel.rawValue:
        message = "The user did cancel"

    case LAError.userFallback.rawValue:
        message = "The user chose to use the fallback"

    default:
        message = "Did not find error code on LAError object"
    }
    return message
}
```

Don't freak out.   I know that was a lot of code to add, but let's unpack it now.

The variable `message` will hold the error message to pass into our alert pop-up later on.
The **switch** is looking for the `errorCode` passed in by
`errorMessageForLAErrorCode(errorCode:)`.
We have declared cases for every case noted in `LAError`, but we have used a neat little
hack to create a custom error code for each error – it's `rawValue` property. Each error has
a `rawValue` property which is of type `Int`.

Let's say that we passed in an `errorCode` of 12.
If `LAError.userCancel.rawValue` is equal to 12, then our message variable will be set to

"The user did cancel" and it will be returned.

We also have identified a default case which will return the message "Did not find error code on LAError object", which is unlikely but it's great to cover all the bases.

One of the last things we need to do is add some error handling.
In the `evaluatePolicy(policy:localizedReason:reply:)` function above we wrote a conditional to determine what to do if we had success or not.
Inside the **else block**, we said that if there is an error that we should do something. Add the following:

```
if success {
    self.navigateToSuccessVC()
} else {
    if let error = error as? NSError {
        let message = self.errorMessageForLAErrorCode(errorCode: error.code)
        self.showAlertViewAfterEvaluatingPolicyWithMessage(message: message)
    }
}
```

If we encounter an error with Touch ID, we will be given an `Int` value from `LAError` to use as an error code. We pass that error code into `errorMessageForLAErrorCode(errorCode:)` as `error.code`.
The return value of that function will set our `message` variable to a relevant error code for whatever went wrong.
Then, we call `showAlertViewAfterEvaluatingPolicyWithMessage(message:)` and pass in our `message` variable to display it.

Build & Run

Now that we have come this far, it's a great time to build and run our app. Let's check to see if different errors are handled properly.

Once **Touchy** opens in Simulator, try to perform various actions that a user might purposefully or accidentally do which would result in an error.
First, click on the red **Touch ID** button in our app. Tap the **Cancel** button on the Touch ID pop-up and an error pops up with the proper message (Figure 5.10.10).
Click on the **Touch ID** button again and try pressing `Shift` + `Command` + `H` to simulate pressing the home button.
We should see an error message that we tried to cancel authentication (Figure 5.10.11).

Figure 5.10.10

Figure 5.10.11

And of course, finally click the **Touch ID** button and send in a successful fingerprint selecting Hardware > Touch ID > Matching Touch (Figure 5.10.12).

Figure 5.10.12

Success!

Wrapping up

We've done a lot of work to integrate Touch ID. This can be used in so many amazing ways in apps – securing content, easy re-authentication, etc.
We learned about **LAContext** and how we must first check to see if we have a Touch ID sensor, then move on from there.

We handled errors in specific, helpful ways to provide the best experience for the user. A confused user is a lost user so letting them know why something isn't working if there is an error is very important. You even learned about threading and how to move some code from a background thread up onto the main thread.

Pat yourself on the back because you just built a really cool app. Nicely done!

Exercise

Extend this app by making it possible for a user to enter their passcode instead of Touch ID. Do some research online on how to do this. If you can do this, it makes for the best user experience because some people are still rockin' the iPhone 5 with no Touch ID sensor. We want to make sure that everyone can use our apps easily.

Chapter 43: Sprite Kit - How to Build a Tiki Bird Game

SpriteKit is a full-featured platform that can be used to build amazing games. We will use it to make an addicting game in Swift.

What you will learn

- How to move an object

- How to animate the movement of a Sprite

- Detecting user taps

- Creating collisions

Key Terms

- **Sprite Kit**

- **SKGameScene**

- **SKSpriteNode**

- **zPosition**

- **SKActions**

- **AKTextureAtlas**

- **categoryBitMask**

- **contactTestBitMask**

Resources

Download here:

We're going to build an awesome game that is similar to the *Flappy Bird* game, with a few changes. Evan has made us some pretty sweet assets to use on this project. Hopefully you have those downloaded already. I will take us through a step by step process and by the end of this tutorial you will have a pretty cool game to show your friends. We'll also have some suggestions for you to make it even better.

Your **Sprite Kit** iOS App (Figure 5.11.0) will have a ground, background, obstacles and a Bird that will flap its wings.

Figure 5.11.0

Creating an Xcode Project

Open Xcode and, from the File menu, select New and then New Project....
A new workspace window will appear, and a sheet will slide from its toolbar with several application templates to choose from.
On the lefthand side, select Application from the **iOS** section.
From the choices that appear, select Game and press the Next button (Figure 5.11.01).
(Apple changes these templates and their names often.

Figure 5.11.1

Under Product name enter *TikiBird*. Language should be Swift. Game Technology is **SpriteKitand Devices isiPhone. Then pressNext`.

Figure 5.11.2

Then select where you want to save your project (you can create a Git repository if you'd like) and press Create.

Under the General tab of the TikiBird target change the device orientation to Portrait and Upside down. Uncheck Landscape Left and Landscape Right.

Figure 5.11.3

In the **Project Navigator** click on the Assets.xcassets folder.

First, delete the Spaceship image that's already there. Highlight it and just press the delete key.

Next, open the folder where you have the assets saved for this game and drag the Ground.png(1x,2x,3x), Mountains.png(1x,2x,3x), and Sky.png(1x,2x,3x) images into the space where the Spaceship image was.

Figure 5.11.4

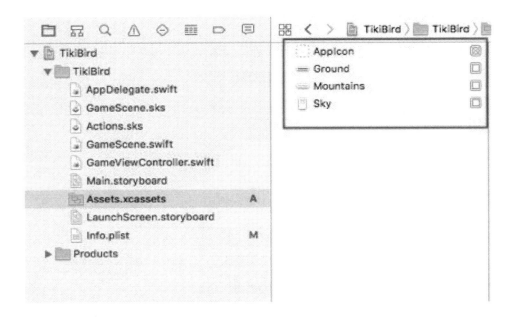

Building the Scenery

We're almost ready to start coding! We will add our Sky and Mountains to the background, place the ground at the bottom and eventually get the ground to continuously move to the left.

Open GameScene.swift. Before we can add our own code we need to delete all the canned stuff apple put there.

Delete everything you see there except for the didMove function and update function. It should look like this when you are done deleting all the nonsense. Also, open GameScene.sks, click on "Hello World!" and press the delete key.

```swift
import SpriteKit
import GameplayKit

class GameScene: SKScene {

    override func didMove(to view: SKView) {

    }

    override func update(_ currentTime: TimeInterval) {
        // Called before each frame is rendered
    }
```

```
}
```

While still inside the `GameScene.swift` file add the following code below the class declaration and above the *didMove method*.

```swift
let totalGroundPieces = 3
var groundPieces = [SKSpriteNode]()
```

Alright, so what we're doing above is defining how many ground images we'll need to use and creating an empty array that will hold these ground pieces. This is how we give the effect of the ground moving.

We animate the image from right to left and once it's out of frame we move it from the left to the right side of the frame. This gives the appearance of never ending ground.

Now we get to add objects to our scene. First we'll add the sky, then the mountains, then the ground.

Let's create a function that will load the scenery for us, call it `func setupScenery()`, place it right underneath the update method.

(Make sure you don't place it inside the update method's opening and closing brackets, though).

```swift
func setupScenery(){
    //Add background sprites
    let bg = SKSpriteNode(imageNamed: "Sky")
    bg.size = CGSize(width: self.frame.width, height: self.frame.height)
    bg.position = CGPoint(x: 0, y: 0)
    bg.zPosition = 1
    self.addChild(bg)

    let mountains = SKSpriteNode(imageNamed: "Mountains")
    mountains.size = CGSize(width: self.frame.width, height:
self.frame.height/4)
    mountains.position = CGPoint(x: 0, y: -self.frame.height / 2 + 200)
    mountains.zPosition = 2
    self.addChild(mountains)
```

You are probably thinking.... what the heck is all this? It's not that bad, I promise. Since the origin (0, 0) of a **SpriteKit** scene's frame and the origin of **SKSpriteNode** is in the center of the object, we're creating a **SKSpriteNode** object for each image, setting the position of the image, then adding them to the scene.

We'll set the sky view to equal the frame of the device and then position the center of the image with the center of the frame (x: 0, y: 0).

We set the mountains a little higher on the Y axis and, since this sprite is not moving, it's okay to hard code it at **200**.

We couldn't just set the Y to zero because the mountains would be in the middle of the screen, so we have to move them down half of the screen height and add **200** to get them where we would like them to stay.

When setting the mountains size, I had to just play around with the height of the mountains until it looked good to me. The **zPosition** is important to add. This determines what layer the sprite is on, the higher the number the closer the image is to you. So setting the sky to **1**, places it in the back and setting the mountains to **2** makes sure they load in front of the sky.

Time to add the ground sprites! We will generate 3 ground sprites and then position them one after the other. We grab the position of the previous sprite to do this. Add this code right under `self.addChild(mountains)` from above.

```
//Add ground sprites
for x in 0..<totalGroundPieces {
    let sprite = SKSpriteNode(imageNamed: "Ground")
    sprite.physicsBody = SKPhysicsBody(rectangleOf: sprite.size)
    sprite.physicsBody?.isDynamic = false
    sprite.physicsBody?.categoryBitMask = category_ground
    sprite.zPosition = 5
    groundPieces.append(sprite)
    let wSpacing:CGFloat = -sprite.size.width / 2
    let hSpacing = -self.frame.height / 2 + sprite.size.height / 2
    if x == 0 {
        sprite.position = CGPoint(x: wSpacing, y: hSpacing)
    } else {
        sprite.position = CGPoint(x: -(wSpacing * 2) + groundPieces[x-
1].position.x, y: groundPieces[x-1].position.y)
    }
    self.addChild(sprite)
}
```

One last step and then we can press run and see what we've done! We need to call `setupScenery()` from the didMove method.

```
override func didMove(to view: SKView) {
    setupScenery()
}
```

Once you do that, go ahead and press the Run button at the top and let your simulator run. You should see the sky, mountains and ground in place.

Figure 5.11.5

Now it's time to get that ground moving!! We're going to use the scene editor to help us estimate some X coordinate values so we know when we can take the ground and move it to the other side after it's out of the view.

In your **Project Navigator** click on GameScene.sks. If you still have "Hello World!" there, click on it to select it and just press the delete key.

Click on **Show Attributes Inspector** on the right side and change the size to **640 x 1136**.

Figure 5.11.6

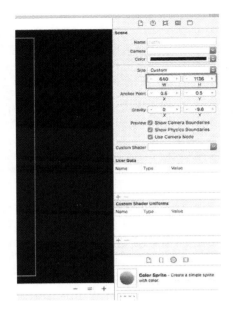

Now drag a `Color Sprite` from the bottom right **Object Library** onto the screen. Change its texture to `Ground.png`.

Since we are generating 3 pieces of ground in the code we just need to find a good X position to make our relocation threshold.

You can quickly duplicate the ground piece **3** ties by pressing ⌘ + d then dragging the pieces one after the other.

-514 on the X position seems like a good number to use (notice how you can see the position on the right hand size in the **Attributes Inspector**).

Figure 5.11.7

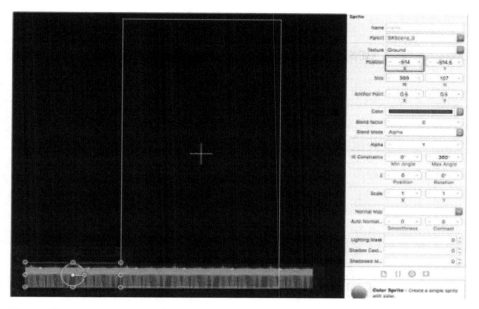

Note: *If you were to run the app right now you would see these ground pieces in your scene on your device. We don't want that because we have already added them in code, so just delete them all from the GameScene.sks. (We only need the X coordinate)*

Moving the Ground Sprites

First, we will get our project organized a little. We will define a initSetup() method to take care of any setup we need to do when the view is loaded.
Then we will create a startGame() method. This will load the scene and start the game. We will learn how to add **SKActions** to the ground images for movement. Then simply continuously monitor whether we need to move the ground pieces back to the starting position.

We need to store *ground speed*, the *actions*, and the *ground reset x coordinate* (that was what the **-514** was for from the scene editor).
Put this code just below the groundPieces array at the top.

```
let groundSpeed: CGFloat = 3.5
let groundResetXCoord: CGFloat = -514
var moveGroundAction: SKAction!
var moveGroundForeverAction: SKAction!
```

Create a initSetup() method, define the actions, then call initSetup() from the didMove method:

```
    override func didMove(to view: SKView) {
        initSetup()
        setupScenery()
        startGame()
    }

    func initSetup() {
        moveGroundAction = SKAction.moveBy(x: -groundSpeed, y: 0, duration: 0.02)
        moveGroundForeverAction =
SKAction.repeatForever(SKAction.sequence([moveGroundAction]))
    }
```

We hard coded the duration of the moveBy on the X coordinate by the groundSpeed in
0.02 seconds.

We then want this action repeat forever. Notice the negative sign before groundSpeed,
this is so it moves to the left.

Now start the actions we created in the initSetup() method in the startGame() method:

```
    func startGame(){
        for sprite in groundPieces {
            sprite.run(moveGroundForeverAction)
        }
    }
```

If you build and run your app, your ground is now moving!
Oh no, wait a second! The ground runs out and leaves the screen! Let's fix this.

Remember that the groundResetXCoord variable we created and never used? Well, now
it's time to use it.

We will create a groundMovement() method that loops through the ground pieces
continually and checks whether they have passed the reset X coordinate.
If they've hit that point we will take that image out and place it at the back of the line.

```
    func groundMovement() {
        for x in 0..<groundPieces.count {
            if groundPieces[x].position.x <= groundResetXCoord {
                if x != 0 {
                    groundPieces[x].position = CGPoint(x: groundPieces[x-
1].position.x + groundPieces[x].size.width, y: groundPieces[x].position.y)
                } else {
                    groundPieces[x].position = CGPoint(x:
groundPieces[groundPieces.count-1].position.x + groundPieces[x].size.width, y:
```

```
groundPieces[x].position.y)
                }
            }
        }
    }
```

Okay, so lets think about what this section of code is doing. We have 3 ground images laying across the bottom in a continuous line. The far left would be index 0 of the array, so as they move to the left we take index 0 and place it at index 2 once it hits our reset coordinate we found earlier.

Lastly, call the `groundMovement()` method from your update method:

```
override func update(_ currentTime: TimeInterval) {
    // Called before each frame is rendered
    groundMovement()
}
```

Build and run the game. You will now have endless ground moving! Pretty cool hey? You can also control the ground speed by changing the `groundSpeed` constant we declared at the top.

Bird Animation

Click on `Assets.xcassets` and click the + arrow at the bottom of your assets window, click on `New Sprite Atlas`, then rename the folder from *Sprites* to **Bird**.

Next, drag Bird-0 (1x,2x,3x), Bird-1 (1x,2x,3x), and Bird-2 (1x,2x,3x) into that `Bird Atlas`.

Figure 5.11.8

Now we need to create a bird node. This is the actual object that will be used in the game.

Then we need a **AKTextureAtlas** for the bird animation frames, and an array to store the frames of the texture.

Add the following code above the `didMove(to view: SKView)` method:

```
var bird: SKSpriteNode!
var birdAtlas = SKTextureAtlas(named: "Bird")
var birdFrames = [SKTexture]()

override func didMove(to view: SKView) {
    initSetup()
    setupScenery()
    setupBird()
    startGame()
}
```

Notice we need a method called `setupBird()`. We will add that now:

```
func setupBird() {
    let totalImgs = birdAtlas.textureNames.count
    for x in 0..<totalImgs{
        let textureName = "Bird-\(x)"
        let texture = birdAtlas.textureNamed(textureName)
        birdFrames.append(texture)
    }
```

```
        bird = SKSpriteNode(texture: birdFrames[0])
        bird.zPosition = 4
        addChild(bird)
        bird.position = CGPoint(x: self.frame.midX, y: self.frame.midY)
        bird.run(SKAction.repeatForever(SKAction.animate(with: birdFrames,
timePerFrame: 0.2, resize: false, restore: true)))
    }
```

Alright, so what is this? We assigned the variable `birdAtlas = SKTextureAtlas(named: "Bird")`.

Since this was assigned in the global scope of the class it will be initialized right when the class is loaded.

Bird is the name of our atlas folder. Remember, when we added the **New Sprite Atlas** and renamed it to *Bird*? The name in this variable must be exactly the same as the **Atlas** folder we created.

Now down to our `setupBird()` method. We first grab the total number of images in the atlas.

We then create **SKTextures** for each of the bird animation frames and add them to the `birdFrames` array so we can use them.

We then create the actual bird object and give it a default texture `bird = SKSpriteNode(texture: birdFrames[0])` and add it to the scene.

Then we set its position and run a repeat forever action that runs the `animateWithTextures` action that will play our animation. Don't forget to set the birds `zPosition` to make sure it's in front of the background!

Let's check out our new animation, build and run the app. You will have a bird flapping its wings in the middle of the screen.

Figure 5.11.9

Bird Physics (Jumping... or flying)

One way to implement physics to the bird would be just to use **SpriteKits**, but we will make our own for this project.

Here's what we need to do:
1. Detect Touch
2. Give bird initial Y velocity
3. Decrease Y velocity incrementally as bird moves up (this is to simulate the pull of gravity)
4. When max jump duration is reached, begin gaining negative Y velocity.
5. Velocity picks up as bird continues to fall.

Above the `didMove(to view: SKView)` method add the following code:

```
//simulated jump physics
var isJumping = false
var touchDetected = false
var jumpStartTime: CGFloat = 0.0
var jumpCurrentTime: CGFloat = 0.0
var jumpEndTime: CGFloat = 0.0
let jumpDuration: CGFloat = 0.35
let jumpVelocity: CGFloat = 500.0
```

```
var currentVelocity: CGFloat = 0.0
var jumpInertiaTime: CGFloat!
var fallInertiatime:CGFloat!

//Delta time
var lastUpdateTimeInterval: CFTimeInterval = -1.0
var deltaTime:CGFloat = 0.0
```

1. `isJumping` is a boolean that indicates if the bird is jumping.

2. `touchDetected` is a boolean that indicates that a touch just occurred so we can manage some things in the update method.

3. `jumpStartTime` is the time that the initial touch took place.

4. `jumpCurrentTime` is how long the bird has been jumping.

5. `jumpEndTime` is the time that the jump ended (when it met it's max duration).

6. `jumpDuration` is a constant that says how long the bird should jump (adjustable)

7. `jumpVelocity` is a constant that says how fast the bird should jump (adjustable)

8. `currentVelocity` is the current velocity of the bird

9. `jumpInertiaTime` is a time frame in which "gravity" should not affect the jump.

10. `fallInertiaTime` is a tie frame in which the bird should float without falling at the height of the jump.

11. `lastUpdateTimeInterval` stores the last time update needed to capture the delta time.

12. `deltaTime` stores the delta time (which is the time difference between current frame and previous frame)

Delta Time Explained

What does delta time mean and why do I need to worry about it? Delta time is the time between the current frame and the previous frame. We need this time to be the same on all devices our game will run on. Some devices will run at 30 FPS (frames per second) and others could be 60 FPS.

This could be a huge problem if we wanted to make our game multiplayer and was running on two devices. On one device the bird could actually jump faster.
To fix this issue we create the variable deltaTime.
We multiply calculations by deltaTime to get the same performance across multiple devices with different FPS.

Change your initSetup method to look like this:

```
func initSetup() {
    jumpInertiaTime = jumpDuration * 0.7
    fallInertiatime = jumpDuration * 0.3

    moveGroundAction = SKAction.moveBy(x: -groundSpeed, y: 0, duration: 0.02)
    moveGroundForeverAction =
SKAction.repeatForever(SKAction.sequence([moveGroundAction]))

    self.physicsWorld.gravity = CGVector(dx: 0.0, dy: 0.0)
}
```

You can adjust your jump and fall inertia as you see fit. Basically, on the jump inertia, gravity won't start taking effect on the bird until the last 30% of the jump. Similarly with the fall inertia, we won't increase downward velocity until we have been falling for 70% of the fall (this is the 0.3 value).

Make sure to set the physicsWorld gravity to 0. Since our bird will use physics to detect collisions he will be subject to **SpriteKits** world gravity. We don't need a value here because we have created our own physics engine for gravity.

Next, change your touchesBegan(_ touches: Set<UITouch>, with event: UIEvent?) method to look like:

```
override func touchesBegan(_ touches: Set<UITouch>, with event: UIEvent?) {
    touchDetected = true
    isJumping = true
}
```

The Update Method

Alright, this is where all the important heavy lifting happens in our game.
The first thing we will do is add our delta time calculation under our groundMovement()

call. (Note, this is being added inside the func update(_ currentTime: TimeInterval) method):

```
//Calculate delta time
deltaTime = CGFloat(currentTime - lastUpdateTimeInterval)
lastUpdateTimeInterval = currentTime

//Prevents problems with an anomaly that occurs when delta
//time is too long- apple does a similar thing in their code
if lastUpdateTimeInterval > 1 {
    deltaTime = 1.0/60.0
    lastUpdateTimeInterval = currentTime
}
```

Remember, delta time = current time minus last recorded time. That's it! The second part of the code deals with a delta time anomaly that can happen when delta time is too long to be effective. So the added code takes care of that problem.

The next step is to do some setup whenever a touch is detected. Place the following code under the delta time code we just added.

```
//this is called one time per touch, sets jump start time
//and sets current velocity to max jump velocity
if touchDetected {
    touchDetected = false
    jumpStartTime = CGFloat(currentTime)
    currentVelocity = jumpVelocity
}
```

We set the jump start time as the current time and then set the current velocity to the max jump velocity so the jump has full force in the beginning.

Now onto the jump, we are still inside the update(_ currentTime: TimeInterval) method:

```
//If we are jumping
if isJumping {
    //How long we have been jumping
    let currentDuration = CGFloat(currentTime) - jumpStartTime
    //time to end jump
    if currentDuration >= jumpDuration {
        isJumping = false
        jumpEndTime = CGFloat(currentTime)
    } else {
        //Rotate the bird to a certain euler angle over a certain period of
time
        if bird.zRotation < 0.5 {
```

```
        bird.zRotation += 2.0 * CGFloat(deltaTime)
    }

        //Move the bird up
        bird.position = CGPoint(x: bird.position.x, y: bird.position.y +
(currentVelocity * CGFloat(deltaTime)))

        //We dont decrease velocity until after the initial jump inertia
has taken place
        if currentDuration > jumpInertiaTime {
            currentVelocity -= (currentVelocity * CGFloat(deltaTime)) * 2
        }
    }
}
```

Remember, `isJumping` is set in the `touchesBegan(_ touches: Set<UITouch>, with event: UIEvent?)` method.

So if the bird is jumping then the current jump duration = currentTime - jumpStartTime. The jump ends when the bird reaches maximum jump duration, so we do a check on that next: if `currentDuration >= jumpDuration`.

If the jump continues we want to set the rotation of the bird (similar to how Flappy Bird rotates when he jumps). The values in this part are arbitrary numbers and can be adjusted to desired settings. We are just allowing the bird to rotate to a max rotation angle (0.5) over a certain period of time.

We then move the bird by adding the `currentVelocity * deltaTime` to the Y position.

Finally, we want to have some gravity kick in! But not right away. We want to wait until the jump inertia time passes and then we start decreasing velocity.

Now if we aren't jumping? We need the bird to fall… so add this **else statement** to that.

```
    else { //If we aren't jumping then we are falling
        //Rotate the bird to a certain euler angle over a certian period of
time
        if bird.zRotation > -0.5 {
            bird.zRotation -= 2.0 * CGFloat(deltaTime)
        }
        // move the bird down
        bird.position = CGPoint(x: bird.position.x, y: bird.position.y -
(currentVelocity * CGFloat(deltaTime)))

        //only start increasing velocity after floating for a little bit
        if CGFloat(currentTime) - jumpEndTime > fallInertiatime{
```

```
            currentVelocity += currentVelocity * CGFloat(deltaTime)
        }
    }
```

So we do the same thing with the bird's rotation as before but instead of upwards we want to rotate it downwards.

We also need that Y position to go down instead of up.

And we also need to increase the bird's speed as the inertia time passes. This acts just like gravity, the longer you fall the more velocity you gain... until you hit terminal velocity of course ;)

Time to build and run this game! Now your bird will fly and fall as you tap on the screen.

Time to add Obstacles

In the **Project Navigator** click on the Assets.xcassets folder. Open the folder where you have the assets saved for this game and drag the *Tiki_Down.png(1x,2x,3x)* and *Tiki_Upright.png(1x,2x,3x)* into the space.
Now your project should look like this:

Figure 5.11.10

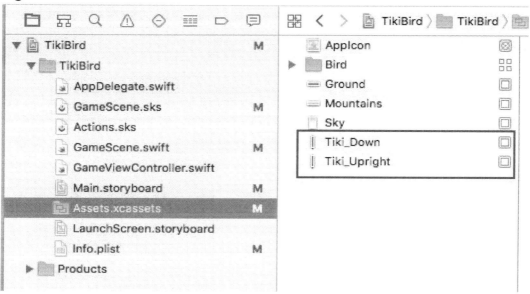

Like we did before with the ground, we need to open up the **Scene Editor** by clicking on the `GameScene.sks`.

Let's add the *Upright Tiki* and the *Down Tiki* to the scene like below. We need to move them around and figure out the **Min** and **Max** Y and the space between the tiki's. The **Min** and **Max** of the bottom tiki is important so we can add it at a random height and then always placing the top tiki the same amount of space from the bottom tiki each time.

Figure 5.11.11

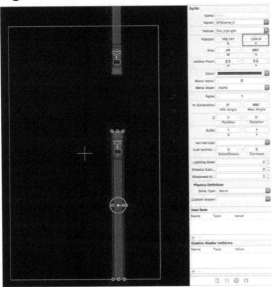

Playing around with the numbers and running the simulator, the values below are what I decided seemed right. You can make tweaks as you see fit. Don't forget to delete the Tikis from the **Game Scene**.

1. Height between obstacles: 907

2. Bottom Tiki max Y: 308

3. Bottom Tiki min Y: -120

4. Tiki start pos: 830

5. Tiki destroy pos: -187

Tiki Code

```
//Obstacles
var tikis = [SKNode]()
let heightBetweenObstacles: CGFloat = 900
let timeBetweenObstacles = 3.0
let bottomTikiMaxYPos = 234
let bottomTikiMinYPos = 380
let tikiXStartPos: CGFloat = 830
let tikiXDestroyPos: CGFloat = -187
var moveObstacleAction: SKAction!
var moveObstacleForeverAction: SKAction!
var tikiTimer: Timer!
```

What these variables will do.

1. `tikis` - an array that holds the active tiki objects

2. `heightBetweenObstacles` - the height between tikis we found in scene editor

3. `timeBetweenObstacles`- the time span between the generation of tikis

4. `bottomTikiMaxYPos`- the max Y coordinate of the bottom tiki

5. `bottomTikiMinYPos`- the min Y coordinate of the bottom tiki

6. `tikiXStartPos`- the X coordinate where the tikis will be created

7. `tikiDestroyPos`- the X coordinate where the tikis will be destroyed

8. `moveObstacleAction`- the action that moves the obstacles by a certain amount

9. `moveObstacleForeverAction`- the action that moves the action forever

10. `tikiTimer`- the timing mechanism we use to create tikis at certain time intervals

Take note that we refactored (Changing all the previous code) the `moveGroundAction` and `moveGroundForeverAction` into `moveObstacleAction` and `moveObstacleForeverAction`.
In this case, we want the ground and tiki poles to move at the same speed. This allows us to use the same actions.

```
//Collision categories
let category_bird: UInt32 = 1 << 0
let category_ground: UInt32 = 1 << 1
let category_tiki: UInt32 = 1 << 2
let category_score: UInt32 = 1 << 3
```

Next, let's add some category constants that we will use for collision detections:
These are bit mask categories that we set on the physics bodies of the obstacles and the bird. They allow us to know when the bird has collided with an object.

Now make a `createTikiSet(timer: NSTimer)` method. What we will do is create a top and bottom tiki, assign the tiki graphic and add physics to it, then add those tikis to a generic **SKNode** that will be created and added to the game.

Add this code to the new method you just created:

```
func createTikiSet(_ timer: Timer) {
    let tikiSet = SKNode()
    //Set up Tikis and Score Collider, bottom tiki
    let bottomTiki = SKSpriteNode(imageNamed: "Tiki_Upright")
    tikiSet.addChild(bottomTiki)
    let rand = arc4random_uniform(UInt32(bottomTikiMaxYPos)) +
UInt32(bottomTikiMinYPos)
    let yPos = -CGFloat(rand)
    bottomTiki.position = CGPoint(x: 0, y: CGFloat(yPos))
    bottomTiki.physicsBody = SKPhysicsBody(rectangleOf: bottomTiki.size)
    bottomTiki.physicsBody?.isDynamic = false
    bottomTiki.physicsBody?.categoryBitMask = category_tiki
    bottomTiki.physicsBody?.contactTestBitMask = category_bird
}
```

First we create a `tikiSet` node that will hold our tikis (and eventually our score collider node to detect when the bird has made it through tikis).

After that, we create the bottom tiki node and set its graphic. We give it a random Y position that keeps within our **min** and **max** bounds and we add a physics body with a size that equals the size of the graphic.

We don't want the tikis subject to gravity or other forces so we set the `physicsBody.dynamic` to `false`.

Lastly, we set the `categoryBitMask` to `category_tiki` and the `contactTestBitMask` to `category_bird`.

By setting the `contactTestBitMask` we are saying we want to get a notification whenever an intersection happens between the bird and the tiki object. We will work on the collision soon.

Make sure to add the tikis as a child of the `tikiSet` node.

Now we will add very similar code to add the top tikis. Place this right under the code we just added.

```
//Top Tiki
let topTiki = SKSpriteNode(imageNamed: "Tiki_Down")
topTiki.position = CGPoint(x: 0, y: bottomTiki.position.y +
heightBetweenObstacles)
tikiSet.addChild(topTiki)
```

802

```
topTiki.physicsBody = SKPhysicsBody(rectangleOf: topTiki.size)
topTiki.physicsBody?.isDynamic = false
topTiki.physicsBody?.categoryBitMask = category_tiki
topTiki.physicsBody?.contactTestBitMask = category_bird
```

Now we need to add the `tikiSet` to the `tikis` array and set the `zPosition` to 4 (behind the ground)

Run the movement action on the `tikiSet`, add the `tikiSet` to the scene, then set it's starting position. Place this under the code we just placed.

```
tikis.append(tikiSet)
tikiSet.zPosition = 4
tikiSet.run(moveObstacleForeverAction)
addChild(tikiSet)
tikiSet.position = CGPoint(x: tikiXStartPos, y: tikiSet.position.y)
```

Now we can modify the code in `setupScenery()` method to add the physics body for collisions.

```
//Add ground sprites
for x in 0..<totalGroundPieces {
    let sprite = SKSpriteNode(imageNamed: "Ground")
    sprite.physicsBody = SKPhysicsBody(rectangleOf: sprite.size)
    sprite.physicsBody?.isDynamic = false
    sprite.physicsBody?.categoryBitMask = category_ground
    sprite.zPosition = 5
    groundPieces.append(sprite)
    let wSpacing:CGFloat = -sprite.size.width / 2
    let hSpacing = -self.frame.height / 2 + sprite.size.height / 2
    if x == 0 {
        sprite.position = CGPoint(x: wSpacing, y: hSpacing)
    } else {
        sprite.position = CGPoint(x: -(wSpacing * 2) + groundPieces[x-
1].position.x, y: groundPieces[x-1].position.y)
    }
    self.addChild(sprite)
}
```

We need to do the same thing for our bird. In `setupBird()` method let's make the same changes.

```
func setupBird() {
    let totalImgs = birdAtlas.textureNames.count
    for x in 0..<totalImgs{
        let textureName = "Bird-\(x)"
        let texture = birdAtlas.textureNamed(textureName)
```

```
            birdFrames.append(texture)
        }

        bird = SKSpriteNode(texture: birdFrames[0])
        bird.zPosition = 4
        addChild(bird)
        bird.position = CGPoint(x: self.frame.midX, y: self.frame.midY)
        bird.run(SKAction.repeatForever(SKAction.animate(with: birdFrames,
timePerFrame: 0.2, resize: false, restore: true)))
        bird.physicsBody = SKPhysicsBody(circleOfRadius: bird.size.height / 2.0)
        bird.physicsBody?.isDynamic = true
        bird.zPosition = 4
        bird.physicsBody?.categoryBitMask = category_bird
        bird.physicsBody?.collisionBitMask = category_ground | category_tiki
        bird.physicsBody?.contactTestBitMask = category_ground | category_tiki
    }
```

The difference to pay attention to, is that we're setting the physics body to be circular and to match the size of the bird.

We are also adding a `collisionBitMask` and setting which objects can collide with our bird. This is the only physics body we'll set this on because the objects should only collide with the bird.

In the `startGame()` method let's get our timer set up so we can see some tikis move!

```
    func startGame(){
        for sprite in groundPieces {
            sprite.run(moveObstacleForeverAction)
        }
        tikiTimer = Timer(timeInterval: timeBetweenObstacles, target: self,
selector: #selector(GameScene.createTikiSet(_:)), userInfo: nil, repeats: true)
        RunLoop.main.add(tikiTimer, forMode: RunLoopMode.defaultRunLoopMode)
        tikiTimer.fire()
    }
```

If we want the timer to repeat, we must retain an instance of it. This is why we have the `tikiTimer` variable.

Build and run! You have yourself a pretty sweet start to your Tiki Bird game!

Wrapping up

We covered a lot in this Tiki Bird Tutorial, all from moving an object across the screen and animating movement of a sprite. We integrated user taps to move the bird, added collision bit masks to it as well, tiki posts, and ground to prevent the bird from passing through. You are leaving this tutorial with enough knowledge to make a fun and simple game.

Exercise

Now, I didn't add everything to this tutorial, it's time for you to make it your own. I think we built a pretty solid foundation for you to make something extra cool.

One thing you should consider adding is the `didBegin(_ contact: SKPhysicsContact)` method, this will be called every time your bird collides with an object. You can have the game end or maybe give an option to restart it.

```
func didBegin(_ contact: SKPhysicsContact) {
    //Add game over here
}
```

Now to use `didBegin(_ contact: SKPhysicsContact)` you will need to add `SKPhysicsContactDelegate` extension next to the `SKScene` of your `GameScene` classe.

```
class GameScene: SKScene, SKPhysicsContactDelegate {
```

Also, in the `initSetup()` method you need to set the `contactDelegate` to `self`.

```swift
        physicsWorld.contactDelegate = self
```

I also included some sounds in the assets. Game noises would be a pretty awesome addition. For instance, if you'd like to add a flap noise every time you tap the screen you would need a `tapSound` variable of type `AVAudioPlayer`.
Place this at the top with all your other variables.

```
    var tapSound: AVAudioPlayer!
```

Oops! We also need to remember to `import AVFoundation` at the very top with import `import SpriteKit` and `import GameplayKit`.

Then in your `initSetup()` method we need to set up the `AVAudioPlayer` to play the sound we want. The sound assets should be dragged into your project either in their own folder or just on the same level as your Storyboard.

```
        let tapSoundURL = Bundle.main.url(forResource: "tap", withExtension:
"wav")!
```

```
    do {
        tapSound = try AVAudioPlayer(contentsOf: tapSoundURL)
        print("DW: tap loaded")
    } catch {
        print("DW: Music not played")
    }
    tapSound.numberOfLoops = 0
    tapSound.prepareToPlay()
```

All we need to call this sound to play is place it inside our update(_ currentTime: TimeInterval) method inside our if touchDetected statement calling tapSound.play().

```
    if touchDetected {
        touchDetected = false
        jumpStartTime = CGFloat(currentTime)
        currentVelocity = jumpVelocity
        tapSound.play()
    }
```

Keeping track of how many tikis you pass. That would be a great way to keep score. Make this game your own with customizing it and taking it to the next level!

Made in the USA
Lexington, KY
18 February 2017